CW00828063

Camel Milk

Solomon Barrani

AuthorHouse™ UK Ltd.
500 Avebury Boulevard
Central Milton Keynes, MK9 2BE
www.authorhouse.co.uk
Phone: 08001974150

This book is a work of fiction. People, places, events, and situations are the product of the author's imagination. Any resemblance to actual persons, living or dead, or historical events, is purely coincidental.

First published by AuthorHouse 11/2/2009

ISBN: 978-1-4389-8175-8 (sc)

This book is printed on acid-free paper.

About the Book

This is not a historical record but a vivid sketch of experiences, challenges, colors, people, sandstorms; the sketch of a country as seen through the eyes of the author over three decades.

The author lived for three decades in Libya, The Socialist People's Libyan Arab Jamahiriya of Muammar Qadhafi.

Witnessed the magnanimity of the Bedouin, his ruthlessness as dictator, the eloquence as a preacher, the dog of the Middle East, according to Ronald Regan, the shrewd salesman of crude oil.

The man who thrived on staged coups, and intimidated, persecuted, imprisoned, and executed his opponents, even murdered persons who survived the gallows.

The student of Jamal Abd-el-Nasser, who believed in succeeding him as a Pan Arab Leader.

The man who substituted normal education with arms training.

The voracious person who inspired and supported every kind of uprising around the world and squandered millions of dollars on terrorism and revolutions. The man who subsidized the devastation of Lebanon and killed every ray of hope for peace in the Middle East, but also fought the so called reactionaries on his own territory, a category broad enough to include Muslim fundamentalists, covetous fellow army officers and members of Westernized business class.

He speaks about the man who wanted to cut off the hand that fed him, the man who wanted to wipe out the West and their ally, Zion.

Also about the man who never celebrated a birthday, because no such records exist for his birthday date. Rumors say that he was born in the spring, or may be in September of 1942, the offspring of an Italian general, and a Jewish Bedouin woman, in the Surta area.

But also about the man who built the infrastructure of his country, built whole towns, road networks, hospitals and brought water from the heart of the desert and provided electricity to the last shepherd's tent.

Contents

Prologue

If atrocities were committed, should not necessarily be attributed to only one person, the Leader.

Under such regimes, many are those who constitute the criminal cabal and settle personal matters in the name of a revolution.

If the cubs superseded their genetic or acquired traits or the instructions handed to them, history will tell, when the desert sandstorm would die off, the precipitated dust though would remain for a long time and rain occassionally falls on the desert, to wash it away.

If the cubic meter of crude soil that will cover the sinners will erase all their sins, only the divines of the upper world may deduce.

Atrocities against people within the territory of the dictator are disputable if committed for a reasonable cause, but when acts that cause suffering to innocent ones, especially alien to the dictator's compatriots are definitely rated as acts of terrorism and should never be left unpunished.

Muammar's have been proven not clean.

Definitely, no civilized nation would tolerate such type of leaders and no such type of leader may rule for more than a few hours over people of a higher caliber.

People that live by the rules of nature are bound to dissuade any sophisticated ideas whether they derive from some ruling body or even religion.

1: Libya, the land of plethora

The Mediterranean Sea has been the cradle on whose borders civilizations have developed, nations been created, dynasties been malleted, religions been founded.

Every gorge, mount, and lowland have witnessed through the ages, gusts of storm, torment by scorching sun, caressing by light rain, and mesmering by starlit skies and flooded by deceptive moonlight.

Geographically, lying between zones of extreme climatic conditions has shouldered the dust-laden gusts of the desert winds and elbowed the biting cold snowdrifts from the north.

Not a single day passed without a forceful change, not a single day of rest.

The harshness of the landscape and the relentless climate forged the people of the region into a hardy race that developed triumphantly into clans, races, nations.

Despite their common ancestry, a distinct diversification has been prevalent along with the multiage history of the area.

The area, known for its instability, but also for the interest of so many other races to invade, conquer, and occupy the states of the area.

Phoenicians, Carthaginians, Greeks, Romans, Vandals and Byzantines, Turks, Europeans, one after the other crisscrossed these lands for various reasons.

Many invaders helped in developing and improving the area and founded cities, leaving behind true evidence of their passage.

The ancient Greeks, a seafaring lot, landed on that North African sandy expanse, founded cities, the Pentapolis on the East and Tripoli on the west. Built monuments, and carved a name for that territory, LIBYA. The name referred to, by the ancient Greek historian, Herodotus.

Sand storms and conquerors forced that name be buried and trodden under masses of sand and conquerors' debris.

As to Libyan history, no records exist as such to go by; warrior like nomads roamed the area, fighting each other. After conquering a site from a weaker tribe, would change names and customs to their liking. In reality, very little would be left from a fleeing nomad tribe.

The name remained buried in that sandy environment, awaiting inspiration to rise through the sand dunes, and elevate its torso and name, in the universe.

The Greeks and Romans built cities, citadels, and infrastructure for those who wished to change their style of life.

Several conquerors of lower nobility destroyed cities, and monuments, and annihilated populations.

The conquerors came one after the other, like the harsh sweeping winds of the desert and forced the inhabitants to subjugate to the whims, the laws, and the frame of mind of their new masters. Repeatedly, had to relocate, like loose sand, dislodged from its habitat, and transferred to a different location, as if the hardships of the inhospitable and arid environment were not enough for them. The new masters tried invariably to impose their alien laws, and above all, their culture and perception.

The Ottomans occupied Libya for centuries, but did not leave a speck of evidence of that long occupation. On the contrary, allowed opportunists of various nationalities to excavate archeological sites and carry away treasures of enormous value in money, history, and culture.

The Turks with their barbaric way of ruling imposed their nota and destroyed what previous occupants built.

Several invasions weathered and eroded, piling monument upon monument.

The Italians moved in, riding on the wings of expansion and domination. The new occupants considered the land of Libya, as the land of promise, for their future generations. Like their Roman ancestors, built cities on the trends of civilization and tried hard to transform the nomadic clans of the desert into disciplined communities.

Transformation is a slow process, where, pressure achieves very little and force creates hostility.

The Italians have tried and succeeded to a great extend. They laid down the plans of the major cities and actually founded those cities. To-day, the Centrum of Tripoli and Benghazi bear the Italian trademark, streets, administration buildings, post offices, hospitals, courthouses, museums, ports, even the cathedrals. Exactly, like their Roman ancestors believed in transforming the arid desert into the breadbasket of Rome.

Moving around the countryside, even to-day, one finds farms with fruit tree plantations, at strategic locations, along with administration buildings, schools, shopping centers, and cafeterias.

Interesting was the idea along the Benghazi-Tripoli road. They built rest houses at every twenty kilometers, a very thoughtful idea considering the strength of the traveler and his animal, under the prevailing weather conditions. In addition, at every forty kilometers built administration centers, schools, and churches.

Many of those buildings withstood the menace of the political wrath, and remained to prove those attempts.

The countryside was developed after careful consideration. They built farms with water wells, houses, and useful facilities. Several of those farms dotted the slopes and vales, others clustered at strategic points to provide cultural and administrative centers.

Although, the Italians tried hard to develop and improve the life of the locals, still bore the trademark of the conqueror. Their laws and organized way of living restricted the nomadic life of the locals. Disobedience flowed through their veins and anarchy was their customary notion.

Thousands of those native persons who defied the power of the conqueror and withstood the sweep of change, were pursued, captured and herded like animals in open detention camps, exposed to the harsh elements of nature. Many succumbed due to lack of water, food, and medical care. Others died through rivalry. The remaining stubborn ones were piled on derelict boats and directed to the sea.

The masters of the solid desert found themselves helpless in the bottomless dark salty liquid; those who made the trip up to the mainland of Italy died there.

Until to-day, the Libyans have a mourning day for their heroic descendants, refrain from work and unnecessary engagements, those that are obliged to do so, raise a small black flag on prominent spots of their cars and bear a black armband. The day is known as, 'The black day of Lybia'.

It commemorates a very bad day for the Libyans. Like today, about seventy years ago, the fascist Italians shipped hundreds of Libyan men, women, and children to some remote Italian islands, where they perished. Till today nobody knows about the fate of those people; how many died and under what circumstances; if there are survivors and if so, there are no records.

Yes, people today, refrain from unnecessary movements, especially by car. If they are obliged to travel, they wear a black arm band and tie a small black ribbon on their vehicles, you must have noticed that.

It took the Italians more than twenty years to subdue most traces of resistance in a country raven by fierce clan loyalties and regional fundamentalism. However, when the occupants considered themselves as the masters of this vast country, the wind of the Second World War raised clouds of unrest from the heart of Europe across the whole planet.

The armies of the opposing giants fought bitter fights in North Africa, waging eastwards for the capture of strategic points. The allied forces predominated and Libya came under British jurisdiction. The Anglo-Saxon race with a worldwide supremacy and an open promise, helped nations, improved the standard of living through peaceful means, and undertook the role of directing people to those channels.

Stability in the Middle East improved only in the last century, through the occupation by more civilized nations. Still such stability did not last that long and the wind of liberation blew harder, after the Second World War.

Better education, improved standard of living matched with nationalism forced the European occupants to depart in a diplomatic way, though leaving behind a bubbling kiln, ready for eruption at any moment.

The yearning for supremacy never died, rather revived with the departure of the last occupants.

Egypt, being the largest country in size and population in the region experienced such ideals, very early.

The one strongman succeeded the other. With fiery speeches and lip promises, lured the masses to follow him as their savior. Very few had enough logic to visualize the aftermath. Poverty and lack of education were deplored. Masses play a leading role in politics.

The manipulated masses had a great impact in the movements; it only required the right person to perform it.

Abd-el-Nasser gleamed in front of the camera operator and his posture traveled across the Arab World. His towering height clad in the new tailor-made General's uniform brazing with the shining insignia, sent waves of chest expansion to millions.

The young recruits straightened their torso and inhaled the new air blowing over their much trodden arid homeland. Time runs when the wind sweeps messages.

Libya received its old name and acquired an entity under the protection of the Westerners.

Oil prospects were promising, but needed substantial amounts of capital and technology, before the black gold could be extracted and traded. Investors were positive of the promising future, but businessmen are always the same. The foreign companies brought in machinery, personnel, and entire ancillary for the welfare of their specialized personnel.

The locals were blinded with the expatriates' style of living, with rented villas, furniture, posh cars, imported foodstuffs, nurseries, schools, hospitals. Such amenities were considered income, deriving from the oil. The young looked at those foreigners with envy and eyed them with a jaundiced eye.

The British managed to bring reconciliation across the vast arid and thinly populated country. Tripolitans, Fezzan and Cyrenaica, three different people with distinct diversities, very little in common with a faint concept that they belonged to the same nation, were brought together.

They reconciliated a noble person, Idris, a grandson of Sayyid Muhammad bin'Ali as-Senussi, the founder of the Senussi Muslim Sufi order, and Leader of the order from 1916, following the abdication of his uncle.

As a Leader, opposed the Italians who terrorized and victimized thousands of his compatriots. Was forced though, to flee to Egypt in 1922, from where he tried to organize a guerilla group to fight the occupants of his country, rather his section of the country. The British acknowledged him as Emir only for the territory of Cyrenaica, a position confirmed by the Italians in 1920.

With the onset of the World War II, Idris advised his followers to fight along with the Allies. In 1942, he returned to Libya, after the British occupied the country. They assisted him to form an official government and unite the three regions Cyrenaica, Tripolitania and Fezzan. From his base of Benghazi negotiated with the United Kingdom and the United Nations over independence. Independence was achieved in 1951, and Idris was proclaimed the King of Libya

The British were ruling, the British were drilling and the British army stood by, the Americans invaded Libya from the back door and worked parallel to their bosom allies.

During the early years, after the coup against King Idris, the locals did not respond to the whims of the new Leader and his revolution.

Thousands of Egyptian fellahin were allowed to cross the vast border and swarm the Eastern part of Lybia.

The greatest employer was the Benghazi municipality: there thousands found temporary jobs, especially before the annual celebrations of 1st September, the revolution day.

The locals refrained from processions and overexcitements. The new rulers though were determined to advertise their ideas and intentions in Benghazi with all the glow of a dictatorship.

Facing the resentment of their people considered the poverty stricken Egyptian fellahin be the right type of people for their processions.

Nasser, attempted such a unification before and failed for various reasons; the most obvious being the idiosyncrasy of the

Arab, with a strong-headed freedom blended by opportunism. For such ambitious dreams money plays a leading role, the masses cannot jump up and down forever with empty stomachs. Hungry bears cannot stand and stare forever.

Nasser helped the new Libyan regime to solidify itself; in return, the new junta invested heavily in Egypt and allowed thousands of fellahin to cross the borders for employment.

Nasser's regime embraced Qadhafi and directed him how to use media and propaganda, to strengthen his grip on power. Nasser provided Qadhafi protection and advice. Exported Egyptian bureaucracy to Libya and helped the Libyan strong man sharpen his focus on Arab nationalistic and revolutionary principles.

With the death of Nasser, Sadat became president of Egypt, mistrusted Qadhafi but agreed a kind of loose union between the two neighbors for a full union at a later stage, with Sadat as president and Qadhafi as defense minister. However, Muammar's ambitions worried Sadat. The embrace though enabled Muammar to consolidate his power, the student had chance to emerge from the shadow of his master.

With pockets full of petrol-dollars dreamed of acquiring the role of the pan-Arabic Leader. He calculated the odds and attempted to use the Egyptian masses, was mistaken, the Egyptian bourgeoisie played a leading role in the background. Differences sparked along and relations strained to such an extend, that the two armies came to confrontation. The odds disproportionate. The Egyptian army with better training and experience along with the numerical difference got ready for the worst. With the first countenance, they invaded the Libyan territory to more than seventy kilometers along the eastern border.

His weakness to fight back, turned to insanity against the ordinary poor Egyptian fellahin working in his country, most of them engaged on temporary jobs in the eastern part of the country, the Cyrenaica bordering the defaulter of the great Jamal Abd-el-Nasser.

Thousands of poverty-stricken fellahin walked hundreds of kilometers across unattended but hostile borders to reach the land of promise. Many Libyans cashed on those illegal intruders through forced labor, prostitution and even street begging.

Army tracks, no more needed for war engagement, were turned into transport cages with iron doors and heavy bolts and a guard's cell at the rear.

The biggest employer in the town of Benghazi was the municipality, employing more than a thousand on a daily basis. With the first announcement that the municipality was recruiting, more than two thousand called for work. Once the job seekers were inside the municipality boundary wall, the gates closed behind them. Armed soldiers sprang from nowhere and the hoarding began. At gunpoint, all work seekers were grouped up, and after being stripped of all personal belongings, were loaded onto the cage trucks, locked up, and with a gunman in the guard cell were driven non-stop for more than five hundred kilometers to the Egyptian border. It was a monstrous sight, those trucks packed with male descendants of Pharaoh; most of them dressed in their traditional gallabia: they looked like upright sardines.

There, they were unloaded, simply unloaded, that is how they were treated and driven eastwards, towards their home country. These beggars had to walk, under the scorching sun, another fifty or so kilometers to the nearest inhabited Egyptian spot, the town of Sallum.

The army, unable to combat the Egyptians, a more disciplined and organized enemy, undertook a cleansing operation in their homeland; thousands of Egyptians were deported straight away, deprived of their personal belongings and many were not even paid by their local employers who cashed on the turmoil.

Several hundreds of detainees confined temporarily, in an army camp, on the Beida road, by the Quefia prisons. A camp with an area of more than ten square kilometers was crammed with scared, hungry, thirsty, miserable Egyptians.

It was here that Mahmoud spent two nights and three days in captivity.

When George was forced to move his operation to Teeka area, to continue slaughtering chicken, advised the two Egyptian laborers, Mahmoud and Gasala working with him, to remain within the farm, until the storm eases off. They were foolish enough to ignore his advice.

Police mounted on horse, began roaming the area; searched farms, fields, and isolated shepherds' places and forced all out of sight Egyptian laborers to the Quarchia police station.

Despite George's warning, the two were foolish enough to leave their place of work and walk across the fields to Faakat, their old working place, where the young wife of Ahmed lured them with her fat buttocks and oversize bosom. The distance was more than twelve kilometers, a long way for normal walking, a distance Mahmoud never made, only Gazala managed to reach Muftah's farm at Faakat.

"Where is Mahmoud?" asked George when unexpectedly saw Gazala on the farm.

With tears in his eyes and scratches on his face, the young Egyptian told them how a mounted soldier chased them.

"We saw him from afar and hid in an old farmhouse, he rode round, determined to catch us. We crept from the back of the farmhouse, he shot at us, in the air, luckily were not hit. I, squeezed myself through an opuntia bush, the pricks pierced my face, my hands, my body, my legs, pushed my way through, the blood oozed on my face but got through, the army bullets were worse than the opuntia prickles. Crawled on my four and hid behind a stonewall, crouched there; a fierce dog came at me, I even stopped breathing. When the beast approached me, lifted my arms and waved them; then gave a shrill yelp and the dog fled as if bitten by a serpent."

"For long seconds, the only audible sound was my heartbeat. At a moment, my puzzled mind sensed the trotting of a horse, lifted my head very cautiously and peeped over the wall, it was my imagination, gathered courage, looked around, and saw the soldier on his horse going the opposite direction. Raised myself to a half-seated position and saw Mahmoud led away: I froze, '*Hamdullah', I said 'Mahmoud is alive*'. Remained under cover, till the rider was far enough; then took a large circle skipping the farms and reached here about an hour ago."

"You walked from say nine in the morning?"

"About seven hours, Boss."

"Where would Mahmoud be now?" asked George.

"All those captured are brought to Quarchia police station," said Muftah, who stealthily appeared from nowhere.

"Can we visit him?"

"No, it's impossible, by the orders of the Colonel, nobody dares to question his decrees".

In that evening, they did not kill any chicken. George went down town, and witnessed the whole drama, with his bare eyes. By the port, two trucks loaded with detained persons ready for deportation parked by, with the guards in position. He did not ponder or looked at the desperate beggars packed in those trucks. The trucks parked temporarily there, in a show of muscle.

At Farag's restaurant, piles of roasted chicken lay in the aluminum tray and the rotisserie stood idle.

"There is no business," said Farag and with a droopy face pointed to the pile of chicken and added, "the Egyptians are deported, once they are gone, nobody else eats chicken."

George discussed with him the situation, and how far might affect their business.

"The situation is very bad, it's rotten, more than half a million Egyptians are driven away by force, farms will close down, and vegetables will become scarce. Many small businesses will close down, like the building activities."

"The decree is not directed only to those beggars but to ourselves also. It was made clear that any Libyan caught employing or hiding Egyptian males or females, is liable to be imprisoned without been presented to court. You know, George, here we have a revolutionary regime, every word from the Leader is heavier than steel."

To relieve Farag from the obligation of canceling his order, George told him that there would be no chicken available the next day.

"I was going to ask you not to bring any for tomorrow, till we see how the situation may develop."

"You know, Hag Farag, you are in the mid of the market, you can sell fresh chicken, I mean non-cooked."

He looked at George, scratched his chin and said, "I have to sell by weight and I do not have a scale."

"They don't cost that much."

"And from where can one buy scales nowadays? Before they were available in every corner shop; you know Shubani used to sell them, he was forced to close down, and the cooperative does not bring them anymore."

They discussed how George could help in order to carry on the business. Farag was one of his best customers, honest, paid on time, and he needed to work, had a big family. George suggested supplying him with chicken of an average weight around one kilo and a quarter, so, he could sell at a fixed price, by the piece.

"Well, I can try what you suggest, provided you bring birds of that weight, otherwise I may be forced to close down, and I have a family of nine, all too young for work."

George assured him, "You know my slaughter house is yours."

"And my shop is yours."

"So tomorrow there will be no delivery."

"Aiwa, Yes, after tomorrow bring me one hundred, I'll try the sale of fresh meat."

At Rue-Sad with Mohamed, the owner of the small restaurant, things were different there. Other nationalities lived around, many Bulgarian families; the males working at the Benghazi cement factory, and chicken was the only meat affordable to their low salary, although Benghazi was literally flooded with Bulgarian lamb at the time.

"Hello Mr. George," bellowed Mohamed from behind his solid bench.

"Hello Mohamed, how are you?"

"Here take your money," he said and pulled a bundle of notes from his pocket.

George got hold of the folded money and pocketed it deep in the inside pocket of his jacket without counting it, trust amongst dealers was of utmost concern, very seldom money was counted, at least in front of the client. In the long course of dealing with his clients, only once, found the money short and in that case only one note of five dinars.

"Tomorrow yia Sidi-Mohamed, there will be no chicken; my laborers have been caught by the police."

"The army you mean?"

"That's right."

"No Egyptian will be left in Benghazi."

"Only in Benghazi?"

"No, not only Benghazi, may be the whole Libya, you better find laborers from another nationality"

"Like what?"

"Have you tried Chadian?"

"Chadian?"

"Yes, but I must warn you, they always carry knives; I do not trust them."

If he does not trust them, how can one work with them, specially a white foreigner; how can he trust them in the middle of the night out in the wilderness.

"Good-night, yia Mohamed."

"Good-night, Mr. George."

"After tomorrow, how many shall I bring?"

"Bring hundred and fifty, and plenty of liver, OK?"

George reached his home by nine, at his coded touch of the bell, was met by the whole family. His three young daughters raced out of the house into the yard, followed by his wife. The moment George pushed the front door open; three young hands grabbed his and moved indoors. He let the girls enter still holding his hands; he kissed his wife, who looked very worried.

"Where have you been George? They say that the army rounds up the Egyptians like animals."

"No, not all of them, just those without documents."

"What documents, which Egyptian has a single document? They say all, without discrimination."

"Who told you my dear, that's not true."

His three daughters always wanted to do something for their father, wanted to make him feel that he was at his own house. So Sonia took his bag, Margarita brought him his slippers and little Mary undertook to prepare for her father his customary cup of Nescafe. She became an expert in this little errand and her father enjoyed every drop of it; she always prepared the Nescafe at the right temperature, the right consistency and the right quantity, the cup was never too full or too low. George enjoyed his family attention; all of them appreciated his hard efforts to earn the family bowl of food.

George had a family night, that night. After super, he and Kate washed up the dishes, tidied the kitchen, counted the money from his customers and joined their girls studying in the large hall.

"Dad I'll show you my composition, the teacher gave me twenty out of twenty," called Margarita.

"Yes, I'll read it in a minute; you must have written a very good one to get such a high grade."

"Yes, although the teacher doubted at first, but when I explained that I wrote it in the class that same hour and was true what I wrote, even I explained where the Libyan lady lives, he accepted it, in the end."

"George you must read it, it is really touching."

George took hold of the exercise book in his hands but Mary pleaded with her eyes to look up her Math exercises first. Being the youngest and her first year at school deserved all his attention; after all, he did not have the chance to be at home so early and spend time with his loving children before they went to bed. Only, every blue moon, he managed to be free.

"Yes, Mary, the additions are correct, you have them all correct, bravo." Said George and gave her a kiss on the forehead. "What else do you have for tomorrow?"

"Reading in Greek, I did that with Mum."

George looked at Sonia, she was deep in trigonometry, "Sonia you need any help?"

"No Dad, thank you, I am on the last exercise, can manage."

She was very smart; George tried to challenge her occasionally, but got his lesson.

"Dad, you promised to read my composition?"

"Yes, my dear I promised and I will do that now."

With Margarita on his knees and her exercise book in hand, and his wife next to him and with another cup of Nescafe, sipped the coffee, drop by drop and began reading, read it to himself. The composition was about a visit by Margarita with her Mum to Zeinab Benily. The family was one of the richest families in Benghazi; they owned an oil drilling company, machinery for road construction, owned more than half of the Omar Khayam hotel, the biggest hotel in the town, along with villas, flats, and farms. Literally, ownedk half of Benghazi.

Zeinab spoke perfect English, understood some Greek, and traveled abroad extensively with her husband either on business trips or for pleasure. They lived in a large villa with gardens all around in west Fuehat. The gardens looked rather neglected since the Egyptian gardeners and house helpers were rounded away.

Margarita was not interested to describe the big house, but what she witnessed at the Libyan women gathering at Madam Zeinab, and wrote it down.

"Went along with Mum to Madam Zeinab where she was invited; it was my first visit to a rich family's house and was curious. We reached the house by five in the afternoon after walking almost a kilometer. My father was at work, at the Benily family farm, where he was a kind of a partner. We owned only one car and that was used by Dad.

Along the streets, our walking drew the interest of many young Libyans. They whistled, gestured indecently, and shouted, "I love you, I love you."

"One of them, in a polished fancy American car, tried hard to persuade us to get in. Mum was very angry; we walked faster and faster, tried to reach the villa of Madam Zeinab the sooner. We had only a hundred meters to walk. Was astounded, large private cars, stopped at the entrance of the villa, one after the other; women formally dressed, descended and crossed the garden gate.

My Mum held me back till the large Peugeot left, we walked through the gate to the veranda, stopped for a few seconds, Mum looked herself in her small mirror, I looked up at her, she was red and exasperated. She hesitated but a soft voice was heard, "welcome madam Kate, please come in," the woman embraced Mum with both hands and kissed her on both cheeks five times, I counted them, she looked down at me and said, "hello young lady?"

We were accompanied inside; women's voices were heard loud and merry. There was such a noise and I thought they were all talking at the same time and none was listening. When we came through the doublewide door of the salon, a deadly silence fell upon them; we were unknown, strangers.

Madam Zeinab, holding me by the hand, addressed the muddled group of women who faced us in astonishment.

"This is a new friend of mine, she is Greek from Cyprus, and her name is Kate." The bystanders close to Mum began hugging her; Madam Zeinab dragged me to another room. There, four children were sitting on the carpet with a bowl of homemade sweets in the middle. All of them were holding sweets in their hands and had sweets in their mouths.

"Ahmed," called Madam Zeinab, "this is ...what is your name?"

"Margarita," managed to articulate.

"We'll call you Rita; the first one is too long."

"Thank you," said nervously.

Ahmed, a boy of nine, nearly my age, rose, offered his hand, and said, "Hello?" took my hand and pulled me towards the others and gestured me to sit down.

"Tfatal, please," murmured a girl of about seven, with her mouth stuffed with cake and lips powdered with white sugar. Sat down, as I was told, but was not ready for the cakes, was straining my ears to hear Mum's voice from the ladies' salon, it was impossible, could only hear high pitch talking in Arabic, interrupted by laughter of equal tone.

Ahmed lifted a large size of a spongy cake dripping with grey syrup and urged me to take it. Looked around for an empty plate or even a paper tissue but saw none, stretched my hand and the whole piece landed in my small palm. Felt the syrup dripping through my fingers, thought of the carpet, and looked down, around the tray were unbelievable, cake bits, syrup drippings, and liquid Pepsi from a tipped bottle by the small fat boy sitting opposite me; the frothy liquid soaked his pants, the debris and the carpet. Could not return the cake; cupped my hand with my other one as a protective cup and began nibbling at it.

"This is your Pepsi," called Ahmed placing down in front of me an already opened bottle. He held it from the top with his sticky fingers, wanted to clean it with my fingers, the syrup was everywhere, took two gulps to clear my throat, and with palms open, ran to meet Mum.

"Here, here wash your hands, here," called Ahmed.

I turned back, got into a side room and washed my hands with a piece of *Dove* soap, dried my mouth and hands on a towel that I lifted from a pile of newly washed, ironed and nicely piled on the marble silt.

In the large salon, found several women sitting on cushions spread over a thick carpet. They were sitting in groups of four or five, Mum was sitting with another two old women. The two were engaged in some gossip from what I understood; were bent forward and talked in low tones.

Mum smiled, when she saw me. Sat next to her. The gossiping from the groups around was loud and noisy.

Where Mum was sitting, lay a large tray loaded with dishes full of home made sweets and cakes, they looked different from what we had across, there was no spongy cake or bottles of Pepsi, crystal glasses were standing in the middle instead. Two of the glasses, were empty, a third one was still half-full. Guessed that was my mother's.

"Did you get something to eat Margarita?" asked Mum.

"Yes, a lousy cake," said in English.

"Please Margarita…many of the women speak English."

"And Greek," added the old woman sitting next to me. Looked at her with surprise, she pronounced the Greek with a different accent.

"We came from Crete," she said.

Ah, yes, she talks like Zacharakis in my class.

The two women were engaged in deep talk but their eyes and ears roamed the room, from time to time stopped talking, and listened to the others.

Sat next to Mum for more than ten minutes; the two kept their conversation with deep concern; spoke in their language, alien to me at the time. We were taught Arabic in the Greek school, but it was too early for me to follow them. At some moment, the one who spoke Greek asked from where I come, how long I have been in Libya and if I liked it.

"No, I don't like it;" I said clearly, "my home was very nice in our small town of Kyrenia, in Cyprus."

"Margarita!" Mum intervened, and to hush me up began telling how we fled the invading Turkish army, how we left our home, how we lost everything, and. and..."

The old woman listened anxiously, and with a witty eye cut short Mum's lamentation, "that serves you right, that serves you right."

Mum almost fainted, the old lady added, "the Greeks did the same to us in Crete, were forced to leave by boat just with the clothes on our backs," she plucked her thick lips, crossed her hands on her fat stomach and remained silent.

Lifted the half-full glass with Pepsi and Mum took a sip of the grey liquid. We were both ready to leave, when Madam Zeinab came into the salon holding a carton with both arms very reverently.

"Here, look at this nice embroidered table cloth, I brought it from Istanbul, from Turkey, where I went with Omar." She lowered the box and one middle aged fat woman opened the flaps and picked it out of the box. Several guests, standing already closed up to Zeinab, unfolded the tablecloth, stretched it to its full length and inspected it carefully.

"Very nice, really very nice."

"Bravo Zeinab, you brought something very nice, not like many who go there and purchase cheap stuff and waste their money."

"How much did you pay for it?"

Zeinab made her calculation and mentioned the price in Libyan dinars.

"Really, cheap!"

"And it's of very good quality."

Mum approached Zeinab and the group holding the tablecloth, she touched the embroidery, looked at it closer, studied the design, frowned her eyebrows, it reminded her of something, "You bought it in Turkey, Madam Zeinab and at a very good price, you said?"

"Yes, I did get it rather cheap; look at the quality, the work put in it, and it's hand made."

Mum inspected the tablecloth closer, the color, the design and the size; I saw Mum with trembling hands turning the cloth over at the corner, and all of a sudden let the cloth go and she dropped flat on the carpet.

A shriek voice said, "Madam, for God's sake, what happened to you, bring water quickly."

Stepped near Mum and took hold of her hand; I screamed at first but then pleaded with her to wake up. Could not say why she fainted. The women rubbed her hands, slapped her cheeks, put handfuls of water on her face.

I began trembling, called out, "Mum, Mum."

She regained her senses, after a while, opened her eyes, smiled when she saw me so distressed, "I'm alright, let's go."

"Please Madam," pleaded Zeinab, "what happened to you?"

"The tablecloth is mine, my Mum made it for me, her initials are stitched here," she turned the corner of the cloth and showed them grandmother's initials.

"Oh, God, Zeinab," exclaimed the ones close by.

The middle-aged woman raised her arms and pleaded to Allah.

"Please Mummy," I besieged crying, "let us go."

"Are you alright now?" asked the middle-aged woman.

"Poor one, poor one," were the exclamations all around.

We stayed there bewildered, the cackling and the gossiping died out, one by one, the podgy women left the salon, was alone now with Mum; Zeinab went to see her guests, when she returned asked Mum incessantly if she was alright.

Mum remained numb; "the dirty Turks stole this from our home and sold it for peanuts."

Zeinab remained breathless.

"I'm sorry, really sorry, but I bought it in Istanbul, I swear, I did."

"I'm not angry with you Madam Zeinab, I'm bitter with the dirty politicians who paved the way for the invaders, who looted our homes, our farms, our land."

Zeinab brought the carton box, pulled out the embroidered tablecloth folded it very neatly, placed it back in the box, closed the flaps and said to Mum, "please, I offer it to you, you can have it, you deserve it, and it's yours."

"You bought it, you did not steal it, you can keep it, but it was mine."

For more than five minutes, the two women tried to persuade one another to accept the looted item, in the end Zeinab's generosity superseded, she handed the box to me, "I offer it to you my young lady, present from me."

I was caught unprepared, looked at Mum, she was motionless, stiff, not an eyelash blinked. Zeinab kept pressing the box into my arms, I closed them, held the box, a tinge of a smile formed on Mum's face, I was relieved, the embroidered tablecloth was now mine, I was the legitimate owner, Zeinab smiled broadly.

"You spread it when I come to your house in Cyprus," she said, "good luck."

She helped Mum to walk towards the door; Mum put her hand on my shoulder.

"I'll drive you to your house."

"We can manage."

"No, let me drive you there, I'll get the car."

We waited in the front of the house; Zeinab brought her car and drove us home.

"Margarita, this composition is one of your best, very contemporary," with difficulty George turned his face to look at his wife and the second daughter of his.

"Your Margarita," stressing the name, "continues the legend, you remember George back in Cyprus when she was attending the Terra Santa School?" said Kate.

"Yes, I do, the day father Massimo phoned up and wanted to see me?"

"And we thought something happened to Margarita."

"And I drove there in a hurry, I told you how they received me in the headmaster's office; they congratulated me, told them, I was not the one who wrote the composition."

"Still you are the father."

"Margarita, I said, I'm very proud of you, and all the teachers in that office applauded her, I repeat that I'm really proud of you my dearest, I'm proud of all of you, my young ladies."

"God bless love," sweet memories came back, tried to suppress them; George did not want to spoil the family evening.

"To-night I'm all yours," he said and took a sympathetic look at his family, "I'm ready for whatever you say, even play chess with anyone who likes to."

"No, no chess to-night," complained Kate, "chess requires concentration, no interference, tonight you are ours, for all of us."

After super, they talked over their daily troubles, about the school the girls attended, the labor problem and went to bed later than usual and enjoyed a nice sleep.

In the morning, he woke up like their neighbor who worked normal hours and enjoyed a normal life.

2: *Hard knocks*

George drove up to Mustafa's office down town, his employment permit and temporary residence was due to expire, needed renewal. Mustafa conceded to keep the visa under his name with no covenant. At the office met the Palestinian secretary reading his local newspaper in English, the only one available in a foreign language.

"It's all propaganda, talks about the Leader, the achievements of the revolution and the atrocities of the colonialists," said Fuad, "but costs only three piastres, less than ten cents."

He rose and greeted George as usual, then sat down and began lamenting about the situation and the problem with Mustafa, who was to loose all his property, the government would confiscate it, and Fuad might loose his job.

"Mustafa, you know is in Italy just now, the situation here is very bad, the Big man will confiscate the property from the rich and distribute it to the poor. Qadhafi slowly and surely reaches deeper into society and imposes the authoritarian system into a totalitarian one, terror reigns everywhere."

"Why doesn't he send them to work and earn their living? Why should they be given other peoples' possessions?"

"You are right, but you know here the system is different, he wants to enforce the communist system."

"Where all are equal but some are more equal than others," said George in an amusing way.

"Your papers for the immigration are ready, you have to go though to Hag Mohamed, you know him, Mustafa's father, I talked to him a few days ago during his visit here and he is aware about your papers."

"I met Hag Mohamed once but where does he live?"

"Oh, you don't know his house, he lives at Berka."

"Berka is a large neighbourhood Mr. Fuad."

"I'll explain, take a piece of paper." He began drawing the street system of Berka neighborhood.

"Is there anybody around here who knows the place?" George knew that the old man spoke only Italian.

"Nobody is here just now and I cannot close the office. Ah! Somebody is coming up, I hope is the boy Mahmoud, I'll ask him to ride with you up to there, you just sit there quiet."

Mahmoud, a young Egyptian, quite literate, was employed as a messenger, pageboy and did all sorts of errands. Padded his low salary with some extras from the little odd jobs he undertook.

Fuad handed him the papers after the customary greetings. He studied them carefully, asked George to sign the forms so they would be ready and when he finished his tea asked George to drive him there and back. George with a twist of his head agreed to the demand, the boy normally rode up and down on an old bicycle.

At the old man's house, George was received with reservation, but politely. During the past year, George delivered processed chicken to the old man, which he accepted with contentment. Normally his daughter, a girl of about twelve, received the bagful of chicken. Today the request involved official concern and Mustafa was not that popular with the authorities.

The old man's third wife, very much younger than him, was seen very rarely, gave birth to four children, the girl, who was born with a certain disability and limped badly, a boy of eleven, another boy of six or so and a baby hanging always on the lap of the girl.

The young Egyptian explained the purpose of the visit and handed him the papers. The old man called his limping daughter to read them aloud to him, form after form.

Tea was brought by the little boy who stampled and almost tipped the tray.

After the tea, the old man talked to Mahmoud in a patriarchal way, the boy listened with his head bent down; shaking it from time to time to assure the old man that he sided with his logic. Then the boy explained to the old man that Mustafa conceded for the visa. The old man tried to turn down the request, the boy indulged once again in his recitation, pleading with the man that the Greek had a family and was an honest man .

At last, the papers were stamped; George thanked Hag Mohamed with a warm handshake, and assured him that he will always remember his benevolence.

From that day onwards, George made customary chicken deliveries to the house. He picked plumb, clean chicken that were always accepted with pleasure and was always asked to step in by the limping girl for a cup of tea, and always turned down the invitation for some other time.

George was happy with his visit to the office and the old man, thanked Fuad, and promised him some plumb chicken, gave Mahmoud the usual charge of twenty dinars and drove back home.

For lunch, they had roast beef with potatoes, fresh salad, home baked crispy bread and Sunshake orange juice straight from California.

George felt relaxed now that his papers were stamped and the residence would be renewed for another year.

In the afternoon, George resumed his old routine. With Mahmoud missing, he brought only three hundred birds, left them on the farm and returned home. Spent some time with the girls, took an early super, and went to bed by ten, since he had to get up at least by twelve midnight. He must have just fallen asleep when the house bell rang intensely.

"Dad, the bell is ringing."

George was already awake by the lengthy ringing, "this must be an Arab," said George, pulling up his trousers.

The intruder, at that time of the night, forgot to release the bell button. From inside, George called out without success, he had to step into the yard to yell, "Who is it?"

"Ibrahim, yia Mister."

"Which Ibrahim?"

"The friend of Mahmoud and Gasala yia Mister, open up?"

George, felt a grip in his stomach, he thought another fearful message.

"Mahmoud returned to the farm, we are celebrating there, open up, yia Mister."

George opened up and the intruder almost fell on him. Breathless, repeated that Mahmoud was really on the farm, that he escaped from the detention camp and was really back.

"*El-hamdullah*, thanks God," said with relief.

"We are having a party there, you must come, and your Mahmoud is back."

"My Mahmoud, ye,s he was working for me, he carried out his duties, but was not my Mahmoud," thought George.

"Switch on the car," continued Ibrahim, "and bring rice, tomato paste, sugar, tea, I don't know what else."

"And salt," George cut him short.

"No, we have salt, salt we have."

"OK, I'll bring meat."

"Yes bring, but do come."

"I'll just put on a shirt, will you wait for me?"

Further back, George noticed a pick up car with its engine still running.

"No. No, I'll go back with Ashiur as quickly as possible."

"Yes, I'll come, thank you for coming, here take money for renting the car."

Coming out of his house met Nasser; the Libyan who lived across the street, came forward and asked George if there was anything wrong and if he needed any help. George thanked him for his interest and got into his car. *This man, most of the time is sitting outside his house, just wondered what he was up to.*

George on his way, stopped at Hag Selim and purchased a bag of rice of twenty-five kilos, ten kilos of sugar since a whole bag weighed fifty kilos, ten, one litre tins of sunflower oil, one kilo of Ceylon tea, ten tins of tomato paste of one kilo, a pack of Sunshake juice, paid the old man and drove off. At Hag Selim one could shop his requirements twenty-four hours a day; he had a bed inside the tiny grocery.

From the distance of more than two hundred meters, George pressed his hand on the hoot of the car and released it only when several figures appeared outside the old house.

George embraced Mahmoud in the traditional Arab way, kissed him five times from cheek to cheek, hugged him as many times, held him tight with both arms, patted his back, looked at him straight in the eyes, and welcomed him. He could do all this now easily, learned it over the time.

Mahmoud was deeply moved, got hold of his boss's hand and moved to the house.

"Gasala! There is something in the back of the car, please bring it inside."

Inside the house and under the feeble light as the single electric bulb was covered with fly remnants, George looked at

Mahmoud closely; the boy looked distressed, unshaved, with matted hair, with scratched forehead, and swollen eyes; looked much thinner, although he was always thin from the hard night work and the constant visits to the neighboring woman. Those three days cost him a lot, very much more.

All sat down on the plastic mat; George looked at Mahmoud again and said.

"Well yia Mahmoud, you had a bad holiday, didn't you?"

"Holiday, boss? It was worse than hell," and went on, told how he was treated from the place he was caught, put with many others in a yard surrounded by a high wall and taken by truck to Quefia.

"There, at Quarchia we were treated reasonably well, they knew you Mister, but at Quefia, *Allah ou Akhbar,* the army was in charge, there. Once out of the truck, were lined up in single file and several soldiers stripped us of all our belongings. They took the wristwatch and my two dinars were pulled out of my pocket. One soldier pulled at my sleeve and torn it off, look at it," he turned his shoulder and showed them the torn shirt.

"After they grabbed what we had, pushed us forward and made us ran to the crowd of detainees."

"Where did you sleep yia Mahmoud?"

"Sleep, Boss? There was no sleep, no food, look at me? Look Boss, I'm not a storyteller and really cannot describe the conditions in that detention camp. Food was brought in limited quantities, if one may call it food, bread two days old, hard as rock, boiled eggs, some boiled too hard, and others like water inside. Grabbed a loaf of bread, one of those round ones; you could throw it as a disc and land without breaking; egg, did not manage to get. As I was walking away, with the loot in my hand, somebody approached me. He walked suspiciously with one hand under his shirt, *you barter, brother,* heard him saying, did not understand, he offered one of the two eggs he had hidden under his shirt, for half of my bread, I was too glad to agree, my bread was hard but his egg was like a pebble.

Water was scarce, the soldiers said that the municipality did not have enough in the area, surely they cut it off."

Gasala brought the foodstuffs in, stealthily George took a glimpse of them, "did you bring all of it boy?"

"Ibrahim is bringing the rice."

"Yia Mister, I killed a chicken from the lot you brought and is in the kettle," said Gasala, in a low tone.

They always took chicken for their needs, many times, more than they needed.

"That's OK," said George, "it's for Mahmoud isn't it, and look how thin he is."

"Same, same Ahmed now."

"Naama sucked your juices," said George and all broke into laughter, it was a common secret that the fat woman satisfied all three of them.

"And how were you released, Mahmoud?"

"Released? Was not released; met two country fellows of mine, from my hometown, and decided to escape. We made a sort of human ladder at the far end of the camp and escaped over the wall."

"All three of you?"

"Yes, the third offered his shoes to an old man; who helped him over the wall. It was about four in the afternoon, at that time many trucks arrived and the soldiers were busy driving people onto the trucks, you know they carry them to the border."

"How did you get here?" George asked eagerly.

"We walked all the way to the *funtuk* from the sea side, there I met Ashiour."

"Ashiour, the neighbor?"

"Yes, being a Libyan, nobody stopped him on the way."

A kettle was brought with steaming chicken stew; the smell of spices, onion and tomato paste filled the small house, reached the nostrils and watered the mouths.

"You have bread, I didn't bring any, at this time of the hour there is no fresh bread," said George.

"Ashiour brought ten loaves from his home."

"And where is Ashiour now?" nobody answered, too concentrated on the smell from the steaming kettle.

"*Tfatal, yia Mister*, please boss," said Gasala.

"Give, give to Mahmoud, I had my super."

"No, you must," insisted Ibrahim, "tonight we are celebrating."

"Of-course we are," George added with zest, "Mahmoud is here."

The kettle was placed in the middle of the group along with several plates, they were actually soup plates, but what did it matter, Ibrahim undertook the task of distributing the hot steaming stew. First, he gave to the two children of Naama sitting on the floor and really staring at the food, then to Naama herself,

"I'll share it with my Ahmed," she said, wriggled a bit her plumb body that sent her ample bosom to bounce and that stirred up the two youngsters.

Ibrahim tried to find the best plate for the boss. He picked the second one from the pile, took a long look with his healthy eye, blew at it strongly, looked at it again, then scooped from the kettle the still steaming stew; he rotated the material in an attempt to pick a good piece for the boss and the supplier of the ingredients.

"Thank you Ibrahim, it looks wonderful," said George, who couldn't wait, the smell was alluring.

"Thank you boss, thank you for the material, thank you very much," said Mahmoud, "this is too much, really too much, take some for your family."

"You are welcome, keep it all, after all you are two now," said George with a witty eye.

The boys giggled softly.

It was a Friday morning when Muftah, the farm owner, came over to the slaughter house with a young woman holding his arm. Fridays were always burdensome, the demand was higher, and the workers demanded free time and the family implored George's intimacy.

"*Good mo'ning*," he said leaning his head forward. All were surprised to see him with a strange woman at the doorstep of the slaughterhouse.

"Good morning Mr. Muftah," said George as politely as he could. His outfit was drenched in sweat and blood and chicken feathers from the defeathering machine, his face was not in any better condition.

"You have some chicken liver for breakfast?"

"Yes, we do, would a kilo be enough?"

"Yes, thank you," he took the bag with the fresh warm liver and led his companion away.

All were shocked; especially Kate; Muftah at his age and seven children, two daughters recently engaged to spend the night in his villa with a prostitute, unbelievable.

George collected the slaughter offal and disposed it at the municipality garbage place. On his way back, drove up to the villa; was flabbergasted, besides Muftah, two girls and another four men huddled in the front room on foam mattresses. Two men were fast asleep with a woman between them, the female half-naked; she must have had a rough night.

The two, were the sons of a neighbour, who owned a chicken farm. They sold their birds at a good price and wanted to celebrate for that; Muftah's villa was ideal.

The smell of fried liver came strong from the kitchen, "add some onion yia Muftah," called Mustafa.

George left them to enjoy their breakfast. Several days later Muftah tried to justify that small gathering.

"You see, when we entertain friends, we like to have around women who have no reputation to lose, a kind of professional ones."

George was not impressed.

"Welcome," said and left them to enjoy their breakfast.

The days rolled by, the work was reasonably good; a decent profit was made. Though the Egyptians were driven out of the city, they were also driven out of the farms, consumption dropped but production was reduced too as the farm helpers were gone.

The revolutionary government wanted to stimulate the interest of the nationals to work their own businesses, including their farms and reap the income. Offered incentives to the farming community; a new gigantic project was implemented, new complete farms were created all over the area of Djabel Akhdar.

Such farms comprised of three bedroom villas with all the amenities, salons, bathrooms, kitchens, garages, with electricity, water, and septic tanks. Apart from the contemporary dwellings, allotted farmland planted with vines, almond trees, fruit trees, mainly apricots, apples, pears, as well as other kinds of trees, imported from European reliable sources. Each farm had its own flock of laying birds, a hundred or so, two cows or twenty ewes.

Besides that, each farmer had a monthly allowance of approximately 250 dollars for the first three years until the fruit trees were established. It was a gigantic project; very few countries offered such facilities on a large scale.

The Colonel spoke continuously and extensively on the national television, tried to inspire his people to accept the offer, the farms on that gigantic project of Djabel Akhdar. He urged them to go into farming and enjoy the healthy life in the open countryside, a far better proposition than swarming in the cities under crowded, unhealthy conditions.

"You will be the heroes of the Great revolution; you will produce our food, our fruit, fresh and succulent. You will grow your children healthy, robust, generation after generation, strong and hurdy, like our distinguished predecessors. Now if you are willing to accept hardships for a time, you can win the battle, but if you persist in laziness and indiscipline, I'm afraid you will pay heavily for your inertia."

He suddenly fell quiet, to create emphasis and declare his seriousness. To night, the subject was on home production. Why shouldn't the followers take advantage of the green revolution and develop their skills and enthusiasm to produce their own food, for their own needs.

"Why rely on an imported tin for your lunch, to morrow you'll open a tin and there will pop up a child with some Asian characteristics. Tell me, has anyone of you planted a tree for production or even for shade; you eat oranges from the trees planted by an Italian countess, shame on you. You very well know that we barely produce the 20% of our food. Idleness is disgraceful. To achieve your goal, you need perseverance and patience. Definitely, nobody can make predictions about the future."

Then, turned downright hostile, created a language of his own, austere and strange, with a taste of spreading in space absolutely that might sound simultaneously profound and absurd.

All the advice and talk fell upon deaf ears, and left many yawning.

Many commented that the wind carried his talk to the desert, the good old habitat. The followers of the revolution showed no interest or enthusiasm to live on lonely farms, although newly built, and many were those who did not trust the fellow. Climatic conditions and poor soils severely limited the output.

The revolutionary committees undertook the great responsibility to deplore poverty and encourage the peasantry to accept the keys of those modern farms and henceforth their management into healthy enterprises.

A peasant is always a peasant, his needs traditionally negligible and his interest in work debilitated, he is contented with a tent, his herd of sheep and most probably a pick up car, not that he needs it but because his adversary managed to buy one. Were accused of being as thick as bricks.

Even if the Italians were long gone, macaroni consumption remained high in Libya and easily may be considered, the stable food in the countryside.

When the Leader saw no response from his disciples, threatened to let these contemporary farms to Tunisians. He would prefer the Egyptians, but due to the political differences with his counterpart, thought of coalescing with this small country on his west, with European orientation. The Tunisians proved too clever, their single blunder might be the concession to Yiaser Arafat, to open an office on their territory.

The witty proclamation sent cold wind up the peasants' pants. They considered the land as sacred and inherited from their ancestors, their Kabilas. With unreserved sheep grazing, over countless years, it would be inexplicable to allow another nationality to undertake these lands; they were Muslims all right, in their own way to be frank, since they drank prohibited beverages by the Holy Koran.

According to the unwritten law, if any one cultivates a piece of land to grow food to support his family, it is in his right and if he manages to cultivate that piece of land for two successive years nobody had the moral courage to drive him off. This may not be written in the scriptures, but is well respected by every believer; mind you, land is so abundant in Libya that very few were interested in cultivating more than what they could cope with.

Fearing, that another nationality might establish itself on their own land and with a few more fiery speeches, the roaming Bedouins succumbed and conceded to undertake the farms of their homeland.

This decision of theirs proved constructive, not only their ancestors rested in peace, but the land did not change possession and the market within a few years was flooded with locally produced agricultural products with vegetables, fruit; even wine was produced along with genuine white spirit from the locally grown grapes.

Tripolitania was by tradition the producing area of agricultural products. All kinds of fruit, potatoes, onions, carrots, alfalfa, olives, just name it. The production did not only suffice the area but sent to the rest of the country.

To stimulate agricultural production in Cyrenaica, a decree was passed that no product that could be produced locally should be brought from Tripolitania or from across the border. The decree did not only create shortages of certain products, but many disappeared altogether, like citrus fruits; not a single citrus tree existed in eastern Libya, such trees were totally restricted to Tripoli area. The locals insisted that citrus trees never thrived on this part of the country, a wrong concept.

It was interesting to listen to the Colonel accusing the Benghazi people of being lazy and indifferent; they frittered their time in unproductive jobs, like street corner shops and failed to plant even a single tree on their multi-acre farms.

"Everybody and I mean everybody; eat oranges and tangerines from the citrus trees that Italian countess planted years ago. This is not only shameful but also absurd. Idleness is disgraceful, to achieve your goal, you need perseverance and patience."

Such were the accusations of the Leader; inertia returned to its lethargic mood, the moment the television set was turned off, everything was put aside.

Nobody attempted to grow onions or potatoes in Cyrenaica, two stable products that vanished from the market after the decree. Limited quantities reached the outskirts of Benghazi across the inhospitable desert roads since the formidable army and the street militia guarded heavily the main ones. Prices soared; complaints were mounting.

Another decree was issued, to alleviate the intermediaries; the farmers should market all agricultural products from parsley to oranges, from tomatoes to barley, by themselves. The marketing of agricultural products got more and more complicated, no Libyan was prepared to sit outside his farm and wait for the customers to buy his meager produce, and none of them had the quantity or the variety to maintain a shop. Very few voices raised their tone to be heard and taken into consideration.

A well-known entrepreneur said that a new law or decree is issued every twenty-four hours; it takes nerves and brains to follow them.

The new decree stated that all agricultural products had to be marketed through a central board and made available through the chain of the People's supermarkets, and here arose the multitude of problems. At the supermarket arrived what remained after the army had the prime choice, the inmates the second, the black marketeers and the traffickers their share.

George walked once into the almost empty supermarket and requested two kilos of tomatoes. Explained that he had a family of four and needed the commodity badly. The person in charge handed him a plastic bag with two or three tomatoes floating in a slimy fluid.

"Are these tomatoes?"

"Yes, don't you see them?"

"These are rotten."

"They are good enough for you, you bloody foreigner."

The blood rose to his head, his nerves tightened, unable to react, placed the bag on the counter and turned away; the abuses were countless and loud.

One could buy limited quantities, from behind stonewalls of farms bordering roads and only during late hours. Prices were exuberant and the quality depended on his acquaintance. Values deteriorated, marketing was jeopardized, and products were contra banded.

George called on an afternoon at the farm of one of his friends, Mustafa; he owned a big farm in Quefia. When the Egyptians were around, the production on this farm was abundant, but now many acres laid idle, bare red soil exposed to the constant blowing east winds.

George tried to reason with the owner that the market was good and should step up his production; the man smiled subtly and said in a whispering tone as if the surroundings were full of flapping ears.

"You see these receipts?" said and pulled a bundle of papers from his pocket.

"These are the receipts they gave me, when I delivered my produce to them."

He meant the Marketing body abstractly, "them."

"Now is the seventh month and they did not pay me a single dinar. Need seeds, fertilizers, insecticides, spare parts, just name it; have to buy these only from them. However, they not only settled their dues, they demanded from me every piaster for their supplies. How clever, from where do I get the money, I have a family, and we cannot eat just parsley and pumpkins day after day?"

"You are absolutely right, although you are obliged to settle your bills, you cannot request settlement for your produce deliveries."

From afar, a Toyota was entering the farm at high speed, "here they come, and you better go inside that shed."

George hasted into an old hangar nearby and kept company to the fat rats for more than an hour. He kept out of sight behind a wooden box, heard footsteps, crouched lower and listened, someone came into the hangar and pissed noisily against his hiding box, two rats fled from under the box, the intruder walked away and the flies swarmed in for a drink.

"Boy come, where are you?" called Mustafa.

George rose to his feet and rushed out freeing himself from the rats, and the ammonia.

"They are bastards, they demanded why I do not deliver vegetables to the board. Told them, the water turbine broke down and do not have money to replace it. I haven't been paid for more than six months; I have no money even for my family."

George looked at Mustafa amazed and let him talk; all he wanted was some vegetables for his family, the man had problems with his own people. Mustafa complained about the system of marketing, the wastage of the products, and the contraband during the nights; he referred to tons of vegetables that rotted at the collecting centre for obvious reasons.

"In the end who pays for all the wastage, the producers suffer the losses, nobody cares for us."

George constrained himself to a compliance with Mustafa's grumbling, nodded his head, wanted to flee from that place. When Mustafa deflated, pointed to the vegetable beds, and said, "Go George, take what you need, at least what is available."

"Ah, some for the family," on his way out, George asked for his friend, he was gone.

"Yia Mister, got money with you?"

"Yes, yia Mahmoud! I think I have."

"Give us one dinar to buy bread."

"You are going to buy a lot of bread then."

"We need some sugar and tea."

"Then you require more than that, my dear fellow. Why you left the okra on the plants? It's overgrowing."

"Not only the okra, the cucumbers, the tomatoes, the pepper, the aubergin, all the produce is in the field."

"Why, yia Mahmoud? Did you quarrel with the Hamed?"

"Not with the owner, he shows great understanding."

"Then, what happened?"

"That son of a bitch."

"Mahmoud what's wrong."

"You know Mr. George; the farmers have to deliver their produce to that stupid organization for agricultural products."

"Well?"

"They do not pay the producers, owe us a lot of money, have not been paid for more than six months, now we do not have money even for bread."

"Come with me Mahmoud."

"Several producers just like us, used to sell some of their produce on Fridays when the municipality police are sleeping. We know that is forbidden, but what can we do, our families back home need money, have expenses, we are poor fellahin, came over to Libya for a few bloody dinars and here we are, cannot sell the produce."

"You sold some on Fridays on the sly, where?"

"At the small square behind the fish market square, you know the place surrounded by those ficus trees."

"Yes, I know the place."

"There, a few bold producers went early, before dawn, took with them what they could, believe me we almost sold it for nothing, people have no money, their Leader scraped it off them a couple of months ago."

"Yes, when they changed the money."

"Exactly, at least we collected some money to keep us going. Last Friday, about ten in the morning, the time people drop in for their purchases, a brand new Toyota rushed through the narrow street and knocked off the stalls, the stands and crushed them along with the vegetables. The sellers, rather the peddlers jumped to safety. I think two or three got injured, but nobody bothered about them. Then, the bastard drove over the pavement, and run over the whole place and smashed anything and everything. I was with Montasef, had to run through the arch to Omar Mukhtar Street, left everything behind, even the funny looking scale."

On pain of imprisonment, Libyans and non-Libyans dared to criticize the government, its political system or its leader, Muammar Al-Qadhafi.

"My God, why?"

"They are crooks, do not like foreigners working here, we've been here, rather going and coming for how many years, more than twelve. We are leaving, let them go hungry, which Libyan will cultivate his land?"

"Mahmoud, feel sorry for you, really."

"Sorry, not sorry, this is the rotten situation, you are lucky; you got a job with their government."

"So, to say, yia Mahmoud."

"Yes, you have your diploma and that counts."

George paid a visit to his old friend Nasser, there he learned that the driver of that Toyota that devastated the producers, was shot dead just outside his house in Sid Hussein and nobody even bothered to investigate his death. Some expressed their satisfaction the way he was treated.

3: *Plucking up the roots*

The Secretary, as was named the Minister of agriculture, heard the complaints of the most audacious farmers, at one of the meetings of the popular committees for agricultural products. A few days later, the marketing board for agricultural products was closed down by a new decree, and the farmers were allowed to peddle their produce in defined places or in front of their farms. The decision legalized somehow the smart ones. In front of the farm wall minimum quantities and varieties were available for sale, behind the wall one could buy products of unknown origin at a premium price, the supply problem was not solved, production was negligible, supplies meager and prices soaring

The Secretary of agriculture decided to solve the problem in a different way. A gigantic project was set up that undertook the production of the most popular vegetables like tomatoes, cucumbers, marrow, parsley, and coriander.

Two groups of green houses were built, one at the Barge area, especially for the needs of the army and one in Benghazi area, on the Tripoli road.

Agricultural production may be planned but not guaranteed; the produce was there and abundant, but vanished overnight. By the second year the Barge area green houses closed down due to poor management and those of

Benghazi area were turned to flower production, mainly for carnations; the supermarkets were flooded with huge bunches of carnations with very few interested to buy, the locals had no affection to flowers, except on special occasions, like decorating the wedding vehicles.

The shrewd and non-aligning entrepreneurs, fled abroad to Malta, Italy or Greece, where many already had business connections or were married to spouses from those countries. There, they either lived off their fat bank accounts or created businesses. Very seldom, the whole family was allowed to travel abroad and the militants were busy in harassing members of those families left behind. The pressure was immense, the weaker ones joined the club, and information was thriving.

Abroad, the dissidents decided to convene to antirevolutionary organizations; some governments promised help but remained at lip service level.

Death squads from the homeland were dispatched to countries entertaining such dissidents with abhorrent consequences, several were murdered in cold blood, and others forced to flee to countries like Egypt under Anwar Sadat, the invincible desert wall between the two countries was formidable.

The second in command, Abdel Salam Jalloud, justified the assassination of dissidents, saying that they fled abroad, took with them goods belonging to the Libyan people, and put their illicit gains at the disposal of the opposition led by Sadat, imperialism and Israel.

In Jamahiriya, that is how the Libyan Arab Republic was declared, though only known as such within its own boundaries, a multitude of organization was in progress, and the military had the priority. For a while, it seemed that all the factories of the Soviet Union were working day and night to cope with the needs of the Jamahiriya military program. Ship after ship arrived at the port of Benghazi, unloaded trucks, tanks, and huge wooden containers. Special tracks with missiles were driven through the city towards Topolino missile base, Fuehat tank unit and the Tripoli road training camps. Others left for Elabiar, Adjdabia or Tobruq. The country was turned to a military base with Russian instructors. Ming fighter planes cramped the Benina airport. Army vehicles were criss-crossing the streets day and night; Libyan drivers traditionally rough and lawless, now became worse. Army tracks became the dismay of the roads; if one did not drop off the road, nobody guaranteed him or his car.

The generation under constant counseling so as to acquire as much knowledge as possible and be able to undertake the future ruling of their homeland was under tight scrutiny. Their mind still green and being like the toothpaste that is easier to get out of the tube than to put in again.

The unrest in the higher institutions obliged the rulers to lay off several of their instructors who expressed enough experience to guide the new generation.

The message reached the den of the ruler, and the reactionaries had to be rounded up and directed to discipline or exterminated. The second was much easier.

Pressure and disciplinary sanctions failed with the hard headed and stubborn students, the race was about power.

The early windfall earnings from oil exports flowed to the broader public under King Idris, through specific channels and education was one of them.

The students got accustomed to a more cosseted lifestyle and any attempt to change the style or impose restrictions, lead to growth of frustration, outbreaks of violence and vandalism.

When classes were suspended and students expelled, hundreds of them rallied towards the town, informing drivers on the way about their cause and shouting slogans.

Mental records were kept by disguised paramilitaries and every single attempt for organized rallies was followed by detention, imprisonment and disappearance.

Foreign students who landed in the Jamahiriya under the cloak of scholarship for Islamic studies found themselves in the heart of the desert in training camps undergoing indoctrination in the use of force, rioting and even terrorism against their own governments.

Mounting discontent spread rumors of an anti-coup; brave dissidents would infiltrate from outside, join those within, with the support of some disappointed army officers would endeavor to initiate the overthrow of the Colonel. The attempt was by members of the National Front for the Salvation of Libya, and fighting took place at Bab Alaziya in Tripoli where Qadhafi's headquarters are, the attempt failed at its nativity in .84. Several fighters were killed.

The United States have been accused of being behind the attempt, discontent and accusations ran high.

A period of terror shrouded the country, hundreds were interrogated or imprisoned, an unknown number executed, army officers were singled out and executed without judgment; some of the infiltrators, were captured near the Tunisian border, two or three were kept alive, imprisoned, tortured bodily in their cells and mentally at the special courts under the cameras. Libyan television broadcasted selected hangings and torturing.

Members of the death squads traveled abroad to annihilate those dissidents who dared to oppose the aims of the great revolution.

How many souls perished aimlessly will never be known. Instead of exploiting those clever brains, have been singled, imprisoned, tortured, perished, what a tragic loss for an upcoming nation.

The United States expelled all employees of the Libyan people's Bureau in Washington and advised Americans working in Libya to terminate their activities there.

An embargo was imposed by both United States and the European Union, in an attempt to curb Qadhafi's terrorist attacks at various parts of the world. The embargo proved too porous, petrol being a prime commodity, many opportunists found ways to circumvent it.

The local television showed it all live and in detail. From their detention cells, the detainees were helped to their feet, and taken to the special courts. Without a lawyer or other legal advisor, were obliged to confess their disgraceful act. Convicted to death by hanging in public, the same old way carried out by the Italians. The Colonel himself, the Great Leader, normally announced the date later. It took almost six months for the announcement.

Then, his menace turned to the affluent families of the large cities. Nobody could drive a fancy private car down the road; those who defied the orders had their windows smashed, their headlamps broken and their tires slashed.

Nobody could open his purse in public, too many prying eyes. A two-piece suit inspired suspicion; a necktie was the symbol of the money sucker. The tying of a necktie was demonstrated on television in a disguised manner. Tying a knot was like the sign of a cross, the cross being the symbol of the Christians, the Christians were Europeans, Europeans were traders, traders were thieves, stole the money of the poor. This was the slogan against any person dressed modestly.

Trousers made of jean cloth became the mark of hatred, jean trousers originated in America, a general name for the United States of America. The Americans were suckers. Anyone wearing such trousers was considered an agent of the Black House, the coded name of the White House; the guardians of the Great revolution roamed the streets, agents wearing jean trousers were attacked, had their trousers slit off above the knee, it was not only embarrassing but shameful too; thanks God this notion did not last that long.

Before the issue of one mandate, a second one slipped down the conjurer's sleeve. This time it was sheer robbery, the rich families were in pursue, these bourgeois deceived the nation and consequently the people of the Jamahiriya, concealed their real revenues, cheated the inland revenue, did not pay their taxes.

Indictment of the bourgeois was organized in great detail. The guards of the revolution, accompanied by armed soldiers of the special squad and a television group paid visits to selected rich families at odd hours. In a boisterous manner, the family was intimidated at gunpoint, and the head of the family interrogated.

Such a visit and in the most abhorrent presentation was contacted at the impressive villa of Fathi Ibrahim, a relatively young civil contractor. When the Colonel was maddeningly expanding his military camps, Fathi managed to get several contracts. Smart, as he was, subcontracted a foreign company to do the jobs. The contracts around Benghazi, at Elabiar and as far as Ajdabia, where the mercenaries' camps were constructed, brought considerable profit to Fathi. As the common saying goes, riches cannot be concealed, Fathi was affected by this maxim.

Along with the military camps, the subcontractors built a specious villa for Mr. Fathi on a specious acreage at the outskirts of the city of Benghazi. In that area, underground water was abundant and that encouraged the owner to develop a nice orchard. One could see vines on trellis covering the farm alleys, citrus trees, banana plants, and a multitude of other fruit trees as apples, pears, plumbs, peaches, mango trees, and palm trees of the newest varieties. He tried cherry trees but the climate was not suitable for such plants that require a term of vernalization for the crop to bind. At a distance from the magnificent villa, an animal station was built, with a small dairy unit, a few goats of the improved breed was brought from Cyprus, three ugly camels and some layer birds. A pigeon loft towered the other buildings and his pigeons again of fine breeds were free to fly to and fro.

Mr. Fathi was in fact well equipped and organized in case an embargo or something like was imposed. That farm complex was an alluring spot for investigation. He was more than happy there, away from the city with his family of four, until the Colonel's militants paid him a nocturnal visit.

The visit was planned in detail. The scenario began by showing the large and impressive entrance with the guard's room, and the vine covered alley leading to the magnificent villa.

The photographer did not miss the orchard with its well-tended fruit trees, flowerbeds, the climbing jasmine, the honeysuckle, and the multiflora rose bushes.

Emphasis was given to the mass of the villa with the marble covered verandas, the large windows, a rarity in an Arab country, and the heavy door made of hard wood with impressive carvings. The camera showed in detail the artwork of that magnificent door, moved to the children's playground, showed the swings, the small water pool with the two white swans floating in a majestic way on the clear water. The docile birds suspected nothing of what was going on and when the floodlight fell upon them, withdrew their graceful necks, moved affectionately close to each other as though performing to an audience.

Inside the house, the camera operator took his time; did not miss a single item. Showed, the shining Italian marble on the floor, the paintings on the entrance walls that extended to several meters and the inner door, so professionally made. In the salon, money was spent lavishly on furniture and adornments. Then, showed the bedrooms, the bathrooms, and the dining room. The furniture from Egypt and Italy and the marble from Greece aroused the interest of the viewers. Fathi put a lot of his money into his own life and his dreams.

Details of the wardrobe of Mr. Fathi's wife full with dresses from European houses of multitude style and fashion, were displayed in front of the camera, with variable comments.

The family was saved the exposition; the local taboos were respected, where no female is ever allowed to be seen by strangers, so Mr. Fathi remained the central figure. The camera now pointed at him; the yesterday's prominent figure, now curled on the oversize armchair like a beaten dog, with eyes turned to the infinite, wide with terror. With a half-open mouth and a pair of hands resting nervously on his knees. He was not given much chance for meditation.

"You seem to be a very wealthy man, yia Fathi," here politeness and respect had no room, "how did you manage to acquire so much wealth in such a short time, how old are you?"

Fathi, the successful entrepreneur, who drove the latest model of Volvo, dressed in two piece suits, drank distilled water, had his groceries delivered, spent his holidays in Europe and entertained the elite of his home town, was now under the fiery interrogation by the son of Ahmed Salem from Timini, a tiny village of shepherds, hundred and twenty miles away. Electricity or running water was still to come in that remote place.

Ibrahim Ahmed Salem, that was the name of the interrogator, since the Leader forbade the use of the tribe name by decree, stared at Fathi like the hawks of his native village, balanced the moment for the attack. He had enough time; it was still early in the night, and aimed at that psychological moment for the dive.

Time at Timini was never a problem; the sheep would roam the bare vast shoulders of the plateau from dawn to dusk, therefore time did not matter here either.

The rough-hewn primitive male whom civilization had not refined-hardness, crudity and vigor, sucking his teeth with villainous sideways glance, sharpened his claws now.

He was a hero in front of the television camera and over the coming days even months, he would be seen by more than a million people; his family might not, neither his villagers, they would get to hear it though. He was chosen to do the job, he took advantage of his position, his cultural traditions of the wilderness, his sharp tongue and claws; the person at his feet was not more than a few kilos of flesh, an easy prey.

With an icy smile began his questions, he was pumped with an excess amount of venom, was obliged to dispense part of it, here was his chance.

Fathi might have had answers; reasonable answers that through the years he grabbed the opportunities offered to him and by professional and experienced procedures earned a decent profit. However, under such humiliation he could not even articulate the simplest phrases. Thought it wiser, to say as little as possible. The time was tense for victim and raider.

Ibrahim shot his first questions and the camera darted from the assailant to the victim.

"Where is the gold?" demanded Ibrahim with rather a soft voice.

Fathi lifted his head just enough to face Ibrahim, the eye contact enraged him.

"Where is the gold *ustad Fathi?* Where are the kilos of gold you bought from Suk-el-dalam?"

Fathi's larynx dried out, his vocal chords shrunk, did not respond to his reflexes. Fathi contracted even more in front of Ibrahim, though the interrogator was much shorter and thinner.

"Gold, which gold? I bought a negligible quantity for my wife when she gave birth to our first baby; this is quite customary in our traditions." Fathi said at last.

"Leave your fake stories aside, where is the golden necklace of eight kilos, where is the diamond studded tiara, where are the heavy leg bracelets, the diamond rings, the necklaces… where are they?"

"I don't understand," tattered Fathi.

The camera, until now was directed at the interrogator, the main actor of the scenario. When turned to Fathi, something must have happened to him in this short interlude, was shown curled on the carpet with his hands between his legs. By mistake, could be deliberately, the camera showed another three persons on the scene, they could have forced Fathi to coil down with body pains, like a badly hit dog.

The interrogator repeated the same stereotype questions twice with no answers, the curtain fell, this act finished. Fathi was dragged along the vine covered alley; he was directed somewhere else.

The whole group was standing on the elevated paved paths. The light breeze caused the vine leaves to move and the lemon tree branches to shake; even those citrus branches showed their respect to their owner, shook their leaves and waved white bunches of flowers, the delicate aroma reached George's nostrils as he watched intensely the television, and that helped him back to his senses.

For a moment the viewers thought that Fathi was dragged away to be hanged right there from his vine supports. No, they had no intention of ending his suffering so soon, instead, they proceeded to a half demolished dome brick oven. The four axe holders were digging and pulling down the bricks, within minutes the structure was a pile of rubble, they cleared the basement and revealed a concrete slap, nothing could resist those diggers in front of the camera, the slab was smashed and removed.

Ibrahim, winked at one of his people, who immediately climbed down the revealed opening, assisted by one of his mates, holding a large flashlight. More lights were lowered and the cameraman descended, the exposed cache was unbelievable. A whole strong room below ground with a heavy iron door, where ustad Fathi systematically stored his treasures.

One by one, pulled out the valuable pieces from safety drawers and presented to the viewers, through the camera's eye. It was a treasure cache. Kilos of golden ornaments were revealed, diamonds of many carats adorned the tiaras, the rings and the necklaces, everything went into a large black bag, sealed on the spot, Fathi and gold were carried away, end of act one.

4: Family life despite all odds

A wave of ruthless terror hovered over Benghazi. The sky was gloomy over Fuehat, the suburb of the rich. The hard wood doors of the impressive villas were forced open in the small hours of the night, the bourgeois were dragged out of exquisite bed rooms, shoved into Toyotas, just in their silk pajamas; inside the "bird box" as those cars were known, and carried away, very few witnessed those scenes.

The heavy iron gate, painted in the revolutionary green color, seldom opened under the rays of the sun, preferred the soft defective moonlight, and acquired nocturnal habits.

The invisible net of the night meant to catch any snippet of information floating in the air and transform it into the intrigue and envy that infest the human soul; the word, reality, was beyond description, those were the circumstances and many turned downright hostile to the slightest provocation, revengeful.

Only the bright sun crossed the expanse of the enormous camp and at that, from a very distant height; the moon in its various faces witnessed the inflowing of the bourgeois brought in at odd hours. The camp was named, Seventh of April.

How ironic, the season of abundance in color and metamorphosis, the month of the birds, as was known to the public. The month of the improved weather, when the soil bursts with growth, the month the birds inspired by the lengthening of the day come closer to each other than ever, build their homes and mate frivolously for their natural conservation.

How tragic, the best time of the year when people freed from the unsteady winter, flow out into the countryside, instead of that, the elite of the town were rounded up for trivial or no apparent reason, carried to that treacherous camp, tortured, humiliated, deprived of their freedom, unable to defend themselves, devastated.

Here, someone was thriving on power, on the pain, and humiliation of the others, and tore them away from their homes, their beloved ones; simply being smart enough, to cash on the wings of development.

Many were brought into the camp; several succumbed from the dreadful physical sufferings. Some transferred to Tripoli for further interrogation, others given long leave to the horrible prison of Quefia. Little or no documentation kept of the inmates on such basic data as crime and condemnation. Quite a number set free, so to say, the freed ones found their businesses closed, their belongings confiscated, their second houses, and even more, their extra apartments taken away, and given to the people. The people that never bothered to work, those who never thought of tomorrow, who never saved a piaster.

George rose every night close to midnight, drove from Fuehat along the Tripoli road, passed the famous camp on the way to his slaughterhouse and back again, when his work was over. He avoided even turning his head towards the heavily guarded camp gate, luckily, it was on his left hand side, and as the road was of a double lane, George passed the place from a distance of more than twenty meters. On his way back, it was daylight and the sun enlightened his thoughts and fears.

During the day, the traffic was heavier and that helped to ease the tension, somehow.

Despite the climate and the terror bewildering everyone, George managed to carry on.

The limited supply of foodstuffs and the awkward hours of the supermarkets, created a heaven for Kate. Developed a small chicken market for herself, the neighbors called for chicken, surpassed their notion that the birds were not killed by the halal way, the expatriates working with foreign companies called regularly for their supplies; were too pleased to buy clean chicken.

George allowed his wife to keep the money she collected, for her personal whims, she was quite happy.

When the bourgeois' businesses were shut down, many other related ones followed suit too. Many employees found themselves without work, that forced them to indulge in such activities that before were looked down, such a set up was the processing and peddling of chicken. Their finished product though did not much that of George and very few of his customers turned to another source. He was the only European engaged in such a messy job, the work was definitely not to be envied but was rewarding. He offered a very reliable service and clean products of prime quality. George came under the beacon of his competitors' eyes, though. The yesterday's friendly and generous Libyans, today, turned to stern rival Bedouins some were even hostile.

George kept an open mind, was friendly with those who understood the difficulties of the times, advised them on the proper killing and marketing of chicken, how to avoid bruising the carcasses, and cleanliness was of prime importance. Very few appreciated George's instructions and many were those who listened and calculated on shortcuts for the simple reason of quick profit, though very short sighted. Being locals, Muslims, with numerous connections, connections to such bodies set up by the Leader with variable political power, which counted a lot in those days.

George kept away from politics, kept a low profile, down to earth, and became a willow. His greatest worry was the traffic police, his car was not only old but also needed repairs badly, denting, and a good coat of paint. He was planning to renew it; it was impossible for him to purchase a new car directly from the new government controlled company. He begged assistance from some friends, with a certain commission of-course; his offer was rejected on the spot on false pretensions, although not forgotten.

Another big problem that hovered over George's neck was the new body of 'the guards of the city'. This was a municipality police force responsible for price and quality control, with great power and unlimited scope of action. The dedicated authority was translated to responsibility and ferocity.

Old Hamid warned George about them, "you see George" he said one afternoon whilst they waited to buy live chicken from one of the farms, "you are the only European in the trade, you are not a Muslim, everybody knows that, you have no license for operating a slaughterhouse and Muftah is a weak person in the town now."

"You know his father was a big electrical contractor and the co-owner of the Omar Khayyam hotel, but Muftah likes his distilled water, you know what I mean. You see, he is on the wrong side and in case of trouble he cannot help you."

George's ears went ablaze with the facts reiterated by old Hamid.

"What do you advise me?" asked George trying to conceal his alarm.

"I'm afraid very little, try to keep your premises as clean as possible, deliver the chicken early, these people start work at eight; and always have a Muslim to kill your birds."

The farm owner called them to start collecting the birds and left their conversation to that. George knew that things were deteriorating fast and badly, he was in the eye of the storm.

Mohamed Morsi, one of his good customers, ran a large restaurant near the fish market; his weekly sales were low, compared to those of Farag only a few meters further along the street, but George liked to supply him, just to keep other competitors away. Most of the times, he was the last customer to be visited and George took his time with him. He was an amicable man, soft spoken, pleased with the chicken he received, and his customers were satisfied with the quality. Many times Mohamed invited George to take a cup of tea and a small sandwich from what he offered for sale at his restaurant, made of fried chicken liver. It was not the best for breakfast but many a times was like manna after the long hours. At one of those days, old Mohamed confessed to George how he acquired his surname.

George, munching his sandwich was more than interested and asked, "Well how did you get it? Is it not your family name?"

"No, not in the least. When young, very young, hid in a Greek boat lying here in the small harbor and landed on the island of Crete. Stayed there for more than twelve years, doing all kinds of errands around the market, mainly carried the shopping baskets full of vegetables to the homes. People talked to me, in Greek of-course, "*ela more esy, ela more esy, more esy, come here you little one, and turned to be Morsi.*"

"Very interesting," said George and called out, "*ela more esy.*"

"Found a new car for you," he said with a whispering tone, "you come in the afternoon to see it when it will be much quieter here."

George drove down town in the afternoon and there was a brand new Peugeot pick up with only a hundred kilometers on the meter. He bought it on the spot, right away, for two thousand dinars, about two hundred above the agency price; he gave a deposit and the next day was registered in his name, the first possession in Libya that legally belonged to George.

Now, with one problem less, he could drive anywhere without being pestered by the notorious traffic police. George gave his old car to Muftah as a gift, though he put a new engine not that long ago. George always liked to help those who helped him. Muftah was thrilled with his acquisition, promised to do the required body repairs and use it for his family.

Within a week Muftah sold the new engine, the wheels a few days later and dumped the rest under the shade on an old olive tree, George was very disappointed. It was though registered in Muftah's name the moment George paid the seven hundred dinars, two years ago.

With a new car, George's image was upgraded among the community, but moreover his family appreciated the new acquisition. Now Kate did not hesitate to climb onto the new car though the passenger seat could not take five persons whatever their age. George promised to acquire a saloon car the soonest. Every time the four passengers piled into the seat, Kate remembered their brand new Bermuda blue Vauxhall, George purchased three weeks before requesting her hand from her father; it was one of the latest models in their home town of Kyrenia before the devastating Turkish invasion.

"We need a new saloon car," George said one day, when Kate put on a brand new dress and had to hold Margarita on her knees for lack of space.

"Yes, George," she said softly, "at least the traffic police will not pester you for carrying four in the passenger seat."

The neighbor appreciated the new car too, and many were those who came forward to congratulate George and inquire how he managed that since it was almost forbidden for non-Libyans to buy new cars, but did not refrain from saying, "*Mabrook*, Good luck."

Nasser, living just across the street insisted to tell him how much it cost with the registration, as he was so much interested, George told him.

"You could have saved up to two hundred dinars if you told me that you needed a new car, the secretary of the committee is a close friend of mine."

George thanked him for his great interest, "Next time, Mr. Nasser."

After dark, the traffic on all roads was scarce but George was obliged to be on the road at odd hours for the family's bread. The work was rolling reasonably well, Mahmoud and Gasala stayed on the farm away from prying eyes but George wondered for how long. He was the only person they met, spoke to and mixed with; at least that's what he thought.

The school year was drawing near; the three Cypriot girls were hard at work for their end of the year exams, tried to help them as much as time permitted; none of them actually needed any help. They were bright and good scholars; throughout the year, studied hard enough and showed no gaps in their homework. Even now at the examining period all three looked relaxed and went about freely, this was George's greatest satisfaction, it reminded him of his school days; he was just as cool and confident.

"Oh! I'm…these walls drive me…"

"Drive you mad, Margarita? Have you finished your homework?"

"Now? Hours ago."

"And you have nothing else, I mean interesting to do?"

"Books, books and books."

"You hear the uproar in the street?"

"They are all males."

"Even at that, they play day in, day out, nothing positive really."

"I agree Dad, take the daughters of our landlord, they are grown up girls with very little in mind, where is their learning, future, targets, nothing."

What a disgrace, what a waste of time. All the neighborhood children, anything from five to fifteen creep out of their homes day in, day out and engage themselves in playing. They play football. If their ball is inflated or not, does not really matter as most of them wear plastic slippers or go barefooted.

The street is wide enough and the house walls high enough to provide ample space for exercise. No gates and the goalkeepers take part in the disorderly game. Screaming and shouting fill the atmosphere. The kids may come to confrontation for some misunderstanding, but very seldom use their fists. Few angry phrases, probably some pushing but soon the matter is resolved and the game continues. Sweaty and dusty faces do not matter, the street not paved yet and the soil turned to powder by the passing cars. The game goes on feverishly until six or until a sister calls that Centipede, the beloved program is about to start and the game drops there on the spot, even the ball is left in the middle of the street. All kids flow to their homes, to watch the series, until the next day the same crowd, the same game.

"Dad, you know that our school is about to close for the summer?" Margarita was not interested in what the street children were pursuing day after day.

"Oh, is it?"

"Yes, Dad, you have not realized that it's June already?" said Margarita, who was playing with her doll.

"Dad, we like to go to Cyprus after the school closes, you think we'll manage?" said Sonia.

"Yes, Dad, here is like a prison."

"After the school closes we have nowhere to go."

"Except paying visits to the J&P camp, and only when you have time to take us," said Mary, who was playing with her watercolors.

"Now, you three, you have nothing to study? Tomorrow aren't you having exams? And the one is drawing; you are playing with your doll and you Sonia?"

"Oh. I'm reading."

"And what are you reading? If I may ask."

"Hawk Finn," she said casually.

"Translated?"

"Dad…no."

"In English? Bravo Sonia! I want you to tell me the story when you are through."

"Daddy, I will tell you the whole story," said Margarita, lifting her head up, her hands still fumbling with the belt of her doll.

"Margarita, it's me whom Dad asked."

"I don't want to hear it, I'll read it by myself when I'll be able to read English," said Mary.

"And understand English," added Margarita.

"Gave your passports for the visas and I believe to have them back in a week's time."

"Oh, yes?" and three graceful shining faces turned up.

"You like to go via Athens or direct to Larnaca?"

There was a pause, a hesitation.

"The tickets do not cost that much more than the direct ones and you can spend a few days with your aunt in Athens."

"Yeees... Through Athens, and I can visit the Parthenon," said Mary.

"Oh, again," complained Sonia, "I'd rather go to the island where my uncle is serving."

"Oh, the island of Lesvos?"

"Yes the island of Lesvos," said Sonia dropping her book on the oversize table; she looked determined to start there on the spot.

"Well, say a week or so in Athens, so Mary can learn something about her famous ancestors and visit the world wide known ancient Greek monuments; you can discuss with your aunt about Lesvos."

"Oh, my aunt never likes to close her pharmacy and take us to any place, never mind Lesvos."

"Now, now don't complain about my sister."

"And our dear uncle will be in Athens studying for his postgraduate degree, like last year," said Margarita grudgingly.

"Well, you take your chances; probably you prefer to go direct. Your grandparents will be waiting for you."

"Yes, and close us in the apartment, my grandfather never has time to take us anywhere."

"Yes, Grumpy always drives the lorry, even on Sundays."

"So, you better go through Athens and spend a week or so there, probably you get a chance to visit the island, it would be great."

"Yeeees," yelled all three in unison.

"So, tomorrow I'll arrange for the tickets, confirm the seats, I'll arrange with Olympic. Oh, another small matter, I'll check for some drachmas."

"Oh, Dad, I forgot to tell you, the consul came to our school and announced that a boat of the Greek navy is coming to Benghazi next week, its taking cadets on an exercise trip round the Mediterranean."

"Oh, that's an opportunity to change some dinars into drachmas."

"Dinner is ready," said Kate, coming into the salon; all this time she was in her domain, the kitchen; she took her time there, put on her expertise, her recipes were superb.

At the table, George repeated what he discussed with the girls a few minutes ago. Kate remained silent, reserved. She would love to go to Cyprus for a month or so, but loved her husband also. Alone in Benghazi with odd hours of work and an unstable environment; kept quiet, even she stopped eating, and now was poking her food.

George noticed her change of mood but did not respond immediately, gave her time to express herself.

"George, if the girls go through Athens, couldn't I go too at least for two weeks and have those blood tests of mine? Gia has very good connections with specialists," said with head bent over her plate.

"Two, three weeks is not a problem, Kate," said George lightheartedly, "and you come back with the cadets on the Karaiskakis."

"Not in your life," and tossed her napkin at him.

All the family laughed at the comment.

"Our mother is the best of the mothers," said Margarita.

"She is Cypriot, not a Greek woman," said Sonia.

"For this I'm more than certain," said George and added, "Was very careful when I chose Kate, to be your Mum."

A soft tear dropped off Kate's beautiful eyes. George outstretched his hand over the table and Kate gave hers, he began singing softly,

"Around the world, I searched for you, I traveled on and all alone for you..." he returned her napkin as more tears flowed down her silky cheeks.

George found in his pitiable home, in the arms of his wife, in the circle of his children and in the labor to support them all, the happiness he searched the wide world. Nothing overflowed more than the quieter genuine emotions, than those features of patriarchal life, thank God, that weaved without affection into his personal way of living.

A prolonged ringing of the house bell shook all of them to reality, George's song was cut short, his family gazed at him, he rose slowly, steadily and walked out into the yard, paused behind the iron external door, the bell rang again, he called "*Aioua,* Yes?"

"Yia, George," he recognized the voice, that of his neighbour and repeated, "*Aioua.*"

"You forgot the lights on," he said in a casual tone.

George felt a relief, flung the iron door open, and saw the car sidelights still on, switched them off and returned to the house, Sonia was at his tail.

"The Arabs have a characteristic way of ringing bells," said George when he was safe in his house.

"How did you forget the lights on, George? You came in early?"

"Yes, now I remember when I parked the car and was ready to get out, this silly boy of Naima stretched his hand, wanted to press the hoot and you know the lights are on the same arm, now I remember."

"Got scared, you don't know what goes on around here," sighed Kate, George reserved himself.

"Tomorrow I'll arrange five tickets, for all the family," said George cheerfully, tried to change the atmosphere, "now, I need an hour's sleep before going to work."

"Daaad..."and all the girls rushed and kissed him.

"Yes, it's almost eleven," said Kate, took her husband by hand, and led him to their bedroom.

"Time flies when we are together," he almost said altogether, he caught himself the last moment.

At Olympic Airways, George bought five tickets, four returns for Larnaca and for himself, up to Athens and back, needed a break, a change, could afford it now after almost two years of continuous work and what work, sixteen to eighteen hours a day, seven days a week.

He called at Mustafa's office collected the five passports endorsed with exit-entry visas for three months. Now all he required was some currency; it was very risky to look for dollars, as for drachmas father Iacovos of the Greek Orthodox Church was apt for that. George took a walk down Omar

Muftah Street, the main commercial street of the centre, where Father Iacovos frequented; the man lived not far from the central post office.

If they had a predetermined meeting point, would not meet so punctually. The old man was more than a journalist. George was on good terms with him. He received his regular quota of well-dressed chicken; his mistress was not such a delicate cook, but father Iacovos was amicable to his congregation.

"All right my son, I'll get the invitations for the whole family, will you be able to meet me here?"

"Thank you Father, what time, please?"

"Oh, my George, say at six thirty."

"Isn't it too early Father?"

"We can go any time, the captain is my friend, and I've met him at the consulate."

"Thank you Father."

"My son, you know how much I respect you, if you require anything else, just tell me, do not hesitate."

Father Iacovos was always kind and warm with his disciples, people felt free to inquire about almost anything, so George considered the moment of their countenance to ask what was at the back of his mind.

"Father, I know the situation is very bad for everybody just now, but I take the liberty of confiding that I'm in need of a few dollars."

"Trust me, my son, how many, say two hundred, more?"

"It would be a service to me if you can secure me with say two."

"Tomorrow, bring your own."

In addition, with that, meant the corresponding amount, the exchange rate was well known and established, two dollars to the dinar; that meant sixty percent higher than the official rate, where was the official rate, anyway.

"Got your tickets, the passports and the invitations for the ship," said George, the moment he stepped into his house.

"Good for all four?" asked Kate.

"For all five," said George with a broad smile. Kate smiled graciously, the girls flowed out of their room, and jumping up and down with glowing faces grabbed their father's hands and said in unison, "We have a great Dad."

"Thank you my darling, my heart is at rest now, but with such a family who couldn't be."

"Yes, George, I'm glad you are coming too, you really need some rest, a change, you deserve it," said Kate with a tear rolling down her soft cheek.

"May not be able to come with you to Cyprus, but for a couple of weeks up to Athens, have to see the bank there."

"You are not coming to Nicosia, Dad?"

"I'm afraid no, not this time; must get back to look after the job."

"Just for two weeks, George?"

"Hopefully, two."

"If we leave on Sunday, we need a few things from the market."

"All right, you make your list, we go through it together and decide what we need, try to keep the list of the presents to the minimum," said George with reservation.

However, Kate dreamed of reaching Larnaca airport loaded with useful and not useful gifts. Everybody likes to carry gifts for everybody at home, and for everyone who calls to say, welcome, but George barely kept afloat with the family's demands, the new car and the uncertainty of tomorrow. He did not expect any reaction to his comments and let the matter pass almost unnoticed.

George met Father Iacovos by the central post office and walked towards the church and the domain of the old clergyman. In his office, father Iacovos handed George the tickets for the ship, who accepted them with great pleasure, the father was pondering on the second request, George looked up to him inquisitively with a broad smile.

"Got you the other stuff also," said the father. "Here," and pulled out of his deep trousers pocket and handed the two folded notes to George, in the most discreet way as if the walls had eyes and ears. He in his turn handed the reverent father an envelope with the agreed amount in local money, none of them counted or even checked the handled material.

"You know George; I do not have any means to go to the ship."

"Father, you know I have just a pick up and that with difficulty takes the family."

"Never mind, never mind, I'll arrange with some other kind person."

The ship was due on Wednesday, according to Father Iacovos, but with boats, nobody could predict their arrival. George considered Thursday, to be the best day for paying a visit around the harbor for the cadets. Definitely, some would require local money for their purchases. He needed just a few drachmas for the family, if the rate was attractive, he would change a lot more, things were so volatile, and drachmas were not a good proposition but in a drought even hale was welcome.

George finished his deliveries and drove towards the harbor, parked his car in a side lane and walked along the Jamal Abdul Nasser Street. There they were, gleaming in their smart white uniforms, walking in groups of three and four and five.

George approached them, greeted them in Greek, they were delighted to meet someone speaking their language; many expressed their desire to purchase imported electrical appliances still reasonably priced. George sold them dinars and got drachmas; few had dollars, but as they were still at the beginning of their trip, saved the hard currency for their next destination.

The majority swarmed the shops selling portable radios with cassette recorders; others were holding clothes irons for a respected mother. Sparingly one could meet cadets holding a television set for their officers; the cost of such an item was beyond their wallet.

The banks were reluctant to accept drachmas and the shopkeepers too eager to squeeze the young cadets, therefore George was their best choice, he needed currency, whatever kind, and opened an exchange kiosk. The weather was not for a jacket, but George put on a light jacket, stuffed his pockets with dinars, and moved from the Christmas tree square along the Jamal Abdul Nasser Street with the most prestigious shops. Then to the small square in front of the huge municipality building and up to the corner of Omar Khayyam hotel, from there to the harbor side, avoided the immigration building, too many secret police around there. Turned towards the central post office; he needed just one or two cadets to have the first transactions. News travel fast, business was conducted under the shade of a tree or behind pillars. Within two hours, George managed to change more than two hundred thousand drachmas, drove to Fuehat and returned with more dinars but was too late, the cadets vanished, went back to the ship; he expected them to be out later in the afternoon; his schedule was rather pressed, time was too limited for George. Had to purchase live birds, dispose the slaughter refuse, and take his family to the banquet of the Karaiskakis' captain.

George was known throughout the community as a hard worker and as a family person. He never got involved in rampaging; gambling was not his line, never smoked and always contributed generously when it came to the community demands.

Kate, was addressed always, as Mrs. Kate, was highly respected as a person but also for her aristocratic posture that contented George to the bottom of his soul. Kate was always proud of her family, expressed it at every occasion, a hard working, and respected husband with three blooming daughters.

With the onset of the revolution, social life diminished, almost vanished, the best, a family would expect was a social visit to another family. At such visits, everything was not only informal but also rather casual, nobody dared to dress up for a coffee at the hotel, and the militants reserved the tables, long ago. To take a stroll to the shops dressed up above a peasant was risky, so tonight was a great opportunity to dress up in a civilized manner and attend an offshore banquet.

"George, what do you suggest I should put on tonight?"

"The only problem will be the strong breeze, Kate."

"Oh, I'm not going for a desk show."

"My dearest the breeze is... of-course there will be many families from the diplomatic community, you know these people are well orientated and well organized. There will be people from the Ministry of the Interior, the police, from the External affairs section, the immigration, mind you only males from those departments."

"Thank you for the hint."

"Thank you for the understanding, Mum."

"Mum, you look wonderful tonight," said Sonia.

"Mind the captain, Mum," commented Margarita with a twitch of her lips.

Mary was too young for any comments; was too occupied with her new dress.

"Shall we go," said George admiring his wife, Mary took her father's hand and pretended to straighten her collar.

"Maryyy, you look great, in this crimson cotton dress, it fits you very nicely."

"You bought it for me Dad, you forgot?"

"No, love, never," George could not keep track of what has been bought and when, all he tried was to satisfy the family's requirements, to help them regain their confidence after the deportation from their home in the north of Cyprus, their little heaven.

"Shall I borrow Hag Nasser's new Nissan?"

"No, ours is much cleaner," Kate cut him short.

Just beyond the customs gate met father Iacovos walking along, slowed down the moment he noticed them, although ahead, some other families were walking.

At the top of the ladder, stood the ship's captain greeting his guests. Greeted George's family warmly and he thought that was because father Iacovos was accompanying them.

"Welcome aboard, father," and shook hands with their companion.

Father Iacovos introduced them all by their names, wreathing their halo, and emphasizing their refugee status from Cyprus.

For a moment, the captain hesitated, looked across the deck, and then said, "It's a kind of early, we can go to my office though, father."

Since he mentioned only, father, George paused undecided. The captain, a person with long experience, noticed the hesitation, looked at the followers with a broad smile and said,

"We'll all go."

Moreover, with a brisk movement, they were climbing more ladders, the captain, the father holding Mary's hand, Sonia, Margarita, Kate and George trailing behind.

In his quarters, the captain was less authoritative, though his smart navy uniform, cladding an athletic body, looked impressive. He offered drinks all around, but contented himself with tomato juice; complained about a stomach pain, that was bothering him.

They talked about his trip around the Mediterranean ports; he outlined the training of the cadets at the Island of Hydra College, and later on the navy ships.

"This particular trip," he said, "is actually a pleasure trip, we were in Cyprus, and have two cadets from your island, from Famagusta actually."

George expressed his interest to meet their compatriots; memories were still high and the invasion wounds still unhealed.

"I'll give instructions to be on the deck at some time later, you know on such occasions all cadets are confined to their cabins, for obvious reasons."

From the bridge outside the captain's quarters, the light flooded deck looked crowded, the majority were males as George predicted, very few young ones and even very few children.

"Let's go and meet our guests," said the captain, draining his last drop of tomato juice.

They climbed down to the deck. Soft Greek music flowed from the loudspeakers over the heads of the guests, over the spotless deck of the destroyer and beyond, over the ripples of the surrounding sea where the ripples turned silvery with the floodlights. Most of the visitors grouped in small numbers with glasses in hand, were discussing minor subjects in low tones.

"Help yourselves," said the captain stretching his long arm towards the beverage kiosk and went forward to greet his esteemed guests.

For a long time George had to taste genuine alcohol and there it was, ouzo, brandy, whiskey, vodka, even original coca-cola along with other soft drinks. He took a double cognac; Kate contented herself with a coca-cola along with Sonia and Margarita. Mary preferred Sprite. The soft drinks were cool, sparkling, according to Kate. George enjoyed his cognac, sipping it slowly, slowly, afraid of finishing it too early, the captain came along.

"Are you still on the first one?. We have plenty, please feel at home."

His friendly inducement lured George for a second one; the waiter told him that the cognac finished, he asked for a double whisky on the rocks. Food was plentiful and lay out conveniently at various spots. Open sandwiches, with various toppings, from anchovies to cheese, from ham to roasted beef, from plain greens to caviar, all was spread lavishly and very tempting.

Father Iacovos introduced George to several dignitaries, the Italian consul and his wife, the Bulgarian commercial attaché, the Turkish consul to whom Kate offered her hand constrained, and to Abdelgader of the customs, whom they knew already.

It was an evening different from the others, people were moving around, talking, joking, laughing, and above all drinking genuine alcohol.

George felt the desire to try a third glass but Kate poked him off, the thought of the road patrols and the obligation to rise for work at midnight put him off.

Kate was complimented by the Greek consul, that she slowly but surely was regaining herself, Kate blushed, shook his hand and invited him to the house for next Sunday, emphasizing to bring his wife along.

Margarita's school teacher took her with Mary around the deck and explained the various sections, the radar, the boat guns, even the lines on the deck, he spent three years in the navy before giving it up to become a school teacher. Sonia found company with her schoolmates, talking and chatting at the far end of the stern.

The two Cypriot cadets were allowed to come to the deck, were more than pleased to join the party and meet some of their compatriots.

"If you did not ask for us," said one of them, "would have been locked downstairs, the orders are rigid, and life is tough on a ship."

George listened to their experiences on a ship and realized that no matter where you are, a prolonged stay, at work or travel, gets boring. They enjoyed an ouzo, normally not only unavailable but also forbidden on a training boat.

5: *Mohammed's suffering*

Hamid Shukri got wind of a new chicken farm near Suluq village.

"George, if you can't find live chicken, come to the farm of Mohamed el Badri, it's a new farm, very good chicken."

"And where is this new farm that I don't know?"

"Just before Jardina village, the way to Suluq, on the right hand of the road, it's the only farm in the vicinity, you won't miss it."

"Trust they have good chicken."

"Yes, sure, guaranteed, I'll be there at around five."

"Now, with the wave of hot weather, make it six."

"Very well, you take no chances; you are considering everything, George."

When George mentioned the farmer's name to Mahmoud, the boy knotted his brows and looked at his boss awkwardly; George shook his head inquisitively and forced a smile.

"You know boss, he was on the television, and is one of those caught, one of the rich."

George knotted his brows now, knew the family, one of the rich ones in Benghazi, but as he does not watch television regularly, missed the show and the information. His interest was focused on good birds, the owner's name was of secondary importance, and if he had any problem with the authorities, it was his personal concern.

On the way to the chicken farm, the exposition of Fathi Milad rotated in his mind.

Hamid was already there, his car parked close to the hangar and he himself under the only tree, an acacia tree big enough to provide shade for two or three persons on that side of the farm.

"*Salam alekoum*, Peace with you, hello there?" said George cheerfully.

Hamid was probably the only chicken dealer that George had close co-operation, he was sincere, more than many others.

"Hello Greeky, you made it after all, come sit down, Mohamed is still asleep."

George took his comment as a joke and said, "still, how is that, it's almost six in the afternoon."

" Come and sit down."

Working with Libyans over the years, George got into their way of acting and thinking, suspected though something wrong. He coiled next to Hamid on a stone that the man pushed forward with his bare foot. Hamid had a habit of dressing himself in the traditional light cotton costume of a baggy pair of breeches and a loose oversize shirt. In this outfit, he cared less where to lay his body, whether it was a patch of shaded ground or a piece of tarpaulin spread out, any place was his natural habitat, here was contented with the light shade of the acacia tree on the bare ground. Flung off his sandals and enjoyed rubbing his toes on the ground shedding off some of his fungi.

Stretched out on his lap with his head perched in his palm, held high up to the height of his poked elbow, continued chewing his tobacco; he disliked matches, smoke and cigarette ashes. From time to time, spat notoriously the placid brown fluid a few feet away and resumed the chewing.

He liked to talk a lot; spoke perfect English and a little Italian. George quite often teased him about his Italian, from where he learned it, was it from his great Italian grandfather. It was a common joke amongst the elders that the Italian officers during the occupation of Libya, paid nocturnal visits to the homes of the locals. The local was obliged to leave the house and his wife to the visitor; the visitor hang his army cap on a peg by the house door he was visiting as a warning for the owner to keep away whilst being busy inside. Many Libyan offspring had blue eyes, fair hair, and white skin. Many laughed with the joke, others got very annoyed. Hamid enjoyed it.

Hamid was quite open in his conversations, criticized matters that contradicted logic and even the Koran. Was well acquainted with the internal situation, as well as what was going on around the world. He listened to foreign stations; preferred though BBC news and commentaries.

His job as a superintendent at the maintenance water section of the municipality, allowed him to move around the city considerably. He saw the negligence and the impotence of the new generation, noticed the degrading social values and the gloom of his townsfolk. Saw the lack of planning and organization, the escalating corruption, the poor maintenance of the water system; his job took him to every corner of the city. Everywhere flooded streets and thirsty households, Benghazi was in the process of crumbling.

"We got derailed, yia Yunani, the departments lost their heads, there are no more competent persons at the wheel, and those who are appointed are interested only to pad their pockets, Libya is driven to a blind labyrinth."

George did not dare address any thorny questions, confined himself to quote that the climate favoured the poultry industry, if such well off persons like Mohammed endeavoured in the business.

Hamid laughed loudly, rolled from side to side on the red soil as if he was rolling in his bed, regained his initial position, stopped laughing and stared at his companion.

"You don't know why Mohammed grows chicken? You do not know why Mohammed el Badri lives here with the Chadian laborers. Where do you live, George?"

George was caught unaware, possibly, as a foreigner was not informed properly, his limited spare time might be the reason of his ignorance, and failed to watch the television, to listen to the radio, or spend time with friends in their evening gatherings. Though he could see undeniable facts, he misinterpreted them because his own mental experience was different.

Unable to give an answer to Hamid, remained staring at his companion intensively who wanted to talk. George invited him through his inquisitiveness.

In the town, persons like Hamid, very seldom find the opportunity to speak, to express their views, to spill their venom; too many informers around. The slightest comment could easily be commuted to the wrong person in the wrong way with detrimental consequences, out here in the open, the wind might carry the conversation to flapping ears, but the chance was remote. With George, Hamid felt at ease.

"You don't know that Mohamed spent more than six months at that horrible detention camp of "*Saba April?*"

George leaned forward as if someone struck him from behind, "My God, that's why he was absent from his electrical shop?"

"Their shop; their shop has been taken over by the People's committee, confiscated, George where do you live?"

"I'm sorry, but you know better what goes on around, I don't go down town that often, and the sparingly short time I have, preferred to spend it at home, with my family."

"I know that and praise you, the town is full of crooks and informers. Ah! He is coming," said Hamid.

George turned himself to the tin roofed hut, turned and what he saw could not believe his eyes. Knew el Badri, a businessperson with whom he discussed the electrical installation for the hatchery of his first employer. The man possessed his profession. As a graduate from the University of London, undertook the family business, placed it on the right track, expanded it, and was thriving with the new electrification program. Was a hearty person with an assuring composure, nicely dressed, soft-spoken. He was a trustworthy person.

Today, the approaching figure resembled someone who escaped from an abyss; looked taller, which could be from loss of weight, his clothes, oh, his clothes were not fitting him, rather hanging on a skeleton, his arms seemed to be falling off their joints, his legs hardly supported him. As he drew closer, tried to smile and his oversize teeth showed badly from his bony mandibles covered with unshaven skin. A pair of feeble eyes blinked from sunken sockets, an untidy crop of hair at the mercy of the breeze fell to one side covering the left ear, exposing the other like an oversize hearing organ. The poor man needed a shave badly, a good bath and some extra food.

Hamid rose to his feet and George followed him, the customary greetings, kisses and back patting went round, with Hamid still holding his hand said in English, "you know the Greek, George."

Mohammed furrowed his eyebrows and his eyes sunk deeper in their sockets, and through a bush of eyelashes, shadowed by overgrown eyebrows, studied the foreigner for a long moment.

George gave him his hand, and with a genuine smile said, "We met at your shop in Omar Muftah Street, a couple of years back."

Took his time, allowed the image to reach his memory system, stretched his hand mechanically, forced his eyes to the extend he could, revealing a pair of pale eyeballs and said with apathy.

"Yes, you were building a hatchery for Abdurrahman, that's right."

Unintentionally, George squeezed the bony fingers, rather harder this time, trying to express his sympathy.

With a jerk of his head, body and arm, Mohammed freed his captivated hand, he feared George might cause him harm.

Hamid broke the tension by asking him about his father. The word father struck him more than a lightning. Restrained himself, and told them that he did not visit his family for the last ten days with the excuse that the laborers were not trustworthy now that the chickens were ready for sale. Hamid agreed that most of the workers easily trade their mothers for a packet of cigarettes.

"George and I, are willing to undertake the purchase of all your birds," said Hamid leaning backwards with his right hand on his chest, a sign of assurance.

"Yes, for sure," added George.

"We take around a thousand daily, how many thousand do you have?"

"The whole batch is supposed to be ten thousand, but that bastard, the son of Warfalli, is a crook."

Neither Hamid nor George spoke; they let Mohamed spit his venom.

"His hatchery is not clean, many chicks died during the first week. I brought Dr. David, he is the most reputable veterinarian in Benghazi, I am sure you know him, he saw my birds, did not need to do any posthumous, he knew the problem, brought medicine by the bag and thanks God saved most of them. Let aside that the counting of the day-old chicks is manipulated. So, say we have about seven thousand now."

George listened to him gravely and sympathetically.

"We'll collect them in say six days." Said Hamid and turning to George added, "alright George?"

"Yes, whatever you say Hag Hamid."

"Just wait, he is bringing tea." Mohammed squatted on a block of brick and over the tea spoke of his 'Saba April holiday.'

"I was taken from my home, would rather say, was dragged off my bed at 3.00 am in my pajamas, thanks God, my wife was not there, she was with her sick sister. Was jostled out of the house and by the time I reached the Toyota, my back, sides and shoulders must have been black from punching and clubbing.

Kept my head down, a single stern look would be enough to strike terror into the heart of anyone.

When shoved in the car, felt a bang between the shoulders and fainted, when I recovered found myself drenched in cold water in a tiny cell. Tried to move, felt dizzy, my legs did not respond and my arms hang limp as I coiled in the corner, it was pitch dark. When began functioning sensually, nausea overcame me. The stench was horrible, the room stung badly from urine and refuse. Twice, tried to vomit but my empty stomach had nothing to throw."

George looked at Hamid; his face was tense, bent forward eager to hear more, his listening ear and excellent perception made him an extremely valuable listener, Mohammed continued with the same bitterness, with eyes wide with terror and reflected the state of his soul.

"My torment started in the morning, around ten o-clock. Two bastards carried me, that's the only way I could be taken to the interrogation chamber, a well planned place for torture, my two bearers shouted '*Fatah el fatah*,' as we approached the chambers, I was silent, they shook me violently and forced me to repeat their slogan

In the room, saw someone standing behind a bare table with an army cap lying on it, all I saw of him, was a sunken face in an army uniform, with some stars on both shoulders. He returned the greeting of his subordinates, and the two haulers released me, I dropped on the dirty carpet, my legs would not support me. The man in the uniform, ordered me to stand up, I struggled in vain; I remember, pleading, "*wallahi,* in God's name, I can't", he grinned and mumbled, "alright."

A flood light came on, as he sat down, could hardly keep my eyes open against that strong light; my two bearers stood by, one on each side, a voice began questioning me, cannot say if the voice was that of the man in uniform behind the table or somebody else's, the light was so strong."

"Your name is Mohamed el Badri?"

" Yes."

"Yes, sir, should be your answer," yelled a voice, probably from the one behind the table.

"You are running an electrical business at No 8, Omar Muftah Street."

"Yes, sir."

"You are selling the products the Great Leader allowed you to import, at exuberant prices. You cheat the working people, this is contrary to the aims of the Great revolution, you do not pay your taxes, you concealed your income, and you misused the money to buy big cars, build a huge villa and lots of gold ornaments for personal use."

"Could not answer any of his questions, never gave me a chance, and tried to react when I was accused of bribing the officials of the Electricity board for awarding us the large contract of Benghazi- Ajdabia overhead high tension system, but the two bravos pushed me down."

The voice repeated the accusation of bribing.

"No, never did such a thing…" instead of giving me chance to finish what I wanted to say, the two bravos grabbed my legs, one each, lifted them high up and with butts began striking my soles. At first it hurt badly, by the time they stopped, did not feel anything. When I was lifted, could not stand, was carried away, my legs followed me instead of supporting me. Outside the room, was thrown into a wheel burrow, with my legs dangling between the barrow's handles, a bystander pushed me away, the ground was rough, pitted and every time the wheel dropped in a dip my head knocked on the barrow's side"

The hush of a new fear gripped him, and the air was darkened with the shapes and phantoms of the terror the cell reminded him and stood for long in perplexity at a loss of words.

"For God's sake," said Hamid and poured himself another round of cold tea, Mohammed and Hamid washed their gullets with the thick sweet liquid, George had no feeling for that, too many flies visited his tea glass whilst Mohammed wanted to extricate, to relieve himself in another language to other persons.

Soon his vocal chords revived and the extra sweet liquid stimulated his energy, shifted lightly his bony buttocks on the cement block, coughed, cleared his throat, sending his Adam's apple up and down and continued; he never asked the liable chicken purchasers, if they wanted to hear his story or not, both of them waited patiently.

"Must have dozed away by the time I was tipped off the wheelbarrow; felt a shock between my shoulders, opened my eyes and heard like a voice coming from the far distance saying.

"You will kill him,"

Some one spat at me, probably the burrow pusher.

"Let the dog die, who cares."

"It's a shame, my brother," said the voice.

"The burrow pusher was on his way, probably had another call. Two or three persons lifted me gently this time and laid me on a blanket, was moaning with pain, in the ribs, the shoulders, the feet, the stomach, can't remember if my head ached, was too vertiginous.

"I was given water, drank whilst lying down, was left to my sufferings, fell asleep. It was dark when resumed my senses, woke up, looked around and saw two persons sitting near me, one was smoking, 'where am I?' I asked."

"You have company," said the non-smoker.

"Tried to elbow myself, but the piercing pain between the shoulders forced me to drop back, brought one hand to my face, moved it round, the pain was everywhere, my forehead, my skull, my cheeks. Moved my hand downward, my chest, my stomach, my legs; whatever I touched reacted with pain, even my knuckles. The non-smoker mumbled, '*Hamdullah*, thanks God, you are still alive,' understood they were detainees too."

"You recognized them?" asked Hamid.

"No, what are you talking about, in that state, not even my mother."

"And then yia Mohammed?"

George looked at the man whose actions and words seemed inconsistent but kept his thoughts to himself, actually a wise course of action.

"Two came with something that smelled like food, "*Hayia yia Mohamed*," called the non-smoker. Strained the eyes and forced my senses to find out who was calling me by my name, on second thought I gave up, he might have heard the burrow pusher calling my name.

He read my mind and said, "welcome to the group, I'm Mohammed Fituri, this is Salah Magrabi, Athman Shaari, Awad Sallabi, came the names one after the other, the roll-call of the cell."

"Good God." exclaimed Hamid. "From what we hear all the good people were there."

"In that cell, yes, many other cells lie around the huge camp, did not have the luck to meet that many. Not only rich people, as you think, simple people detained for various reasons, tortured, terrorized, enforced to follow the will of the Leader. No documentation whatsoever of the inmate population, dissidents or not, treated alike."

George could not recall any of those names, remained neutral, considered himself organized, kept a schedule, consulted his wrist watch twice, the second time confirmed the reading with Hamid but Mohammed failed to notice the gesture, he was eager to tell them more of his 'holiday'.

Hamid rolled out in Arabic, criticized the revolution, but was bitter with the street people; they devastated the aims of the revolution, all agreed that they were responsible for what was happening, and rose to collect their chicken.

Hamid explained the way, he and George operated, the day's purchase remained on credit until the next day and so on, Mohamed agreed without any comment.

Mohammed bid them farewell, they promised to be there the next day at the same time, God willing.

The next day, Mohammed was not there, orders were given to the laborers, the chicken were delivered, but Hamid didn't trust the Chadian for the money, luckily Mohammed arrived only minutes as they were getting ready to leave; they settled their bill and promised for the next day.

Hamid and George bought all the birds without settling their account; both were trustworthy persons. On the last day, they called at the farm. Mohamed was waiting for them. A mat was spread under the acacia tree, the area sprayed with water, foam cushions were laid out. As if by intuition, Hamid arrived only minutes before George and was on his cushion already. George joined the banquet; tea was brought and served twice. They talked about the market, chicken meat was in great demand as mutton was very expensive and imported veal was just enough for the privileged ones.

The topic, like everywhere, was the deteriorating situation in every respect, at every level and every aspect of life. Everything seemed infected and all looked yellow to the jaundiced eyes. The people's committees were fraud, the secretaries double faced, which made everyone around shrink in his cocoon. The militants were brazing their muscles, ears dropping was common and God, too far for mercy on the branded ones.

Mohammed reiterated his experience during his 'holiday', an experience he never wished to his worst enemy. Spoke about personalities with dignity, wealth, and prudence, being wheel burrowed from the interrogation chambers and dumped into the open grave at the far north of that camp.

"One day, when these bastards will go, those graves will be dug up and bones, I'm afraid, only bones will be exhumed. Pray to my God for their punishment. Wish to be alive and witness His lightning sword strike those treacherous ones."

6: The airport experience

Kate was to accompany their three budding daughters to Athens. George was obliged to postpone his travel. Their neighbour, Hag Nasser volunteered to take them to Benina airport in his Nissan 180G. With gratitude accepted his offer, as the roadblocks to the airport were formidable. Might not encounter any problem but nothing was unpredictable.

Despite the queues at the checkpoints on the Benina road, Nasser swerved his car right to the front; presented a small white card to the obnoxious guards and was through without second word. He repeated the same at both checkpoints close to the airport. Nasser dropped them at the main entrance with instructions to wait for him; left to park his car in the strictly forbidden area.

George pulled the luggage inside the hall, the commotion, there, was beyond description, piles of luggage were all over the overcrowded hall, rows of suitcases lined the front of the only counter not wider than six meters. Four rows of baggage were lined, but nobody could make out which line was for which destination. To approach the counter for inquiries turned to be a nightmare. Passengers drenched in sweat, jumped over suitcases, over boxes of various sizes and bundles of many shapes, and carried their belongings over their heads, handing them from person to person up to the airline scales. The crowd near the counter, the shouting and the arguments put off any sensible person of traveling, right there on the spot.

Hag Nasser found his passengers crouched over their luggage, too scared from that chaos. Twitched his nose and asked them to wait there. Took the tickets and passports and pushed his way to the far left side where the crowd was thinner. George watched him with anxiety. They traveled several times before from Benina airport but today the commotion, the shouting, the arguments, the stench of sweat was beyond fantasy.

More and more passengers were swarming through the entrance, mostly Arabs of various nationalities. From Sudan, Egypt, Syria, dragging massive bundles of materials tied in a crude way with nylon rope. Due to restrictions on money transfer, the illegal immigrants carried whatever considered saleable in their country and bought it. Even the airline companies made concessions to these troubled people with overweight bundles.

None of George's family spoke, the dismay was hanging on their sweaty faces, Nasser was lost through the crowd, beyond the sea of heads and overhauled luggage. George focused his eyes at the spot he last saw him, there; he was with one hand clearing the bystanders and with the other waiving for his group to proceed, gestured them to bring their luggage forward too.

Margarita with Sonia braced hands and carried two small handbags, Kate got hold of Mary's hand who was clutching a doll to her chest and dragged a suitcase with the other hand, George lifted one suitcase and pulled a second one by its strap, went along pleading and shouting at the same time. Nasser managed to squeeze his way towards them, took Mary by the hand, and pushed towards the narrow entrance to the customs counter, there he waited for the rest dragging their luggage and dripping with sweat.

Nasser smiled at the immigration official, handed him the passports and motioned the family ahead. At the entrance, he paused and talked to the sentry; the fellow stood by and let the group pass through. Beyond the sentry, they lifted their luggage onto the customs counter, Nasser greeted the customs officer by his first name, and the luggage ticked OK, taken off the counter, placed on a trolley, "yia Nasser, bring the labels from the airline."

"Yes, you are right," said Nasser and looked at George, the luggage was not presented to the company's counter; only Nasser could explain why. He paused, bent forward and whispered to the customs official, the man looked at George and waved him to proceed for the waiting hall; Nasser was lost in that sea of anarchy.

George directed his family to the overcrowded passengers' hall, searched for a seat without success. The hall was packed. Luckily, at that very moment the Syrian Arab Airlines announced the departure of their flight and a current of persons, men, women, children and handbags, flowed to the exit. The speaker stressed in his announcement twice, women and children first, his request fell upon deaf ears, the door kept closed since the whole group of passengers tried to squeeze through a door of not more than a meter and quarter.

The police stepped in and forced every single passenger back. Those passengers preparing for departure were forced to huddle in the narrow space between the rows of seats, since the seats have already been taken up by the wave of inflowing passengers. At last, order has been imposed and the women pulling along two and three children each, squeezed through the door into the scorching sun.

Minutes later, Nasser appeared unnoticed in the waiting hall, holding high above shoulder the traveling tickets, he was drenched in sweat, but the broad smile never dissipated from his face. He did not go straight to them, instead passed by the refreshment counter, and brought along the badly needed drinks.

Kate was the first to express herself, "without your super help, I don't think we would be able to board the plane today."

"Oh, I'm glad I was of some assistance," said casually, "These are all my friends," and distributed the drinks.

Nasser had an affection to little Mary and always teased her, she responded to his friendliness and out of the blue, she said, "Next time I hope Amina and Salha come with us to Cyprus."

He was moved, caught her with both hands lifted her high and said looking straight in her eyes, "yes, for sure, first we see how their mother's health will develop."

"I pray to God, Mouna gets well and we all go for a holiday to Cyprus, you will all enjoy it" said Kate.

"Thank you, Madam, I have my reservations with our doctors here, I'm arranging to take her to London next month."

"May God be with her and return cured and in good health, I like her very much."

"She likes you too."

"I know! She is such a kind person."

The departure of Olympic Airways was announced over the loud speakers, with great relief to the absolutely packed passenger hall, mother and daughters trailed to the exit; the order was more systematic this time. George and Nasser helped them with their small baggage up to the exit, both bid them a safe journey, and to see them back revived.

"My wishes for quick recovery to Madam Mouna," begged Kate and vanished in that flow of human beings.

The two men trailed back through an ever-increasing crowd to the car. Nasser presented his white card, the guards saluted him and through they were.

At one checkpoint, Nasser left the curious white card on the fascia of the car and George lifted it, tried to read it with little success, as it was all hand written.

"*Shukran yia Nasser*," said George to his companion, "thank you Mr. Nasser," and dropped the card in his shirt pocket.

"Even if you keep it, I have no problem in moving around or going through any check point or whatsoever. You know what it says, "thank you Nasser, your help was great, Muammar."

The moment he translated the hand written card, George pulled it out of his pocket faster than he dropped it in and returned it on the fascia.

Nasser explained how the Great Leader awarded him the card, for his contribution, during the early days of the revolution.

"At that time," he said, "I was working at the Libyan broadcasting service and was responsible for the news section; you know George, how important was to keep the people informed, properly informed. The great Jamal Abdul Nasser provided material and directed us in a big way."

He was right, *properly informed*, George looked at his companion, and simply smiled in appreciation, that man was in the right circle, and one had to be very careful with his comments.

At the major checkpoints of the Benina road, the queues were long, but they went through without even stopping, Nasser was gliding on the higher ranks of the revolution, George was obliged to be on good terms with him, in every respect.

7: The booby trap

With his family away, the house was empty, his errands increased and the long hours at work became intolerable, he despised to stay longer in the house than needed, though he required rest, sleep.

More and more customers kept coming requesting for processed birds. Every new customer extolled George's sincerity, punctuality and so on. Fake pretensions, simply to be supplied with plumb, clean chicken. George learned his lesson over and over with many of them, the moment they turned their back, their long speeches vanished with the first whiff of the breeze. George though, listened to them tentatively, noted their names and location of their restaurant, whatever it was and promised to visit them the next day for the details of the probable transaction; they left with an innate hope for a closer cooperation. It was impossible to increase production under the present situation; his old customers demanded an increase in their orders also with little success.

George was alone, one person, one car, had to bring water, live chicken, to work along with the laborers at night, deliver the meat, go round the customers in the evening to get their next day's orders, settle accounts, settle complaints and meet his personal requirements.

George discussed the requests by many of his clients and their excuses with Hamid. Warned him of the continuous inspections at the slaughterhouses, and advised him to keep the premises clean, deliver early in the morning, and never issue any receipt.

The problem was the early delivery. George considered the addition of another employee, but with the prevailing conditions, such an idea would be out of question since almost all the Egyptians were bundled away. He prayed to God and carried on; praying to God in that situation was a sheer fallacy.

The dreaded day came sooner than he expected. On July 13, two disguised inspectors approached George and asked for his ID whilst he was delivering chicken to Farag near the fish market, after the ID, asked for his health certificate and the license from the municipality for operating the slaughterhouse.

His health certificate, that never existed, pretended to have it in his home, as to the license that was with the Libyan partner.

"I'm in cooperation with Muftah and the license must be with him."

Muftah never dreamed to apply for such or any license. Like all Libyans, despised to have any dealings with any authorities. An application for a slaughterhouse license had to be accompanied by the land registration certificate, building license, health certificate of the owner and above all a tax clearance certificate, such a long list of required documents never existed. Many Libyans, like Muftah never paid any taxes; they evaded taxation at any cost.

The inspectors looked reasonably polite, but one may say they had an evil face smoothed by hypocrisy; George naturally despised them for their imperfect manners. They forced George to stop delivering and asked him to take the whole lot of killed chicken to the central office of theirs; one of them squared himself in the passenger's seat and chain-smoked. George kept as cool as possible despite the horror that settled in his stomach.

His co-passenger directed him through the guarded gate to the place, asked him to park the car in the parking lot. The chicken meat was left exposed to the burning sun from above. George was asked to accompany him to the superintendent's office, through a corridor where more than a dozen inspectors were sipping tea in the most noisy way, and commenting on their achievements.

The second inspector, who intervened half an hour ago, was already there, taking his tea. When he saw George, told the others sitting around, how they caught him with more than four hundred kilos of chicken on a Peugeot.

As they passed by, all stopped talking and drinking and stared at George with a glint of triumph, the second inspector offered tea to his victim in a rather ironic tone.

"Thanks," snapped George and continued for the den of the inspector.

"This is the Greek; we caught him selling chicken meat without the proper license." That's how, George was introduced, then turned and left.

"Good morning Mister." A customary greeting to a foreigner.

George greeted his interrogator with a forced icy smile

"Where is your identity card?" was his second question.

"He took it from me."

"Yia Salah," shouted the officer.

"*Aioua, aioua,*" and came running.

"Where is his ID?"

"*Tfatal,* I'm sorry."

There was no chance of creeping away now; the ID was in front of him. He pulled out a ruled piece of paper, placed a carbon paper over it and added a second piece of ruled paper on top, lifted the lot tapped it on its narrow end, placed them back on the desk, found a pin and pinned all three together; he was ready for his interrogation.

All this time, he did not leave George from his eyes; studied his face for any reactions but did not disclose his intentions, lifted a ballpoint pen, looked at the contorted face of his captive and began his questioning.

The interrogation began like any other but for George, who found himself in such a place for the first time, the seconds seemed longer than hours. After noting his name, nationality, mother's name, religion and address, stopped, looked at George, hesitated for a split second, realized that his captive did not master the official language, commented that a translator should be present, pondered over the idea, was more interested in completing his job the soonest, probably aware of the judge's verdict. From experience, he knew that the judge cared very little what has been written in the reports, the ruling would the same, so he decided to question George and note what he considered not only essential but also just enough to convict him.

"Who is your patron, how many birds do you have on your car, I mean how many kilos and what do you intend to do with them."

George gave him straight answers and he scribbled what he liked. Stopped for a moment and commented that he visited the slaughterhouse, congratulated George for the cleanliness, but scorned him for the open ditch behind the building overflowing with feathers, bits of flesh and chicken heads. George kept cool, looked straight at his interrogator with a sad face.

"What are you going to do with the chicken on the car?"

George got tense but kept his posture, thought for a long moment and at last said, "I'll pour diesel over the bags of chicken and throw them at the refuse disposal of the municipality."

The man remained skeptic, doubted the answer for a second, then asked, "and where is the dumping place?"

"At Terria, about twenty five kilometers away, along the sea road."

"Are you not going to sell it?"

"Would you buy such meat, would you buy it for yourself or your family?" asked George composing himself in the most serious way.

"No, I wouldn't," answered the man and knotted his brows.

"So, I will relieve you from the disposing problem, I'll dump the meat at Terria after pouring over it enough diesel so that nobody may take advantage."

Without turning his eyes anywhere, the interrogator said, "you know I hate, detest and can't bear a lie, not because I'm straighter than the rest of us, but simply it appeals to me," and ordered George to sign the report, by pushing the papers in front of him.

"I cannot read Arabic, so if you kindly read it out for me, I will sign."

He got disturbed, looked tense and said; "you know I can lock you up till the day you are presented to the court for hearing?" one could read the signature of Satan on his face.

"Yes, I do know this," George was cool, "only requested you to read me the script and I will sign."

Swallowed his pride, looked at him without turning his head this time and George noticed the white of his eyeballs, the vehemence radiated through those eyes, then he read the whole report slowly and clearly, another lawbreaker in the bag.

George pretended to understand what he had been accused of and signed, the man returned the ID to the owner.

"Thank you," said George after signing, got up and without looking left or right, hurried to his car. The bags of chicken were black from the multitude of flies that swarmed them. George took no notice of those flies, drove out of the parking lot, forcing the cloud of flies to rise and disperse; he threaded his way through the dedaloid streets and came to one of his wholesale customers. On his way to the dealer composed a story that due to electricity cut around the farm, was dilated and so on. The man helped George to unload the bags full of chicken, placed them on the scale, weighed them, piled them on the trolley, and pushed the whole lot into the cold room.

George noticed that they weighed only eleven bags, where should have been twelve, infuriated, spat in the air and said, "crooks are always crooks, a bag had been stolen from the car whilst it was in the police car park."

George became bitter and distrustful of people because somebody betrayed him. He was going to hate those who evaded the regulations and continued working. He was too insignificant to bring any change. The city was no longer the city he conquered with his high quality products, the yesterday's clients, and friends, today turned remote, untalkative, and ironic. Kept out of George's way, afraid that closeness to him might infect them by his unlawful dealings. Considered that personal bias could distort his understanding of how people behave in different circumstances, so tried to keep an open mind. He was more confident of himself, possessed enough knowledge and money to continue and make amazing progress and the accomplishment could give him the energy needed to keep at it, sort of self-fulfilling prophecy, but in a good way.

After the delivery, George drove to Muftah's house, found him flat on a foam rubber mattress under the vine tree. He reiterated what happened, the Arab listened carefully and said, "For this, I can do nothing, its very bad for you and for me, we must see a lawyer, I have a very good friend, he speaks English."

"Is he a lawyer, and how much will he charge?"

Muftah meditated for more than five minutes, then said, "from hundred dinars, we'll ask him, you come at five here and we'll go together to see him at his farm in Faakat."

"Docs hc live there?"

"No, but he always goes there in the afternoon."

George felt his loneliness, his hard luck, had no one to lean to, except Muftah, after all he was the farm owner who collected his monthly rent and took his chicken quota every week.

On the way, George thought of Hag Nasser, when he reached the neighbourhood his car was not there and did not dare to knock at his door, considering any possible misunderstanding.

Inside his empty house, George felt the problem more seriously, he was hurt much more, and was lonesome, he sighed, and the echo reverberated in the empty house.

Hamid's words buzzed in his ears, "you are a foreigner, and you are not Muslim."

If Kate was there, could have shared his worries. In times of crisis, she supported him despite her delicate character. She was in Athens now, in a cosmopolitan city, in a free country. Felt hungry, ate a piece of bread, few black olives, a piece of cheese and a medium tomato, very lightly.

He looked at his watch, it was only four, he rose with a heavy heart, got into the car, and drove to Muftah's ramshackle in Rasa Beida. He crossed the narrow alley to the narrow door that lead to Muftah's courtyard; found him propped up on the same mat, sipping tea. With strong puffs from his cigarette tried to scare off the numerous flies that abounded for an afternoon sip. He was not surprised to see George, greeted him with the two words he knew in Greek, that was more irony than sympathy.

"What is the time?"

"Just after four."

"Too early."

"By the time we reach Faakat…?"

"Sit, sit, tea?"

George needed his help badly, had to abide with his whims, so he lifted the overturned tea glass from the wet aluminum tray with a blobby sound, and held it for the traditional thick liquid called in Benghazi, tea.

Muftah was in his late fifties, belonged to the old stock where tea was poured from the height of half a meter to create froth. The tea was lukewarm; George poured it down his throat in two gulps.

"Another?"

"No thank you, we better go," did not like to stay any longer, his multimember family might start flowing out of their beds into the yard, which might delay their departure, and manners had to be applied.

Muftah rose, slipped his callous feet in a pair of plastic slippers and without informing anyone of his absence, left with George for Faakat. Along the fifteen-kilometer road, none of them uttered a single word; they drove past Muftah's farm, turned into a narrow alley good enough only for horses and came to an iron gate leaning on its pillar, badly rusted. The alley led them to a small house with a mud roof. The plaster dropped off from most of the front wall and the mud bricks showed badly, such huts could survive only in hot dry climates, thought George.

A fierce dog recoiled at the sight of the car from under a thorny bush and barked viciously, revealing its sharp teeth.

Muftah reached for the car hoot, pressed it twice in a prolonged way, the dog startled for a second stopped barking, made a move to run away but soon regained its ferocity and yelled again, this time from some distance.

George was depressed since the morning and now at the sight of his survivor's dwelling, his heart sank deeper, almost reversed the car to leave and he would have done so if Muftah did not open the door to climb down. George froze in his seat, his feelings declined to the surroundings' level.

Now the dog became a real animal, with lips pulled back, his fierce flanks went up and down showing two rows of sharp teeth and with saliva dripping from both sides, barked at the top of its wildness.

Muftah was pinned just a few meters from the car, the dog attacked him, he fought back with his plastic slipper in hand, the dog turned away, Muftah must have managed to hit it on the snout. The wild beast did not expect such a strike and retrieved embarrassed.

George pressed the hoot vigorously that gave a shriek bleep louder than before; a short man appeared through the old wooden door of the hat. He screamed at the dog, threatened the animal with his bare arm and the ferocious animal just minutes ago, left with a complaining growling, and crawled under the thorny bush.

"Hag Awad," hailed Muftah, unimpeded now that the dog was at a safe distance.

"Her, yia Muftah," said the man from the doorstep, he was bare foot, did not dare to walk beyond the hut entrance.

Muftah slipped his foot back to his slipper that he used a few minutes ago to fend away the fierce dog and reached for Hag Awad.

George from his safe seat could not make out what they conferred, only guessed; spent the first five minutes for the customary greetings, how was the old wife, the sheep and the terrible weather.

Everything was going according to the will of the Almighty God, on which there was definitely compliance and after such an agreement, the burning subject was tackled.

After seven whole minutes of close discussion, George was beckoned to join the open-air conference. By that time, the whole matter had already been discussed, the fee agreed,

George's name and nationality noted mentally and that the accused did not speak Arabic.

"Hello George," with the accent on the *R,* the short man put forward a fatty hand for the customary handshake. He studied his client from head to toe, forced a smile, and began to explain the routine in such complicated and formidable cases.

George listened intensely, how the short man and his future lawyer for the case, eluded through the intrigues and difficulties of representing foreigners in the courts of the Jamahiriya nowadays. George thought not only of the short man's fees but also the commission to his patron, Muftah.

"You have to sign the form that you appoint me as your legal advisor, you give me one hundred dinars and leave the rest to me. Do not worry at all, the judges are my friends."

George struggled the way a condemned man struggles in the hands of the executioner, knowing that he cannot save himself without some external help.

The comment of friendship sent two messages, either there was no law and order or the man was bluffing, the second was more liable. George forced a smile, cursed himself for his poor knowledge of Arabic, asked the short man for his office to sign the appropriate paper, and deposit the agreed amount of the hundred dinars.

Muftah prompted to direct the whole endeavor, which sent George to second thoughts. They left before the dog revived.

Stopped at the farm, the two laborers were not there, the slaughterhouse door was flung open; the wind blew hard at it, sending it from side to side with a bang at each flapping. The blood rose to George's head, his eyes blurred, swallowed his saliva, and remembered what the officer told him, "We visited your place, it looked pretty clean."

George went inside the house, the equipment was all there, Muftah walked round the house and pissed in the open ditch, that way nobody could accuse him of indecent behavior. Exiting the slaughterhouse, George stopped at the entrance, looked around, a feeling flowed through his whole body, that he might not work this place again, confusion and sadness returned to silence, fought hard to overcome this sensation. Ahead in the bushes, saw two figures, waited, his two laborers crept out of their hiding place, they hastened their pace, approached, were pale, scared.

George smiled at them and asked why they were hiding. They looked at each other and then at George. Mahmoud, with trembling low voice reiterated about the visit of the inspectors, more than five of them.

"Came in a Toyota, we remained inside our room, silent. They searched the place, it took them just less than ten minutes; we waited, the Toyota sped away, listened intensely, nobody was left behind, we crept out and hid in those thorny bushes, we saw the door of the slaughter house left open but did not dare the attempt of closing it."

"I think they went up to the house," said Gasala.

"Yes, I know, noticed the tire marks."

Their limbs trembled; their hands quivered and showed signs of intense inside agitation.

"We are afraid, cannot kill chicken any more," said both of them with quivering voice.

"Yes, we'll stop for a while," confirmed George.

"Boss, we want to leave, we are afraid, we'll go back to Egypt."

"Don't worry," Muftah intervened, "they will not come back."

He needed someone around his house; house breaking became a habit lately.

"I'll try to bring you your pay one of these days," said George in his cool casual manner

George visited his lawyer's office signed the paper of attorney and handed the requested hundred dinars. Despite the short man's assurance the worries did not lessen, George was labeled, he breached the laws, and will never be able to kill any more chicken. Was accused of killing birds in the wrong way, not the Muslim way, possessed no license, Muftah was weak, negligible in the town. George was forced to give up his source of income, the support for a family of five.

In Cyprus, nothing left from the invasion, a rented flat bestowed to his deported parents in law. His ambitious move to Libya with an uncertain future saw his hopes being shattered and his expectations betrayed.

Pictures of the past paraded before him, one after the other. The scenes began with the most recent ones, concerning time and then back to more remote- to better days- when he was manager in that big farm, taken by force by the invaders, and stopped there. He struggled, the way a condemned man struggles in the hands of the executioner, knowing that he cannot save himself; anger and bitterness choked him. The unanticipated and unpleasant event really upset the relatively peaceful course of his life. Nevertheless, he was though healthy, professional and determined to resolve in his future and redeem the past.

His lawyer assured him that it was a minor offence and he would most probably settle the case without appearing at court. George never had any dealings with the law till then, and had no experience with lawyers or courts.

Called at the slaughterhouse; Mahmoud and Gasala were ready for departure, already collected their scanty belongings, waited for their pay and take the long journey of return to the country of theirs, Egypt, the land of Pharaoh.

They helped George store the cages, barrels, water tank, and the defeathering machine into the house; then loaded the gas ring, gas bottles, and knives onto the car. Paid them their dues, offered an extra bonus to each one of them; they embraced and kissed him with tears rolling down their eyes. George prompted to give them a lift up to the bus station; thanked him sincerely, and said that they could manage by themselves and no need to bother him any more.

George drove away with mixed feelings, in the driver's mirror saw them picking up their only handbag and fleeing through the neglected, scruffy olive trees; headed eastwards as though picking the shortest route to their homeland. George was so moved and preoccupied with his mirror, he almost hit an olive tree a few meters off the alley.

At the farm exit, George met Muftah getting off the municipality bus, waved his hands vigorously, George backed the car into the farm, Muftah greeted him in his casual manner.

"Shall we go to see the lawyer?"

"I saw him already, paid him his fees and signed the paper."

"You gave him hundred?"

"Yes, that's what he asked, isn't it?"

"If I took the money to him, might bargain somehow."

George sensed his intuition, dug out of his pocket the last twenty-five dinars and handed him twenty, held back one five-dinar note discreetly, wanted him to get the message of money shortage.

"What's this for?"

"You may need it for traveling expenses," said George.

Held the money in his hand for a few moments, looked at it, looked at George, did not utter a word, George had to be careful with money, a turbulent period lay ahead.

"Will call to his office tomorrow and find out what he can do, I don't want to go to court," said Muftah with a hoarse voice.

"Please do, I don't like courts either," said George and offered to give Muftah a lift upto his house.

"Yes, please, because the next bus will be in over an hour."

On that long way to Rasa Beida they exchanged nothing, George was not that much interested in Muftah's dealings. Dropped him near his home, as the street leading to the side street was cut off; a neighbour was giving a banquet for the marriage of his son, a custom that permitted the entertainer to block the street and use it for the party. Of-course it was simply another egoistic way of expressing to the vicinity that a party was in progress.

Back at Fuehat, George met Hag Nasser, referred the problem to him, his answer was, "You are not a Libyan," George thanked him and rushed to the cold dull place, called his home.

Telephones in Libya were a gift for the privileged, if one needed to communicate anywhere, had to call personally to the telephone exchange down town, which meant traveling several kilometers for obvious reasons.

The house bell rang at 1.30 pm. The ringing was prolonged like any other Arab, as if all graduated from the same school for practical training. George hurried to the door; Muftah was leaning against the wall smoking his local cigarette.

"Her, yia Muftah, I hope nothing serious."

"Her yia George, the case has been fixed for Saturday the 17th, at 9.00 am, you must be there sharp at eight."

"Can you come along?"

"Up to the court, but not, in the court room."

"What are you afraid of the judge? It's me; they are accusing and not you."

Puffed at his heavy cigarette, smiled and showed his deep yellow teeth and looked in the distance.

"Well that is fair enough, shall I pick you from the house?" a promise was one undertaking, to be there was entirely another, George was grateful for Muftah's concession to be at the court.

"No, don't bother, after all is not that far from my home, and I want to see the lawyer before hand."

George was skeptic about his friend's visits to the famous lawyer but refrained to express himself. There was a growing fog of pessimism hovering over George, he considered a good idea of taking out his optimism umbrella and shield himself from the downpour.

At 8.00, George set off for the courthouse, parked the car more than three hundred meters away, and walked to the courthouse, expecting the exercise to relieve some of his tension. He felt weak before the towering court house, needed more adrenaline in his blood stream, had no way of forcing that extra quantity, Almighty God perfected the human body in such a way that hormones be composed voluntarily, it was one way to delete the animosity from the human being.

At the court entrance, George met the two Palestinians, engaged in the same trade, and reported for the same offence. "Come on Yunani, they called your name, you are late," shouted Salem.

"It's your name they announced," Said George, "and I came round to inform you." They gave their hands.

"The dirty bastards, they chase only us, the foreigners."

"But you are not foreigners," said George casually.

"The Arab has no brother," complained Ahmed, and winked with his left eye.

"Do you know which courtroom?"

"Yes, at the second floor, No 14."

"We might as well make a move," said Salem, "nobody can be sure of these bastards." He stressed the epithet.

George looked around for someone overhearing. All three climbed the crowded stairs to the second floor, to No 14, but was locked; they hanged around in the littered corridor.

The place was crowded with persons awaiting prosecution, friends who came for support, lawyers, solicitors, assistants that hurried hither and thither with files under their arms and officials in untidy uniforms run up and down with contorted faces, pushing their way through, disregarding everyone in their way, it was a very depressing place.

George walked along the corridor but turned back much faster, the place was swarmed with armed guards in front of heavy iron doors. Right down on the floor and very close to the armed persons, some colored women were down to their knees, weeping and pleading, probably Sudanese, the sight was disgusting. George turned back for No 14, looked for the two Palestinians, but could be seen nowhere, the time was approaching, the door was still closed, he felt a cold shiver down his spine, looked for Muftah in that disorderly crowd without success, not even the well paid lawyer was to be seen. He decided to search for a familiar face, at least his competitors, the Palestinians, after all who declared the No 14 to be the courtroom. He walked down the stairs searching in the frenzy crowd for his Libyan or the lawyer with no luck, the time was past nine, he hurried back to No 14; a guard spotted him and asked him why he was hanging around there.

"I have a court case at No 14."

" From where this report?"

"From the municipality."

" Not here, today the judge will be at No 12, you better hurry up."

George ran for No 12, as he had no idea where this courtroom was. He kept looking at the door number scribbled in those funny Indian figures that the Arabs considered theirs until a court case was won by that German telephone company at the International court of Hague.

The Germans installed a new telephone exchange system for Libya along with thousands of telephone sets. When the sets were delivered with the internationally accepted numbers, one high-ranking idiot refused to accept the telephone sets for the only reason that the numbers on the dials were not Arabic. The supply company took them to the International court and won the case and got its money, the Libyans swallowed their venom and the Leader proclaimed by decree that those numbers were the pure Arab numbers. This decree though has not yet reached the citadel of law, the courthouse of the city of Benghazi. George was running out of patience, he got No 10, but the next consecutive two doors were not only locked up but had no numbers written on them.

Where is Muftah, where is the prepaid lawyer, he pocketed hundred dinars equal to a three month salary of an Egyptian laborer. Back up the steps for No 14, who was that bloody guard who chased him away? To his surprise, the corridors were empty, except the guards, they bunched in small groups half way down chatting and laughing aloud. George turned back before his guard spotted him, decided to return to the main entrance for a new search.

People were coming, people were going, the commotion was awesome, George had to fight his way through, and the guard at the bottom of the stairs let him through without hindrance. Out of the building looked around for his defender, no sign, the breeze from the sea across the road blew cool and helped George earnestly.

"Yia Yunani, you Greek," came from a voice, from the middle of the crowd, George lifted his body of one meter sixty-five trying to locate the caller, and saw a hand waving. Buttered his way towards the voice that summoned him; it was Salem, "hello Salem."

"Come, let's go to No.12 at the second floor, its still early, they will start at ten."

A wave of relief flowed through George's body, "you have the same problem, Salem?"

"No, not me, its Ahmed that was caught by those dirty bastards," went on cursing those who reported his friend for selling chicken packed in burlap bags, George remained apathetic, it was not a place for criticism. Both went upstairs for No 12; George was surprised to find some of his competitors sitting around the wooden benches of the courtroom.

"Come, George come," called Ahmed.

"The whole of Benghazi will be without chicken meat," said Saeyed the Egyptian.

"They will give us the government slaughterhouse at Benina road, we'll work it as a co-operative, and I'll be your boss." George said.

"George, there is a rumor that they are building a brand new slaughterhouse at Quefia, you'll be taken there as the manager." Salem, teased him

"Inside the prison compound, or outside?"

"No! Inside."

"Better inside, there are so many convicts who specialize in knife jabbing; I'll employ them free of charge."

"Ha, ha, ha," all of them laughed, their laughter agitated the skinny militant, he approached in his urban gait, Saeyed changed the talk to an old woman trying to catch a train followed by a fierce dog.

The militant paused for a minute, listened to the story, pulled his face and walked away, the laughter turned to a roar.

Muftah appeared all of a sudden from nowhere, went to George, sat next to him. Since most of the competitors never met him before, they stopped talking, joking or laughing. He bent forward and said in a very low tone, "Awad is here, he went to see the judge."

George did not show his enthusiasm or his sadness, he said only, "good."

Muftah asked George to move to another bench, at the second row from the judge's podium. The cage was on the right, with a wooden door that opened to an elevated tiny room surrounded with wooden slaps fixed vertically. The lacquer was peeling off, the three or four slaps facing the judge were the worst.

"How many sticky hands grabbed those slaps of wood, how many were closed in there in agony?" thought George and searched for his handkerchief.

A thumb by the orderly on the judges podium, forced everybody to rise. There was tension, an old figure appeared through a back door carrying some flat files, proceeded to the desk, gave a quick glance to the standing crowd, forced them to envisage his outfit, nodded his head that made his white hair jump up and down and all relapsed to their seats noisily, except the orderly by the cage door.

After thumbing through his files, he looked up, was commonplace in complexion, in feature and in voice. There was an inexpressible faint expression on his lips, something stealthy, a smile, not a smile, George remembered it, but could not explain, he inspired not love or fear, or even respect, spoke sparingly and even when he opened his mouth, it came like opening a door into the darkness. He called in a feeble voice, "Ahmed Suleiman Ahmed."

Ahmed rose briskly and moved fast to the cage, the sooner he entered the judge addressed him and within a minute the verdict was decided. Was accused of selling poultry meat for human consumption in dirty burlap bags, did not posses any license for operating a slaughterhouse and his premises were very dirty. Ahmed was not given the slightest chance of admitting, apologizing or defending himself; was fined for each offence one hundred dinars plus two per cent for the stamp. The amount of three hundred and six dinar had to be paid right there.

George was reported for delivering poultry meat in burlap bags, did not have a license, but his premises were clean, he estimated two hundred dinars fine, plus the stamp.

The next one was a Libyan selling eggs above the fixed price. He put up an argument of the difficulties of the trade, lack of feed, medicine, even egg trays. The judge took no notice of the problems the farmer encountered; he fined him with two hundred dinars plus the stamp, payable there on the spot.

His dignity looked over his spectacles and settled his eyes on George, "George."

Before pronouncing the full name, George moved briskly to the cage. The Libyan coming out blocked him, and then all of a sudden, somebody grabbed him by the arm violently and forced him to enter the cage. George did not resist, the cage was littered with a good layer of dust, and bits of paper, and it smelled badly from sweat. George faced the judge, tried to force a smile and above all control himself.

"You are George..."

"Yes sir."

"You understand Arabic?"

"Not much your highness."

"I stand for my client," said Hag Awad and stood up. The judge turned to him; George was darting his eyes from the one to the other, depending who spoke.

George understood the accusations, three in line, for killing birds without a license, delivering them in an open car and selling above the fixed price. Hag Awad conceded to the accusations. His dignity turned to George and recited the accusations, followed by the verdict, one hundred dinar for the first offence and two hundred for selling poultry meat above the fixed price, a serious offence in the Jamahiriya.

"Do you have anything to say," and pinned him with his gawky eyes from behind the spectacles.

"No, thank you, sir."

"Relieved."

George stepped off faster than he was pushed in there; Hag Awad stepped forward took his client's hand and ordered Muftah to lead him to the cashier.

Saeyed the Egyptian, was summoned after George, he paused for a second, eager to hear the punishment, was fined three hundred dinars without being represented by a lawyer, it cost George four hundred with a first class lawyer. The tariff on that day was three hundred dinars no matter what the accusations were.

With Muftah guarding George, they reached the cashier's office, paid the full three hundred and six dinars, and hurried to escape from that dreadful place, the House of Justice. Muftah had a job to keep up at the pace of his companion.

"I have some urgent work at the Greek embassy," wanted to free himself from the parasite. George decided to give up killing chicken at his farm; was no more his patron.

Sometimes people learn best when forced to deal with consequences of their actions, thought George.

8: Becoming a Phoenix

On his way met Aly, a neighbourer at Fuehat, who lived in a side street from George along the way to the Greek school. He spoke perfect English and worked as grain inspector, for the Ministry of Agriculture. After greeting George warmly, invited him to purchase live chicken from the farm he was running as a side business with a certain Mohamed Benily.

Like every farmer who finds difficulty in marketing his produce, tries hard to attract buyers by exaggerating the quality that is what Ahmed did outside the courthouse. He explained the location of the farm, the prime quality of his birds and promised to help with the price. George listened carefully, but his mind was on other topics.

At the agreed time, George drove up to the farm; it was not that difficult to find it. Stood in the middle of nowhere, in a barren area of red soil with a high stonewall around it. Aly was there, showed his new customer the birds, that were really of prime quality, George promised close co-operation.

"How about the water supply, you get enough water here?"

"The water comes from the huge main water pipe from Benghazi to the numerous military camps, a reliable source."

They walked up to the main water tank of the farm, an old freight barge placed under some overgrown acacia trees, and water was overflowing. A sensation, that George had not felt for a very long time. Water the source of life. The virgin soil and an abundance of sweet water were perfect for trees like acacia to grow to several meters high.

"Why don't you kill yourself?" George asked.

"You see, I'm a government employee and we are not allowed by law to carry out any other activity, if they catch me, I may loose my job and even put in jail. We have a slaughterhouse, there," and he pointed to a stone building some five hundred meters away from the large six chicken hangars.

Both walked to the house, it was a perfect, properly planned slaughterhouse, with tiled floor, tiled walls, killing stand with cones, a plucking machine of the latest models, dressing table, two bath tabs with piped water, George did not resist to open both taps and feel the running water.

"There is a septic tank outside, large enough for daily killing."

"Aly, the whole place looks great, how about the owners?"

"Reasonable people, but I tell you George, they are business people, and understand nothing beyond money."

"Could I kill chicken here, your chicken? At my place, water is a big problem; I carry water from Hawari, by my Peugeot."

"George, you carry water for a slaughterhouse, daily?" asked Aly staring into George's eyes with amazement.

"Now yes, before we had water from the municipality but the water man of Quarchia turned it off."

"I know him, Muftah."

"No, not Muftah."

"Muftah, that's his name, not your Muftah, he is known as *the water dragon,"* said with anguish. "You better go and see Hag Mohamed at his office in Juliana, he is the owner."

"OK tomorrow, may be," said George casually.

Aly was too eager to sell the chicken, the news traveled fast about the municipality.

"We better go together," insisted Aly, "you know we have three hangars full of ready for the market chicken and I'm worried with the hot weather, a heat wave may devastate any farm."

Hag Mohamed was still in his office at 6.00 .PM, a rare phenomenon with Libyans, and more over the rich ones. Aly and George crossed the empty secretary's office and entered the office of one of the top businesspersons of Benghazi.

On their way to the office George, said to himself, your attitude is right on target, and won't take much effort at all to step over the sunny side of the street.

The man seated behind a large dark polished hard wood office in an expensive rotating chair. Welcomed the visitors, the Arab language predominated for more than ten minutes; Hag Mohamed was briefed about his chicken farm, the condition of the chicken, the amount of feed available, the daily consumption, the market, the weather and the stranger standing by. George understood most of the discussion, the poor market, the intentions of the visitor, that he was a poultry expert, a good man and a neighbourer of Aly, with a respected family.

Hag Mohamed pierced George with his canine relatively small eyes, and then stood up to greet him. He ordered tea by calling out and an old Egyptian arrived with a tiny teapot and three small glasses. With a gesture, the tea man filled the glasses the customary way and the thick grey liquid frothed to the brim.

"Mr. George, welcome," the visitor was addressed politely in perfect English.

"Nice to meet you, Hag Mohamed."

"Mr. Aly tells me that you visited our farm, saw our birds and my slaughterhouse."

"That's right, the chicken look very good."

"You are killing chicken on a daily basis."

"Yes, seven days a week."

"Why, you don't kill on your farm?"

"We have no water, and you know without water one cannot do the job properly."

"You saw our slaughterhouse, what do you think of it?"

"With a couple of good workers, one can operate it nicely."

"Do you have laborers?"

"No, not now, they were Egyptians without proper papers, and left before being caught."

"Regulations these days are very strict."

George let the comment pass away.

"We can let you kill chicken there, but only from our birds, you understand?"

"Yes, I don't only understand but agree too."

"I want to make it clear that we will allow you to kill birds on our farm, to purchase and kill."

"Definitely, to buy and kill," there followed a short laugh and Hag Mohamed played with his short trimmed grey beard.

"You will pay the laborers, how about the other expenses like water, electricity, cleaning up?"

It was George's turn to let a laugh and he did.

Aly intervened to explain that there was no separate electric meter and would have to go on the general farm expenses, the same for the water, changing into Arabic reminded Hag Mohamed of the bad market situation and it was a good chance for them to allow the killing of chicken on the farm, if possible that very same day.

"I intend to start tomorrow, with say five hundred chickens if the Egyptians are willing and know how to kill chicken."

"Mr. Aly will explain them, and when they hear of the extra money, they will do it."

"I am not that sure."

"Anyway, you can show them, at the start, you are the expert."

George was aware of the difficulties, knew his ability, but through his mind flashed the liable income; the market was empty, and competition scanty. Probably remain as such for several weeks before the scared off chicken peddlers resumed work. George considered the idea of supplying only the wholesalers, with variable time of delivery; Hag Mohamed noticed his meditation, "and you made your calculations Mr. George?"

George tried to rid himself of any self-doubt lurking in the dark corner of his mind.

"The biggest problem is the municipality."

"We have a license and you can use my name."

"Was told such stories before, just lip service."

"No, I will help you. I can give you a paper to supply my hotel with chicken, the Omar Khayyam; at least it was till recently." Said Hag Mohamed and his face turned pale, his eyelids shriveled and moved his hands nervously.

Hag Mohamed's bitterness reminded George of another hotel owner, that of hotel Montaz, that was confiscated recently by the state in the name of the Great revolution.

"I will get it back one day," sighed Hag Mohamed, "these people will not live for ever."

What an irony, an old man of seventy expected his much younger ruler to go and get back his property, revolutionary governments normally last for more than a generation; the old man reacted momentarily or was an old man's perseverance.

George felt proud of Hag, the same bitter feelings electrified his body, and the old man reminded him of his lost property, presently under the Turkish occupation back at his home island. With sad feelings, but determination for a better day, George rose to his feet ready to start organizing himself for a new era, under a new umbrella.

"Thank you for the customer, Hag Mohamed," said George politely and held his hand for a farewell handshake.

"Wait, I'll write a note for Amin, the man in charge on our farm."

"So, you decided, you will start tomorrow," said Aly.

"Yes, I will give it a try, I'm sure it will succeed."

Hag Mohamed handed the folded glossy paper and said, "good luck", shook George's hand heftily, then turned into a shower of advice to Aly, in Arabic, insisting that he should be there at the delivery and, and… George walked out of the office with a paper in hand and an obligation to resume business.

On the way to their neighbourhood in Fuehat, Aly broke the silence, "The old man is not only careful but a shrewd business man too. You know how many went to him to rent the slaughterhouse and sent them away?"

George made no remarks, just turned, and looked at Aly.

"With you, I don't know, he trusted you from the first moment."

"Thank you Aly, will try my best to fulfill his expectations."

"I'm sure you will," said Aly and dropped off for his house.

George back in his empty house felt the emptiness. Now he was sad and alone and what happened to him in a single day. Made himself a Nescafe with extra coffee, but the taste was far from the one his Mary made for him every afternoon. Over his bitter coffee made a strenuous attempt to recollect the day's chronicle.

"Within two hours rose from my cocoon, transformed from chrysalis to a butterfly, from a beaten dog to a formidable trader, from the accused foreigner to a respectable poultry expert, it was remarkable. Did all this happen out of the blue? No, it's the careful behavior of the whole family over the period they lived in the area. Aly, very seldom spoke to George before, apart from a greeting, had no other countenances.

Crept out of the courthouse, accused, judged, fined; left the depressing building, met a neighourer who through respect and recognition, led me to one of the richest businesspersons of Benghazi. There, within an hour agreed to a new era, ready to embrace surprises with open arms."

Felt like the old phoenix rising triumphant from the ashes. Now his coffee was not that bitter.

"I'm still young, full of spirit, with enough money to start afresh. Never thought of counteracting my pursuers but to proceed decently and earn the necessities for my family."

With such thoughts, George leaned back, closed his eyes, was not in the least mood for a replay of his envious past and dosed away.

It was pitch dark, when he woke up, felt hungry; pulled out of the refrigerator a big piece of pasticcio, his dearest wife stored for him and placed it in the electric oven, the microwave has not reached Libya yet. Enjoyed his pasticcio, picked the car keys, closed the house door as softly as possible, and stepped into the front yard. A strip of concrete led to the exit door, to the left, sand was spread over the red soil covered by a weak vine plant that battled to spread on the trellis, near the boundary wall a few geraniums procured their feeble blossom. Down near the roots, a few tortoises that the girls collected on their last trips to Shahat, were nibbling at what was left from Kate's mint plants. That struck George, since his family left, forgot the green for those docile creatures, well; he would bring them lettuce, first thing in the morning.

A noise drew his attention, sounded like the shouting and clapping of a crowd, tilted his head and tried to locate the source of it, he was puzzled, actually no processions took place in that sleepy neighbourhood of theirs. At closer concentration, the noise came from just across the street, from his neighorer's house; it came in waves, sometimes loud and at others not at all. He reached the exit iron door and pulled the latch very carefully, opened it slightly and pushed his head through. Looked across the street, Hag Nasser's door was wide open, the television set showing at full blast the Colonel talking to a frenzied crowd somewhere in Libya. Hag Nasser wanted the neighbourhood to enjoy the Leader's speech. George closed his door quietly, crept back to his home, opened his set to a volume just enough for him, both channels presented the same program; dish antennas were unknown in Libya and strictly forbidden.

The Leader, accompanied by three aids, took the center of the podium. Faced the frenzied crowd, half smiled and raised both hands high above his face, clenched them in a handshake, the symbol of togetherness.

Many were those who stepped on their seats and leaning forward shook clenched fists forth and back, screaming the revolution slogan, Fatah, al fatah.

The Leader neither encouraged nor requested them to sit down or terminate their affection to him.

Today the speech was against the bourgeois. Standing on a platform staged like a Bedouin's tent, in his native costume, either thrust his tight fist up in the air or thumbed the cheap table, which made a devilish sound at every bang.

At specific moments the cameras showed scenes from the prewarmed frenzied crowd, where every group of around twenty had their own leader, armed with a microphone and made their heroic voices heralded all over Libya.

Since George did not understand that much the language and today already paid his share to the aims of the great revolution, switched off the set and found his way to his bed.

George, within a single day, arranged everything for killing chicken on the farm, despite the difficulties and limitations, the farm labor resentment to work overnight, and the fear of the dreadful municipality inspectors.

Three days later, George called at Hag Mohammed; found him alone in his office. Over the cup of tea, George suggested to Hag Mohamed that he could undertake the running of his chicken farm Aly decided to give up the co-operation fearing the law.

The old man meditated for a few seconds with closed eyes and unexpectedly he said.

"Are you ready to deposit say two thousand dinars yourself as capital?"

George made a quick calculation, that amount, might derive from the killing of the Hag's chicken; he agreed to deposit the two thousand, if they put down as much.

"You know George the farm belongs to my sons, I'll inform them about our agreement, and my friend Aly will inform you accordingly."

"That will be fine," agreed George, "he knows my place."

The proposition was made officially at a meeting with Hag Mohammed presiding, in the presence of his two elder sons, Abdullah, a physics postgraduate from Cambridge and Omar, a mechanical engineer from Austin Texas.

Abdullah tried his characteristic expertise, tried to manipulate the newcomer in his circle of influence; George congratulated him for his degree from such a notable university but told him bluntly that Glasgow was an excellent place for an agricultural degree.

He eyed the Greek through his dark rimmed spectacles and pulled at his goatee beard, Omar showed a better understanding.

George was compelled to accept a third of the net profit, to bear the wages of the laborers, to manage the farm at all levels and deposit all the income from the sale of the finished birds to Hag Mohamed. He accepted their terms; made his calculations, although nobody could predict the outcome with the Leader on the television.

Hag Mohammed stated that in a previous meeting George agreed to deposit two thousand dinars.

"That's right," said George emphatically.

"Well, you bring the money and we'll start," said Abdullah.

"Have planned to go to Greece for two weeks, upon my return I'll bring the money and finalize the agreement."

"You called us here and I considered the agreement finalized," said Abdullah to Hag Mohammed, then turned to George, "how do I now that you come back?"

They were kind to him, but they would have been just as kind, George thought, to some miserable big dog that has lost his master, found him promising but the moment they get tired of him, would kill him out like a stray dog, he was underestimated, felt manipulated and insulted.

To give an end to oscillations, George almost told them that he was not an Arab, but on second thought, offered to deposit the money before leaving, if they gave an official receipt.

Hag Mohammed reproached his eldest son that was too quick in his conceptions; George considered that, as an Arab maneuver.

Abdullah pardoned himself to his father in Arabic and before they dispersed, George stated that he would bring the money first thing in the morning.

"Did you bring the money, yia Yunani?"

The impersonal attitude of the rich always enraged George and very much more this time, almost replied negatively but looked at the challenge from a different angle, wanted to go ahead with his life and considered that could only happen if he created a strategy of brainstorming, took a seat, and pulled out the agreed amount from his bag.

Hag Mohammed counted the money slowly, slowly, and then called his cashier, asked him to count the money and issue a receipt in George's name.

George watched the people who use their hands when they talk, their expressive mannerism might be contradicting their words, and revealing their lies.

Still, saw the stars sending some extra merrism and bonus brightness as the day began and that was a gift. Suddenly the world was full of opportunity and brightness.

"It will be his share of capital in the farm at Ganfooda." His sarcasm was beyond George's imagination, the instructions to the cashier were to put the money in the cash box, "the Unani will try his luck with the farm if he succeeds, good for him, if not, and God is great."

The fat cashier laughed ironically, George paid no attention to that behavior, sipped the tea and waited speechless for the precious receipt. Within a few minutes, the cashier returned with the receipt, handed it to his boss, waited until he read it and left without a word.

"I hope he wrote exactly what we agreed," said George with reservation.

"You must trust me Mr. George," said Hag Mohammed in a sweet tone.

"I trust you very much, but that was my family's savings," said George sternly.

He passed the receipt over his desk, "here is the receipt, he wrote what we agreed, and you can read it."

"I can't read Arabic."

At that moment, Omar came into the office, at his father's instructions, translated the writing on the receipt with the excuse that his father's English was not that good. Correct or wrong George pocketed the receipt and hurried to catch the plane for Athens.

9: Getting some fresh air

Back at home, George filed the receipt, packed a few things for a two week stay in Athens, after all his sister was there, Gia stayed with them for more than three consecutive years back in Kyrenia whilst she attended the secondary school in that town.

Then he called at Hag Nasser, wanted to inform him of his absence, and request him if he could park his car on that side of the road, near his house.

"George by all means," said Hag Nasser, "You can put it in the garage, if you want to."

"Whatever you advise me, Hag."

"When are you leaving?"

"Tonight, with the Olympic Airways."

"You want me to take you to the airport?"

"Please do not bother, now I'm alone, can take a taxi."

"Today there is a lot of checking towards the airport, you'll be drained."

By 6.00 PM, George was at the Hellinikon airport, called his sister at her pharmacy.

"George, where are you? We have been wondering what happened to you, where have you been these days?"

With emotion, heard the voice of his younger sister.

"I'll pick a taxi, where do you want me to come?"

"You can come to the pharmacy; I'll be here till eight."

"If I'm delayed will you wait for me? You know Omonia square is jammed with traffic in the afternoon."

"Yes, I'll be here, kisses."

Along the whole way, no roadblocks, no checkpoints, no gawky eyed armed soldiers, no stray cows crossing the streets and the drivers followed a reasonably driving behavior, what a difference.

Driving down Syngros' avenue, the cool afternoon breeze, the hustling traffic, the rows of flowerbeds and the evergreen changed his mood. Straight ahead was the Parthenon, the gem of Athens and one of the wonders of the world, glistening at the top of Acropolis, the Lycavitos mount with the tiny church dedicated to St. George perched on its ridge, what a difference, what a sensation!

They passed by the Greek parliament with the monument of the Unknown Soldier guarded by two smart gilt wearing soldiers and a cloud of pigeons flying from place to place picking the best feeding spots. To his left, down below the rows of trees and umbrellas where hundreds of tourists and visitors enjoyed their afternoon coffee, their drinks and beer, George said to himself, *is this another world?*

"The pharmacy is off St. Constantine Street, you said?" the driver cut short his daydreaming.

"Yes, that's right."

At Omonia square, the traffic was worse than he thought, despite the efforts of the traffic police, drivers were as lawful as in Libya, every one tried to force his way, even the fountain did not approve the chaos and rocketed up and down with an occasional splash onto the passers-by.

"Hello, my dear brother," Gia greeted him with affection, "welcome to Athens."

"I'm glad to be here," said tenderly, and embraced his sister, hugged her and kissed her on both sides of the face with her long hair falling all over.

"Kate and our girls left for Cyprus four days ago, we tried to ring you up but never succeeded, your friend's telephone is out of order or what?"

George said only, "May be." He did not want to go into details about the situation in Libya, an entirely different country, to people living under a democratic constitution where the last person had voice and dignity; they could not visualize the image of dictatorship.

On their way to Gia's rented appartment at Acharnon Street, they stopped at a corner grocery; it was not more than twenty square meters but its shelves were piled with so many kinds of foodstuffs that George got puzzled. If he began picking stuff, might pick more than a hundred items that he did not taste over the last two years; simply let his sister buy what was necessary; the shop would be open the next day also.

"George, what do you like, take what you want," she urged.

He reached for a bundle of Fix beer.

"We have plenty at home, but take if you are that thirsty."

"Anyway another six...."

Further along, from a side street stall picked not less than six kinds of ripe juicy fruit, produced locally.

At home, by the time Gia prepared something for supper, George took a cold shower with soft sweet water and slipped in just a pair of shorts. From the fridge picked a bottle, popped off the stopper, and enjoyed the frothy beer in a proper glass.

Gia's husband, a lieutenant in the Greek army was serving on the island of Lesvos down the Aegean Sea and was not due for leave at the time. With the beer in hand, George picked up the phone and rang Cyprus, from the first trial, spoke to his sweet wife and his father in law, the three girls were out on a visit to some old friends of theirs.

He finished one bottle of beer and helped himself to a second one, the cool liquid with its low alcohol invigorated him; aimed for a third one and would have had it, if Gia did not intervene with her sisterly concern, "George don't get drank, here, I saved something for you." She brought semi-dry wine from the island of Lesvos.

The steak was delicious, the Greek salad topped with feta cheese was appetizing, and the litre of wine flowed freely; they sat on the veranda but the noise from the traffic was annoying.

After supper, Gia suggested, to take a walk up to Castella, the tiny peninsular over Piraeus, it was a wonderful idea. They sat in an open café, and really enjoyed the ice cream. The cool breeze caressed their faces.

Gia, there on the spot suggested to her brother, to accept a job in Greece, reasoned her gnome on various concepts, education, communication, and civilization. They discussed the possibilities for a job, she was proud of her brother, a well-known poultry expert over the Middle East. Discussed the merits of living in a free country like Greece, and the expected income. They speculated on jobs and localities; he reminded her of a previous attempt to several poultry units four years ago, the salaries were not even a third of what he was earning in Cyprus, and that was before the invasion of the island. She agreed that salaries in Greece were not so promising and realized the difficulty of a married employee with a family living at a remote poultry unit. She tried hard to win him over; George promised to visit the Poultry Growers Association at Agios Constantinos street first thing in the morning.

The time was near eleven when they leisurely walked back to the apartment; George enjoyed a restful sleep, no slaughtering at twelve, or the Imam calling at four in the morning.

Breakfast was simple, "I have to open the pharmacy," said Gia, "we can always eat something from the market if we want to, and the neighbourhood is crowded with all sorts of restaurants."

George had a pastry stuffed with cheese, around nine; he did not enjoy it, tasted too cheap.

Later, he walked up to the National Bank of Greece where he kept an account in local currency; was misinformed when he called there two years ago for an account, the advice to deposit his currency in Drachmas proved misleading, the drachmas was sliding badly.

"George, would you like to go to the theatre tomorrow night, a very nice drama is on, *Electra.*"

Theatre, the word struck his ears, fascinated him, "Theatre," he said, "I haven't heard such a word for more than two years."

"Don't they have theatres in Libya?"

"Oh, yes, there is one in Benghazi, but you know they play the locals and not very often, nowadays."

"Let me see if Tim is coming for the weekend, we'll arrange something." Gia rang up her husband at the military offices on Lesvos Island. George walked to the veranda but was summoned back, his brother in law wanted to say hello from Lesvos.

"Hello Tim, how are you, how is that tourist island of yours?"

"Its great, now is the tourist season you know, why don't you come for a couple of weeks?"

George's schedule was tight, had to arrange a few outstanding matters, get a few medical supplies for personal use in Libya and …and needed some rest. A trip to Lesvos would be a great change but decided to stay with his sister in Athens, might be of some help to her at the pharmacy.

Tim could not leave his post as his assistant was on leave for some family reason.

They dropped the idea of the theatre; George saw this Greek drama back in the sixties, preferred to rest as much as possible. After four days though got bored with nothing to do, at the pharmacy daylong dispensing medicine to sick persons who cried over their ill health, and the high cost of medicine that did not cure them. The doctors prescribed the medicine; Gia simply administered it and just advised on the dosage, that was all.

George enjoyed the evenings; the atmosphere was cool and had plenty of beer, one, two, three, then a walk to the toilet and back again. Dosed off when his sister reiterated her poor economic condition, she complained of the double expenses with her husband far away and alone.

"Are you worried, being alone, young and smart?" he got no answer; she brought more meze and another cool beer.

George contacted his family in Cyprus, Kate wanted to leave the girls with her parents for the whole summer and join her husband now that he was undertaking a new adventure.

"Can manage for a month or so," he explained, "it will take time to stock the farm," she knew the sequence of poultry raising: he appreciated her comprehension.

The two weeks ended faster than George realized, thanked his beloved sister for her hospitality and patience, and promised to return soon. With tears rolling down her cheeks she whispered, "George take care in that wild country, this was the least I could do my dear brother, kept a diary for my long stay with you and your family in Kyrenia."

"I hope you noted the bright side of your stay."

"I had a great time altogether and always confess that I'm greatly indebted to you personally for my upbringing during those crucial juvenile years but also to Kate who considered me as her second sister. I never forget that my further education was purely your determination."

" I'm inundated with happiness simply by your acknowledgement."

The taxi blipped twice, they embraced and hugged, and let the tears flow freely, George ran for the taxi and Gia waved her hand, he cannot say if her blurred eyes saw him going.

10: Setting up the farm

George picked a taxi from Benina airport; the driver spoke little Greek and kept practicing it on the way. Through the checkpoints passed easier than expected, the driver spoke to the guards very amicably, they returned his greetings the same way; he must have been one of them.

Later in the evening, George called at his neighbourer, Hag Nasser and offered him some feta cheese from Athens, got a very warm welcome, they drank tea, talked about the deteriorating situation and George received his keys.

Early next morning George called at Hag Mohammed, found him alone in his office killing time with his chaplet.

"Good morning Hag."

Without urgency raised his face, withdrew himself from meditation and bead dropping, and said, "Ah, you are back," hardly remembered the person who greeted him.

George thought there must be a language that does not depend on words, if he could learn to understand the language without words, he could learn to understand the world.

"Enjoyed your visit in Athens? Lucky you, we are doomed to rot here under this narrow-minded regime. Jamahiriya, the ruling of the masses, where are the masses, what do they know about politics, about governing, about administration, planning, creating, respect to the citizen, his thinking, his expression, where, where?"

Hag was carried away. Before the coup, the old man traveled all over the world for his business and his pleasure.

The United States was his habitat, had close business relations with oil companies; his children attended American institutions one after the other. Now, exit visas were issued only for Saudia, unless you wore the green color of the revolution.

"Revolution, look at our devastated condition, how things stand?" the faster he spoke the faster moved the beads of his chaplet.

"Hag, we cannot change it, better follow the trend and hope for the quick change."

"Have you been at the farm, or not yet?"

George drove down town.

"Greeky, where are you?" that's how George was known to his customers, "we heard you've been caught, jailed and about to be deported, thanks God you are still alive."

"Well as you see, I'm still alive, shake my hand."

All shook hands heartily and laughed at George's mishap, "here they come every day, are just beggars."

The word beggars surprised George and asked, "Do they accept…"

"Within a few months every single Libyan will accept, we wish we'll be around."

George got good orders from all his wholesale customers, the market was empty, and nobody dared to kill chicken.

"Do you accept in the afternoon?"

"You want to kill at daytime, the flies will eat you first and then the meat."

They were right; it would be impossible to kill during daytime, even at Hag Mohammed's place with the fly net all around. He took the operation for granted, the birds on the farm, the water at the turn of a tap, the laborers available. Matters were not as such, was compelled to accept inferior birds to start with, be very careful with the counting and weighing, the cleanliness and the worst the lazy Egyptian workers. To kill five hundred birds had to employ four instead of two, they demanded food, drinks and trips back and forth Benghazi for all kinds of excuses.

George could not accept the situation, called at Hag Mohamed, who listened carefully but lectured George instead and confessed that their biggest problem was labor too.

"If you don't talk to the Egyptians to work to my standards, I'll stop killing birds at your farm." The old man got the message, sent his younger son, a Garyunis university lecturer in economics, the fellow gave them a good telling off with little effect. George gave in to their demands and killed chicken by the thousand.

"It's already three days that I returned," George lied, "I've been on the farm arranging the hangars."

The old man retrieved to normality when he heard about the farm, his poultry business. Dialed a number but got no answer; looked at his wristwatch and mumbled, "Abdullah is never here on time."

The coffee man brought a glass of tea, Hag Mohammed stopped him right there on his tracks, asked George if the tea was to his liking; He approved it after an artificial tasting and the coffee man was released.

George tried to reason with Hag about his planning, the number of day old chicks to be ordered, how many to each hangar, the schedule for the batches and the whole concept of programming. George depicted right from the start that Hag Mohammed would never dream of endangering any of his money. He kept advising on starting carefully and going slowly, his cunningness did not go beyond George's capacity, all he wanted was to operate the farm on somebody else's money. Well, he was not aware of George's experience and abilities in poultry husbandry despite the numerous references.

George pressed and got him to agree to place an order of ten thousand small chicks to start with, the plan was to place the small chicks, purchase part of the required feed with the deposited money, and draw from the other party's capital for purchasing further feed, the objective achieved.

"I'll pay for the petty expenses, like disinfectants, small quantities of medicine or diesel oil from my personal money and account for them per batch, of-course receipts will be obtained and presented accordingly."

"You can do that," said Hag Mohamed and asked his cashier to call Abdullah at his home.

Abdullah was not to be seen and George was in a hurry, wanted to call at the farm and assess the condition of the hangars, the equipment, the water supply, and the laborers.

Drove up to the farm, ignoring the guard, entered the farm by jumping over the perimeter wall, wanted to see if what he requested during his absence was done.

Two Egyptians were employed as watchmen, though should have been alert 24 hours a day, it was ten o-clock and the only one present just managed to get his breakfast, the second one was away in town for some dubious reason.

When George spoke to the one available about the program of chicken growing, the worker said, "wait till Ibrahim returns and we'll see."

"And where is Ibrahim?"

Was annoyed at the question and said in a husky voice, "he went to the house from yesterday, hopefully returns today."

"Which house?"

"You don't know the house, the house of Hag Mohammed."

George left him with his teapot, the tea glass and the flies; toured the hangars, inspected them, checked the equipment, feeders, waterers, gas brooders, the water supply, the electricity, found it all in good condition, then found his way out as he entered and drove back to Hag Mohammed.

Without any consideration of the rules of behavior, George slipped into the big office and said categorically, "the farm workers are not used to work."

"Why, Ibrahim is good."

"The good Ibrahim left for the house two days ago and never bothered to call back."

Abdullah greeted his father solemnly, then George casually, he just arrived.

"I know you are a manager, but managers start work before the employees."

"Not at this time," said Abdullah.

"The Greek does not like the Egyptians you have on the farm."

"I don't like them either," said that because it was true, he said it to please George or to oppose his father; it was a gamble, "well he can bring his own," added indifferently.

Right from their first meeting with Abdullah, George considered him as an adversary. Felt a grip in his stomach, pushed his hand in his pocket to search for that piece of paper stating that they received his two thousand dinars. None spoke; Abdullah remained standing, Hag Mohammed looked at his chaplet, the inert beads. Family relations were not that bright.

"Go and arrange as you consider it best."

"Thank you Hag Mohammed," and hurried out before he changed his mind. Drove to the importer, ordered the ten thousand day old chicks, hundred kantars of feed, twenty starter and eighty the grower type; bought English disinfectant,

Italian vitamins and Belgian medicine. Drove to the farm, nobody was there, the second Egyptian was gone, returned to Hag Mohammed, informed him what he did. The old man congratulated him for the positive way of starting the business, asked him to arrange for laborers, as the two Egyptians might be sent back to their village. Upon his instructions, the cashier issued two checques to enable George settle the cost of the feed and that of the chicks.

"Bring receipts, George."

" Yes, amel Hag, yes dear Hag."

Egyptian workers were hard to find; reliable ones, George thought of another nationality, Chadian would be a solution, from that country people were allowed to enter the country at least from the part bordering Libya, were considered Libyans. George drove to a village not far from the farm he already undertook, met Ibrahim Tardy who employed from that nationality as far as he remembered. The farm was outside the village, George drove there, and found Ibrahim drenched in sweat feeding his own chicken.

"Her, yia Ibrahim," shouted George through an open window.

"Oh, Greeky?"

"Need any help?"

"These bloody Chadian are good for tending only camel, nothing else."

"What happened?"

"They got paid, asked to go to Benghazi for some reason and never returned; it's more than three days now."

"How much do you pay, I'll work for you."

"You, to work for me? Never, how much do you want?"

"Only half of the farm."

"Take all of it; I'm fed up, no laborers, bad quality chicks, bad feed, bad…all bad."

"Was passing by," said George, "and dropped in to see you."

"You are welcome, may be you advise me with that hangar there, have many dead chicken."

"If you like me to have a look, I will."

The birds were a month old but retarded, on post mortem George noticed intestinal infection and requested to enter the hangar for a closer look, the problem was evident, it was coccidiosis, "you better bring and give the medicine today otherwise the whole flock is liable to die."

George scribbled the medicine on a piece of paper in English and said,

"First clean your water tank thoroughly and fill it up. Dissolve the medicine in a bucket and add it to the tank, stir it well and let the birds drink medicated water for three days. Then plain water, just water for one day and repeat the medication for another two days, anyway I may call the day after tomorrow if you want me to."

"Where do I get this medicine?"

"You can find it with Abdelhadi, you can refer my name."

"I'll get it today as soon as I finish the feeding; these bloody Chadian are useless, only for money."

George never mentioned the purpose of his visit, drove to the town, paid for the day old chicks, the feed, and drove to the city centre, the fish market square. There had an acquaintant from Nigeria, who promised to help with labor if needed; now George needed it badly.

Bob was working for the People's foodstuffs co-operative for more than two years; with the present shortage of foodstuffs the work was almost non-existent, was glad to see George; at least, that's how he pretended. George was glad the man still remembered him.

"You need any milk powder, cheese, we received some yesterday, and they are still available."

"Yes, I would appreciate some, if I'm not causing you any problem."

"Well, can manage a tin of milk powder and..."

"Kilo of cheese would be fine," said George, the amount was doubled, placed in a carton box and dropped in the car. George thought that the man would ask for a reward for his service, he was too moderate for that, despite the insisting.

"You know Bob, I'm looking for one or two good workers for the farm, do you have anyone in mind?"

"Can you come tomorrow, same time; I will look around for you."

"Yes, thank you, I'll be here tomorrow the same time," said George and walked up to the restaurant of Farag, only the helper was there. "Where is Farag?"

"He no come, no chicken, you no bring chicken, Farag very angry, he like see you."

"I will come tomorrow," said George and hurried away.

Back to the farm, when the iron gate squeaked on its hinges Ibrahim jumped out of his cabin, "*her yia Mister*."

"Her."

Ibrahim was dressed in his traditional gallabia and bare footed, quickly pushed the gate open, "please Mister."

George ignored the Egyptian and drove away to the hangar, the easternmost one. George planned to start from the east one and work westwards considering the wind direction, since the hangars had no positive ventilation, one had to rely on the natural one, and the westerly winds prevailed in this part of Libya. He wanted to start growing from the east to avoid the dust from the older birds been blown over the birds of a younger age.

Ibrahim came running, George was inspecting the hangar when he arrived panting heavily as though he ran the sprint and in his working outfit, "you will bring small chicks Mister?"

"Hope so."

"I and Ziad will grow them, I know the job."

"Thank you."

"You want us to do something today, now?"

"Yes, I want No 1 and 2 be swept clean the ceiling the walls, floor and the front. I want the dried grass cleaned around both houses to ten meters."

"Show me only how you want to do it and we'll start now."

Hag Mohammed, must have talked to them, there was no other explanation. Ibrahim expressed his willingness to do all what George asked, which was a change.

"Will start now and if not finished by tonight, we'll do the rest first thing in the morning. By the time you come everything will be as you told me, what time are you coming tomorrow, Mister?" His question left many doubts about his promises.

Although George knew the exact number of the feeders, he took time counting them over again; wanted to check on Ibrahim's promises. Ziad joined him, began sweeping down the dust from the iron trusses, George left them fight their way in a cyclone of dust, Ibrahim was too quick, ran, caught him before driving away and requested for some foodstuffs.

"You look after the work and I'll arrange what is available in town, you know the situation here." George cut him short.

In the afternoon George called at the Fish market square to see Bob, it was still early and the normally crowded square stood almost empty. Found Bob unloading bags of sugar; was drenched in sweat. Despite his hurry to finish the unloading, smiled when he saw George, smiled and showed the white of his eyeballs and his two rows of white teeth. "Ten minutes," he said under the weight of a fifty-kilo bag.

George walked up to Omar Mukhtar street and the central post office, it was closed as well as the shops around there, only the old peddler at the corner was sitting by his cart dosing away under the shade of the ficus tree. It was a common joke that old Mohammed never left his post day or night. He was fat and repulsive. The worst of him was his lower lip, it must have weighed more than three hundred grams, this, along with his droopy cheeks brought memories of the long vanished Ottoman Empire.

George's idle walk took more than ten minutes, just about the time that Bob required to unload the load of sugar. Back to the People's co-operative, met Bob drying off his face, another broad smile, George shook his hand, "you know sir, I talked to two of my bothers, just now they are having their final exams, they may finish in two or three days."

"What examinations, Bob?"

"At the university, Sir."

"Are they students?"

"Yes, they are studying."

"Can you ask them to meet me here on Thursday evening?"

"Yes, I will, yes sir."

George picked whatever foodstuffs he could find and drove to the farm, to his great surprise what he instructed was done, the houses were swept clean, the perimeter cleared from the brush and the rubbish was lying on top of a bonfire. A sweaty couple greeted him with broad smiles, George returned their smiles, and walked to the second hangar, which was cleaned too, he could disinfect both houses now.

"Ibrahim, is there any small water pump here?"

"No, boss, no."

Instead of disinfecting the houses with the customary disinfectants that were hard to find, George thought of spraying them with diesel oil, it was cheap and had a strong cleansing power, could destroy the wax-coated coccidia, one of the major diseases in poultry, in warm climates.

The idea sprang up after his visit to Ibrahim's farm two days earlier. He estimated the required amount; about two hundred liters for each hangar would be enough. Now, he needed two big oil drums, a small size pump, tube, and nozzle. He discussed the matter with Hag Mohamed, "we can give you two empty barrels, and you arrange the rest."

At the rubbish dump laid many empty barrels that was easy, for a pump and the rest George had to look somewhere else.

From his friend Milad near the Fish market, George bought a pump, fifty meters of reinforced tubing. For the nozzle he needed, had to be brought from Europe or Japan. George would innovate something; in the worst case, he could use his thumb to regulate the flow of the liquid.

Called at Bob's place, he was unloading boxes full of bananas. Despite the heavy work the smile was his companion, "my brothers are just there," he said and pointed at two Africans standing under the shade, at Bob's signal both approached.

"Good afternoon, how are you?"

"Very well, thank you."

"Bubaker," a man in his forties, thin and sinewy stretched his long arm for a handshake; his characteristics were between an African and a Mediterranean.

"Izzy." muttered the second one, though standing in the shade, insisted of wearing his dark sunglasses. Was much younger, heavier and of slower motility, he smiled and shook George's hand vigorously, tried to impress him of his physical condition.

Under the shade of the enormous ficus tree, George learned that they were students at the University of Garyunis, scholars from Nigeria, taking religious studies on scholarships from the Great Leader of the Alfatah revolution. He congratulated them for their success to obtain scholarships and be able to study abroad.

Both admitted their achievements but complained the way they were treated here in Libya. Were given assurance for exclusive treatment, but all those promises turned out fake.

George was not there to discuss their problem; he was there to ask them for work.

"Yes, please."

George explained the situation, the kind of work, the system, the place of living, the salary, in general the chances and limitations. The elder one, having his wife and a kid with him was eager to accept any conditions. Izzy looked unreliable. George considered Bubaker as a gang Leader; he liked him from the first moment. He explained that two Egyptians were already on the farm, Bubaker pleaded at least for part time work. Although they were in the middle of their exams, agreed to work in the afternoons. George promised an answer in two days through their brother Bob. Izzy complied with the idea but Bubaker was disappointed. As George was leaving, called Bob and handed him twenty dinars to be given to Bubaker, in a gesture to help him out.

At the first petrol station George was not allowed to fill both drums with diesel oil, at the second one there was no electricity, he had to drive along the Tripoli road to fill up the second drum.

At the farm, George advised Ibrahim how to unload the heavy oil drums.

"Place the big tire near the car and drop the barrel onto it; the tire would act as a cushion for the full drum."

Ibrahim helped to arrange the pump, the tube and a suction tube from the drum, the problem remained who was strong enough to suck diesel from the drum to feed the pump for the start.

"I will, yia Mister," said Ibrahim

"Ibrahim please do not swallow the diesel, brought it for the hangars." He chuckled away but even at that, took a good swill, because he coughed badly later on. The tube suction tube was now full. George slipped it onto the pump; the motor squirted slightly but began flowing. He ran to the far end of the hangar, grabbed the tube that was swerving from side to side like the tail of a rattlesnake, he did not want his trousers get soaked with the turbid liquid. Despite his precautions one of his legs got soaked, he felt it hot a few minutes later.

With his thumb, managed to regulate the flow into a thick spray, it was good enough for the purpose but felt his thumb itchy and cold; changed thumbs, tried his left one with little success, the right thumb had to stand the encumbrance. By the time he sprayed the first hangar his thumb was so numb that he could not feel it.

George advised Ibrahim to close up the hangar and nobody should open or enter for the next two days.

For the second hangar Ibrahim undertook the handling of the tube, George remained by his side to make sure the job was done properly. Two hundred liters of diesel was just enough for the hangar with careful handling of the tube, he wanted the same procedure be followed for the second hangar, Ibrahim proved reliable.

Evaluating the labor problem George had to work with the Egyptians in hand, at least for the time being. The next morning he called at the farm, the program was how to disinfect equipment.

"Yia, Ibrahim?"

"Yia, Mister at your service."

"Look, I want you to disinfect the feeders, waterers and all other equipment used for the hangars. This is the concentrated disinfectant, its very expensive, you have to follow the instructions, are you listening?"

"Aioua, yia Mister."

"First you wash all the equipment thoroughly, and then prepare the mixture this way. You see this mark in this plastic container, you put water up to this mark, then in a bucket with water you pour a measure of disinfectant, this is the measure, you got it?"

"Aioua, yia Mister.

"Then stir the mixture thoroughly and dip one by one the feeders, the waterers, scoops, buckets and all the rest you have washed, place them on a plastic sheet to dry somehow and afterwards take them into the house. After you dip the equipment in the mixture, you can wash the equipment for the second hangar, and disinfect them in a newly prepared mixture exactly as you have done with the first lot. You got it?"

"Aioua, yia Mister."

Ibrahim was clever enough; he caught easily and was interested in learning the sequence of the work.

"Yia Ibrahim, Hag Omar will bring a load of feed today, two kinds of feed, some for the small chicks and some for later on when they grow up. Hag Omar knows the difference, just show his people where to unload it, half of each kind in the two hangars,"

"Aioua, yia Mister."

"Now the gas brooders, I want you to wash them also, but you have to be careful with the ceramic, it breaks with rough handling. Come closer I'll show you what I mean."

Ibrahim followed George to the store, "what a mess, why didn't you store each item separate, feeders, gas brooders, plastic waterers all piled up like this?"

"Boss, I'll separate them."

"You better do! Come here, you see the gas brooder, you see this part here, this is the ceramic where the gas spreads over and burns, if this breaks the gas will not burn properly, some may escape unburned with unexpected danger."

"It may explode Mister."

"Yes, and may burn you before you are able to run far enough."

"Aioua, yia Mister."

Ibrahim was very submissive, and this worried George, Egyptians by nature were deceptive, they needed someone always at their tail. He should visit Hag Mohamed and ask him to talk to them if he had not already done so; he was the only one who could handle them, since their residence was in his name.

The way, the gas brooders were hang from the ceiling was not that practical, and since these had to be moved from time to time as the birds grew and the space was enlarged for them, George had to innovate another method. He came up with thin rods of iron with hooks on either end, he tried once and the idea was wonderful; several rods were prepared, the Egyptians were astonished with the idea; were rubbing their eyes.

"You know Mister the chain was good but in order to change its position one had to use a ladder, now with a simple handling the hook is hang where needed, safely and quickly."

Gas was brought in cylinders; Ibrahim undertook the loading of the empties and insisted to go along to the petrol station for handling the full ones too. George appreciated his willingness, on the way back George bought him a full pack of Rothman cigarettes. He was thrilled. By the time, they returned with the gas, the feed was brought and unloaded according to his instructions.

George caught Ziad ready to discard the used disinfectant; he stopped him on the spot,

"Ziad, if you wash your veranda with this mixture, you will kill many microbes and no fly will come anywhere near."

Ziad hesitated; the plastic container was too heavy to carry on a wheel burrow. George asked them to lift it on the car. He helped them. The spraying proved beneficial, both Egyptians adored George and his ideas ever since.

"*Yia mudeer*, big boss you were right no flies and no mosquitoes come near us that was a very good idea."

Wood shavings in Libya were a permanent problem with very few trees and with restrictions on imports, made the commodity scarce. George visited several workshops with disappointing results; at each workshop, a pile of empty sacks lay disorderly. He decided to use another material found in abundance in Libya, sand.

Libya is covered with the material, George ordered two loads of it and asked his workers to carry it inside and spread it evenly on the floor, to three centimeters thick.

"Boss, shall we grow the chicks on sand?"

"On sand, Ibrahim, on sand."

"Boss, excuse me for asking, may be I'm stupid, but how does it work?"

"Ibrahim, you are very clever and never reproach yourself, the matter is simple, here we have a dry climate most of the times, the feces from the chicks will drop on the sand will dry out and dissolve, no dirt and no smell. The sand is cool in summer and the chicks get the benefit of it in the hot season."

Both Egyptians stared at George with open mouths.

"You will learn a lot if you stay long enough and listen to what I advise you; then you go back to Egypt and start your own farming."

"That's what Hag Mohammed said too," added Ibrahim. George looked at him with appreciation.

Abdelhadi informed Hag Mohammed by phone that the plane from Holland would be arriving on Thursday evening; the message was passed to George through Omar who called for a visit and an investigation.

"George, the chicks are arriving at Benina airport on Thursday, you will have to go there alone, please do not take any workers with you, they do not have proper papers, but make sure you take the original receipt with you, that's a proof for the authorities." Omar passed the information and left faster than he came in, none of the sons liked the farm, this was to George's benefit, and he could do the job with the least interference.

"Ibrahim, come here both of you."

" *Aioua yia Mister.*"

" Tonight I'm going to the airport to bring the small chicks."

" Welcome."

" Come with me down to the hangar."

Both Egyptians followed George into the hangar; he switched on the lights for better inspection but also, to check if the electric bulbs were still in their place.

"Things look in order, now I want you to fill the small waterers with fresh clean water to which we'll add some sugar."

"Boss, do the chicks drink tea like..."

"Yes! Like the Egyptians."

"Fill the plastic barrel with water and dissolve this bag of sugar in it, stir it properly with your hand, then fill the plastic drinkers and place them on the small wooden slaps in the way you arranged them, I mean do not change the place of the slaps, you got it?" George remained around, he saw the drum being filled up, the sugar dissolved and get into the drum, and the waterers being filled up and capped properly. He explained that the drinkers had to be absolutely horizontal, otherwise the water would run off, wet the litter and leave the chicks thirsty. George had to be strict with them, he couldn't take any risks.

George passed through the check points with no difficulty and reached the last gate leading to the airplane parking area, many farmers were idling there, most of them Libyans, one or two Palestinians; he knew most of them, he greeted the few nearby and listened to their gossip. *The feed nowadays was not that good, the chicks too small and the medicine was simple kaolin, never cured sick birds*, such were the complains of the farmers.

Abdelhadi, the importer of the day-old chicks was not to be seen yet, George kept guard for him, it was his first time at the airport, was not familiar with the procedure, he remained near his car and kept his eyes open and his ears flapping.

Abdelhadi arrived with his helper Issa the Palestinian, simple and modest. Greeted his customers in general, but did nod shake hands with anyone of them. He explained that the customs official needed the official receipt to allow the entrance, "this is the law, and I think is right," he said plainly and walked along, he spotted George and asked him in English if he brought the receipt, with a nod assured him about it.

"Just show it to the guard and that's alright."

Many farmers stared at the foreigner who endeavoured to grow chicks in Libya, a difficult trade in a difficult country. George climbed to his car, he was ninth, or tenth in row; kept alert for his turn, with these people, nothing was civil.

When George reached the loading bay, many farmers were piling carton boxes into their vans, almost all, worked in couples, they were locals, brought with them a brother or a son; he was alone, by himself.

He approached a pallet still full with chirping chicks, must have just been offloaded, the noise was deafening, the forklift was busy. As he closed unto the pallet with the chicks, the heat emitted was too high, with the airplane engines switched off and no ventilation many chicks may succumb from overheating and lack of oxygen.

When on the ground the cool breeze helped a lot, the chicks could breathe and that quietened them somehow; he watched the anarchy at the loading bay with the officials darting here and there uttering instructions with the forklift operator being the main figure. Farmers were shouting and arguing for no reason, Issa and his boss, in vain tried to bring order, George was at a loss.

"Benily?" called a voice, it was Issa, "bring your car here," and pointed to a pallet full of boxes from which a devilish noise was rising, Abdelhadi approached calmly and advised George to wait, "let the people from afar load first."

"They are welcome." George said, positively.

As he went by the pallet, the heat emitted must have been more than hundred, was glad he did not take his from that lot.

Issa signaled George to a newly offloaded pallet, there was less chirping, one would think either the chicks were mostly dead or too weak to cry or the pallet was in a better position in the plane. George reached the pallet, lifted two, three boxes, tilted them one by one, and listened, dead chicks tend to be heavy, his heart throbbed when the small chicks tried to cling to their position, and they used their tiny claws. He began loading; within minutes, took all the cartons from that pallet.

"Take another twenty boxes from here," called Issa. George carried the twenty boxes near his car, they were his now. He did not pile the cartons in his car with any haste; loaded half of the bottom part of the car, then placed planks of wood above and secured them on the sides of the box of the car and on top of the planks piled boxes to the roof.

Two Libyans watched him from afar and approached, they studied the system and said, "you see the Greek, he does not pile the boxes high, and so the bottom ones do not get crushed; we never envisaged such a concept."

George heard them but let them get some new ideas; they helped him to load his chicks and thanked him there on the spot for his advice.

George finished loading and lowered the rear part of the tarpaulin then closed the rear door, the farmers were still standing by, momentarily one, stepped forward with his hand raised, as he wanted to say something.

"I say, yia Greek, thank you for your wonderful idea, one last question, do you add anything in the water for the first days?"

George smiled approvingly; they are after me, "yes, as a matter of fact I do give sugar in the water for the first six hours or so, and then I give some ordinary antibiotic for two days, have to go now otherwise the chicks will die in the boxes."

"Tfatal, tfatal and thank you very much."

George drove away. This was his first attempt to grow chicken in Libya with Hag Mohammed, actually with his own money. A failure would be disastrous for him as a farmer and as a scientist, had to succeed. All the way to the farm, he was tense, but when the small chicks began running happily under the gas brooders, George's heartbeat returned to normal. From the ten thousand he bought, found only five dead, two of them choked with their heads under the lids.

Sweet memories overwhelmed him; the chirping of the little devils reminded him of his own farm back in Cyprus, now under the army boot of the invader.

"What is this?" asked Ibrahim when George hung up a record sheet on the wall by the door.

"Yes, Ibrahim, this is a record sheet, onto this, we will record all activities going on in the hangar, as the number of dead, which I want to see, the number of bags of feed given to the birds daily, the medicine administered and so on." Both workers stood with their eyes directed to the sheet of paper and their mouths half open.

"Even a pencil is hung for the purpose," exclaimed Ziad.

"Yes, and I want the pencil there," said George sternly.

"Aioua, yia Mister."

By the time they unpacked the small chicks, it was almost midnight. He wanted to stay around to keep an eye at the thermostats; pondered around for more than an hour, Ibrahim brought tea, the water plastic drums were refilled with fresh water, George explained once more about the amount of medicine that had to be administered, Ibrahim nodded positively and George decided to leave. On second thought, he turned back and made a point on how to fill the waterers and how to start. With his finger pointing at the circle of drinkers distributed around the gas brooder, advised them to start from one end and follow clockwise. In this way, he explained you won't miss any and the chicks will be moving ahead of you, try not to step on them yia Ibrahim."

"No, yia Mister."

"Ziad, go and bring your blanket, you sleep in this hangar and Ibrahim in the next one, I don't want a single chick to die through your negligence, you got it, is it clear? Allah, help you."

"Yia Mister, nothing will go wrong, if it happens you talk to Hag Mohammed." Said Ziad, Ibrahim left for the blankets.

11: Nasser and his friends

Nasser, their neighbor completed his three-story building and moved from the second floor to the ground one. They were always on good terms and whenever he saw George, called him from afar and loudly, "Come Mr. George, come and have a look at my newly finished flats."

The flats were enormous but the plan was not to his liking, the two oversize salons dominated almost half the area, another big portion was turned to the main bedroom, leaving two small bedrooms and a relatively small kitchen. Nasser led the way, explained about the rooms and the spaces and followed George's eyes, tried to read his response. George congratulated him for his achievement; and commented that the flats were very well planned, pointed though that the kitchen was rather small.

"I'll be renting them anyway," was his answer, George left him and drove to his work.

A few days later Jamal, Nasser's younger son came running to George, "Uncle, my dad wants you now, you have to come."

George crossed the street and called from the gate his friend's name, to announce his arrival. Nasser answered from inside the house and the youngest son came forward to meet George and lead him to his father.

Nasser was in the big bedroom among some peculiar parts of furniture and some carton boxes.

"Hello Hag."

"George welcome, they brought me a new bed from the army stores; I need your help to assemble it."

"You have any drawing, any catalogue?"

All he had was a glossy piece of paper with a photo of a bed in vivid colors and a slim attractive young woman in a prostrate stance.

"Hey, you got all the parts here," said George and pointed at the feminine figure.

"That will come later," said Nasser and winked his eye.

The bed consisted of an oversize steel frame of an oval shape. The headpiece consisted of three portions, the centre one decorated vividly, the other two side portions had sound speakers, telephone and an electric control, that George took as the motor regulator. From the description that was in Italian, George figured out that the bed could be rotated to a ninety degree and rocked to about thirty degrees. The end piece had in the centre a television screen seated between parabolic mirrors. A kaleidoscopic light was available to be fixed at the ceiling; George teased Nasser about a red light for the door.

"Yia George, you came here to help me or what?"

He explained that all his friends had a bed like this one, therefore he got one too, and his long caged devil came out now roaring. Both toiled to fix the bed, had tea twice, the middle-aged Egyptian housemaid brought in. Nasser employed her a few days after his sweet wife died of liver cirrhosis.

After they finished the assembling, went to the sitting room with the modern Italian armchairs and sofas, really were marvelous, the drapery on the walls was of heavy material and matching with the tapestry. The Arab salon spread with flat cushions all around, with a local carpet spread from wall to wall, a very relaxing place, thought George. On the east wall, a huge portrait of the Leader hang rather too high, purposely or not, the portrait was at that height and the Leader looked down in a despotic posture, dressed in the legendary outfit.

Both times that George was invited to sit with Nasser's friends in this salon, the guests were sitting directly under the portrait, from that position they did not face him whilst drinking their illegal alcohol.

Nasser asked George once, to have a look at his cooking oven, he was shocked. The whole kitchen was not more than ten square meters; the space looked smaller with a gas stove, a small table, some kettles piled in the corner, and a water tap over a carved limestone basin full of unwashed dishes, cups and kettles. The stove was out of use, covered literally with burnt food debris and overflowed oily material. He had to dismantle the burners and give them a good scrubbing before reassembling. What a contrast between the bedroom and the kitchen.

After George fixed the gas stove, decided to fix the dripping tap; it needed a new washer, he brought one from his toolbox, the smell from the food debris, the blood and fat from chopped meat over the sink was unbearable. Cleanliness seemed to have been neglected for quite a long time.

"I think it works now," commented George to his friend Nasser, standing by.

"I do not understand much about such things George, anyway I'll call you whenever I need you."

George eyed him from the corner of his eye and added, "Please do, at your service."

"Let me call Naima, she knows how to operate the oven."

The Egyptian housemaid came along, lit the gas burners, one after the other, then the oven, looked up, smiled and approved the job. Nasser's face turned red, and that certified his incompetence, "come George, come let's sit in the salon."

Nasser led the way, both got into the salon; a fragile scent of flowers hang in the air, George looked around for flowers, but could not see any, an aerosol flask stood on the floor. The JVC color television stood on its polished stand with the video recorder underneath, both gadgets crept into the souls of all Libyans. By extending the electrification scheme, television sets found their way in almost every house, tent and sheep pen. People needed entertainment and the Leader gave orders for the supply of reasonably priced television sets. Television became the main means of communication with the Leader since the majority of the fellahin followers were illiterate.

Nasser tuned on the television set; the sound was loud enough to be heard from across the street, the owner enjoyed it that way. This time a boy of around seven brought a tray with two small glasses of a greenish liquid, placed the stainless steel tray on the floor and muttered the customary, "please, *tfatal*.' His father commented on something in Arabic that George did not catch, the boy turned red and mumbled, OK, OK then fled away barefooted.

The pale green liquid tasted like lemonade, was too sweet, lukewarm and without flavor, George sipped it slowly, slowly.

Channel 1 was showing folklore in genuine Arabic from the heart of the desert. Hag Nasser commented that those people, only recently allowed the camera operators enter their private life.

A simple band consisting of two drums, a flute, and a violin played a repetitive tune to which a couple of women dressed in their legendary heavy clothing curled and twisted in harmony. If they were a bit taller and dressed lighter, the dance would have been more appealing. They moved their arms up and down exhibiting their golden bracelets. One of them wore leg bracelets of some width just above the ankle of her bare feet. The tune was monotonous and so was the wriggling.

Hag Nasser switched to channel Two; this channel was meant for expatriates working in Libya. The program was stereotype; the Leader was either shown talking obviously in Arabic, or a Maltese group singing antiroyalist songs, "the crown tumbled down, etc," or exhorting the merits of the Great revolution or documentaries from the National geographic magazine.

News were limited, as to what the Leader did over and over, a few phrases about the Arab world and time permitting some extracts from the National Geographic were shown on a repeated basis. The whole program for the foreigners lasted only for two hours.

"Yia Nasser, yia Nasser," somebody yelled from the middle of the street, George got frightened, thought that something serious happened.

"*Tfatal*, Come," screamed Nasser from the heart of the house. He rose quickly and barefooted threaded his way through doors and corridor, "be seated yia George, be seated."

From inside the house, doors were heard been closed in a hurry, a stranger was coming.

George remained glued to his seat, heard the loud voices, and tried to figure out the unexpected worriment. Several voices could be differentiated but was impossible to figure out what was the discussion about, all were talking simultaneously and fast. The blabber got more and more intense as the group was entering noisily the house. George shriveled in his crouched position, did not even turn to face the approaching regiment, that's how it sounded, although no footsteps, only high pitch voices, they flowed into the salon conversing at the same aptitude, one, two, three and Nasser, all of them dressed in their native outfits of light white cotton, probably manufactured in China.

"My house is not that rich but you are welcome to what we have."

Nasser wanted to introduce George, who rose to his feet.

"*Her yia Greeky*," cackled one of them, from his towering height.

"Hello learned one," a respectable way to answer a dignified Arab.

"Greeky?" asked the second, a middle-aged man.

"Yes, George is Greek," explained Nasser, "Greek Cypriot, a brother."

"*Yiasou ti Kanis*? How are you?" he greeted George in Greek.

"*Kala euharisto*, very well thank you."

"Abdullah is half Greek," added Nasser.

"Is he?" asked George with reservation whilst shaking hands with him.

"This is Mohammed," said Nasser, "sit down yia Mohammed and make yourself small."

Greece being the nearest European country, with six flights weekly and with a strong Libyan dinar, Athens was like their backyard picnic place. Most of the elders made several trips to that city in a year, either to saw their wild oats or to contact some kind of trade. They picked the casual phrases and mumbled them whenever there was a chance, at conceded audacity.

They did not feel comfortable in the salon with the sofas and the armchairs, and did not sit down.

"Let's go into our salon, yia Nasser."

"There is no air-conditioning there yet."

"Come to us and take two, yia Nasser."

"Will you be there Abdullah?"

"If I'm not, Abdelkerim will be, one of us is always working."

"That's something new," said the tall fellow, and all cackled noisily.

"All right just sit down and make yourselves small."

"Comfortable?" said Mohammed and pushed the sofa backwards, dropped on the thick carpet and rested his head and arms on the sofa, "I can sleep for days, here."

The other two followed Mohammed.

The third visitor, a young fellow in his mid thirties with dark grizzly hair and a nicely trimmed moustache was very quiet. Simply sat down on the carpet, with eyes darting from speaker to speaker, did not utter a single word, simply played with his moustache.

Now, four bodies stretched down and four pairs of bare feet formed a small circle in the salon, eight toes pointing to the ceiling, George's toes were imprisoned in a pair of grey socks, at least the flies did not tickle him that much. Though, those toes looked clean enough the flies were not fooled, at first one, two, then more landed on toes at random, and the toes in turn, moved back and forth and feet changed places.

Nasser lifted his scented aerosol and gave a liberal spray over all the feet, George got the most, he was sitting opposite him, sneezed twice, and Abdullah joined him.

"Sit still yia Nasser, this bloody aerosol is too strong, isn't it yia Greeky."

"Somehow," said George.

Channel 1 was switched on and the Leader was in the middle of one of his lectures.

"He is a professor now," said Mohamed.

"He solved all the other problems and..."

All cackled loudly but left it at that, too many around for any personal opinion; George remained silent, waited to find out what was on their minds, and gave them space to figure some things out.

The TV showed the Leader, with no smile on his face whatsoever, standing in front of a big board painted green, the cloth covering the podium was green, and the ruler in his hand was green.

"Is the chalk green, yia Nasser?"

"Where are my spectacles?"

"If you need spectacles to see the Colonel, you are finished."

"Greeky, here we are all brothers," commented Mohammed with a twitch of amusement.

"Yes, thank you, I just feel like that," gave himself a break, and gave them a chance to soar.

The Leader tried to explain to a gathering of about hundred persons, all males, and the word democracy. Half of those present held tiny green flags on tiny masts with the Leader's portrait printed in the middle, and wore green shawls either round their necks or around their heads, it was a sea of green.

The Leader tried hard to persuade his disciples that the word democracy was pure Arabic; a compound one, consisting of 'demos' and '*karasi*', where 'demos' meant the people and the second part 'seat', a wave of green ebbed hither and thither for several minutes, shouted the slogan, '*Alfatah abadan.*'

"Enough, you hungry beggars," called Abdullah.

"Louder, yia Abdullah, they haven't heard you."

"Sheep, brainwashed idiots."

"Shut up Abdullah, he is about to start," said Nasser.

"To-day I'm happy, because you are happy," said the Leader.

Another wave of screams and flag swinging.

"To-day........."

The group leaders, with both arms raised, waved the subordinates to shut up. When silence was imposed, the Leader with an expressionless face looked at his disciples and began his speech in a monotonous tone.

Mohamed gritted his yellow teeth, "that's rubbish, isn't it yia Greeky? O.K.?"

George turned and simply looked at him.

"The revolution is for ever," said Nasser, the guests agreed by just nodding their heads, a silence fell in the salon.

"You see our professor," said Abdullah, "he will steal all the Greek literature from you, wants to explain the word democracy."

"The man who does not know where he was born…."

"And when?" cut short Mohammed.

"Turned himself to an academic and tries to teach us the meaning of expressions he does not understand."

"It's not for you Abdullah."

"He talks on the air, to his nation."

George avoided even the slightest muscle movement; his eyes though darted from speaker to speaker. Cupped his glass with the forbidden beverage and felt the change of temperature as the ice cubes melted. His pretended apathy did escape the inquisitive eyes of his friend's guests.

"Why does he not explain the word megalomania?"

A roar of laughter filled the salon.

"What do you say, George?"

"We have plenty anyhow, let the Leader borrow some," said George in a low tone, avoided any feather ruffling, a sensible man should regard the small things and rate himself accordingly, did not want to play the cultured Greek amongst the followers of Muammar.

"Yia Nasser there is nothing else? Try the second channel."

Nasser responded to Mohamed's request, and switched to channel Two, the same program, rather clearer, the laughter rocked the salon again.

"Don't you have a satellite yia Nasser? Go to Abdelkerim," said Mohammed and that brought another roar.

"Tea, I ran out of tea," apologized Nasser.

"Bring the water," groaned Abdullah.

At his advice, not only bodies rocked but also the feet rose high up, the gallabias rolled back and disclosed hairy legs.

George half raised himself, was ready to leave, Nasser pushed him back, "you are a brother, sit down."

"Welcome," said Abdullah and smiled at George winking his eye at the same time.

George returned the smile and guessed what they were up to; the tray arrived with a stainless teapot and short heavy glasses.

"So you are from Cyprus, Greek?"

"George speaks Arabic yia 'Abdullah."

He asked, the same question twice, George paid no attention to his inquiries.

"And this is just the tip of, what do you call it Mr.George, the iceberg?"

"What are you talking yia Abdullah? Here we don't have even ice cubes for our drinks and you refer to icebergs?"

"Ignorant? Please George; explain him, what I meant to say?"

"I'll try to explain in broad lines, and it's not a question of knowledge or ignorance. If we look at the desert, one can see a sand dune protruding, it consists of sand, but just a small portion of sand is visible, compared to the amount of the stuff lying below and around that sand dune. The same applies to a floating iceberg; one can just see moreless a third of it above the water, the bulk is below the surface. By this, one means that what we hear is not the whole story."

George used his diplomatic skills to create a dialogue, and did not like to come off defensive; wanted to come off mature, intelligent, and dedicated.

"Thank you Mr. George, tell me, have you ever worked as a teacher?"

"As a matter of fact, I did, several years back."

"So, tell Abdullah, what we cannot see?"

"The Leader has many thoughts and as many plans for changes in our lives."

"What, first he took the money, then the property..."

"Then will close all the shops, the workshops and any other small business; and the list gets longer."

"Well, he forced the farmers producing cut flowers to close down."

"And opened his own."

"And the people stopped using cut flowers for decorating bridal cars; turned to plastic ribbons and balloons."

Ha,ha,ha... the laughter was loud and raucous.

"You care for another drop? Lift your glass."

"No more bridal cars and no more brides"

"What, people will stop getting married?"

"They will get married, but you see, he closed the coiffeurs."

"And the Egyptian hairdressers make more money now, by calling from house to house."

"Two days ago, some of them were caught, jailed, treated accordingly, and deported."

"Two deported, ten entered the trade, there are Yugoslavs, Bulgarians; too many needy ones."

"That is true."

"You heard him giving instructions and recipes how to make cakes at home?"

"That was one of the funniest speeches I've ever heard."

"He said those women sitting in the house could do something. It is very easy to make a cake, flour from France, butter from Holland, and sugar do not remember from where, mix them up, stir the mixture well and bake it. Gas, we produce our own gas."

"Yes, Naima made a cake the other day; it tasted like mashed potatoes, even the children refused to eat it."

George was listening with skepticism, and was amazed with what he learned and always ready for a sympathetic ear. If the government undertakes the trade, the imports, the distribution, closes down confectioneries, hairdressers and corner shops, how a person could make a living.

"George, what are you thinking? Things will change; we are just going through a transition period."

"What transitory, my dear friend, nothing will be left standing, nothing will remain normal."

George lifted his face, the locals stopped and waited. He had something to say.

"Last week, I called at the Benily pharmacy, the one at Pepsi road, and asked for a toothpaste. I know both persons running the pharmacy."

"What kind of toothpaste do you want George?" asked Fattallah.

"Normal size, please?"

"The two looked at each other, smiled at me and said, yia Hussein, is there anything normal here in Lybia, just now?"

The laughter was resonant.

"Mr. George, I wouldn't worry, if they close down your chicken farm, will arrange employment for you with our Leader, just talk to Nasser."

"What, teach the Leader Greek?"

"Yiaaaaa…."

"Thank you, yia Abdullah; I'll bear it in mind."

"Now, enjoy your drink, till to-morrow, Allah ouakbar, God is great."

"That is true, definitely true."

"You read the Green book?"

"Read parts of it, conflicting and ambiguous."

"The second part is rather directive, 'The solution of the economic problem' gives power to confiscate private businesses, nationalize private property and cap the income from the natural resources."

"Another big issue will be the involvement of the female population, labeled them as feebler sex and berated as black Africans labeled a lazy race liable to multiply without limit."

George smiled.

"His wife," and Nasser pointed at George, "is helping him everyday on the farm. I see them riding on the Peugeot every day."

The whole group stared at George with appreciation.

"Not like our ducks, who do nothing beyond eating and sleeping," said Mohammed.

"That would be a real change in our traditions."

"Yes, the women, let's call them females, will have to learn a lot more beyond their traditional skills of cooking, cleaning and growing children."

"Are our women inferior to our men, are the men better-stronger in muscle than a normal woman, in mind or operation, can they not ride a horse, drive a car, serve a person in a bank, municipality or a shop? The judgment of women is likely to be as good as that of men, sometimes better."

"Endeavor to involve women in the machine of development and life change, will give them a broader span of interest, broader view of the human life with other fields of engagement and interests. To have fewer children, using logic means of contraception and be able to pay greater attention to their family as a whole and moreover the upbringing of children with regards to care, health, education," said Mohammed.

"This may create a controversial debate as to what right development could be implemented to meddle in the hierarchy of our community." Abdullah added.

"Education is the means to improvement but involves western concepts and standards that clash with our traditions and religion."

"We all agree with you Ibrahim, but you cannot have everything."

"The question is, would a westerner understand the local cultures and traditions of our community and if women acquire the universal right of total social equality. If the transition is gradual, the new ideas will filter into the legendary culture and the marriage of such traditions with the modern and improved western ideas will prove the benefit."

"The basic and most fundamental tool will be education, education implemented by local personnel who will feel and understand the local culture and traditions. It is scientifically indent that close inbreeding throws out, discards, all non-natural traits and brings forward body, mind, and stature to near perfection, body with a harmonious symmetry. Definitely, such traits highly selected by nature exist in our community and educating such persons whether males or females, the dedication to economic progress will be positive."

"Needless to add, that there is a great potential reservoir of women all ready to advance, the only thing is to tap that reservoir in a positive manner and raise the awareness of the benefits. This will lead to an untapped reservoir of job creation, economic growth, and national cohesion.

Concurrently, the women involvement will play a role of promoting economic diversification and development.

However, education at all levels will increase the awareness and motivation among girls, and acquire tools and skills, will enable them to participate in-group endeavors and join associations.

At a later stage, such talented women may endeavor private entrepreneurships with the help of foreign expertise to bypass society obstacles.

To foster economic diversification could be achieved by building along with a public affairs policy. To publicize through the media the success of such strategies and plans for a broad view the sunny side of the movement."

"Did you hear the Leader talking over the television a month ago, if I remember right?"

"About the Italian sorrellas in Beida, who work as nurses with the lepers there, and still do not contact this horrible disease?"

"Heard it quite clearly, but I doubt if our girls would like to do such jobs."

"It is done in every country of the world, isn't it yia George? Do your people in Cyprus bring Philippine nurses or Bulgarian? Just to name a few."

"No, no, nurses are local, and the females are engaged in so many other jobs and trades."

"And they drop that veil. One cannot find the beauty and attraction with veiled women," said Nasser, who kept quiet for quite a while.

"You heard the news Mohammed?"

"What, about the houses?"

"So you heard about it?"

"If Mohammed does not know, who would," said Ibrahim, "I forgot that you are a member of the people's committee."

Nasser came in silently, had no shoes on, with a tray holding a bottle of Johnnie Walker, five glasses and two glass bowls with roasted groundnuts.

"Where is the ice yia Nasser? Or you don't have a refrigerator?"

"Go to Abdulkerim," said Abdullah.

Before Nasser returned with some ice cubes, four glasses were quarter full with the forbidden liquid. George was handed one.

"Wait for the ice, this stuff is terrible when is lit."

Nasser served the ice with his fingers, but as he dropped the cubes, the pale liquid danced up and down in the glasses.

"Nasser you like some of this?"

"Just for my throat," exclaimed the proprietor.

George waited for the ice to melt somehow and cool the drink but proved too slow compared to the two visitors, they had already drank theirs.

Abdullah helped himself to a second one and replenished the other glasses.

"Drink yia Younani," ordered Abdullah.

"You drink your own way," adviced Ibrahim, then turned to George and added, "they do not know how to drink."

Abdullah got hold of the half-empty bottle, "no more for Ibrahim, he does not know how to drink this water."

Ibrahim made no comments.

Abdullah initiated the conversation about the important news. He tried to explain to Mohammed that this movement was wrong.

"Why wrong?"

"All those citizens who own more than one apartment, house or villa, have to submit it to the committee; every single citizen, no exceptions."

George looked at Nasser; he owned three, remained motionless with the glass just below his chin.

"Yes, all extra houses will go to the committee. The committee will undertake to rent them to institutions, committees and to poor people who do not possess their own, even the foreigners who work officially in Libya are entitled to proper living quarters."

"Just like that, take the extra houses and rent them?" asked Abdullah.

"So all those who built appartments or extra houses for renting, will have to abandon them to the hands of the government?"

"Not the government, to the committee."

"What committee yia Mohammed?"

"Do you have an extra house?"

"Yes I do the chicken coop."

"Is it made of masonry or chicken wire?"

"You.......... my best friend."

"Any villa at the farm?"

"I have a Greek one, my prick."

Ibrahim laid down his glass, pursed his lips and asked if the new regulation concerned any extra buildings on the farms.

"No, not the farms or the villages. This regulation doesn't apply."

"Who has an extra house in a village?"

"You know the regulation has been studied carefully by the general committee in Tripoli, they investigated the matter carefully."

"Like what?" Abdullah asked.

"Yia Abdullah, look, the old system, I mean the system of the King, the few smart guys borrowed money from the banks, exploited the poor Egyptian workers, and built multistory buildings, like boxes one on top of the other. Such housing complexes are met in every country like Greece, Italy, Germany and even Cyprus, is that right Younani?"

"Yes, unfortunately you are right, box like flats and people are obliged to live there."

"Like rats," commented Abdullah.

"Rats, no rats, that's the new trend, but this is not the point."

"Haram, wallahi haram, it is sheer larceny, by God, larceny."

"Haram not haram, no rich stone can stay in its position, wealth is power, and power is dangerous."

"Yes, this is true," all agreed and Nasser poured another round.

"We are brainwashed with the green revolution and our Leader leans towards the red ones, he got color blinded."

"They are the strong ones around here nowadays and since we are part of our world, our Arab world, we have to climb on the same train."

"I'm inclined to say that such kind of flirting is contrary to our religion, our culture and I dare say to our future. Have you seen those ships in the harbor, one after the other unloading armaments?"

"They are supplying us with a full range of weaponry, along with missiles that have a huge range."

"What is their range, Mohammed?"

"This is a military secret."

"Keep your secret; I hope will not need to use them."

"Are you talking about the long range SA-Vega, or the SA-2 Volchov?"

"No, I' am talking about the anti-aircraft ones, like the SA-3 Neva, the SA-6 Kub, the SA-8 Osa-Ak."

"You forgot the Crotale II."

"Are you going to give us another drink, yia Nasser?"

"The fellow is confronting foreign policies and growing a friendship with the reds."

One has to apply his logic for their strange ways of communicating.

"We have haragin, it's ready, shall I bring some?"

Ibrahim kept quiet but Mohammed and Abdullah requested some, not that much.

George thought Nasser would bring something to match the scotch; he was wrong. Nasser came in with an enormous bowl of hot chopped macaroni.

"Move your legs yia Abdullah."

Legs withdrew and the stainles bowl took the middle of the carpet. It was hot, steamy and the vapour krept to noses, and mouths began watering. The smell of spices, animal fat, and chili pepper filled the salon.

Nasser's son followed with a flat tray with spoons, table serviettes, water glasses, and pewter with water.

"Take," Nasser distributed spoons and table serviettes, pointed the place for the tray with the water and glasses, the boy placed it down and turned to leave.

"Bring the meat boy."

Astonishingly with a simple twist, the Libyans rotated their bodies; legs turned backwards and bodies forward, spoons in hands and scooping started.

"Come on yia Yunani, this is very good."

George joined the group, it was delicious, properly cooked, not too spicy, not that hot, with chilli to his taste.

Abdullah asked for green pepper.

The loud orders, were executed intastaneously, the green pepper was brought in a porcelain bowl floating in water.

Abdullah lifted one short stout green pepper, shook off the dripping water, broke it in two, dropped back the tail, and bit the other piece with his mouth still full of macaroni.

"Ah………. from where is it yia Nasser, its hot."

"From the market, I have no farm."

"Where is the water?" Abdullah lifted the pewter and quenched his thirst liberally but left the outline of his lips, on the perspiring glass.

Ibrahim caught George watching Abdullah, gave a wink, and continued to stuff himself.

"Jamal?" cried Nasser, the boy came in a hurry, lifted the empty bowl with some left over fatty juice and five spoons swimming in it.

Mohammed and Abdullah finished the water jug. George felt for a drink of water, Nasser lifted the jug and called Jamal.

The boy returned holding the same jug with both hands; George expected him at least to wash it, was disappointed, lip marks were all round now.

The moment, the jug was returned on the tray, George dived for it, filled up two glasses, and returned it to its place.

"Thank you yia George," said Ibrahim.

Nasser placed the bowl with the meat at the same position; five chunks of pouched veal were sitting in a circle.

As Nasser lowered the tray, he twisted it so that the nicest cuts faced Abdullah and Mohammed.

Hierarchy is hierarchy, passed through George's mind.

No forks, no knives; fingers did all the work

"Tfatal folks, help yourselves."

Each one lifted the piece of meat lying in front of him.

"Take yia George," invited Nasser.

George lifted his and followed the pattern.

The meat was well cooked, juicy, tender, and tasty.

When they were halfway, Ibrahim broke the silence.

"Meat will be scarse shortly, I'm afraid we will have to satisfy ourselves with simple macaroni."

"What are you talking, Ibrahim?"

"Well things are tightening up, matters are getting worse, you will see."

"Speak up man, what do you mean?"

"You people at the central bank, what are you cooking up?" Nasser asked.

Now with his belly bulging out with meat and macaroni, floating in scotch, his tongue was released and protruded.

"Rumours going around the treasury are that very soon money; I mean paper money notes, will be replaced."

"This is quite normal."

"No, you no understand, I did not make myself clear, bank notes of five and ten dinars will be replaced by new ones. All citizens will have to produce their money to a bank, any bank, there every head of family proving himself by bringing his family book, may exchange one thousand dinars"

"That's why those rich ones smuggled lots of their money abroad."

"And that forced the Leader to order depreciation of our money abroad."

"It was never that high, anyway."

Both Abdullah and Mohhamed let their meat drop noisily back to the stainless bowl with a splash.

Nasser and George kept hold of their half-eaten pieces with one hand and stared at Ibrahim who got another bite after his small speech about money.

Since Ibrahim was chewing calmly his veal, George joined him, so did Nasser. Mohammed lifted his and licked off the remnants.

Abdullah leaned back to his sofa holding his greasy hands in the air and trying to lick his lips clean.

"Jamal," another short cry from Nasser, the boy rushed as though he was hiding behind the door, lifted the bowl, leaving the three delayed ones to finish off with a meaty bone in their hands.

"Bring water and towels."

"I can't, its heavy."

Nasser rose to his feet, got hold of the tray, passed it forward and one by one dropped what was left from the half-kilo pieces of meat into the thickening fatty liquid of the bowl.

The host brought a very interesting contraption; it was a large aluminum bowl with perforated cover, on its apex was a depression holding a piece of soap. Jamal followed his father with a large bronze pitcher and several towels. The father got hold of the pitcher, approached Mohammed who lifted the soap, streched his palms over the bowl and Nasser poured water in them; Mohammed washed his hands clean, picked a towel, and dried both hands and lips.

Abdullah, Ibrahim and George followed the same procedure.

As soon as Nasser released the pitcher, George lifted it and offered his services to Nasser.

"Thank you George, thank you my brother."

"So you want to say that, if I have 1.000 dinar, I have to go to the bank with my family book and exchange it for the newly printed ones?" said Abdullah.

"Yes, that's right."

"And if I have more than this amount?" asked Mohammed.

"Here is the catch, you bring all your money whatever you have in five or ten dinar notes, you will be handed 1.000, just 1.000 and the rest will go to the treasury, maybe the balance be registered in your name for the future, God knows."

With Ibrahim's clarification, the drunkedness from the scotch liquid vanished from everybody's head

All three became conscious of the matter and demanded a more detailed explanation.

"There are no details; Libyan money belongs to Libya, to the great Alfatah revolution and not to individuals"

"The tess, what is he trying to do?"

"If you remember in one of his speeches, he mentioned that some people, and meant the fat merchants, collect the money from the people, they actually steal the money and store it under the tiles of their villas," said Nasser solemnly.

There was a pause, all tried to recall this utterance.

"So, he will try to collect all the money and get everybody flat and manageable."

"Well?"

"Say yia Ibrahim, if I have as a foreigner...,"

Ibrahim cut George short.

"Foreigners working in Libya, properly registered and pay their taxes, their social insurance and all other dues, may exchange only 250 dinars per passport, I mean the head of the family, if the employee has a family."

The flash of red must have given George's worries away.

"George, do you have more than that?"

"Ah! Not much," George tried to be cool; he must have had more than 5.000.

"I'll tell you, if you have, you better deposit it, you never know, there are rumors of house to house search and anyone caught withholding money in the old currency may have consequences.

So, you deposit your money and come later for any salaries not transmitted or obligatory expenses."

"George if you need any help, please do not hesitate," said Nasser.

"I appreciate your willingness, thank you for your understanding."

Tea was served in the customary way.

Visitors and host had enough of everything. It was after midnight, everybody was ready for a visit to the toilet and a good sleep.

George was the first one ready to depart, Abdullah recoiled to his feet and so did Ibrahim.

"Mohammed you need any help?" laughed Abdullah.

"Away you go, you old man," scorned Mohammed but streched his hand, Abdullah grabbed it and Mohammed came to his feet.

"Good-night all, good night Hag Nassser, and thank you very much."

"Thank God, God is great."

The three visitors lingered behind George, Abdullah tried to balance himself, Mohammed kept teasing him. George walked out, into the street; three brand new cars of the latest model, a Peugeot 505, a Volkswagen Passat and a Mitsubishi Gallant were competing in size and gloss.

Across the street stood George's old pickup, checked the car doors if properly locked, opened his house entrance, closed it calmly, and paused behind the door.

The street was dead quiet, Nasser's visitors were still his, and George entered his desolate house and within minutes found his bed.

Although it was almost one after midnight, George did not feel sleepy; his mind was overburdened with what he heard. Rotated in his bed for more than ten minutes, then decided to apply his own psychomethod of appeacement.

"George you cross the bridge when you come to it, now you start counting till Morpheus embraces you and one, two, three......... 317..."

"George I'm coming with you," said the second son of Hag Nasser and without any approval climbed into the seat. He was the son of a revolutionary; George bowed his head, since times were very difficult for everyone.

On the way to the farm, George was seldom stopped at the Tripoli checkpoint.

On that day with little Abdullah in the co-driver's seat, the armed soldier raised his arm.

George lowered his window, forced a smile, and waited for the customary questions, where you come from, where are you going, where you work, and finally what is your name.

"Is that your son?" snapped the guard of the revolution.

"No, he is the son of my neighbor."

"Where do you live, yia Mister?"

"Fuehat garbia."

"Hello young fellow?"

"Hello," answered the boy in his smart manner.

"What is your name?"

"Abdullah.........."

"Are you Libyan?"

"You mistook me for Egyptian?"

"Where do you live, the color of your hair is different."

"That's from the new green soap."

The man was either satisfied with the boy's answer or irritated by his impertinence and with a hand gesture, ordered George to leave.

"Bravo Abdullah, you answered him the right way."

"I put him in his place, you want to say."

George side looked the boy and felt an innate satisfaction.

"You know today, was a big day, George."

"Eh! What happened today?"

"Today we feasted on Pepsi...."

"What happened?"

"Normally we get one sandwich and just a bottle of Pepsi, today we had two sandwich each and two bottles of Pepsi and anyone who felt thirsty could take a third bottle."

"And for what reason, Abdullah?"

"Today, we paraded and shouted slogans against the bad Americans; all the boys shouted 'down, down America, go back to your Black House, down with Regan, whatever his name is."

"Abdullah!" exclaimed George, the boy upturned and stared at George.

"George, the Americans are bad, they are very bad."

George honked twice for the gatekeeper.

12: *Black April*

Private enterprises were thriving, the petrol boom of the late seventies helped considerably. The prominent ones turned to imports of consumables or semi durables. The first automatic washing machines appeared on the market, larger size refrigerators, air conditioners, saloon cars and so many other commodities. Import duties were negligible, and goods reasonably priced.

Foodstuff prices were really low, needless to talk about the basic foodstuffs imported by the national company and distributed with a liberal subsidy. Corn oil, flour, rice, tea and sugar, all these were imported by the NASCO, in abundance and anyone could buy them at the corner shop.

Any one could purchase Italian furniture, or bring to order at good prices. Like these, many other goods with worldwide known brand names were imported. Samsonite bags from the States, knitwear from Britain, perfumes from France, diamonds from Belgium, gold pieces from Italy, cars from Germany, Italy and Japan.

The exploring of the desert lured millions of Arabs, mainly Egyptians. This influx of people created street jobs and helped the development of farming.

Although, these immigrants created a boom for food and consumables, such goods were imported, imports demanded currency, the workers demanded currency, and the country went into draining of its income.

As though draining was not enough, smuggling thrived in parallel. Goods worth millions of dollars found their way along the desert caravan ways towards Egypt, Sudan and even Tunis and Algeria.

The system got out of control by late 78; it was then, that the government decided to impose measures for restoring order and control the country's economy.

The declaiming actor on line, who believed his audience wanted to hear, undertook fiery speeches. Such one was not to be forgotten by those who took the time to do so; the one about food production and food imports.

The Leader went over the problem, point by point. Analyzed the list of imported foodstuffs and the cost to the country; then stressed the wastage of food. The fallacy of cooking very much more that was actually required for the family and the rest dumped in the dustbins. Tens of dogs feasted on damped meat.

He went on to reproach his compatriots on their inertia, their laziness. Instead of making proper use of the fertile soil of their farms, passed by the food shop and carried home boxes full of tinned food.

At one moment he stated, "Tomorrow you will open a tin and extract a baby from it with Asian characteristics, as though you are unable to produce babies by yourselves."

He condemned them on their failure to plant even a tree to provide shade for themselves. Instead, ate the citrus fruit from the orange and lemon trees that the Italian Countess planted in Tripoli area more than fifty years ago.

"Look at our main streets," he said, "the eucalyptus trees you see, can you tell me who planted them? You have no answer, I can tell you, the Italians and now you are lying in their shade, whenever you go for picnics."

Moreover, the measures came fast. The foreign investors were driven away, shut down all private enterprises, and changed the color of the whole lot into green. The merchants could not import ad lib, the banks were instructed to impose restrictions.

The merchants with the fat bank accounts answered back by over ordering and for prolonged periods. The government permitted them to place their orders but seized the goods upon arrival and concurrently created sizable supermarkets on a national basis and those goods were available to all people living in Libya.

A key driver of the green revolution was to improve the potential to produce food for all.

Euphoria of goods was available, priced reasonably, people moved in and out loaded. Corruption commenced spontaneously, goods found their way across the desert.

When the matter got out of control, they imposed restrictions and rationing began at the supermarkets. Persons could purchase only the permitted quota according to the family book.

Rumors, that at specific supermarkets, such and such product would be available, brought endless queues outside the gates from the early hours of the morning. Hooliganism was at large, coercion prevailed, and fights occurred on a daily basis. It was risky to join such lines of angry customers. Most of them were foreigners and the bulk Arabs, Palestinians, ill bred, ill mannered. The more impudent used their four, climbed high up on the steel gates, like baboons. Several times, the product did not arrive and even worse, the gates never opened for days. Survival became a huge problem for the suckers, a title for foreigners, the parasites.

George was lucky enough to be involved in the chicken business; they had a constant supply of meat and traded poultry meat for other foodstuffs. Many were those who bartered products acquired legally or not.

The number of goods diminished along with quantity. Quality still had its luster.

The supermarkets proved uncontrollable and non-manageable, small cooperatives were created in the neighborhood. Here, they followed the Marxist system; only the natives could become members and purchase the available goods by providing their family book. The family book, booklet bearing detailed information of the family with the head of it as patriarch, almost replaced the Shari'a. George managed to acquire such a family book through a neighbor.

The street and corner shops closed for obvious reasons, the illegal suppliers could not find much to trade, and several goods in such places could only be purchased from under the bench at premium prices.

The restrictions aimed to stimulate the nationals to engage themselves in food production.

It was near ten in the morning, when George accompanied by Aly the foreman of Hag Abdusamad, drove upto the municipality cold stores by the harbor.

Hag Abdusamad hired one large cold chamber for holding meat intended for his oil company clients in the desert.

George and Aly were surprised to find a bunch of people standing in the middle of the street, staring at two ships overloaded with containers in the harbor.

"Yia Aly, what are all those people doing there at this time of the day, under the scorching sun?"

"Really, have no idea, but nowadays too many idle people."

"But they are looking at the ships over there."

"Ah, those ships brought gas cookers from what I heard."

"What, everybody's gas cooker broke down?"

Aly laughed his head off, was not sarcastic but solved George's curiosity.

"The Leader wants every household to acquire the essential house appliances and started with the gas cookers."

"Very interesting, and what are they going to do with the old ones?"

"The smelting factory will collect them."

"Where is the smelting factory?"

"Sorry, not the smelting factory, I meant the crusher."

"To compress them for melting, you mean?"

"That's right."

"The one at Quarchia?"

"Yes, the small one, you know the bigger was at Beida but burnt down within a week, after been commissioned."

"What the operator got drunk with tea?"

"Let's unload the chicken, I have to go."

George drove along the one-way street and tried to go through a disorderly crowd that stared frantically at the ships.

"The boats are Italian," mentioned someone.

"No, the boats are Greek; it's the material from Italy."

"No, the equipment is German, I'm sure," another onlooker intervened.

"No, you are wrong, Abdulkerim told me, the equipment is Italian, but good quality."

"If it's Italian then I do not want any."

"Wait till they offer you one and then reject it, there are too many eager ones to trade them."

"You remember what happened with the refrigerators; Muammar brought many more than the households of Benghazi and the suburbs."

"And half of them were smuggled to Egypt and Sudan," shouted a tall fellow with a fez on his head.

"Those from inside, they are able for anything."

Khalifa was a small broiler grower by the road to El-abyar in Benina; nobody would miss him, had a high pitch voice, and always voiced his opinion. Belonged to the group and always wore the wristwatch handed to him with the Leader's picture. Once he boasted of his Chadian passport and that, he was ready to go into battle against those savage desert bastards who massacred the Libyan warriors in full daylight.

"Yes, caught them drunk in their tents."

"No, the Chadian disguised themselves into Libyan commandos and approached in full day light, opened fire and killed all those on the west side of the dune."

"The bloody Americans helped them and its them who carried our warriors through west Africa to their America, and imprisoned them there."

"Who cut off their genitals, ears, and noses and sent them to Tripoli."

"Shameful bastards, will pay one day, God the most gracious and most Merciful will punish them one day, the great day they reach heaven."

"What are you waiting for, Greeki; you are not entitled to any of that equipment."

Before George managed to answer, a thin tall fellow with inch stubble on his hawky face, said, "Bloody foreigners are not allowed, parasites," and spat on the tarmac.

"Not George; I'll bring you one if I manage."

"If not, I can always repair a used one."

"I know you can repair a gas cooker," said Khalifa and turned to the bystanders, "he repaired my gas brooders."

The line of cars trying to get through grew longer and longer, the honking became unbearable, nervousness rose high, one rushed through, the crowd opened frantically, George caught the opportunity and drove away.

On the way, Aly commented, dropped the customary greeting, and without reservation kept asking anyone if he managed to get such and such equipment or foodstuff.

"You know George, you are my friend and I trust you, whatever we say remains between us."

George turned and smiled, assuring Aly of his integrity.

Aly felt easier and said, "You know last week, I stood in a queue to buy bread, nowadays there is a shortage of flour and the bakeries, we call them ovens, make less bread."

"What happened yia Aly, did not manage to find bread yesterday and today, I don't know."

"I'll give you some from the store; we get them overnight for our customers in the desert."

"I'll appreciate it, will save me the sun and the abuses, we are bloody foreigners."

"As I was telling you, stood in the line, the line was more than twenty meters long, there came someone, who seemed to be in a hurry to get bread, stood in line; after a few seconds whispered to the one in front of him that the jamaia, the co-op, brought bananas and gave them by the box. The man left his position and rushed to find bananas, a commodity that disappeared months ago. The man used the same trick and sent most of the fellows to get bananas. He reached me, the line was moving rather slowly, before he mentioned bananas, asked him if he got apples, beautiful apples, he stopped abruptly and inquired in a low tone. I sent him to the other side of Benghazi, never saw him again."

George laughed his head off, "bravo Aly, bravo."

They reached Hag Abdusamad's store, George stopped, Aly rushed for some bread that he promised, came running with something in a Burlap bag, opened the side door, dumped it in, slammed the door, and vanished.

George's family enjoyed bread for the next three days.

A slogan passed around that everybody was born free and nobody should be a servant, it was not ethical, Allah did not like it. The respectful Libyans were obliged to send their servants away; the females stay at home and carry out all the household chores. The respectful, showed no respect to the promulgation and the farmers closed their farm gates to visitors, friends were not trusted, could be informers, could have lost their aids.

Friend thrives with equality and the gap widened between the favored and the ordinary people.

The numbers of illegal foreigners increased instead of diminishing. Action had to be taken.

Sadat succeeded Nasser and although the two Leaders agreed to unite their countries and their people with Sadat president and Qadhafi minister of defense, Sadat mistrusted Qadhafi and remained so, since, 'The messenger of the Arabian Desert' that's how he dreamed and overwhelmed by megalomania. Considered himself another Shishonk, a Berber officer from what is known today Libya, by legion found a dynasty in Egypt around 750 B.C. The union though enabled Qadhafi to consolidate his grip and power, and the student had the chance to emerge from the shadow of his master.

Anwar Sadat sensing the return of his millions back to an agrarian Egypt was not happy at all. Libya closed the borders, at least at Tobruq area and at few other places along the thousand-kilometer desert line.

.

Stories referred to young Egyptians crossing the desert, walking for weeks under the scorching sun to reach the land of abundance. Tension was mounting between the two neighbors. Egypt, with its 65 million fellahin against the 3 million of the Sahara Bedouins. The odds were obvious. Population wise the answer was simple, but water flows in the land of Pharaoh whilst black gold flows from the scorching desert.

The West was squeezed out, Shell, Mobil, Esso, Occidental gave way to local companies. The area was free for the East. U. S. S.R. moved in with its massive military machine, supplies after supplies reached from Russia. From uniforms to airplanes, from rifles to tanks, just name it.

Germany supplied just the Mercedes and the States the D10 caterpillars.

The Russians came along with the Mig and the missiles, the East Germans undertook the Leader's security, the Austrians his secret hiding homes.

Russia undertook the training of hundreds of Libyans. The radicals embraced the country's security, joined the army and enjoyed the benefits and the good salaries, the given away household furniture and fittings and bagfuls of foodstuffs.

The Italian exporters, crammed the military stores with the latest models of furniture, rocking beds of all sizes equipped with video and television sets, with adjustable mirrors and muslin canopies. Along with all the rest, supplied also semi durables, ready-made garments, and gold ornaments. Quite well known tailors undertook the grooming of the Leader and the elite of the military.

The younger Libyans rushed for a second marriage, gold for them was available at half the market price.

Libyan women, like all their Arab counterparts, are by tradition gold addicts. If someone tries to reason that craving, gets various interpretations.

She begins with her wedding demands; one may say demands, because the amount of golden pieces offered at her wedding and nuptial intercourse being the appreciation of her family towards the bridegroom.

Annual births follow the wedding, this had to be consoled with gold, and there isn't an ever-ending demand. A second wife would enter the competition in actions and the subsequent with the first one, with money being the prime requisite.

Many were those who exploited the lower gold prices. The shrewdness of some went beyond imagination. When a bridegroom of a lower rank applied for gold, several friends provided extra money for a heavier purchase. His friends always had customers at a substantial profit. That is how the revolution angels protected their economy. Their salaries had to be padded with side businesses.

Corruption was spontaneously thriving, foreign companies could secure no contract unless Uncle Mohammed had his share, and he preferred dollars abroad. Sporadic skirmishes were subdued at their nativity. Controlled checkpoints were permanent on all exits of the city, along the roads and at road junctions.

Any suspicious movement was trucked down, God help if there were any family differences, such ones were settled on political grounds, needless to say that the country was raven by fierce clan loyalties and regional factionalism.

Religion was always the fulcrum for leveraging resurgence; was the grant cause for untold power and was not forgotten. Qadhafi has sought to dominate not only the political society but also the religious life. The Senussi teachings that preached austerity, simplicity and the free interpretation of the Shari'a law did not comply with the Leader's ideas. He began to saturate the Libyan media with condemnation of spirituality and introduced Salafist rhetoric advocating obedience to the rulers.

Forgot completely that tribal customs and undecendants are more important than sectarian beliefs in maintaining unity among people. Koran is God's revelation, is not secretive or allegorical but philosophical according to the reasoning of their Leaders, fanaticism and social antagonism of ages of degeneration.

Bedouins tend to follow tribal customs, rather than Muslim jurisprudence and know little of religion beyond the recital of words they have memorized but scarcely comprehend; they are chiefly concerned with deriving a scanty living from the hostile desert. For them, water is more important than religion.

Instead of that, street posters procured by the regime carried slogans, "obey those in authority" and "every shepherd has his own flock."

He sought suppression of the independence of the Senussi preachers, razed the Senussi mosques and university, and desecrated the graves of the Senussi family.

Qadhafi used the cloak of religion to propagate his politics, found a society called "The Islamic Call Society" whose character was to proselytize Africans and elsewhere. Anyone who gave up his religion and became a Muslim would automatically be given the Libyan citizenship and ten thousand dollars. Joe working on the rig of an American company was lured by the offer and conceded to it. When he tried to leave the country was caught, treated accordingly and jailed.

The role was expanded to include subversion and propaganda.

Under the cloak of religion, adopted a guise of religiosity to affirm his rule and intimidate his opponents. Substituted the existing sheikhs with his own, believed to possess religious endowments; they enjoyed a certain popularity that made them imagine that they were powerful and influential, temporary mistaken impression. With diverted talent, distorted and adulterated by lying hypocrisy and intrigue.

With messianic megalomania paralleled himself to Jesus and Mohammed. Named himself, "Messenger of the Arabian Desert" and called his green book as the new gospel that would catapult him to the level of the giants, again implying parallel to Mohammed.

Even issued stamps, depicting Qadhafi on a white horse, leaping into the sky, an allusion of al-Buraq, the white winged beast that Mohammed mounted on his overnight journey from Mecca to Jerusalem.

Qadhafi wanted to cleanse the chief factors affecting the Muslim society, to reduce contacts with the West and their western ideas.

Anyone riding on a big private saloon car was considered bourgeois and the action squads slashed tires, smashed windshields, and headlamps.

Though toleration of other faiths was permitted, still occassionally such religions did not escape indirect attacks.

Those that wore a necktie were Christians, the media showed in a crude form the way a tie was knotted, it resembled the cross, the sign of the westerners, the merchants of the west, the suckers of the fellahin, such ties were chopped off with sharp scissors, and jean wear tore with sharp knives.

Alcohol consumption was strictly prohibited and many were those who tried to cash on the good prices, those caught were imprisoned, their belongings confiscated, and if they were foreigners, deportation was imminent.

Continuation of the past served the purpose, so the drop of the headscarf was an offence; the schools and university were watched for the disobedient.

Long and fiery speeches by selected preachers tried to sway the believers to the right path to heaven, a disguised subversion.

Overwhelmed by an unrestrained megalomania, Qaddafi seems to be impervious to changes.

Fiery speeches came over the mosque pulpits and played on people's fantasies. Imported Salafist Sheikhs invigorated the Muslims on Friday gatherings. Installed extra loud speakers around the mosques; special aids, kept records of attendances and visits were paid to selected homes of absentees. The faltering had to be herded to the confines of the Most Gracious, and most merciful.

Ephemeral success was obvious but even the hard liners are demanding substance. Spirited preaches are good for the soul but the body is materialistic. The Most Gracious did not pass free handouts.

Sheikh Mansur, with a family of nine, was given a bonus but the attempt of extending his dwelling to another story remained without doors and windows, the doves found refuge in an Allah fearing surroundings.

It became a custom for government employees to leave their jobs with the simple excuse of pray, of course at the mosque; their home was nearer than their office.

Driving along any road, one would encounter the faithful praying by the roadside, very often one could see persons praying perched on top of the elevated manholes with the car headlights on, guiding their souls to divinity.

The non-Libyan Arabs sensed the trend; they would leave their job, seeking seats by the roads and swarm the mosques. The protests of the locals were incipient but this was religion, no discrimination was acceptable.

Discontent among the upper social level was mounting; the ones with fat dollar accounts abroad, fled with their families to Greece, Italy or even further to England and the United States.

Abroad, named themselves anti revolutionaries; several attempts to group into cliques failed, and who can fight a terrorist. Several joined the Libyan Islamic Group and other related groups, but members of his special squad were dispatched abroad, and annihilated the confused ones, those that could not envisage the virtues of the green revolution. They struck the shepherds and the sheep scattered. Their kins who were not allowed to travel abroad were harassed and discarded from the devotees. Off-hour visits to branded families, forced them to spend the rest of the night seated on their toilet seats, kept them on suspended terror.

At the cooperatives, their share of provisions was either reduced, or even refused all together. Fear and terror hovered over the city.

In the countryside a planted army general handled matters differently, wore several smirks.

Poverty was deplored.

The farmers needed animal feed, seeds, fertilizers, insecticides; such merchandise could be available to some but not the reactionaries. Managed to pinpoint each man's thumbscrew. In an urban community, just a word was enough to disgrace the yesterday's respected families.

The climax was with the seven adversaries accused by a special court of conspiring with the enemy to rebuke the people's rule and the progress of the green revolution, Kaddafi's speeches reflected his ruthlessness. He could at any moment, send anyone who tried to organize politically, to face repression, send him to the People's court, which would issue a sentence of death based on this law, because execution is the fate of anyone who forms a political party and backed the threats with actions.

The verdict was cast, execution, by hanging the defectors in public on the spot of their diabolic acts or nearby. The abhorrent act was to take place on Thursday, April 7; it was the last day of the Arab week and the Greek orthodox were grieving Jesus Christ's crucifixion.

The appeal of the Greek community to postpone the decree for religious grounds failed. The answer was absurd.

"Our Greek brothers, who enjoy the fruits of the green revolution in our great country, may attend the executions and proceed to their church in the right mood." That was the preposterous answer.

The act was announced over the state run media, with a brief but fiery commentary of the accusations, with instructions to all dignified citizens to be present at the judicious disposal of those devious.

For the government officials, all what accounted, was another day off, the problem was the people, had to be dragged from their homes to witness the act. The shopkeepers were told not to open their shops on this imminent date.

Just before midnight a strong east wind prevailed, by the morning became stronger. Came from the desert as a fierce blast galloping and spattering, brought so much red fine dust with it that shrouded the town, the sky, one could hardly see the sun. The elders prayed to Allah, the more superstitious took this as a bad omen; others said that the noble sun did not wish to witness the deeds of darkness, of abyss.

Before dawn, the gallows were ready in position, three in front of the grand Cathedral, and two within the Benghazi university grounds, one near the seaport and one at Benina Airport.

The condemned were to be executed at the place of their deeds.

By ten o'clock, in the morning, a bunch of laborers from the municipality were directed to the scene. From the several thousand employed by the Mayor, less than hundred or so were rounded up and marched to the small square with the old grandeur.

All passersby were forcibly stopped, and advised to attend the abominable act. The convicted were transported under heavy escort. Several Toyotas manned with automatic weapons accompanied them. Around the execution place, tens of armed soldiers and the special squat dressed in civilian took position.

In this way, the people of Libya would realize that it's the people who brought them to justice, it is the People's court that found them guilty and it is the people who executed them. After all a disguised person in the Bedouin outfit can hardly be recognized, as his face is wrapped up in two meters of shawl. Muammar got others to do the job.

The convoy stopped in the street, the environment was still, tense, nobody moved, nobody spoke, eyes strained towards the armored car, lips smacked, even breathing was concealed.

The padlock lifted but allowed to drop back to the iron door, the sound aroused the tension. At the second attempt, it was unlocked, pulled off its slot but dropped to the ground, deliberately or not. The bolt handle was lifted and swung up and down, then pulled backwards with a squeaking shriek. Even the cold lifeless iron shrieked, sending the macabre message past the numb crowd and beyond, to the distant Ades.

Ears strained, eyes goggled, lips pouched, nerves taut, and bodies stiffened; the militants clutched their Kalashnikovs. The door was flanked open, three mummies were helped out of the car, they could hardly walk by themselves, each one was carried off by two aids, and their feet barely touched the ground. Nine figures moved slowly, slowly, each trio to its destination. Only the heads of the crowd turned and followed speechless the slow procession of the phantoms.

With predetermined accuracy, the three mummies were positioned in front of the gallows. The guards now formed an ellipsoid circle round those gallows.

A militant in tight Bedouin outfit and dark glasses, stepped forward and read in a low tone the laconic charges and the verdict, the crowd was motionless like a bunch of statues.

The condemned stood in apathy.

"Must have been dragged," murmured the most courageous. The mummies were ushered backwards up the three steps in front of their personal gallows, and the loop passed over their heads and brought under the chins.

The militant who read the verdict left a sharp short, "*Fatah*" and the steps swept away from below the feet of the convicted, a short ruckus was their last valediction to this erroneous world.

Most faces turned away from the dead, and silently fled way, only the militants stood rigid to guard the three immortals. History, one day will identify them as defiant of the tyrant, revenge may not be sought, who can tell where the souls of their executors will land.

Later in the evening, George with his family drove by on their way to the church; the three were still hanging from the gallows; only the militants remained to guard the dead mummies.

The streets were empty; Kate had her reservation to proceed for the evening mass.

"We're almost there, so let's go and see," said George with skepticism. The church was open, the sermon was in progress but very few Christians braved to come.

They returned home before nine, the city looked as under curfew, a ghost city. When they stopped outside their home, their neighbors were under the ficus tree outside Nasser's house. George greeted them, opened the door for Kate and his daughters, crossed the road and joined the group, nobody spoke, all were looking eastwards beyond the street.

George tried to envisage at what everybody was staring at. Several men were strolling up and down under the dim light of the deserted street.

"Where have you been at this time of the night?"

"We were at church."

"At this hour?"

"We the clever ones, pray at night. We are in the holy week of Christianity."

"What, the resurrection?"

"Yes, exactly."

"You don't all Christians celebrate concurrently this holy event?'

"Well, the Latin pray at a different time, they do so a month earlier than the Orthodox."

"And who is the right one?"

"It's hard to say, Hag Nasser."

"You do not agree on such simple matters and you try to advise us how to behave and how to rule ourselves?"

George was caught in the welter of controversy. Nasser was a Libyan Muslim, George was a Greek Orthodox, immigrant to this peculiar country. Swallowed his saliva twice, smiled at his neighbor. Nasser did not stop at that, demanded a reason from George about the petition of the Greeks to the Leader for postponing the executions of those convicted in public. George remained silent, his neighbor had every reason to question him on the matter, he was one of the group. Then he explained that the one hanged at the square, was the owner of the house at the corner; his kins were hoping for permission to fetch the body to his home, "that's why we're watching from here."

George stayed with them until Sonia called, "Papa."

"George, go inside, you better go," said Salah.

Inside the house Kate switched on the television, the whole act was repeated in detail with very few comments.

"We have seen it with our own eyes," said George, "we better get some supper and go to sleep," he wanted to add, "Hopefully there may be no reprisals."

"Just wait a minute, they are showing scenes from Tripoli," Kate intervened, "isn't that Muammar himself? He, the mastermind, is kicking off the stool from the condemned one, wretched person!"

"Please, we've seen enough."

In the morning, driving by that square on his way for the delivery, he glimpsed sideways, only the gallows and the soldiers. The bodies have been removed, it was never revealed where they were buried or how, even tradition vanished in front of the Kalashnikovs.

The month of April has seen the worst abuses of human rights in Libya. Arrested suspected political party members, executed military officers within a couple of years.

The madness of Muammar and his regime culminated into reserving April for persecution of Libyan students and other dissidents inside and outside the Jamahiriya.

April 7th was commemorated in Libyan universities annually, with arrests and pubic executions of students. April was the active month for 'physical liquidation' campaign against Libyan dissidents abroad. The long list of April victims includes students, teachers, and other civilian professionals assassinated in Europe and the Middle East.

13: Farming challenges.

The killing of chicken continued and George had good income. He purchased an old Peugeot and returned the car to Anwar.

At nights, the patrol and checkpoints were intensified, but very seldom stopped anyone on the road. At the checkpoint of Tripoli road, George was always worried, until Abdu Salam, a tall black lieutenant from Gimmines asked if he could have a couple of chicken for their late supper.

George did not have much choice, he explained though, that the processed birds would be ready only in an hour or more; in vain, he tried to elude.

"I follow you," he said, "just go ahead."

At the farm, all tried to prepare two good chickens for him, just to get rid of him the soonest; ever since it was a quota, every night, two good chickens found their destination to the Tripoli outpost.

When Abdu Salam was not on duty, it was Salah and if not Salah was Mohammed, almost every time each one of them got hold of the chicken, smiled and asked in a polite way, "you need any help?"

"*Salamtaq, wallahi,* my greetings, by God."

Ahmed was always skinny, you thought a strong gibli would carry him away, but he managed to work, until one day he got sick with a severe cold, George was worried, he worked for him, if something happened to him, who would be responsible? For two nights Ahmed did not kill chicken, George had to kill them, using a sharp knife.

George managed to find two young Egyptians who crossed the border deep in the desert; they must have walked for weeks to reach Benghazi.

Mahmoud and Gasala; the second one was a Coptic Christian with a tattooed cross on the inside of his wrists.

They needed to work and George treated them reasonably well. He arranged for them beds, a small gas ring for cooking as well as a kettle, teapot and some plastic bowls, they brought their tea glasses. Their menu was chicken, fried liver and occasionally chicken gizzards; they ate what they wanted, George never objected to that.

Living next to Ahmed's family, a friendship developed amongst them and shortly both boys moved and lived with the family. From what George gathered, they slept just inside the house entrance. To his surprise the steel beds and foam mattresses that George brought for them vanished, they slept on a wooden double bed roughly made; to his inquiring, was told that they offered them to the two kids who till then slept on the cold floor.

"You have done very well, but you should have asked me, the beds and mattresses belong to me."

"*Malesh yia Mr.*," was all they said, "never mind boss."

George, could do nothing now, the beds were gone.

When George referred the event to Muftah, he said, "it's that bitch, you know, they screw her day and night, she is a scam."

"As long as they do their job properly, I do not care," said George.

"She manipulates them," said Muftah.

George suspected that birds were missing, daily two, or three, but as he was buying by weight and selling by weight and was not absolutely sure about the number of birds he bought, kept quiet.

Ahmed recovered from his bad cold and moved about, but could not work. Even after two weeks when George asked him to work for his benefit, for his family, the man refused. He begged George though to give him a few pullets to grow them for eggs. He prepared a tin shed nearby and George provided the five pullets, he requested.

Normally the broiler birds for processing have white plumage, but occasionally due to gene interaction a few colored birds do hatch, apart from their feather color they are alike all the other birds in many respects. One may get a tinge of red or black, very seldom, the phenotype resembles fully one of its predecessors; such birds have the plumage of the North Holland Blue. Whenever George spotted such one in the flock he was buying from, picked it up, that reminded him of his young days when he was an apprentice at the poultry unit of the Athalassa government farm just outside Nicosia in Cyprus. At that time, the English fellow who headed the animal section, imported such birds and introduced them to Cyprus, new breeds, as the White Leghorn, the Indian game and the North Holland blue.

As an apprentice student, George was explained the merits of each breed. The White Leghorn was an egg machine, the Indian game was a compact meat bird and North Holland blue was a dual-purpose bird with a soft but very tasty meat. He was assigned to grow all three breeds; all the birds were not more than 520 including the males.

When the birds grew up George was eager to taste the meat and verify the texture, if one was compact, and the other soft and tasty.

As a young bachelor living on the farm, George managed his own cooking, had the chance to find out the merits of both birds. What he actually did was punishable but by the intuition of the unit manager, they shared the outcome of pilferage.

With such memories George selected the blue striped broilers and carried them to the slaughterhouse; the more colored birds brought George the less they killed. When he asked the two Egyptians, they shrugged their shoulders. George suspected Ahmed, but the laborers were living with his family, nobody could extract any information from them. Any inquiry might force Ahmed to refrain from his habits though only temporarily.

One night, a strong gibli was blowing hard. It swung the towering palm trees from side to side, carried empty plastic bags, and slashed them onto the dwarf olive trees; even Ahmed's tin shed did not stand the menace. It was blown down.

George arrived a few minutes after the shed was torn down; when the floodlights struck the yard, he noticed several of his colored birds running around, trying to shelter themselves.

Just behind George was the police car, they followed him to get their quota of chicken. When George saw five to six colored birds loose, stopped his car with the lights on, jumped off and began catching the stray birds, Ahmed was also up collecting birds, and already had two in his hands; the police officer drew close to George.

George did not hesitate, called Ahmed; the man froze on the spot but still holding onto the two colored birds.

"So, here you kept the stolen birds?" said George, and moved towards him, catching birds as he went along.

Ahmed tried to tatter something, but dropped the birds and fled towards the house. Gasala stopped his job and rushed forward, "please mister, let him alone, he will not do it again, we know what he did, is wrong."

"And you knew all about that?" asked George.

"No mister, wallahi no."

The police officer stood by, but sensed what was going on.

Two days later Ahmed collected his meager belongings and left for his homeland. George saved his chicken but his laborers lost their mistress

If Ahmed disserted Libya from fear of his stealing, from his wife's misconduct or from fear of his ten-year-old girl, could not say. Budding girls are vulnerable, mistreated, raped, George never bothered to find out.

At the time of departure, Naama, Ahmed's wife, came to greet George, wearing a cheap fancy dress with sleeves pulled up; revealing two brand new golden bracelets on her right arm, normally such ornaments are worn on the left arm.

She shook George's hand vigorously, the bracelets moved and made the characteristic sound, she looked at them, being proud of her acquisition.

George noticed all what happened, but said nothing; he bid her farewell and a happy life in her hometown.

Later in the evening Muftah met George, who told him the golden bracelets were confiscated by the custom authorities at Benina Airport, she could not prove how such bracelets and such valuable pieces were in her possession.

George did not share Muftah's expression, he felt sorry as much as he felt the first time he saw the golden bracelets. Everybody thought that Ahmed left dragging with him a few of the problems. George pluralized the matter because Ahmed, his wife and the children were a menace to all, in different ways to different persons.

A couple of days later and right in the heart of the night George's group was besieged by a bunch of police and the city's special guards.

"We began working, Kate was catching the live birds handing them to Mahmoud, he was killing and dropping them in a bottomless barrel and I carried them to the dipping place by using a wheelbarrow. Apart from a couple of electric bulbs that lit a limited area, the rest of the farm was dark. I was pushing back the empty wheelbarrow when I noticed several shadows approaching; I stopped and strained my eyes, within seconds four or five persons stepped forward with automatic weapons in their hands; they greeted me and I returned the greeting."

"Are you the Greek?"

"Yes I am."

"You slaughter chicken?"

"Yes, I do."

"Who slaughters the birds?"

"Mahmoud."

"Where is he?"

George pointed the place and they rushed forward, Kate was lifting and handing the birds, Mahmoud was busy with his knife. At their presence Kate froze, Mahmoud cut the throat of the bird in his hand and turned towards them.

In an authoritative way one asked Mahmoud, "what is your name?"

"Mahmoud."

"You kill chicken in the wrong way."

"How, this is a sharp knife, it has three studs on the handle and I cut the neck by Halal."

"No it is not, Halal, where is the east? By Halal the animal has to face the east while it's been killed and the prayer should be said."

"With bigger animals, that is the right way; with chicken I say the prayer at the beginning and repeating every five or six birds."

"You are not facing the east."

"With chicken, as far as I know it's not always the case."

"Halas, come with us, you kill chicken in the wrong way."

They were determined to drag Mahmoud, George felt himself sinking, and Kate froze.

George recollected all his energy, his Arabic and his subtlety. With his arms raised stepped forward and pleaded,

"Here, as you see we are working with my wife. Can you think of any other woman coming out of her home at this time of the night to work under this terrible cold and under such bad conditions? This is our livelihood, have three small children to feed and God knows what they need, please, if you take Mahmoud now, and I know you can take him; just the two of us will not be able to clean these 300-killed birds. Please, Mahmoud did not really do anything bad; let him help us to finish these birds."

Kate gathered courage; she stepped forward and in her scanty Arabic pleaded too. The lieutenant hesitated for a moment, he looked at Kate, saw the splattered blood on her overall and spoke in a poignant and authoritative manner.

"Halas, this time, but this is the last time." and addressed Mahmoud in a severe way, "if I catch you killing chicken in the wrong way, I will put you in jail the same moment."

"It will be done as you say."

"*Salam alekoum*, good bye to you," and with a signal all his battalion crept away and vanished in the darkness of the night.

The group continued their work speechless, only when the birds were in the bags Mahmoud broke the silence, "these are bad people, but they never come by themselves, there is always an informer."

"It's the one eyed beggar," said Kate.

"Could be," answered Mahmoud.

"Anyway, he is gone now."

"But spat his venom."

George passed by Muftah at Rasa Beida, took with him five nice chickens and referred this event to him, he promised to see the people, they were his acquaintances; if he ever did it, was up to him.

The work continued with a steady market and a reasonable margin of profit. They toiled at work but were rewarded; at least that is what it looked like.

14: Water supply problems

George talked to Hag Ibrahim, a respectable person of the neighborhood, living across the street. According to Hag Ibrahim, the holy month of Ramadan was the most sacred month of Islam. Referred to the five pillars of Islam that every adult has the occasion to reinforce the Imam by sanctifying his spirit and soul and to eliminate the evil influence of the wrongdoings he gets involved. He would follow the scriptures of the Holly Quran, to realize and understand the hardships a poor person may suffer when he has no food to eat.

When the rich apprehend the poor fellow's hardships, Allah will counsel them to share their belongings with the needy ones. The rich ones must give the needy ones 2, 5% of their total assets, a good Muslim follows the five pillars of Islam, one of them being the Zakat, to provide for the needy ones"

"So the holy month of Ramadan is the holiest month, Hag Ibrahim?"

"Yes, it is. I must go now it is praying time, God bless you. I believe you follow the rituals of our people."

"Definitely Hag Ibrahim, I do, God bless you."

The holy month of Ramadan as commonly known, is actually a lunar month of normally 28 days but may extend to 29 and even 30 depending on the moon. During this period, everything slows down, government services operate in limbo, and many are those who take advantage, absenteeism for faith. Rumors go round that video cassettes are in great demand, and even the forbidden ones.

Saber the Egyptian butcher gave his own explanation.

"You see in the very old days, most of the population was fellahin, agrarian. They worked in the fields and their sucker masters forced them to toil in the fields from dawn to dusk without food or water. Working under such long hours produced very much more without any real expenses, but when prophet Mohammed saw these miserable conditions made it clear in one of his preaches, the holy month of Ramadan must be strictly respected by all without distinction or status, master or slave, learned or naive and ever since all follow him except the wretched ones."

During the holy month of Ramadan after the evening meal, known as fetor, people take about an hour's rest, and then the employees call for work, their obligation is for about two hours. At work they gather normally in one office and gossip on all sort of subjects, what they ate or not ate, they drink tea after tea, smoke a lot and promise to meet the next evening at that and the same place.

After these late office hours, join their families for visits to friends or kins, carrying kilos of sweets. They may spend hours talking, watching television, or dozing away. The elders tell tales of those imaginary good old days and the youngsters listen vaguely, television is more attractive nowadays.

People move endlessly, driving in a very bad way, circumvent all traffic laws. It is dangerous to be on the road during this holy period. The worst time is just before the evening fetor, when everybody drives outrageously to reach home, minutes before the Sheikh calls for prayer and super.

It was half way during the holy month of Ramadan, George went to purchase chicken from a farmer at Maxaha, nearly eighty kilometers from town. It was a hot afternoon, but due to the day's holiness, the birds had to be collected before sunset, so the believers had enough time to wash, pray, and take their fetor, the first meal with the fall of the sun and after the Imam calls from the mosque.

George met another three persons waiting to buy chicken. As they were sitting in the shade waiting for their turn, one after the other went up to the water tap washed his feet, his hands, his whole head and took gulps of water and spat it forcibly.

It was really a hot afternoon, George got so thirsty, could not stand the heat any longer but did not want himself be branded as insurrectionary. He talked to Hamid, he knew the man long enough, and he spoke perfect English.

George leaned forward, talked about the market, the price of birds, and asked him if by chance a believer whilst washing his mouth on such a hot day drinks some of the water.

"It'll be good for him," he said and left for his car.

George followed his advice and quenched his thirst by gargling noisily as every other believer in the name of God.

It is evident, once in the eye of the law, you are followed thereafter. Despite the lieutenant's threats of returning to check and enforce the halal way of killing birds, nobody saw him thereafter. The interesting was that after that midnight's visit the people at the Tripoli road checkpoint who called constantly for their quota of processed chickens, stopped coming. In some way, George had the saving of nearly hundred dinars per month. The appeasement did not last for long.

Winter in Libya does not last more than forty days, according to the elders. When it comes though, the rain lashes on the bare, overgrazed slopes and having nothing to withhold it, rashes downwards in a torrential way. Within hours, the dry creeks begin flowing and carry all kinds of garbage, plastic bags, empty cartons, dry weeds, animal carcasses, and a lot of fine red soil.

On this February day, the rain came down in bucketfuls and the lightning and thunders intensified in the afternoon.

George requested his wife's opinion, if he should purchase live birds to kill overnight.

"I don't think the rain will last that long and the mud roof of the slaughter house is half a meter deep, it will not likely leak."

"So, I'll bring, say just three hundred that will not take us more than three hours to kill them, pluck, and eviscerate them."

"Yes, George, that may be good enough."

George, returned home a little after seven, drenched from top to toe, had to remove his rubber boots outside since every slight foot movement made funny noises, his feet were floating in there.

"George, there is hot water, you better take a bath."

"Thank you, I'd rather take a quick shower."

After a light supper, George went to bed, setting his mental watch to rouse him just after midnight.

Both husband and wife dressed themselves somehow heavier, got in the Peugeot, and began battling with the flooded dirt street of their neighborhood. None of them spoke, watched the windscreen wipers moving up and down at a devilish speed to keep the shield clear for the driver. The street, full of patches, depressions, and floating debris made the car rock at every meter.

Not a soul on the main road Benghazi-Tripoli; the tires made a splashing noise trying to cut several centimeters of floating water.

At the crossroads, towards Hawari, the armed soldiers took shelter in their temporary sheds, nobody moved. When George approached, raised his hand, saluted them, and turned left. The level of the water along this country road was deeper;

George had to press the accelerator to add power to the engine.

"My God, this road is really flooded; wonder how will it be towards Faakat?"

"You may be right, that road runs north south and definitely will catch more water."

George, kept a watchful eye on the turn, any fault might throw the car on the soaked dirt pavement with unforeseen consequences. Took the turn carefully but to his surprise, could not differentiate the road from the fields.

"If you could drive, I could have walked ahead to direct you."

"Unfortunately, but I can get off and walk along."

"You were afraid of thundering once."

"Tonight I'm not; I'll do it for you and for our three children."

George stretched his hand and touched hers, she looked at him straight in the eyes, and he smiled in appreciation.

Kate climbed off and battled with water up to her knees to locate the safe part of the road. The headlights competed with the lightning. The glaring from the reflection on the turbid water made matters more difficult for George.

At a moment, Kate slipped and almost fell, George left a shrill cry, a cry that never reached his wife who tried to balance herself and continued her difficult role.

After battling for more than fifteen minutes, reached higher ground and George blipped twice, Kate got in, was trembling.

George grabbed her wet cold hand, pressed it affectionately, she forced a smile and begged him to proceed.

They reached the farm gate and turned right across the flooded field, trying hard to steady the car on the slippery soil, the olive trees guided George to the slaughterhouse.

His two local laborers were there, the father smoking and the boy huddling close to the burning gas ring for the hot water.

George got off and greeted them.

"Very seldom we have such rain," commented Mohamed, the father.

"And such thundering," added the boy.

"You are soaked, did you walk here? Come close to the fire, you'll catch pneumonia."

Kate without a word approached the gas ring, and squatted to catch the heat emitted from the gas ring under the water drum.

"You stay here," advised Mohamed, "we'll kill the birds."

Normally, Kate picked the birds from the cages, held them by the legs with one hand, and with the other held the outstretched wings. Mohamed grabbed the bird by the base of the wings, upturned it, with an expert movement caught the birds head, and turned it back, the hand holding the wings caught the beak leaving the neck outstretched. Mohamed slit the throat just at the base of the head and before the bird realized what happened, he dumped it into the open barrel. There the bird died of bleeding.

The three hundred birds were killed and George carried them into the slaughterhouse, using a push burrow. Immediately the job began. Mohamed dipped bunches of birds into the hot water, stirred them with a heavy stick, and upturned them so the bottom ones do not get overheated. Would pause churning for a moment, and grab a couple of primary feathers from a protruding wing and pull, if the feathers felt loose, he would scoop them out and drop them on the floor. From there, George would lift one by one, run them over the circular defeathering machine, and then Kate took over for the evisceration. The boy was responsible in separating the edible innards from the intestines and prick out the gall bladder from the liver.

To their hard luck, a lightning struck the nearest transformer throwing everything into darkness.

George did not manage to obtain any portable generator and more than half of the birds lied on the ground.

Kate began lamenting.

Mohamed added that the birds lying on the floor were too many to be plucked by hand.

George tried hard to figure out his next step, always thought in silence. Came out with a brainwave, to take the remaining birds and go to Ahmed, a friendly Palestinian. The man hired Khalifa's slaughter hut near the sea.

Kate objected first for the bad steep road and her other worry was the availability of current in that remote seaside place.

"He had a small portable generator, from what I remember."

"I hope the fellow is there."

All four gave a hand to pile the stiff dead birds in the box of the Peugeot and agreed that Mohamed and his son would stay behind to finish off the plucked birds, put them in burlap bags, fifty in each and take them to Benghazi.

Kate would accompany her husband in an attempt to reach the other slaughtery.

With great effort and difficulty reached Ahmed's place. The rain eased somehow but the roads were still bad, specially the piece leading to the slaughtery. Thundering was not that bad, the sea though was furious, wanted in every way to gobble the land and the few palm trees growing scattered near by. Under such adverse conditions, the Greek couple struggled to earn their living in that alien country.

"Her yia Ahmed."

The Palestinian stopped the defeathering machine and looked amazed at the Greek couple roaming in the early hours of that morning in such a hellish weather.

"Her yia Greeki, what devil brought you here?"

"We have no current in our place and have some killed chicken to pluck," pleaded Kate.

"Yes, but I still have my own."

George estimated the birds on the floor, must have been around two hundred.

"We'll help you, yiahabibi, my dearest."

Ahmed was working with his son, a boy of not more than twelve; normally killed around two hundred and fifty birds, enough to cover the family expenses.

George with Kate dug into the work.

It was after five, when George dipped the first lot of his in the hot water. Kate was unable to operate the machine, the first attempt proved that, the drum turned at such a speed that caught the bird and the poor thing landed ten meters away.

Aly prompted to operate the machine, within an hour and a half the chicken were ready. The day broke, the rain ceased and the first sunrays glistened on the clean palm fronts.

"Leave the refuse; I'll come back for the whole lot."

"Thank you Mr. Aly, you've saved us from real catastrophe."

"George, we are brothers in this place, have the same problems and you've helped me before, you remember with that lot of sick birds, you saved them."

George smiled with apprehension, "Tried my best old friend."

"We better deliver these bloody chickens before the guards of the city wake up."

"You are bloody right."

It was Tuesday night, mid November, whilst George was driving into his farm, sensed trouble right from the gate. Noticed too many tire marks, broad ones, made by tires used by four wheel-drive Toyotas. Near the slaughterhouse noticed the light on. Why, he thought, the two workers are normally fast asleep during Ramadan, something has gone wrong here, reduced speed, turned the wheel left and right tried to scan the surroundings, but did not see anything upnormal. He got off the car with a lump in his stomach. Mahmoud and Gasala were drinking tea in the slaughter shed. George approached them, they were drenched in sweat, before George asked, "Thanks Allah you came only now," said Gasala.

"What happened, the police again?"

"Yes, but this time from the traffic section."

"What, you were pushing the wheelbarrow without a driver's license?"

"An officer from the traffic called at his friend's farm for a cup of tea after the fetour. The farm is on the east side and adjacent to Muftah's property, to our bad luck a strong west wind was blowing, the smoke and the foul smell from the underground incinerator reached his nostrils."

"Stars on the shoulders mean power, such power embodied with law becomes mighty, and authority is enforced."

"The officer with several of his friends crossed the fence and spotted the volcano, with shouts and abuses dragged us out of our beds and forced us to put out the illegal fire according to the officer. This kind of burning annoyed and distressed the serene night of the officer. We carried the two tons of water destined for the slaughterhouse by bucket after bucket and poured it down the well; the fire had to be put out. The officer could not drink his tea. We dug soil and threw it down the pit, the fire is still on," said Mahmoud.

"That fire needs a whole bowser to be put off," said George, "and now we don't have water that means we cannot work."

"We will bring water from Barwin farm."

"Al-right, let's put the tank on the car."

With the empty water tank drove to Barwin's farm, a kilometer away, woke up his labor, started the small diesel generator and filled the two-ton tank; brought it back and after drinking a cup of tea, they killed the quota of 400 birds.

The offal could not be thrown in the pit; the officer might like to drink tea under the palm trees of his friend.

"Take them to Terria," said Gasala.

"The municipality damp?"

"Yes, it's not more than 50km."

Another burden on George, had no choice, the officials were scavenging.

The piped water from the mains got less and less. One afternoon George decided to check it up from the mains to the farm; the pipe ran along the village main road. He opened up the manhole, disconnected the regulator, to his surprise the key connection was blocked with a plastic sheet, when he pulled the plastic sheets out the water flashed.

He did not manage to finish the reconnection and a Toyota stopped upraptly, a fellow climbed off the car and began gesturing and talking loudly, George did not answer until the man was close to him, he was busy connecting the regulator.

"What are you doing, you are stealing water, this is the job of the water board and the water is for drinking."

"Yes, that's right, but was blocked and no water was coming, we like to drink too."

"From where are you?"

"I am Cypriot."

"Which side of Cyprus?"

"I am a Cypriot," George tried to keep calm.

"Are you Turk or Greek?"

"Greek."

He scorned at George and left, the water stopped coming completely, George spoke to Muftah, he promised to check with the village authorities, but never had any answer.

After this George decided to carry water, drove up to Hawari and met a friend, Hamed, it was not that far from his place.

When the man asked about the quantity, George explained that he killed chicken and needed two tons daily, the man offered this small amount free of charge, provided he purchased live chicken from his farm when available. George agreed on the spot, requested to have a look at the farm; it was well managed, the chicken looked healthy. The man promised to talk to his laborer in charge, who was running the farm, the man was Iraqi. It was a solution but not the solution.

15: *Family news*

From the central post office, George managed to call his home in Cyprus, had to wait for more than an hour to get the line.

"Hello Sonia, how are you my dear?"

"Papa, we're having a grand time, but we miss you, all wished you were here, together."

"How is Mum, Margarita, Mary?"

"They're fine, the two are playing with the dolls on the veranda, and Mum is in the kitchen, ah, coming."

"Dad is on the phone."

"Hello George, how are you, love?"

"Oh I'm fine, just a bit lonely."

"We're coming next Thursday; I've booked with the Libyan airlines."

"Oh! Very good, I'll meet you at the airport."

"What do you need, I mean personally, to bring with me?"

"Bring me a few disposable blades, two shaving creams, five tubes of toothpaste, I wanted a tooth brush and …."

"And what?"

"I cannot think of anything else just now."

"I will bring the underclothes I bought for you and the shirts I bought from a Limassol factory, four short sleeved and three long sleeved, do you need more?"

"No, no these are more than enough."

"How is the situation?"

"Everything is fine, quiet and…"

"George is there any problem?"

"Oh no, not in the least, just come whenever you like, of course the weather here is hot."

"We had almost two months, its enough, you have greetings from my Dad, Mum, George and little Notis they are all well; ah, Mary and Margarita are here they want to talk to you."

"Please, give them to me."

"Dad I love you," Margarita was always warmhearted.

"Hello love, are you enjoying your holiday?"

"Very much Dad but I miss you, we're coming this week, we are coming."

"I'll be waiting for you at the airport, I miss you very much. Margarita, your tortoise gave birth, rather the eggs hatched, and three tiny ones are moving about the yard."

"Daddy, really, please put them in a box inside the house, the cats or the rats will eat them; they are so tiny I suppose."

"Yes all right, I'll take them inside; I hope their mother does not bite me."

"Dad, she cannot bite you, she's too slow."

"Where is Mary, can I talk to her?"

"Yes sure, but Dad we're coming."

"Daddy, my barby lost one leg, the left one."

"Mary, my dear, dolls do not lose their legs."

"Daddy she lost it, I tell you."

"I brought you a new one, a bigger one; leave the lame one in Cyprus.

"Daddy, love you daddy, we're coming, I don't know when exactly but we're coming. Mum wants you, bye Daddy."

"George your daughters missed you very much."

"Yes I know, yes Kate."

"As I said, we're coming next Thursday, I will bring some foodstuffs, my father bought for us halloumi cheese from Athienou, looks very nice. He also bought new pure olive oil; I thought of bringing some salami, cheese, and bacon; should I bring any of these?"

"Better not, there is a….."

"What did you say?"

"Do not bring any of that kind of meat, please."

"Hello Unani, what family coming?"

George was surprised; the officer at guard asked him if his family was coming.

"Yes I hope so," answered smiling.

"Tfatal, go inside, they may need some help."

George crossed the forbidden entrance, meant only for exit.

The plane must have been full; a rush of passengers was heading for the immigration table.

George passed the immigration table just by greeting the officer and pushed his way to the passengers' entrance. His people were trailing at the rear of the mob, from Kate, to little Mary, were loaded with handbags.

"Hello Kate," George called. She was surprised to see him at that place.

All were perspiring and all were punting.

"Hello Sonia, hello Margarita, how are you my little one, Mary."

"Please give me your passports; we have to fill in the forms for the arrival."

"Oh, I have them all here, passports and forms, a Libyan lady filled them for us."

"This is great, it will save us time."

George pushed through the crowd and to the same officer, greeted him and deposited the bundle.

He looked up, "Ah! Unani?"

George smiled again.

He did not even check the passports, thumb, thumb; he stamped passports and forms, teared off the bottom part of each form, stuck it in the passports, and said, "Tfatal."

"Thank you, thank you sir."

"Best regards to Hag Nasser, Nasser Merussi."

George was caught unprepared.

"Sure I will, for sure," he said gleaming.

"What did he say?" Kate asked.

"Hag Nasser must have talked to his friends."

Passed the immigration, and turned right for the customs. A pandemonium was going on at that section.

As there was no delivery belt, all luggage was loaded on a trailer drawn by an old Massey Ferguson.

Large bags, small bags, bundles of all kinds, shapes and waight, and boxes, piled two meters high on the trailer. No porter was available for unloading.

Passengers went round and round the trailer, stumbling on some who spotted their luggage and struggled to pull it off the untidy mass. Handles tore off and landed in the scuffle's hands.

The top bags tumbled down; insults and sweat aggravated the hour. Politeness crept away from the scene, was far too humiliated.

George stood aside, confused.

The uncultured ones pulled their bundles, boxes, or bags and headed boisterously for the customs bench.

"That is our bag," hauled Kate.

George stepped forward and pulled it aside.

"How many bags do you have, my dear?"

"Seven."

"Just stand there and point them to me." George retreaved all the seven bags, one by one.

By now, the mob abandoned the trailer, a porter appeared from nowhere; George slipped a dinar note in a sweaty hand, he looked up and asked "where?"

George with his index finger ascribed a circle around their luggage.

"OK," he lifted two and George another two. Kate lifted one but George stopped her.

"Please stay around; we'll come back, Sonia, Margarita, please come with me."

They placed the four bags on the floor near the customs bench, left the two girls next to them and dashed back for the rest.

The porter dropped another two next to the first lot. Another dinar saved George the pain of lifting and removing them from the bench.

He gestured George to leave the luggage and rushed for a cart. George did not see a single cart rolling till then, the man appeared through the back door with an almost new cart.

Up he loaded the luggage and undertook to push it out of the building.

"Just stay here, I will bring the Peugeot."

Onto the Peugeot the same old way, in the passenger's seat four souls piled for the twenty kilometer way and the three checkpoints.

"God help," George murmured.

"Welcome home," he said loudly to his family.

"George how are you, you look thin."

"I am not, not in the least."

"Dad, we brought you shaving blades, you really need a good shave," said Margarita.

"Daddy, I've brought you some cheesecakes from granny," said Mary.

Every minute or so an announcement came about such and such item or such and such subject.

They passed easily through the checkpoints,.

"My family just arrived from abroad," said George to an inquisitive soldier.

"Al-right, al-right, Tfatal."

By the time they reached Fuehat and their home, George heard all the news, about his family, Kate's family, and all the gossip from the relatives. He listened to the problems of the people in Cyprus, simply heard them, he had his own to solve.

"Now you go to take a shower, I have roasted a chicken with potatoes, and I'll prepare a salad."

"Dad, I'll make the salad," said Sonia.

"Come on then, one by one to the bathroom."

"You know Hag Nasser is a big shot."

"I brought them a large box of chocolates."

"Later, we may go for a visit."

"Leave it till tomorrow; I'll go to see Unissa."

"For this bastard, the landlord?"

"He does not deserve a thing, but I brought them too, a nice box of chocolates."

"No, give them the chewing gum," said Sonia.

"Not the chewing gum, it's for us, for the school."

"Even if you don't give them a thing, it does not really matter."

"I did not tell you my news; we have our first lot of baby chicks on the farm, actually the first ten thousand."

"Really?" Kate goggled her eyes, but looked pleased.

"And they are doing very well,"

"George, two hangars?"

"Yes, 10.000 in two hangars."

"God bless, I wish you have a good start."

"Up to now they look good; will try to look after them."

"Daddy it's not only to look after them, and I'm very proud of your knowledge about poultry, the question is the feed, medicine, vaccines, are these materials available?" Sonia asked.

"For this lot, managed to secure what I believe will be needed. For the future batches, will see; things are changing fast in every walk of life."

"Virgin Mary, George, are we heading for a second time?" Kate asked with dismay.

"No, no I don't mean that, never said anything of that sort."

After a good sleep, all of them felt much better.

George was ready for the farm, whilst Kate was ready for her cleaning, Margarita and Mary got hold of the tiny tortoises.

"Daddy they're so cute," said Mary.

"Thank you Daddy for taking care of them." said Margarita, "if left outside some cats might feast on them."

"Daddy is here, he likes animals," said Sonia.

"All kinds of animals Dad?" asked Margarita.

The day was brighter with all the family together.

"Hello Madame Unisa?"

"Hello Madame Kate, welcome."

After the fifth kiss and hug, the two women got apart.

"Tfatal?" Unisa asked Kate to sit.

"How was your holiday, how are your parents?"

"They're good, but you know Cyprus now is not as before the Turkish invasion with more than 200.000 persons deported from their homes, life is very hard."

"There are no jobs, people are begging for food, you know people who lived before in villas with all kinds of amenities now stay in tents, and one can imagine the problem."

"God is great, God will help them."

"And how are you Madame Unisa?"

"Well, I'm not so well."

"What happened?"

"I have a problem with my stomach; rather above my stomach. The doctors say could be my liver."

"Oh my God, what did you do, you had x-rays, analyses, what did you do?"

"The doctors made all kinds of investigations; they say, I have to go abroad for surgery. London would be the best, they say. I'm waiting for my visa."

"Will you be leaving soon?"

"Any moment, I am worried more for my four little children."

"Can I help in any way?"

"Thank you, my mother will take care of them."

"Will she come to stay here?"

"No, she does not like Nasser."

"We have to take them to her home, near El-Badria mosque."

"The way to Benina Airport?"

"Yes, that's right."

"Oh, I am really sorry, I hope and pray to God to help you come back cured."

"I hope so too and thank you for your prayers."

"If it's anything I can do, please do let me know."

The bell rang and the house was flooded with visitors. Two cars brought some seven women. In that commotion, Kate excused herself and got up to leave.

"Thank you Madam Kate, thank you very much and welcome."

"We must register you at school my young ladies."

"Yes Daddy."

"Daddy, can I come with you?"

"Of course, yes Mary, get ready, take your school report with you. Here put them all in this plastic folder."

Downtown they stopped by Umma Bank once known as Banco di Roma, Father Iacovos was more than glad to see them. From time to time, he had his share of poultry meat;

if he did not eat all of it by himself, was none of George's concern.

"Hello trio Thio?" Father greeted the three daughters, "you came for registration, Mr. Kallos I believe has done it already."

"How come father, good morning to you."

"Good morning Mr. George, the young ladies at the top of the entire school."

"Now, now father."

"The results talk by themselves, so Mr. Kallos registered them already."

"How about the fees?"

"Later, later, he's not here just now, the whole of his family went to Derna from yesterday and may not return till Saturday, they have doctor Santos there, you know."

"Well, thank you very much Father, good bye."

"Come I'll make coffee, its coffee time."

"Some other time, Father we have to do some shopping, thank you very much."

"As you wish, my kindest regards to Mrs. Kate."

"Sure, I will tell her, goodbye."

"Goodbye young ladies."

"Goodbye father," all together greeted the church representative.

They walked up to the fish market square to look for stationery, the shop was almost empty.

"We have very few items, if you want exercise books for the school, you better go to Pepsi road, and there the government opened a cooperative for such items."

"You know where about this cooperative?"

"Near the villa of Abd Ishmael, an old man is in charge, Ibrahim his name, I think."

"Thank you very much."

As they headed for the car, bumped into Sonia's schoolmate, Barbara.

"Hello Sonia, welcome back."

"Hello Barbara, how're you doing?"

"Hello Margarita, hello Mary, you are growing, aren't you?"

"Hello Barbara, yes I am growing I enter the second class."

"Hello Mr. Andreas? Come to our house my mother would love to see you."

"Now may not be the right time, will bring them one of these afternoons."

"Yes, please do, it's a long time since we talked ours," said Barbara taking Sonia's hand.

"By the way, you know any place for school stationary Barbara?"

"There was this big shop in Jamal Abd-el-Nasser Street."

"We can see it on our way."

Traders, shopkeepers, salespersons, even pedlars smell their customers, as soon as they enter their shop. The old man behind the glass bench that served as a showcase greeted them warmly; before George even asking, he predicted their question.

"About school stationery, we have a very limited quantity, if you let me have your requirements, will try to help,"

The once very active entrepreneur now was sitting like a nailed figure on a wooden stool and watched his customers creeping away.

George had his reservations about Mr. Ibrahim of Pepsi road, he asked for a piece of paper scribbled about half of the year's requirements and handed it to the old shop owner, then drove to the new stationary cooperative, they spotted it very easily.

Pepsi road was once humming with shoppers, now very few cars parked here and there and the scanty shoppers moved at ease with meager items in their green translucent plastic bags.

At first George thought of visiting the shop by himself, then had second thoughts when the girls hurried out of the car.

Very few customers were in the shop, Ibrahim, an old man was serving a stocky fellow who stood in front of a wooden table; behind him was a woman, who waited for her tern.

George stopped behind her, forming a queu.

Queuing was the latest notion in Libya. The woman took her turn and then George moved en masse forward, now could get a better view of the person in charge.

He looked at George and the three girls, lifted his eyebrows in a greeting and smiled.

George recognized him, he lived on the same row as Hag Nasser, was one of the neighbourhood.

George did not have any close relations, as his house entrance was from the other end of the vertical street to theirs.

The old man greeted them and shook hands with George, then asked him in a pleasant way what they wanted.

George had a liberal request, from exercise books to ballpoint pens, rulers, and color pencils. Without hesitation, the old man brought what George asked and what he thought they might need. Brought a pile of material, actually.

"I'll put it all in the carton box," he said, "its not nice for you to carry it in plastic bags."

George guessed his precautions, paid the bill, and lifted the box to the car.

"Dad, I was skeptical when we entered," said Sonia.

"He is the father of Magboula, the nice looking girl who greet us every day in the street," said Margasrita.

"It's good to know people," said George, trying to appease his girls.

16: Civil socializations

"Daddy, to-night can you take us to Costas."

"Who is Costas?"

"Mary's boyfriend,"

"He is not, he is only my classmate, and he's not a good pupil at that."

"Catch it Sonia," said Margarita.

"He has two sisters in the elementary school."

"Another five cousins of them are coming to our school."

"So, you have eight pupils from this family?"

"Yes, I believe their fathers were born here, they are Libyans," said Sonia.

"The eldest cousin is in the fourth form, one of the girls is in my class," said Margarita.

"You know them well enough then? If so I will take you, you know where they live?"

"Their fathers own a coffee grinding shop near the fish market square."

"Ah! The Sirocco coffee, is theirs?"

"Yes, their surname is Sirocco," said Margarita.

"We are home, let's discuss the matter inside."

Kate was glad to see them back, "where have you been, you left me here for hours? What is in the box?"

"Many things have changed here, even for a few school stationary one must have a middleman to obtain what he wants."

Kate was caught unaware of the situation, "how did you get all that?"

"From Ibrahim, our neighbour, Magboula's father."

"The family across, I think her mother is called Amna, she has rheumatism, or something with her legs, I met her once at Unisa."

"So you know the family?"

The girls pulled the box in the big salon and unpacked all items onto the oversize table. Sonia was busy distributing them according to each of her sisters' requirements.

"The rest, we'll close it up in the box for our future needs." Sonia was straight in her decisions and adamant.

"Sonia? You are like Mum."

"Daad?"

"Mother has set the table, let's go"

"Mum, can we go to Sorocco tonight?"

Kate heard the request with some skepticism; looked at George, he smiled approvingly.

"We don't know them well enough, so to call for the first visit without prior communication? I don't know."

"In Libya everything is excused, we do not have a phone for such purposes."

"Al-right if you like so."

"After I get some rest, I'll go to the farm and when I come back we can go, say at eight."

All agreed to the arrangements.

"Daddy, can I come to the farm?" Margarita asked.

"I want to come too, want to see the small chicks," said Mary.

"If we're going for a visit you better stay at home, take a shower in time and be ready."

"Mother they're only kids, let them come with me."

"You always give way to their demands, you are spoiling them."

"No my dear, let them come, they have no school now."

"Now you just keep with me, small chicks are easily scared, any abnormal movement may send them to the corner, if they huddle even for just a few minutes may suffocate to their death."

Margarita took Mary's hand, wanted to control her sister and avoid any misbehavior, in fact Margaria needed attention; she was the most active of the three. Now she undertook the motherly role.

Margarita always respected her father, now with imminent danger to her father's livelihood, had to respond to his advice.

Both flocks of chicken looked healthy, vigorous and within minutes shook off the fright from the newcomers, resumed their happy chirping, dashed around and began approaching the zinc sheets that confound them to the limited area near the gas brooders.

Margarita began chirping and dozens of them responded to her imitation, cautiously approached closer, and strained their fluffy necks with beaks half open, turned their heads to one side, and with beady eyes studied the figure that chirped almost like them.

She did not resist, knelt down, stretched her hand and grabbed the most courageous that defied the danger. Once in her hand, began crying loudly, sending the whole lot in alert and rushing away. Margarita in desperation let the fat little bird jump off her hand to land on its belly with a loud complain.

George from a few meters away kept an eye on the girls, in such cases the poultryman must act with consciousness.

It is funny though to see hundreds of plumb little chicken trying to flee. Their short legs moving fast and open their featherless wings in an attmpt to fly, lose their balance and land on their backs with the following ones to stumble over and within seconds piles of three and four birds deep are visible.

It is a common saying that members of the feathered world once disturbed hide their heads somewhere and remain inert as though the danger has vanished. Ostriches are known for that, although being the largest representatives of the feathered uniform.

"Come along, come along," George repeated the same calmly.

As soon as the tiny chicks realized that there was no actual danger, stopped running, the unfortunate ones struggled to their feet, looked back over their shoulders and joined the ones further back.

Once order returned to the crowd, George walked closer to the two girls, they looked more scared than the chicks.

Mary was in Margarita's apron with face hidden in her sister's breast.

George placed his hand on Margarita's shoulder and delicately turned Mary out of her hiding place. Both looked at him in apology.

"Such problems do happen, like in every walk of life, the question is how to remedy such mishaps." George never used his hands on his children; mistakes are not solved by punishment.

The red of their faces returned to normal, soon they realized that their father had no intention of any disciplinary measures.

"You know small chicks or even older birds confined in areas like this get used to a program of visitors or workers, who are in the same outfit, to regular feeding periods and even voices.

Say if I talk to them, as I did a few minutes ago, they are accustomed to my voice and show no fear or even pay attention. However, if another person talks with a different picth of voice, may send them all in that corner, if they have the stamina to reach it; otherwise, may pile up halfway with catastrophic results.

An uprapt movement may send them alight too. Every movement has to be done cautiously and in slow motion; say if I want to catch a chick for fun or for inspection, I enter the surrounding, lower down, let the chicks relax, get accustomed to my presence, come close to me and simply I cup one with my palm, if you stop here, will show you."

George entered the enclosure as he explained, waited, and cupped a vivid one.

"Once in my hand, I cover its head with my second palm, with a covered head cannot see around and does not chirp. When it does not chirp, none of the others knows that it is in captivity. When the fear vanishes, can hold it very easily, you see it's very happy."

"Dad always admired you as a poultry expert, but now I admire an expert in handling mishaps," said Margarita with pride in her eyes.

"OK. Let's have a look in the second house."

There the chicks were happy, chirping, running, drinking, charging occassionally at each other, they were happy.

Ibrahim waited outside the hangar, very seldom an Arab will approach strange females, whatever their age.

George talked to him about the preparation of another two hangars for a second lot of day-old chicks. Ibrahim caught up with the system of preparing hangars, but complained of too much work.

"Boss, now with the small chicks we have to spend many hours in the houses, to clean another two at this period would be a problem."

"Let me see the houses and see how much work is there?"

"Boss, both hangars have a lot of litter that has to be removed; you told us old litter is a danger to small birds."

He had a reason, but was always ready for an extra dinar.

"Al-right, I'll come back tomorrow."

George thought of the Nigerian students, they would like to earn a dinar or so.

He drove directly downtown and met Bob, after a short talk he agreed to find two of his brothers that were eager for a job.

At home, after a shower and a light supper, all piled into the Peugeot, determined to find where this Mary's schoolmate lived with his family. Sonia knew moreless.

They circled the area twice with little success; streets actually had no signs and no house numbers. Muammar ordered the removal of all street signs because they were in Latin and the new signs in Arabic had to be brought from abroad.

Sonia, who undertook to guide them, suggested inquiring at the neighborhood grocery.

When George asked, the young fellow behind his loaded bench smiled, "are you Greeks?"

George smiled back, "yes."

He was the best person to inform them.

George drove back to the area they passed twice, now stopped, and rang the bell.

A rush with girlish voices was heard from behind the iron door. The door was as high as the two-meter wall that surrounded the building

Heavy barking accompanied the girls' voices; from the tone, the dog sounded one of the large types.

"Who is it?" asked one of the girls fighting with the rest to keep quiet.

"George, please, good evening."

"Mr. George?" giggled the girl.

"Wait till I tie the dog."

They heard the pulling of a chain. "Come here Pluto,"

The heavy iron door was pulled open and four young faces hang forward. "Margarita, Madam Kate, come in please, come in."

"Mum, Mr. George is here," called the second who run towards the house to announce them.

One of the girls pulled Margarita past the threshold, Kate advanced with Sonia, and George took Mary's hand knowing how much she was afraid of dogs.

Three smiling girlish faces stood aside as they passed.

George kept Mary to his side away from the enormous German wolf. Everybody was glad; the dog was tethered to a chain.

George did not resist though whistling in a characateristic way, which the dog understood and returned to its den, in surprise to all.

"Bravo Mr. George, it's the first time our dog behaves to the directions of a visitor."

George whistled again and Pluto left a wheen of recognition, received the message.

Were directed up the steps, then to the right and into a posh saloon. A small chandelier was set alight.

They sat on new sofas that were still hard, not for daily use, thought George.

The saloon was flooded with girls; George counted five and three of his own

Anita, a girl of fourteen with sparkling eyes, sensed his thinking and said with a laugh throwing her legs in the air.

"There is another one Mr. George, my cousin Nina; she went to town with her mother."

"I was not counting you, I enjoy the fever of all you, young girls," tittered George.

"Thank you Mr. George, you know we like your daughters, all of them! And I'm happy you paid us this visit, I hope, you come more often."

The girl looked smart for her age and environment.

"Costas went with his mother to Merry, they will soon be here, my uncle stayed with them, and they will soon be here."

"Hello Madam Kate?" a friendly female voice spoke from across the door, a woman of forty entered, swaying her short plumb hands back and forth a boxam body. She looked attractive despite her quick hair do, with a round face with half hidden eyes and straight black hair, combed in a hurry.

"Welcome to my house," she said with a broad smile.

Kate rose to exchange the customary kisses of welcome; George gave his hand for a hearty handshake.

"I'm really glad that you came, wish you'd come more often and bring your lovely girls with you."

"Sure I will, thank you, thank you very much," said George in a persuasive tone.

"Pease be seated, Dino will be with us any moment, now he's in the shower, you know my husband is always late with his work."

"Let him take his time, they have a hard time all day long. I was down at the shop the other day, it's a hard work."

"It is a hard work Mr. George, we all know that, but thanks God they earn a good living."

"I hope to God."

"Anita, bring some soft drinks," ordered her mother.

"Mum can you ask first, Madam Kate may like something else, and so is Mr. George, for my young friends, will take care of them."

"It's OK," said George casually.

"George we're in the home of the best Benghazi coffee grinders, let's have one of them."

"That's what I was going to request."

"Mum, take it now, they want coffee; you go and prepare it."

Anita sounded the favoured one, thought George.

"How do you like your coffee Mr. George?"

"Medium please."

"The same for me please," said Kate.

Mariam lifted her weight and in short steps, moved away promising not to be long.

"Good evening, welcome," a man's voice was heard the moment Mariam managed to pass through the door.

George rose to greet him.

"My dad," pronounced Anita, "Mr. George and Madam Kate, Dad," she added.

George rose, shook a bony hand with long fingers; the man had a tanned complexion with wavy gray hair. He looked a drained person, took the sofa next to George's and faced him

He offered George a cigarette.

"Thank you, I don't smoke,"

He lit one and the girl provided him with an ashtray.

"Saw you down at the shop," he said mildly.

"Yes, that's right; came for some fresh coffee, heard very good comments about your products."

"We roast and grind coffee, only."

"Yes, but this is the best in the whole of Benghazi," said with zest.

"Sometimes we have problems with delays and long queues."

"The people like your product, let them wait."

"People do like our coffee, we bring Brazilian No 1, and I roast it. Yianni grinds and retails. We are just the two of us."

"It must be very hard, specially the roasting, in this heat."

"It is hot, what can we do, we inherited it from our late father, God bless his soul, we must carry on the legion, we are obliged to."

"So your father was a coffee man also, Mr.Dino?"

"Yes, people know that place by our father's name, 'Andreas el Kahoui,' he died now, God bless his soul, it's more than eight years."

"God bless his soul," repeated George.

Plumb Mariam came with an oversize silver plated tray, but the size of it was lost between her hands.

"This is Andrea's coffee, ground by my husband."

"And prepared by Madam Mariam," added George, "must be one of the best."

She cuckled and almost tipped coffees, glasses and cakes onto Kate.

"Careful now," came short from Dino.

Mariam blushed; George lifted his saucer with the gold-rimmed cup

Anita was always at hand, she brought a low table in front of the visitors.

"Help yourselves to cakes; I made all of them by myself."

"Yes, thank you," said Kate, "they look lovely."

"Dino, these are the girls your daughters always talk about."

"Yes I see them."

Mariam sat next to Kate, they talked their own, recipes were going and coming, comments about item shortages, the dusty atmosphere and the poor schoolteachers' performance.

Mariam did not hesitate to complement Kate for her perfect appearance.

Conversation with Dino was laconic, George knew very little of the man, so subjects were limited.

A Greek video cassette was switched on; George joined the girls for the laugh of it.

The dog barked wildly, some visitors must have been crossing his surroundings.

Two of the girls rushed out of the room but were cut short by talks in the corridor.

Costas with his mother Renio were heard inviting somebody to enter, “come in doctor,” the invitation was in Greek.

George looked forward to someone that could help. He despised television.

To his surprise, it was Dr. Leventakis with his two children, Costas and Niki. Everybody rose to his feet, Dino, the girls en-masse, Kate, Mariam and George.

A warm welcome awaited the newcomers

George met many times Dr.Leventakis outside the Greek school where he called to collect his children. Felt a lot easier when he saw him; with him, one could hold a conversation for hours.

Renio accompanied the doctor and his children, she greeted all of them warmly, excused herself for a few minutes and left.

Dino was the proprietor, and George expected him to get the initiative, instead, he lit another cigarette and stared at the television.

“Well Mr. George,” said Dr.Leventakis, “I haven’t seen you for a long time.”

“Yes that is true; we have not met since the school closed for the summer vacation, as a matter of fact.”

“We have been outside for a while, Kate and the young ladies returned just a few days ago.”

“It is nice to travel whenever a person can do it.”

“Surely it is,” said George, “you begin with thr preparation for travel, and you get the taste of the airport difficulties…”

“Yes but you are rewarded with the holiday outside this country.”

Leventakis, a general practitioner, lived in Benghazi since the Second World War; this country was his country. He served as a personal doctor to the late King Idriss. Unquestionably, he had sweat memories of the palace, the elite life, the honor, the prestige, and the parties of those days.

Now he advises people to take a holiday outside this country.

Apart from his profession, he served this country as a consular representative here in Benghazi.

His status, his profession, his family life, made him the most eminent Greek in the town.

George talked with him about Cyprus, the political problem, the refugee problem, the indifference of the world's powerful personalities, their interests, and the political chessboard of the big people.

Dr. Leventakis was well acquainted with the political arena; but could not enter this field in somebody else's house.

Renio came and asked all the children to go downstairs to Selma, her sister in law; she was a very good cook.

Renio had known Dr.Leventakis for years, delivered all her four children, and doctored them for years. They had common interests for the school, the church, and the community.

The conversation began with the school and developed into an argument.

Leventakis supported the consul as the one responsible for the community in general and definitely for the school.

Renio insisted that the consul's assignment had nothing to do with the education since he was a representative of the Minister of exterior.

It took some effort to persuade Renio to accept that the community and its activities were under the consul's jurisdiction.

Leventakis brought forward many examples of his long service as a consular representative, before the Greek government had enough currency to open a full-scale consulate in Benghazi.

Dino suggested a drink of arak.

Dr. Leventakis rejected its consumtion altogether, insisted that fermentation was not complete and the spirit produced contained methyl alcohol, which was detrimental to the health of the consumers.

Dino eyed him from the side and lit another cigarette; his ashtray was full of stubs by now.

Time passed fast with Leventakis on the arena.

George questioned the credibility of the community committee, were suspected of embezzling the funds.

Everybody promised to be present at the next elections and combine their voices with many others whom Leventakis promised to talk and warn the members of the degradation.

"We're the ones to challenge them, we have our children at school, and we must alert everybody the dangers of degradation in all respects from the committee to the school teachers and the embezzlement of the funds of the community."

George suggested that an investigation should be carried out. All the community's property be registered, the icons and relics of the church the assets, the buildings and shops, the schools with all the furniture and equipment.

"Why nobody thought of it before?" Leventakis asked.

"Probably the previous persons who handled the community's assets were reliable and honest," said George with some reservations.

"Yes you are right Mr. George," said Renio

Kate suggested ways of increasing the community's income by indirect means, like dances or bazaars. Leventakis was so pleased with Kate's interests, and promised to support her for a membership in the school parents association.

Kate gleamed with Leventakis recognition of her interest.

"It's a very good idea, it is though necessary for a collective attempt, and we tried before with not any real success." Renio said.

Yianni, Renio's husband did not present himself at all, his wife pardoned him on grounds of tiredness. Dino eyed her in disapproving way.

They all bid goodnight to the proprietor, his wife, and Renio and promised to call more often.

"At least, for the sake of the children," said Renio, "I love to see my children mixing with children like yours Mr. George," added with a sigh.

George did not really understand her perception for such closer visits.

"You can bring your children to our home too," Kate said.

"Yes thank you very much, but I don't drive and they're all the time busy."

George called his three children, and Leventakis his, passed the house guard, the fierce dog and drove away.

On the way everybody was quiet for a while, everybody watched the traffic, it was heavy with locals at the wheel and was abominable.

Only when they were almost near their home things eased off; so did the talking.

Kate broke the silence first; asked the girls what kind of delicacy they ate at Selma's apartment.

"Ooh, macaroni, hot and greasy," scorned Sonia.

"Yes too much pepper in it," said Margarita.

"I'm glad I did not even taste it," said Mary, "who asked us, who asked her to cook for us?"

All three giggled at Mary's statement.

"Dad, tomorrow can you take us to the church?" asked Sonia. "I believe some of my school mates did not leave for vacation; hope to meet some of them there."

"Yes al-right, I'll drop you there about 9:30 am, is that good enough?"

"Yes it's wonderful, and then you pick us at 10.30."

"Al-right I'll do that, I have some work downtown."

When George went to pick them up, they were not there, but father Iacovos was in the community's office. "Mr. George welcome, you look for your girls? They went to Mary's place, you know where it is?"

"Yes I know."

"They have just gone, join me for a coffee, or it is still early."

"Father you are always obliging."

"Not to everybody," said with a chuckle.

Mary, as many other children of Greek origin born in Libya, grew there and lived there; it was their second country. Normally such children were registered on their mother's Greek passport; this allowed them to move in and out without hindrance, even now with the strict travel regulations.

Mary's farther, Andreas, boasted of being in Libya for 54 years. He remembered the large Jewish community, the Italians, the Second World War, the King, the pig farm he ran as joint venture with a Libyan and the revolution.

His hearing was somehow impaired from the days he crossed the weird desert of more than a thousand kilometers under all kinds of weather conditions to deliver the subsidized foodstuffs to the remote oasis of Qufra, near the Sudaneese border.

He was trusted the contract of delivering scarse foodstuffs for Libya beyond the heart of the desert. Due to his ill hearing, nobody could stop him from orating about his long experience in Libya, his long living there, as well as his trips across the inhospitable sea of sands.

An Athenian newspaper named him, "the master of the desert." Both he and his Cretan wife were kind to George's family and their two grown up children were good friends. Many a times, their daughter Mary lunched with Sonia and her sisters.

George prayed to God, when he rang their bell that old Andreas would not be at home; to his surprise, the old man opened the door.

"Good morning Mr. Andreas," George greeted him loudly.

"Come in, come in, I invited your daughters to come, they are inside with Mary."

"Good morning Madam Angela, how are you doing?"

"Ah! We are good, the children are all inside, I made for them a small toast and some milk; after the sermon, was the right thing I believe."

"I'm sure it was, but you should not trouble yourself."

"This is no trouble for me, it's a pleasure, and I love your girls."

"Is it, because they come from an island?"

"Yes, that's right; Cyprus and Crete have a lot in common."

"That is true," said George approvingly.

"Come in, come in, shall I make coffee for you? We're having one, my husband does not like the coffee but I do."

"Yes thank you, Madam Angela."

Their rented apartment was clean, but hot, even with most windowpanes open.

They sat in the saloon; the aging sofas creaked as they dropped on them.

Angela hurried to her kitchen through a door on the left; a toilet was heard being flashed and girlish laughter from behind the door to the right.

George guessed the apartment was small for a family of four with two grown up children of different sexes.

Old Andreas sat at the far end enjoying his toast with plain hot milk He dipped the toast into the glass of milk, shook it slightly up and down, lifted it carefully, lowered his head, turned slightly to his right, opened his mouth wide, bit off the wet and munched it noisily.

Angela appeared disturbed with coffee on a tray, "my husband will never learn," she said, "with his hearing problem, cannot hear his noisy manners."

"Please, let Mr. Andreas enjoy his breakfast."

"He enjoys it alright," said with a twitch of her lips.

George was glad that Angela did not treat him to more than one coffee.

The girlish laughter came aloud and louder.

"The girls have a lot to say, listen to them."

"Yes, I do Madam Angela, they sound happy."

"Youngsters, no problems."

"Their turn will come, now let them enjoy life."

"How is your beautiful wife?"

"Oh, she's toiling in the house," said George with a smile, was quite pleased whenever complemented of his family.

"Clever daughters, beautiful wife!"

George felt appeased, said to himself, 'you are striving hard, hard for your family;' he finished his coffee and begged Angela to call his girls.

"It's too early, listen to them. Leave them here for the day."

"Please, not this time, we'll arrange on some other day, soon, the girls will love the idea, now their mother will be waiting for us."

"Only for Madam Kate," she said and rose to her feet.

"Mary, Mary," she called without moving a step forward; when she got no response, moved briskly towards the door from where the laughter was heard.

Unintentionally George followed her with his eyes but stopped before old Andreas. Above him, high on the wall, were three framed enlarged photos. Though glass framed, they faded considerably.

Old Andreas caught George spying his prized photos and rose to his feet. His eyes stopped at the first frame when old Andreas approached.

"Here, this photograph," he said with pride, "was taken when King Idris called me to the palace, there he awarded me the contract of delivering foodstuffs to Qufra."

George rose to his feet, approached Andreas, and strained his eyes to identify who was who. He never saw his Highness, only in newspapers, so he could not make out who was the King even who was Andreas.

"This is in 1966, in September of that year; we had to deliver foodstuffs to Qufra across the desert. Were hit by the worst east wind; Gibli as the locals call it. The wind was blowing to more than eighty miles per hour; the sand hit us so strongly that even with covered faces felt the sand particles as stones."

"It blew for four days and four nights. The dusty wind blew up to Benghazi, across the sea and up to Greece. A thick layer of dust covered Benghazi. Everybody thought we were lost in the cataclysm. Our Land rovers were covered with sand. The endless and free desert turned to a fearful and impenetrable abyss."

"Andreas, now it's not the time to tell your story," Angela called from behind them.

When George looked back, his three daughters, Mary and Costas, the brother, were standing in a circle listening to the speaker.

Old Andreas disappointed with his wife's intervention stopped and looked out for support.

"It is very interesting," said George loudly to his companion and that revived him somehow.

"I was telling you of the gibli, this is another photo taken at the same place but on a normal day, you see how beautiful the desert is?"

"The third photograph here is at a party given for our safe arrival after the ordeal of that unforgettable journey, down at Qufra."

"So the desert is beautiful but treacherous." George said, leaning forward with great understanding.

There was no response.

"We must come another time; you have very interesting experience not only of Libya but also of the beautiful desert."

"We have to go; your Mum will be worried."

Angela invited them to call more often and take Madam Kate with them; Old Andreas accompanied his guests out of the house and into the side street, the place looked awful, debris everywhere, the stench unbearable, the girls brought their hankies to their noses, the old man noticed it.

"Before the town was clean and smart and the people well mannered and respectable and everyone knew exactly his place, look now, how they managed to make people indifferent without respect to environment or neighborhood. They taught them to be cowards, opportunists, and hypocrites."

"You know Mr. Andreas; I visited Libya in 69 and remember a few things. Something that struck me was a butcher selling pork meat at the Fish market square."

Old Andreas leaned forward, looked at his visitor intensely, cleared his throat, and said, "That was our butchery, we ran a pig farm in Hawari area at that time."

It was George's turn now to strain his ears and listen to the man who ran a pig farm in a completely Muslim country.

"You ran the farm, legally, Mr. Andreas?"

"Definitely, yes."

The girls gathered and seemed eager to leave, three pleading pears of eyes demanding something and George had to comply.

The old man remembered of the old worldly standards that crumbled like ancient fragile buildings.

George shook hands the with old man and promised the next visit to be a long one, to hear about his beautiful desert and the good old days.

The old man smiled but his face remained contorted.

"Where have you been, what time did the sermon finish, was worried, your father with his job, I thought he forgot you there in the street."

"No mother, no, Mr. Andreas invited us to their home," said Sonia, "and Angela sends you her best regards."

"From Mary and Costas too," said Margarita.

"Thanks, lunch is ready."

"Come on Margarita, let's set the table."

"Go and wash your hands first."

"I like to do something," complained Mary.

"Yes, put the knives, the forks and ….."

"I know and the table serviettes."

17: Small chicks made everyone happy

After a nap, George visited Hag Mohammed. Instead of him, met a young smart fellow; when he greeted him in Arabic, "*lavoro*" was the answer without lifting his head from some papers in front of him.

"So is everybody," snapped George back and turned to leave.

"What do you want, please?"

"Came to see the old man."

"He's not here, tfatal."

"I'll come back tomorrow."

The man murmured something is his language; George left him at that.

At the farm, the two Egyptian workers got the knack of work and followed the instructions. Apart from an overflowing waterer, the rest looked reasonably good.

The two hangars were prepared for the next batch of chicks, the program was moving, George was quite satisfied; the small chicks grew up so the barriers were removed, there was freedom now, the birds roamed all over the hangar.

The hot weather was oncoming, there was no positive ventilation in the hangars, and this kept George in deep thoughts.

Under the latest restrictions, everything became scarce, sizable extractor fans or any kind of fans were not to be found. George thought of spray nozzles, such an installation required capital, which the farm owner was reluctant to provide. He managed to secure a small water pump from an old friend; placed two large sized drums at strategic positions in each hangar. There, with the help of the small electric pump and the long plastic tube, one could spray the birds whenever needed; this was the simplest and quickest way to get organized for the hot weather.

"Welcome yia George," said Ata, Abdulhadi's accountant, "this time I'm afraid I'm going to disappoint you."

"How, you do not want to sell me any day-olds?"

"I wish I had any and you could have a planeload."

"Then what is the problem?"

"The Minister of agriculture took over the poultry business."

"What do you mean?"

Abdulhadi came in at that moment, "hello George, how are you, how are your chicken?"

"They're fine; really good, came for some more."

"God is great, come in, let's have a cup of tea."

Inside his office, talked about the changing situation in the country and the wind of changes affected the poultry industry too. He explained to George that for any future chicken requirements had to apply to the government poultry organization, at Buatni.

"Anybody there? Whom can I see?"

"Oh yes, your friend Ahmed."

"Ahmed, oh Ahmed?"

"The one, who married a Greek lady."

"Ah, sure he's an old friend."

"You know, he was sent to Egypt on a scholarship to study poultry which actually did, but also got married to a Greek woman from Alexandria."

"So with one trip arranged two matters."

"And what is their program?"

"It is still obscure, but what I heard from Khalifa, the Minister of agriculture of Benghazi, is this. "Any registered poultry farmer can order his day-old broiler chicks from them but has to deliver half of that number to their slaughtery."

"I see, so they want half the quantity back and at what weight?"

"Average weight of 1, 7 kgs, I mean live."

"It will be a complicated program."

"What do you mean Mr. George?"

"First of all what is the capacity of the slaughtery, then how would they collect the birds, what about quality, time of killing, deaths en-route to the slaughtery and who would be the favorite farmers?"

Abdulhadi looked at George stanned, "yes you are right, many questions to be answered."

"And the most important, how would the payment be and when?"

"Many of these matters have to be sorted out by personal contacts."

George left Abdulhadi's office skeptical, he had just begun working and the problems started.

Drove up to Benily's offices, hoping to meet Hag Mohammed, he was lucky.

"Good morning Hag."

"Hello George," he said inquisitively and called the teaboy, who was not to be found; any way he tried to offer George a glassful of tea.

"Hag Mohammed, I've just come from Abdulhadi."

"You ordered new chicks?"

"Wanted to, but things have changed."

"Yes, I know nothing is left in its place, that strong bastard took over everything. Nationalized our houses and apartments, our hotels have gone also."

"I'm sorry to hear it," said George with great sympathy.

"Sorry or not sorry, they took our hotel, not one but both of them, the one in Gamal Abdel Nasser street and the small one at Mohammed Farah street."

"Yes I know that one too, I stayed there for more than a week back in 69 when I first visited Lybia. It was not a very large hotel."

"It was the best and cleanest in Benghazi at that time."

"Yes it was."

"Okay, the hotels are gone, now what about the chicken farm?"

"Abdulhadi was well informed, he told me that we can order day-old chicks only from the poultry organization but have to give them back half the quantity at an average weight of 1,7 kgs live."

"And their price?"

"This I have to find out, but I believe will be a fixed price."

"And how will they pay, when will they pay?"

"This I'd love to find out too."

"You know anyone with a name Ahmed; he is in charge of the organization."

"Half of Benghazi is named Ahmed; it is a very common name you know."

"I don't have his surname, but will find out."

"When are you going there?"

"It's already one of clock."

"These government employees do not keep the timetable, oh, time table, they do not keep anything," said Hag Mohammed and bent his head down.

George rose up slowly and quickly left the office.

He reached home somehow distressed, the situation was deteriorating, the revolutionaries wanted to control everything. Limited knowledge, little experience is always dangerous.

Whatever was his personal condition or feelings, always tried to enter his home with a smile. George avoided whatever discussions, arrangements, or bad feelings before or at lunchtime. Tried to convey this procedure to all his family. Everyone had the right to enjoy his meal. Mind and stomach had to be at ease.

Up to this moment, despite the turmoil over the last couple of years, he succeeded.

Certainly the news of to-day's were not that bad at least for George, he would meet Ahmed, talk the matter over, study the opportunities and the problems and act accordingly.

As far as the confiscation of Hag Mohammed's hotel, was not his concern; it might turn out to his benefit, the family having lost the hotels might pay more attention to agriculture with all the limitations. He had to take on some big challenges right away, hoping the universe would respond to his elasticity and adaptation skills. George followed a positive attitude and that proved contagious, always spread his thinking around and was a bit of a cheer leader for the folks being doubters, never stopped halfway, liked to pull out all the stops, and show them that he was someone they could depend on to get things right the first time. He was poised to impress even those rich people.

George followed the road to Benina Airport trying to spot the offices that would bear an effect on his future. He inquired at the Buatni butchery, "oh Ahmed Bukana, yes the big new office block on your right."

George paid the four pieces of bread with ten piastres and drove forward.

The gatekeeper stopped him at the entrance, "I would like to see Mr. Ahmed."

"You have an appointment?"

"No, not for to day."

The gatekeeper noticed his accent, "from where you come?"

"I'm Greek," said George with a smile trying to gain his favor.

"Tfatal," he said and opened the gate.

George looked up at the three story building and guessed that more than 50 offices could easily be housed, he paused for a while, avoided to ask any official from there not knowing their reaction.

People were climbing up and down the fitted carpet stairs.

George followed three newly arrived persons, whom he guessed as poultry farmers. Were dressed in the customary cotton two-piece outfits with plenty of red dust on the trousers and long shirts, their sandals assured anyone where they've walked.

George followed them up the steps enjoying the thick carpet covering the marble stairs. They vanished through a door that closed behind them.

George gave them a few minutes, then followed the same route; was amazed when he opened the door; behind the new desk stood a very smart and beautiful secretary. He smiled and she returned a broader one showing two white rows of teeth circled by two red colored brimming lips.

She spoke in English with a shining face.

"Are you Lebanese?" asked George politely.

"Yes, how do you know? So you want to see Mr. Ahmed, from where you come, which company?"

"I come from Cyprus, I'm Greek."

"Your name please?"

"George,"

"George?"

"Yes."

She lifted the phone and announced that a Greek with the name George likes to see Mr. Ahmed. "Please," she said politely and moved briskly to open the door for him.

The door was flung open, and another surprise awaited George.

The office was enormous with a conference table at the front, with expensive chairs that stood at the form of capital T, in front of a heavy hard wood office.

At the far end, a kind looking person was discussing something with the three farmers; the ones George met on the way.

He put up a broad smile and proceeded to greet the person in charge of this modern clean, cool, and orderly office.

"Yasou, ti kanis, hello, how are you?" he greeted George in perfect Greek with a foreign accent.

"Here, we have cakes, please help yourself,"

From a tray on the conference table visitors helped themselves to fresh sweets from El-shams, the best confectionery in Benghazi.

George answered in the same language, that he was in perfect health, then changed into English and after the warm handshake asked George to take a seat behind the two farmers already engaged in some discussion.

Waiting there, he could not help listening to the questions and the answers. Ahmed was explaining them the program of the poultry organization. George heard how they could order day-old chicks, from where to be supplied with feed, with medicines and whom to see for delivering the live birds for slaughtering and learned the price of the live birds weighed at the weighbridge of the organization.

"When I saw you, I thought you represent some exporting company," he said politely.

George explained that he was a poultryman and worked with the Benily family.

"I know these people, even visited their farm."

George noticed his positive attitude.

"So you came to order some small chicks?" he was in the picture.

They discussed the newly implemented program and George inquired for clarification as to the way of arranging the deliveries of live birds and the most important the mode and time of payments.

"For your day-old chick orders, you see Mr. Abdulhalim; for the deliveries, first you discuss the matter with Merry and finalize it with Abdulhalim."

"And where do I find Abdulhalim?"

"My secretary will introduce you."

"Annette?" Ahmed called on the interphone.

The Lebanese appeared smiling and wriggling along the sizable office, she was a figure.

Instructions were given in perfect English, George rose to his feet, thanked Ahmed with a hefty handshake, smiled at the secretary who was already hopping out of the office in steady strides.

Out of the office, down to the first floor, she led George to Mr. Abdulhalim.

A short man of his height, with big spectacles on a round face, rose to his feet the moment they entered his office, greeted George by his name; must have been briefed for the arrival.

"Mr. George," he said with a broad smile and provided a fat hand for the handshake.

"Then I must be going," said Annette.

With a smile, George thanked her.

"She's Lebanese, you know," said Mr. Abdulhalim with a smile.

"Sure she is...."

"Please take a seat," the office was in proper order, apart from several empty tea glasses lying at various places.

"What can I do for you?"

"I heard about your poultry organization and your new program, it looks wonderful."

"Yes! Thank you."

"Mr. Ahmed told me that I can discuss with you for some day-old chick broiler orders."

"You work with whom?"

"With Hag Mohammed Benily."

"They have a big farm on the Tripoli road; I visited it, when I had to sign for the approval."

"So you do know the farm?"

"Oh yes, I know all the farms, at least those who have a license."

"Yes if I wanted to order, say 10.000 day-old broilers, when can you accept the order?"

"Are your hangars ready?"

"Yes they are, even fumigated."

"You like next week?"

"Yes, it would be just right."

"So I'll register you temporarily for 12, July."

"Why temporarily?"

"Till, you bring a bank certified check for the cost of the day-olds."

"And how much would that be?"

"For 10.000, the amount is 2.200.LD plus 2% invoice tax, which means 2.244 LD."

From a quick comparison, George noticed that the chicken came out cheaper than from the private sector.

"Can I bring that tomorrow?"

"Tomorrow, after tomorrow, for you no problem."

George was quite satisfied from the response he had all the way through their meeting.

Driving back, George tried to draw conclusions. With gross calculations, he expected a reasonable profit, if mortality was below five percent and the food conversion around two to one. Another challenging factor would be the delivery of the finished birds to the poultry organization. With the income from the organization, George would pay the major costs like feed and small chicks. From the net profit, George was entitled to a third. His obigatory expenses were the wages of the two Egyptians and his traveling expenses. The organization provided the vaccines free of charge. Wood shavings were direct expenses, though George used sand for bedding.

The farm consisted of six hangars newly built, with all equipment new, plenty of pure potable water, away from any other inhabited area, with the set up he could run at least twelve batches in a year, with 10.000 per lot.

Now he had to persuade the farm owners to invest for day-olds and feed.

Instead of going home, he called at the owners' offices, hoping to meet the old man alone.

"If I get him alone and in a good mood, might sell him the program," thought George.

"Hello George?" Hag Mohammed greeted him with good spirits.

"Selam alekoum Hag," said George and seated himself opposite him, the old man very seldom shook hands, though a normal custom with Libyans.

George told Hag Mohammed, what he did at the poultry organization, whom he met, how he was accepted and that he ordered another 10.000 small chicks for 2.244 LD.

"And how are you going to pay this?"

"They accept only certified checks," said George with a low but clear tone.

"They're clever. I'll see Abdullah to arrange it."

"I must deposit that tomorrow."

"You already committed yourself."

"I work with a big family," said, "had to act big."

Hag Mohammed straightened himself in his swivel chair, gave himself a proud posture, and said in slow tone, "at least our name is there."

"Sure it is, Hag," said George reassuring him, "and tomorrow will be another day."

Hag Mohammed went into a monologue that an honest man like him is not afraid of youngsters with brains still green, that times will change; his only complaint was his age.

George waited for the right moment to intervene and his last sentence provided the chance. "Come on Hag Mohammed, yesterday's bridegroom is not that old."

He laughed instinctively. The old man got married only six months ago to the youngest sister of his son's wife. "You know that Amina is pregnant?"

"Well, there you are!."

Moreover, who does not appreciate compliments?

"You said for 10.000 they ask for 2.244 Libyan dinars only?"

"Yes, here is the slip of paper, I noted the sum."

George searched for the paper, did not remember if he ever took anything noted on paper.

Sensing that George could not find his paper, Hag appeased him by saying that he takes his word.

They discussed the advantages and drawbacks of the program. George managed to persuade him of the advantage with such program.

The best part of it, a farmer could plan the running of his farm. If they accepted all the production on fixed dates, the farmer could plan for the new batches. The main objective was to produce healthy plumb chicken in the shortest possible period. With a good product, George had good chances of depleting both hangars in three days. A great advantage arising by selling to the organization was that they kept both delivery cars and cages at a level of hygiene, not like the peddlers who roam from farm to farm with dirty cages.

"You think these pedlars carry chicken diseases?"

"Certainly they do, microbes cling to cars and cages and infect chicken in another farm."

"Many of these peddlers do not wash their cages but you did, I remember."

George laughed at his comments.

"Yes I remember that, instead of allowing a bonus for keeping my cages clean of microbes, you deducted two kilos from the tare for every six cages, you remember?"

"Your cleanliness, this particular detail struck me and here you are now, you know how many people came to rent my farm, and I refused?"

"Yes, I imagine," said George will reservation.

"Come tomorrow and I'll get the check ready."

"Have to deliver it by ten, tomorrow."

After lunch and some rest, George took his calculator along to the farm for a more detailed account. He estimated, if luck was on his side, might make a net sum of 600 dinars per flock of 10.000. Two flocks per month would mean at least a thousand dinars.

Employees with foreign companies were satisfied with barely 300 per month. Certainly, they had a steady salary, but George was not afraid of work, he knew fairly well the poultry industry, even counting the odds.

At home, George spoke as little as possible; could not promise shovelfuls of money.

Back to Mr.Abdulhalim the next day with a certified check, George received a receipt for the payment of 10.000-day-old broilers on 2 September. George talked with him about the already under growth flock of 10.000 broilers.

Mr.Abdulhalim rang up Merry and the outcome was that if the birds after inspection would be acceptable, they would receive them.

They agreed on the date that George would call at the offices of the organization and an officer accompany him to the farm, and if the man would be satisfied with the inspection, the organization might accept the whole quantity.

Everything went to his expectations.

Back to the organization, George met Merry who explained the procedure.

"Two lorries from the slaughtery loaded with plastic cages, accompanied by the farmer to his farm at lunch time. The lorries remain on the farm and the drivers taken to their home in Benghazi. The Farmer would be responsible to fill up the cages; the drivers call at the farm by their own means and deliver them to the slaughtery by 7:00 am, being the starting time of operation. Lorries and birds are weighed, the birds are slaughtered, any dead or discarded by the veterinarian are accounted to the farmer along with the tare of the lorries and empty cages."

"OK, understood."

Everything went to schedule; the problem was who would fill up the cages in the middle of the night and load them in the middle of the night. The two Egyptians did not show any enthusiasm, they tried to exploit the occasion.

Down to Hag Mohammed, another two workers were assigned from the large house with a payment of five dinars each. George had to agree; needed the extra hands.

When he paid the outsiders, his workers demanded the same; George agreed but decided to look for another set of workers They could be of some other nationality, these resented organized work; expected to go free for ten to twelve days between batches, which George could not afford.

The first trip with the two lorries went perfect, not a single problem, the second trip would have gone as well, if there was no problem with a punctured tire, which delayed the delivery by almost half an hour. The delay cost the lives of thirty-two birds.

George demanded the value of those birds, Merry compromised.

The profit was more than expected, Hag Mohammed gave a speech to his eldest son that George made more profit from just one flock of 10.000 than what they did from 25.000 under his management.

Abdullah was a pessimistic person, all he said was, "wait to see," and left.

"Let him go, whatever you need, whatever you do, you discuss it directly with me." Hag Mohammed assured George.

With the sale of the birds they bought more feed, Hag Mohammed wanted to invest all the money in feed, but George suggested to split the profit, not to purchase too much feed, it gets spoiled under hot conditions and the rats of the whole vicinity would come to the farm for a feast.

Hag agreed.

George was happy with the program. He managed to secure day-olds, feed, the sale of the finished birds, but the labor problem remained a headache. George discussed the problem with Hag Mohammed but even he could not help.

Turned his attention to Bob at the fish market square. Bob was happy to see George, even before he offered him a new model of sunglasses; promised to talk to some of his brothers, needed two or three days.

George arranged for an appointment, so that the brothers would be available when he would call back.

Bob being Nigerian, acquired the mentality of people under British rule, he kept his promises.

When George called on Thursday, at four in the afternoon, three of his brothers were sweating under the shade of the ficus.

The two appealed to George, would accept them at least for trial; the third one looked too soft for farm work and was not wrong. Discussed with them there on the spot, the details of the work, the place, the living quarters, the living conditions, the work, the responsibility, the long hours, the loading of live there in the middle of the night, the cleaning of the hangars. Wanted them to realize from the start that farming was not like college attendance.

The two listened carefully, made questions about the salary, and if there was any bonus for extra hours and food allowance.

The salary was normal wages, for bonus one had really to prove his ability and responsibility for such an allowance. George promised a limited quantity of food per week. He explained the foodstuff shortage in Libya. They appreciated his reasoning and agreed for a trial and that they would inform Bob about the date of engagement.

On his way back, dropped at the owner's offices, met Hag Mohammed and discussed the labor problem, then informed him of his arrangements.

"Go ahead, send those Egyptians to me, I will send them off, grew lazy."

The change of labor went smoothly. Now instead of Egyptians with a language barrier had two English-speaking Nigerians.

Bubaker, a man of 40, won a scholarship in religious studies from the Libyan government. Moved to Libya three years back with his family, a very solemn person, quite hard worker, posed as gang leader.

Dandy, whom George thought Nigerian was actually Ganean, he was not more than 23, dropped college after the students' riot at Beida university of religious studies. He spoke how the caterer cheated on the supplies, how the students, all black from African countries, chased him, how they overturned and broke tables, chairs and kitchenware at the university cafeteria, how the police moved in and how nearly all escaped. Most of them came to Benghazi, several registered there at the Garyunis University but quite a number, roamed freely and worked, like Bob.

George asked Bubaker why the police or the university did not punish them for their atrocities.

"You see Boss, we are scholars from Muslim communities of African countries, if they were to punish us, our ambassadors would turn it into a political dilemma, and that's how we got away."

"Is that the only reason?"

He hesitated for a minute, George waited for him, had more to say.

"You see boss, the scholarship for religious studies was the cover for bringing us here."

"What do you mean Bubaker?"

"Whilst studying at Beida, once, maybe twice per month, army officers would call at the university and pick out 40 to 50 students, take us down in the desert. There we lived in tents and had fanatics lecturing rather trying to brainwash us on political subjects."

"Like what political subjects, what could you, or how would you get involved?"

"Not for here, we were doctrined on rioting, on opposing our systems of government and even in guerilla warfare."

George stared astonished; what the Leader could not achieve over the Arabs, tried to stir up African governments. African countries ranking as third world countries, underdeveloped, poverty-stricken would be easy targets for a few crumbs.

George admired those boys who endured such pressures, not only endured but had the guts to revolt against the caterer who stole their food, the instructors who cheated them on the promised curriculum, the system that lured them to this country with false pretensions.

Their endurance against all these sent George a message too, that he should make it clear about the work, the conditions, and their salary.

Both of them easily caught the knack of looking after chicken. George was not worried about their ability to do what had to be done or what he requested them to do, his problem was their reliability of living on the farm and staying there overnight; did not want to police them. To be on the safe side though, talked the matter over with them and both agreed that farm guarding was part of the deal.

George suggested that he would give a lift to anyone down town by his car, provided they returned to the farm before nine in the evening. It was made clear to them and they agreed. George never wanted to patronize them.

Good and honest workers were becoming scarce; George had to play equals

When the day came to load chicken overnight, requested Bubaker to hire another two of his brothers for two nights to help with the extra work.

"If I go down town, I'll manage," he said calmly.

"I'll drop you down, where do you prefer?"

"Up to Bob's place."

George dropped Bubaker near the fish market square, who vanished through the dedaloid streets for his home, George turned back for his home. On the way bought two foam mattresses, two pillows and two blankets, George was careful with the workers requirements.

The delivery of another lot of good chicken to the poultry organization made all of them happy. Merry with the prompt delivery, Ahmed with the quality of the birds and Hag Mohammed with the income.

Small chicks were brought in, feed was carried, birds grew to market weight with a reasonable food convention; the business was flourishing.

Within a few months, George collected several thousand of dinars, being his share.

Apart from the running expenses of his family, Kate was more than pleased. George worked less hours and earned a steady income.

At her request, they visited not only the remaining shops for clothes, shoes, and underwear but also the jewelers. Also allowed them to indulge in the purchase of some pieces of gold, for the girls and their mother.

The steady income revived her; she went about the house cleaning, cooking, washing, ironing, and singing; almost retrieved her old self.

The girls seeing their mother contended spent their energy on studying instead on agony.

One evening after supper, George reminded them of his promise to provide the same conditions that they enjoyed in their home city of Kyrenia and even better.

Kate rose from her seat, came over to her husband, leaned, embraced, and kissed him with tears rolling down her cheeks.

18: The Nigerians

George hired two extra workers on a permanent basis, actually needed only one, but considered it safer to hire two, Dandy and Rahman, both Ghanaians. Their food requirements increased beyond their needs. The most expensive and scarce was the milk powder; sugar, rice, flour, and tealeaves, they managed to scrape off Bob from the cooperative he worked. Meat, they had more chicken than they ate in their whole lives.

Bubaker the most academic, requested permission to refrain from permanent employment due to the increased lectures he had to attend, he was in the last year of his degree. Wanted to complete his studies, obtain a good grade degree and return to his country.

For George three workers were more than enough, was not interested in crowds.

Bubaker was available for part time errands, he had the family to support, was accorded.

George talked to Dandy to adopt the role of the Leader and promised him a financial reward. Despite the young of his age was reasonable and diplomatic, he could manage.

"Hag is not here," said the watchman, "you better go up to the house, the big house, there they are having a gathering, Abdullah is going to Saudia, to Hajj."

"Is he really?"

"Yes he is."

"God bless him, I hope you are the next one."

"Thank you Unani, I pray to my God, I'd love to visit Saudia, to Hajj."

The dream of every Muslim is to visit Saudia, but with Abdullah, a young laureate on physics from Cambridge University, came more than a surprise to many of his friends. Abdullah, according to his father was inert, lazy, stubborn, and very tough with people. A young intellectual like Abdullah, who studied abroad and definitely interested in modern sciences and accept the modern scientific outlook, how could he reconciliate with religion, and get engrossed in traditional religious learning where every word and every phrase is ambiguous. He studied physics, one of the most applied sciences where a scientific formula is undisputedable. Probably may return from his pilgrimage as a thinker, with familiarity in both fields and could attempt a synthesis, which could open up new horizons in a country struggling to set a foothold in the new era of the world.

George drove up to the big house, definitely there was a gathering; despite the restrictions and limitations, many cars of various sizes were parked around the house.

It was called 'big house' according to Abdullah, because of its size and the two storey, it was drowned in green. A thick green fence of jasmine and honeysuckle, dwarf cypress and oleander, four huge conifers stood one on each corner of the garden towering high above the roof of the two-story building. Ahmed the Egyptian boy, who gave a hand for collecting the chicken for the organization slaughtery, came forward to welcome George.

A young Libyan directed him into the house.

Talking, laughing, shouting, and joking came through a heavy door that stood open.

Shoes, many shoes, sandals of all shapes and styles lined up at the entrance; George had to take his off. He removed his shoes, but when he bent down to line them up with the rest, noticed that considerable dust shadowed those shoes, the difference struck him, he came from the farm, they came from their houses for a special visit.

Abdullah was to be seen off for the trip of his life, an honourable trip.

George laid his shoes by the wall near by and briskly walked into the crowded salon. All guests were half stretched out on cushions with Abdullah sitting on a double cushion between his father and an elderly person.

George greeted loudly enough but the visitors were engaged in talking amongst them in small groups and very few noticed him crossing the saloon towards Hag Mohammed and Abdullah, the two he knew best.

Hag Mohammed full of joy with gleaming eyes stretched his hand for a handshake

"To- day," he said, "is the happiest day of my life, my eldest son Abdullah is proceeding to pray at Mecca, you are welcome," and shook George's hand vigorously

George spoke in English fearing of any language mistakes, "with God's will," he said and turned toward Abdullah sitting higher than the others.

He looked sober, quiet, and rather mystic.

George did not dare to tease him for his transfiguration, but smiled to him in an enigmatic way and bid him farewell.

Hag Mohammed asked George to join him, to sit next to him; after greeting the second next to Abdullah, squeezed himself besides Hag Mohammed.

Hag seized the opportunity to turn George's presence into a happening, an event. He spoke loudly and almost all visitors turned their faces towards them.

"Religions," he said, "do not have real differences, if one studies Judaism, Christianity and Islam will find many agreeable similarities."

"Sah, sah wallahi, true, true by God." it was a general acceptance.

"And here," Hag continued, "George, a Christian, a Greek orthodox, one of the most radical sects of Christianity, came to greet his brother, a Muslim going to Mecca for pilgrimage."

"Bravo, bravo," was the epilogue. Now for whom were the exclamations, George could not say.

Helpers circulated huge trays with tens of tea glasses full of frothy tea, another group offered homemade biscuits. The guests were drinking and wishing Abdullah a pious pilgrimage and a safe return.

George lifted a glass of tea, looked Abdullah straight in the eyes, and offered to drive him to the airport.

"I already bought two new white handkerchiefs to tie them on the Peugeot."

He caught the tease, rolled his eyes and contended himself by saying, "thank you."

"When do you expect to come back Abdullah?" asked George.

"The pilgrimage takes normally one month," he said solemnly.

"I'll meet you at the airport."

"You will not recognize me even if you come."

"In a month, will you change to that extent?"

"You will see."

"I hope to my God." Hag Mohammed sighed.

More tea was served; this round was mint tea and more scones.

Just after the mint tea, every single visitor rose to his feet, including Hag Mohammed and Abdullah, George rose too.

Abdullah moved forward and one by one and in ranking order kissed and hugged Abdullah and bid him farewell and safe pilgrimage.

George was the last but one to approach him, shook his hand, and told him, not in Arabic, that he had enough kisses to last him for the pilgrimage.

A couple of days later George called at Hag Mohammed Bruki, he carried with him the usual chicken quota. As soon as he stopped his car near the house, the little son stopped playing with the other barefoot kids of the neighborhood and came running.

He produced his dusty and sweaty hand and George gave his, he held it tight and pulled him towards the house entrance.

George carried the chicken in a green plastic bag with his left hand; the boy thumped the door with his free palm, that usual way of knocking the sun drenched wooden door with the olive green paint peeling off, because the dirty wet palm left its marks on a particular spot.

The girl opened the door, greeted George with a smile, and limped away; she had a polio attack several years back that left her rather deformed.

Whenever George called at the house on previous occasions, this girl was more candid and always took the bag full of chicken. To-day her demeanor sent needles down George's spine.

George handed the bag to her brother, it was heavy for him, he lowered it to the tile floor and pulled it behind him. The tiles were worn out, the plastic bag did not stand the friction, and a trail of chicken fluid followed the bag.

George stood inside the entrance in front of the large hall for more than five minutes.

The girl appeared from a narrow corridor with a key; she unlocked the usual room that Hag Mohammed held his meetings and asked George to enter.

He smiled approvingly, sat on the old sofa, and waited another ten minutes before he heard the drugging of slippers.

The boy led Hag Mohammed to the room; George rose, approached the old man and greeted him warmly.

George had to catch the old man's hand with both of his for the customary handshake, as the man's eyesight deteriorated to a great extend.

He grew very much older since George last saw him and that was not more than two months ago, he kept quiet and waited.

"You know George things are not good at all, no; you know Mustafa was forced to leave Italy, after these bastards killed two Libyans from Benghazi living there. Here we have to close the office, which was the best thing to do and therefore I cannot sign for the renewal of your residence visa, you look for somebody else."

"I am sorry to hear that, Hag Mohammed and I feel pity for those militants who are blinded by animation. Please convey my kindest regards to Mustafa and may Almighty God help him and his family."

"Thank you George, but nobody can see him now, or when, I do not know. Now these bastards are riding for good on our backs."

"Now you cannot arrange for at least another year's residence, Hag?"

The old man focused his sightless eyes towards George with anger and compassion, paused for a long minute, and uttered a dry 'No.'

George wished him health and long life, thanked him for his valuable assistance and that he would call from time to time for his advice and company.

"George, I understand your problem under these bad times and I know that the east wind brings nobody good. I want to tell you frankly, and I swear to my God."

At that very moment, the Sheikh from the Berka mosque was heard. Hag Mohammed lifted his eyes and murmured the typical, "Allah ou Akhbar, God is great," and then lowered his eyes again trying to focus them on to George but while he communicated with Allah, George stepped sideways and now Hag Mohammed was actually focusing the picture hang on the opposite wall.

"I want to thank you, that's what I meant to say before the calling for pray was heard. I am an honest man you know and Allah loves the good people, I want to thank you for the chicken, it's the only meat I can eat, you know very well lamb and veal are getting not only expensive but scarce too."

"Hag Mohammed, I offer you from what we produce and I will continue to help you as much as I can, want to thank you again and wish you good health."

"Maasalamma yea ibni, good buy my son."

George called at Hag Mohammed twice after that, the third time a strange fellow asked what he wanted in the area, since then he stopped calling, Hag Mohammed died before the winter of that year.

Instead of going home, went up to the farm. He paced up and down the dusty yard, walked up to the water tank where the occasional overflowing water gave life to the shrubs and the acacia trees that overgrew and shaded the huge iron tank. Even trees express their gratitude to their benefactor, that's what ran through George's mind when he climbed onto the tank and sat in the shade.

Dandy sensed his funny behavior. Normally, whenever he called at the farm, used to inspect the flocks, beginning from the youngest, but today he paced up and down and then sat in solitude over a tank hundreds of meters away.

"Hey Boss?" said Dandy as he climbed up the ladder, "it's cool here, and it's comforting."

"Hello Dandy?" said cheerfully, for he always kept his problems to himself, "how are your chicken?"

"They're fine."

"Where is Izzy, where is Bubaker?"

"Izzzy is still feeding, I think Bubaker has gone for a shower, he wanted to go to town."

"He has a family," said George quietly.

"Oh gosh, I forgot to tell you that I may have a family soon"

"Dandy what do you mean?"

"Oh! You see Boss the girl I met at the post office."

"Yes, you mentioned her, I remember."

"She likes me and wants me to meet her family."

"You do what? To meet her family?"

George stared at Dandy standing on the ladder with both hands resting on the iron top of the water tank.

"And where is her family?"

"Oh, at Ajdabiya."

"You mean she comes from Ajdabiya, works at the post office, owns a car, and drives around Benghazi?"

Now Dandy stared at George.

"I promised to meet her next Friday and drive to her home town."

"You want my advice?"

"That's why I came to you, Boss."

"All right, you meet the young lady; go to Ajdabiya, meet the family, whoever may be but for God's sake do not stay there overnight. They may press you, as you said she is a widow. Pretend that you may lose your job or something; find an excuse because if you sleep with her, you are caught for good. If I may ask, have you gone to bed with her?"

"No Boss, I swear not"

"Not even once?"

"Never."

"I'll see you on Saturday morning with all the truth," said George in a strong tone.

"Yes Boss, do you need anything from me?"

"Just keep your head on your shoulders."

"Are they that bad at Ajdabiya town?"

"They have a deleterious name."

Dandy slipped down the ladder and George followed to inspect the flocks of chicken. In the third hangar, he met Izzy shaking off the feed dust from his jeans.

"Hello Izzy, boy."

"I'm fine Boss."

"You finished feeding?"

"Just now."

"You know, but tomorrow you can do it, lift those waterers a little bit; I think, I explained that the lips of the waterers should be at the height of the back of the chicken, I did, didn't I?'

"Boss, you did, you want me to do that now, I will do it?"

"You do that tomorrow first thing in the morning; did you have any dead today?"

"One, just one."

"Where is it?"

"It's here in this plastic bag."

George inspected the dead bird, it was a bad doer, should have been culled long ago.

"You should have removed this bird long ago, such weak chicks are disease carriers."

Izzy took the dead bird, returned it in the bag, and hurried to throw it in the pit.

George followed him to make sure that he threw the dead in the pit. It was a venture, disposing dead birds; the boys used to cover their nose and mouth with a handkerchief before pulling the disposal pit cover and dump the dead in it.

"That's another good reason, better take care that birds do not die."

"Yes, you are right Boss."

On their way to the rooms met Dandy, he lingered around to catch up on him.

"Boss you know Dandy got a girl friend?"

"I think he found a headache," said George.

They walked speechless for most of the way; George turned to Izzy and asked him, "how about you?"

"Not in this bloody country," said categorically.

"Come, come Izzy, I only teased you."

"I know, but here they do not like black boys."

"Come on, Dandy is not that white."

"Dandy honestly, is your girl dark?"

"No Boss, normal color."

"And what is normal color?" Izzy asked.

"Remind me to bring a paintbrush tomorrow."

"Boss, are you going to paint me white?"

"Any color you prefer."

"Except green," he said emphatically.

"Or black."

"Our boss is in good spirits," said Dandy.

George was about to get into the car when Bubaker shouted from afar. "Mr. George, Mr. George?"

"He wants you to drop him downtown."

Bubaker like the other two, liked to shower twice daily and now he was hurrying with his towel around his waist; as he walked, the wind blew the towel away showing his thin long legs.

"Al-right, Al-right teacher, we know, you have attractive legs," teased him Izzy.

"O! Ah, do I?"

"Mr. George, can you drop me downtown?"

"Up to the bus stop of Tripoli crossroads."

"Thank you, that's good enough for me."

"I'll wait for you to cover up yourself."

"That means half an hour," intervened Dandy.

"I got married long ago."

With Bubaker on board George bid goodnight to Dandy and Izzy.

"OK, Izzy?"

"Boss, I will do that, first in the morning."

Izzy had a bad record of keeping promises.

"Mr. George, do you have any money with you? I need say ten dinars, may be."

"I think, I have something, when we stop."

"Life is not easy, foodstuffs are scarce and expensive."

"You are right."

"I cannot find baby food now."

"Oh, didn't I bring you some a couple of days ago?" George said in a sympathetic tone.

"Can you not register, say at the university's cooperative?"

"Nobody listens to us, we are black."

"About baby food I cannot promise much, here is ten dinars and God is great."

"Great or not great, we are suffering." Said Bubaker; the scholar of religious studies.

George dropped Bubaker at the bus stop, buses were still circulating, though many were using the private transportation, there was no control.

19: More changes

About the meeting with Hag Mohammed Bruki, George kept it to himself, wanted to ask Hag Mohammed Benily, the farm owner, for transferring his visa on his name, Kate was kept out of the problem.

Hag Mohammed Benily was a businessperson, he figured out everything with a pencil in hand. The poultry farm was doing well; George was running day and night to manage not only the day's program but also the problems created by the situation.

When George requested him for the transfer of the visa in his name, the old man promised to help and arranged a meeting with his accountant for the purpose. After discussing the matter, Hag Mohammed accompanied George to the income tax office. There through a friend of his, George was registered and paid his income tax for the last three months; then with a note from the tax office George called at the Wahda bank where he opened an account. This was his first significant account, was registered as a reasonably high salary employee from which he could transfer 90 percent, which was a decent amount; George was satisfied with Hag Mohammed's response.

Afterwards, arranged the usual medical tests certificate like every foreign employee and prepared all documents for the registration with the Labor office and thereafter with the immigration. Matters were moving at a very reasonable pace.

In the neighborhood, people were going about their daily occupations, the males to their work as before except Hamid who transferred from the broadcasting section to the newly formed Housing department.

Nasser instead of going to his mysterious work was getting ready to take his wife to London for medical treatment. Unisa had a serious health problem.

Kate visited her several times after her discharge from the Hawari hospital, the woman complained of chest pains and a swollen belly.

Kate tried to console her, but the problem according to the Yugoslav specialist was pretty serious, and advised them to seek further medical examinations in a European country and possibly medical treatment.

Nasser with his connections had the paperwork concluded within days, the London hospital, the currency, and even the doctors for the investigation.

Kate offered herself to help Nasser's four children; Unisa was moved by Kate's offer to undertake four uncontrollable children during her absence. She thanked Kate with tears in her eyes, called the two elder children, and in front of Kate instructed them in case they were not happy with their grandmother to return home and Madam Kate would take care of them.

Both kids Jamal and Nadia kissed Kate and thanked her.

Hag Nasser was a prominent figure amongst the revolutionaries; he could be a pier for any future matters.

Hamid was appointed as head of the investigative group in the housing department. His authority was broad and variable; he would investigate and confiscate any extra house or apartment. Was authorized to break into any suspected dwelling and identify the occupant.

He broke into villas occupied by foreigners who left either for vacation or for work and removed furniture and accessories at will. Such movable furnishings and materials found their way to black marketeers. Within weeks he drove in a Chevrolet, wore two-piece suits, double furnished his ramshackle with expensive sitting rooms, dining rooms and stereos, and God knows what else.

Besides, he acquired several mistresses, Egyptians in majority. He spent very few nights with his nine-member family.

Every time he parked his acquired American car outside his old house, his elder sons would wash it and rub it with woolen cloth until the sun reflection would dazzle the neighbors.

Though Hatitjia, his Bedouin wife, wore less color than he did, he neglected her and abandoned her, left to prepare pots of homemade pastry for the multi-member family.

Kate with the soft heart handed her four to five chicken weekly. Hatitjia, with a trembling voice and running eyes, kissed her on both cheeks.

When George talked to Hamid about an apartment for a good Cypriot family friend, he remained aloof. Even when George insisted for his help, he treated Vassos absurdly.

George arranged with Hamid an appointment, when Vassos called as agreed; Hamid was too busy locked inside with two Egyptian women searching for something, probably a house for them.

"Nobody is here," said the tea boy at Benily offices, they're all at Abdullah's house, he returned from his pilgrimage."

"Oh, Hag Adullah returned?"

"That's right, Hag Abdullah now."

"When did he come?"

"More than three days, now."

George thought that was the right time to call upon Hag Abdullah and welcome him.

He rang the bell at Hag Abdullah's house, once, twice, three times but got no answer.

He walked around to the garden; the Egyptian was watering the flowers, "not here, everybody at Hag Muftah's house, Abdullah's father-in-law, you can go there," said the Egyptian as soon as he saw George.

Wanted to ask a few questions about the customs when someone returns from his pilgrimage but the worker turned his back and continued his job.

Hag Muftah's house was not very far, George decided to drive up to there. Very few cars were outside the house, George said to himself either Abdullah returned secretly or the party was over. The second concept was the correct.

The entrance was open, so he walked in freely; he heard somebody talking and called out 'hello.'

A woman met him at the hall; George took her as the house cleaner, but noticed that she was a disabled person with a handicapped arm and crippled hand.

"Abdullah," she said softly.

George followed her, he felt strange, very seldom a woman answers the calling of a stranger and more to a foreigner, it seems the prohibition does not apply to disabled family persons.

Abdullah was sitting on a cushion in the corner of the large salon with his father along with two strangers unknown to George. Probably discussing something personal, because they stopped abruptly at his sight.

Abdullah wore the traditional embroidered three-piece assembly, grew a goatee beard, had his head shaved and covered with a towel that hang down to his face. He looked amusing with the noble outfit, a shaven skull, half hidden by a greenish cotton towel where the tips of it mixed with the goatee beard.

He was solemn when George bent down to greet him, so restrained himself from any indiscreet expressions.

"Welcome, Hag Abdullah," said George in a blithesome way.

"Thank you Mr. George, thank you very much, I wish you go for a pilgrimage to Jerusalem or wherever Christians go."

"Thank you very much, my people ceased going to such places long ago."

"I do not think my son would like to go," Abdullah was astute.

Hag Mohammed eyed him sideways; he belonged to the old stock where the addition of Hag to the name meant affluence, respect.

"Times are changing father," said Abdullah.

"Yes, but the pilgrimage to Mecca will never die out, it's the proof of Muslim coherence."

"From the third world countries yes, but from here I doubt it very much."

"A Muslim is a Muslim," said Hag Mohammed.

"A Muslim was a Muslim," added Hag Abdullah.

"Well, shall we stick to religious rigidity?"

"Would you prefer scientific monomania," Hag Mohammed said.

"I wouldn't go to religious fanaticism."

"Even religions are changing," said George.

"Faster than before. Many factors are influencing religions, like communist doctrines, increased education, increased contacts with the West, admission of females in higher education and even the study of ancient philosophy that goes far back before religions have been carved on stones. The matter requires a good thinker who has familiarity with both fields and could attempt a synthesis, which would open up new intellectual horizons," added Hag Abdullah.

The old man was side looking his sibling that has just returned from a pilgrimage.

"As history moves on, people have to change roles and beliefs. The fundamental problem in Muslim culture is that the political and social conditions that are necessary for the development of a culture have not existed," George said.

Tea was served and Hag Abdullah pulled out his silver beaded pulpit and began dropping the beads one after the other, rather noisily.

"So, how was your sacred pilgrimage, Hag Abdullah?"

He eyed George from behind his spectacles, his eyeballs seemed larger and he looked funnier.

"You see George, at this time of the year many people call for the pilgrimage, more than two million from many countries, like Indonesia, Pakistan, India, China, even Japan. You cannot tell the difference with sculls shaven and dressed in the holy long robes, the Ihram as is known, and then you have all those from the Middle East countries, from Nigeria a lot, even from Europe, the United States; from many nationalities with variable customs of different standard of living and acute diversity of education."

"You mentioned Ihram."

"Oh! Yes, is the dress that every pilgrim wears, and that shows the equality for a prince or a pauper."

"And you know," Hag Mohammed intervened and added that when the pilgrim wears the ihram, cannot shave, clip his nails, wear deodorant or perfume, may not swear or quarrel or kill any living creature."

"Or engage in sexual intercourse," Hag Abdullah added.

"The ones who cash on that are the Saudis. The charge for a single room, for two persons with no private bath or toilet, for a week, is much more than you may pay for a whole villa here for a whole month."

"Really! And where is the brotherhood?"

"Brotherhood! Only to get people there."

"You spend fifteen days approximately at Mecca, this is the ritual program."

"I did not see you going round the Kabbah?"

Even Hag Mohammed was agitated by George's questions.

"You would not recognize me even if you saw me; hundreds of thousands of people go round the Plaza of the sacred stone, every minute."

"And they throw stones."

"What does it really symbolize this stoning?"

"Ah! To kill the devil."

"Is the devil still alive, for how many years the pilgrims stone him considering the multitude of stones thrown at him."

"Really where do they get the stones from?"

"You buy them my dear, everything with money."

"Actually, they come from the mount of Arafat."

"How many times one has to go round before is entitled to touch the holy stone, Hag?"

"Seven times, counterclockwise."

"Is this a ritual?"

"Of-course, everything is ritual."

"And have to kiss the Kabbah."

"With more than two million pilgrims, is impossible for all those persons to kiss the holy stone, may align themselves and point to the stone."

George was learning about the rituals of a Muslim pilgrim.

"You know a bottle of water and I don't think is always certified bottled water, costs as much as a metric ton here?"

"Would you call it sheer exploitation?"

"Well…"

"Al-right if a bottle of water is so expensive, how do the poorer classes of pilgrims manage?"

"Oh! There is piped water at a distance but many thieves go there; you hear stories of stealing and your hair will stand up."

"If any hair left on the heads for the occasion," said George.

Hag Abdullah pulled the towel forward and covered his bear scull; the beads were going and coming.

"Well after the two weeks in holy Mecca?"

"Ah, you have to go to Medina, the next holy city where the conditions are worse. It is a much smaller town with fewer facilities, but there, one may spend his time at his room with one of two visits at will to the holy places."

"Well, are these the obligations, or one has to attend sermons and preaches?"

"Oh yes, they do not let you in peace, the sheikhs and the loudspeakers are busy day and night."

At this point, the two visitors departed casually. There remained just the three, farther, son and the Holy Spirit with George teasing Hag Abdullah.

"Now, you, as a rich, educated young person, what have you acquired from your pilgrimage, Hag Abdullah?"

"To tell the truth, not much, when a sheikh climbs up the pulpit and preaches for hours about the proper way of killing animals, for me is too much. I understand that the meat we eat should come from animals killed the halal way, but that is neither proper nor the right time for preaching over thousands of people."

"There is nothing wrong to that?" said Hag Mohammed.

"I agree, but was not the right time. The worst was, when the same sheikh talked about fish killed the halal way. I got mad; wanted to leave not only the ceremony but drop the whole idea."

"Maybe the sheikh was directing his preaching to third country pilgrims," added Hag Mohammed.

"Third country people tend to follow their customs, many times their tribal customs, rather than Muslim jurisprudence and know little of religion beyond the ritual words they have memorized but scarcely comprehend; they are chiefly concerned with deriving a scanty living from their occupation. For them, food is more important than religion."

"Still they go and are the majority," Hag Mohhamed added.

On the way home, George considered the outcome from such pilgrimages; it was hard to decide, being alien to the religion with a different mental approach probably misinterpreted what he heard at Hag Mohammed's house.

"Where have you been?" said Margarita, as soon as she opened the door.

George took her hand and went inside. Kate was in bed with a wet towel on her forehead, she had a bad headache.

Sonia was helping Mary with her lessons.

George kissed his wife; she woke up, smiled at her and asked if she needed any help.

"You're late George, dear."

"Went to visit Abdullah."

"Oh! is he back? I hope he changed."

"Yes he changed; he looks rather funny with a shaved skull and the new outfit."

"A Muslim is always a Muslim."

"Well, it's none of our business."

"What is wrong Kate?"

"I have a bad headache."

"Whenever there is a gibli coming you are suffering."

"The desert wind kills me."

"All right, let's go to eat something. Sonia, can you set the table, please?"

"Yes Mum, it's ready."

20: *Change of Libyan currency*

On Thursday evening, a heavy announcement over the television informed Libyans and non, that as from Friday morning the existing money notes of five and ten dinars would be no more valid.

It came as a sledgehammer on the head of almost every person living within the Jamahiriya. By custom, the locals did not show any interest or trust to carry their transactions through the banks, preferred to keep their money at home. A common joke was that the rich had no more tiles in their kitchens to hide their money.

It was clearly stated that the respectable Libyans and all those foreigners working legally in the country, should call at any bank within a week to exchange their money. Every Libyan was entitled to one thousand dinars and those aliens holding a valid working permit to two hundred and fifty. The announcement brought chaos.

Those who had money panicked and those who did not have caught the opportunity to cash on the turmoil and the bank officials crept undercover, too many criers.

George went early to the farm. He was not surprised to find the workers dressed up and ready to go, they had some money to change.

"What happened?"

"Boss, you didn't hear the news?"

"What news, Izzy?"

"The Leader wants to change the money."

"He wants to change everything."

"Except our color," said Izzy amusingly.

"Go to the car and bring the brushes and the paint."

"Boss, is it white, or...?"

"Why, white...?"

The laughter was unbelievable.

"Somebody is coming."

"Hello Salem?"

"Good morning, how are you folks?"

"You heard the news…?"

"Yes. I came to pay my dues."

"Have you changed money?"

"To-day is Friday."

George looked at Salem disappointed. The man owed several thousands from his last purchase and now he came to get rid of the old money.

In a cold atmosphere, Salem handed the money, George placed it in a plastic bag without even counting it, Salem was on his way, George looked at the paper money and thought,

Another pile of useless paper, there was nothing he could do, had to accept the settlement.

"Boss, we want to go to Bayda."

"Why to Bayda, this is a simple transaction; anyone can go to any bank and exchange the allowed amount."

"Boss, where do you live, this is an Arab country. We want to go; there we have our people to help us."

"Boys, I cannot cope with all the present load of work. Wouldn't it be better for all of us if two remained behind and go as soon the first ones return?"

Eyebrows turned to knots and eyeballs to the sky, revealing a lot of white.

George remained silent, expected an understanding. In the end logic prevailed.

"Boss, we'll do that just for you and not for the Libyan farm owner, he does not respect us."

"Thank you; you understand my position, as to our friend, that's your opinion."

All walked up to the hangars, the day's work was already completed. George tried to kill time, which proved impossible. The two, trailed George around, he reached the car, tried to make them understand that he would be back in the afternoon, they insisted to ride with him, get their pay and push off to Bayda. George was trapped, gave in, drove to his house, paid them, and let them go.

In the town, people were dashing in every direction asking for information that nobody could give. Nobody had any answers.

The poor ones clung to one another like terrified mice, whispering in an uncomfortable way. No Libyan goes against his government. Some people are excitable and rebellious by nature, but the Libyan keeps his head down his whole life long, so he can eat.

It was clear that the five and ten dinar notes were valid no more. All this kind of cash had to be deposited at the bank. The Libyans would be given a thousand dinars in the new currency and the aliens two hundred and fifty, provided they had a valid working permit. Any amount beyond that would be deposited in the owner's name and pray to Allah.

Rumours spread quickly and renowned names of George's neighbourhood delivered to the banks bagfuls of money, money dug out of the kitchens, out of the hideouts, out of the bunkers. A certain Abdussamad loaded a pick up with more than eight million, delivered it to the bank, received the permitted amount of one thousand, returned home, climbed to the top of his three-storey villa, and dived to his death.

Another well-known citizen, Mohammed Sunki, took the long road to his huge farm, lost control of his expensive car, toppled over and remained crippling on the wheel chair.

George finished the work on Saturday and drove down town, wanted to see with his own eyes what was going on at the center, where the banks were. Unbelievable, double lines cordoned the banks. People standing in position for hours, waiting patiently their turn to enter the holy place for their hard way earned money.

The line hardly moved. The friend of the friend crept through the back door, was served, and exited like an individual; the secular had to pay their dues to the blazing sun, the lukewarm soft drink, and the stale round bread.

Many were those who cashed on the occasion. The smart ones undertook to change the extra money with a share of fifty per cent.

George had some extra money from his dealings. He thought of requesting the help of his patrons, they were locals, definitely would be able to assist him at this difficult time.

Called at Hag Abdullah, took tea with him, and requested his help.

"You know Mr. George; I have some extra myself and to tell the truth, thought of a close relative of ours. He is living off the alms he takes from us, is actually a beggar. You know according to Zakat, the rich people are obliged to give two and a half per cent of their income to the poor, and as a good Muslim, gave this relative my share. When I asked him to help me, you know what he said?"

"I have myself more than three thousand and don't know how I can change it, do not want the bank and eventually the Leader to know of my possessions, may cut off my allowance."

"You see there are no poor people here, do not listen to the criers."

George left wiser but disappointed.

"Mr. George, good afternoon."

"Good afternoon Hag Nasser."

"Have you changed your money or not yet."

"Thank you, Hag; I did, as a matter of fact."

"Any problem?"

"I'll tell you if anything crops up."

"Come in, got some friends coming for a cup of tea."

"I'll come in a few minutes; let me wash up myself now."

" Don't delay, a big car is coming, I think it's them."

"Hello Unani, how are you, have they skinned you?"

Although, George knew those people well enough to express himself freely, still they were loyal to the revolution.

"Even if you deposited any extra money, don't worry, Nasser can help you."

"What are you talking about, yia Abdullah, he is not a Libyan. He will not go to Hajj, he will not get married to another woman, he will not build his house and cannot draw money for higher education of his grown up children."

"Still, he is working here legally, has his valid working permit, can transfer delayed salaries."

George listened carefully the two talking and relaxed somehow, could be able to transfer the extra money deposited at the bank. Could he trust those friends? Several times, they gave away some forth-coming calamities, Nasser proved reasonably positive.

George sitting with Nasser and his friends thought whatever he liked but was obliged to behave like the others, he talked and laughed as the others, those who had a secure job, a house to live in and took life as it came to them, if time mattered or not, that was another question. Only tea was available today.

"Yia Nasser, you ran out of water?"

"The tap dried out, yia Abdullah, and to-day you'll just get water and a very nice piece of cake."

George heard Nasser promising cake to his friends, wondered if the cake was the one that Kate prepared for Amina's birthday, sipped his tea and waited. He was right, that was the cake.

"Nasser, where did you get this wonderful cake, it looks excellent, professional. Is it from El-Shams?"

"No, they closed down, like all the other confectioneries in town."

"Honestly, from where? Really looks very well done, with all the shortages in the country."

"What did the Leader say in his speech about the confectioneries?"

"Yes, he said, 'how does one make cakes, mixes flour from France, butter from Holland and sugar from Cuba, I don't know exactly and the cake is done,' he forgot the water and the essence."

"The women could do that in their homes, what do they do all day long?"

"Mabrouka tried to bake cakes; she baked them but came out harder than bricks."

"And where was your first wife?"

"Oh! She is just a Bedouin."

"This is marvelous, isn't it? Thank you Madam Kate."

"Poor Amina, we ate your birthday cake," said Abdullah.

"Yia Yunani, you don't brew firewater? Nasser has run out of whiskey."

"George does not even drink alcohol and is not a Muslim, yia Abdullah."

"Thank you Hag Nasser, as a matter of fact I do not drink, not even when I go outside of the country."

"I noticed that last time we met here, is that right yia Nasser?"

"You haven't seen Kerella lately; he used to bring this stuff from Tobruq."

"They transferred him from there, more than two months now."

"He made a mint from there over the last year. Sold the bloody scotch for sixty dinars a bottle, stuff that he got for nothing."

"You know how they traded sugar, oil, and rice with the Egyptians across the border?"

"They found a donkey…"

George must have reacted at the word donkey, because Nasser stopped talking and looked inquisitively.

"With Kerella is different. You know they trained the animal to cross the border all the way of no-man's land and reach the Egyptian outpost, there the oil and other foodstuffs were unloaded, the animal was given food but no water; the Egyptians placed whiskey, cigarettes and God knows what else, and let the animal loose. As it felt thirsty, took the way back to drink water at the Libyan outpost, carrying its precious load along. This went on for God knows, how long."

"So, that's how Kerella got the scotch and the rest."

"And the house."

"Good for him, too many fools around."

The change of money turmoil has not yet died out and the topic of the extra apartment or an extra house began bubbling. A lot of talking, many hypotheses, and considerable volume of tea drank, and many cigarettes smoked; the extra housing asset went to the new Housing Department. People realized that they depended on someone for their housing needs, had to go to him for that. He was the one who stirred up the waters to catch fish.

The Leader preached the need for change, was though careful, reforms followed a succession, avoided too much at a time.

House parties and family visits kept to the minimum, the Libyans who rented any kind of housing did not want the informers see those foreigners going and coming to their property.

The house owners accepted the fact that nothing could not be bypassed and laws are not fixed, so began finding ways of evading them.

The decree stated that every Libyan was entitled to a house, did not specify the size of it, so people got busy pulling down walls and turning two and sometimes three appartments into one, big enough to house twenty grown ups.

George's house owner turned from a friendly person to a hostile one. At first stopped greeting his tenant, then made it a habit to climb on the roof of the second floor just above George's flat and crush small stones to make gravel for some reason. It was not only annoying but deafening too. George complained to him, he simply laughed his head off. After that began knocking down the middle walls next to the staircase and made a habit to lie on a foam mattress with his Bedouin wife, very embarrassing and indecent. George smelled trouble, talked the matter with several friends, but got no answers.

It was Friday afternoon and George started his car, to pay a visit to the farm. The moment he set off, his house owner followed him closely. At such times, on Fridays, streets are deserted and people scarse, George felt the bitter threat of a Bedouin drove slowly and watched the car behind him. He reached the main road and decided to drop at the petrol station, wanted to make sure, if his follower really was after him. The man did follow him closely, the moment George stopped by the pump, he drove to his side and bellowed in English twice, 'I'll kill you,' and drove away fast.

George froze; the pump attendant noticed the scene and heard the threats.

"Who is he? What does it mean, kill you, kill you, Mister, what does it mean?"

"You heard him; he is the land lord and wants to kill me."

"You go to the police; I'll testify what I heard."

"Yes, thank you, what is your name, please?"

"I will, do not worry, you lost your color Mister. My name is Mohammed."

"Another Mohammed, thought George," and drove away.

George got very scared and instead of going to the farm, afraid of lonely roads where humans have no value and may easily vanish with no one to search or find them, turned back drove to his old friend Yianni.

On the way called at Hag Abdullah. His wife came to the door, when she saw George's face bent forward and asked in a pleading tone, "What happened, you look very pale?"

"Is Hag Abdullah home, can I see him?"

"Yes, come in," and almost took George by the hand to help him inside.

The once active, Cambridge laureate and shrewd entrepreneur was barefooted lying on the thick carpet of his huge salon shrouded in melancholia.

George told Hag about the threat from his house owner, did not express any interest, simply advised George to look for another place to live.

"The town is rotting; nobody can predict their next move. Dismantled the private enterprises, demolished the private workshops, confiscated private housing, changed the money, rounded up the young ones, blindfolded religion, personalized the country's income, and sent everybody begging for food and commodities."

"Manipulates water and electricity," added George.

When George pleaded once more to him to intervene for the sake of his family, the answer was that according to their religion, they do not go for the women.

"It is in our religion," added casually.

George was on his feet, with Hag Abdullah's statement, almost sent him and his belief to the bloody hell, instead swallowed the lump, and took the way out and considered of knocking at another door.

Pressure was applied everywhere, the huge revolutionary machine tumbled down dignitaries and families with power and dominance.

People now were equal, if there is ever such an equation. All penniless, homeless, without any occupation; their workshops closed, their farms depleted from labor, their scanty produce traded by the government controlled organizations, their sons recruited in the army, their mouths closed, their ears blocked, their eyes went color blind, saw only green, their minds confused, too many laws issued day after day, no life and no foresightedness, no future.

Eccentricity, fanaticism, and hypocrisy brought decline, depression, gloominess, drowsiness, melancholia.

The snippet without thought or screening became an elephant and the animal trotted without discrimination intellectuals, sane, morons, smart, lazy, thrifty, industrious just name them.

In the late seventies, persons who struggled for two decades to get established, found themselves in fathomless surroundings and quicksand, mainly in Cyrenaica, the township of Benghazi, once the center of the late kingdom of Libya.

"Klaus, you are here, I want you to investigate that clan of Warfallah, the one with the reactionaries. Get Farag to sum up the strong clans in all my country, I want the plan..."

"To-day, Great one?"

"To-day I'm busy, got to pay a visit to the souq ad dahab, the gold market, they tell me that some of those cunning ones use their spouses to trade gold ornaments."

"Ah! You mean family, traditional belongings, their last valuables?"

The great Leader side looked the East German technocrat heading a group of advisory experts to the revolutionary government.

"I want your suggestions by tomorrow night, now I have to change into some kind of outfit, may be Bedouin."

Klaus called his collaborators and began scrutinizing, gathered information, and personal experience from his own country.

"First of all, we'll try to isolate each group leader, study him, pin point his favorites and shortcomings, including marital, financial and social status, investigate for any defaults and if not plant one or two."

Those were the instructions and the intelligence machine got down to work.

"Great one, we've studied the three bigger clans and probably the most influential, with the Warfallah acting as the leading one."

"All those who hold key positions will be either transferred to some distant place or forced to resign, if they accept long term leave would be as good."

Those engaged in trading, will be forced to look for some other way to make a living.

Family members being within the range for army recruitment will be called for registration. In the army will be under direct, strict control, being males or females. If members are transferred to a remote place, away from their normal environment, that nullifies their authority and influence.

Henry has a wonderful idea, to issue a decree forbidding the use of the clan name as a surname and so neither recognition nor influence may be implemented."

"Klaus, that's a great idea, cut the nomenclature to say, three names, many of my people are called Mohammed, Ahmed and so on."

"How about those customary intermarriages?"

"Intermarriage is a great bond of cohesion. It may not be that easy to break down, it is a long-term process, and customs need time to change. A normal way is through education, both sexes pursue further education, in such institutions, vigilance is closer, and youngsters tend to look for their partner, ignoring parental interference. Marriages between individuals from different clans help reduce friction between the clans and simultaneously weaken them. Clans tend to group since their nomadic life and live collectively. If you bring the housing under your control, may regulate the provision of roof and closer supervision. Confiscate the extra house and apartment in the name of the needy ones, in the name of the revolution."

"Klaus, you are genius, anything else up your sleeve?"

"Restrict traveling, going abroad they gather ideas and meet with the reactionaries."

"Good afternoon, Hag Nasser."

"Hello George?" answered Nasser with a droopy face; did not even turn to see the man who greeted him.

George sensed that something serious must have happened and Nasser was in such a cloudy mood.

He crossed the broad dirty street to greet his neighbor in private.

"Her yia haboob, hello my dearest?"

"Tea, yia George? Sit, there is an extra cushion."

"By God, I have to go to the farm, but I'll take a glass of tea, if it's ready?"

"There, the tea kettle is there."

George lifted one of those tiny tea glasses off the water flooded tray and poured himself some lukewarm tea.

"You heard the news, the bad news, George?"

"Not really."

"Didn't you hear about the plane brought down, just before landing at Tripoli airport?"

"Heard about a plane crash."

"What crush George, it was shot down, and all passengers and crew died within minutes."

"God bless their soul, the most gracious, and the most merciful."

"Rubbish the plane was knocked down by his Tripoli bastards."

"Anyone from the family?"

"Here in Benghazi, all of us are one family. You remember Abdullah, my friend you met here in my house."

"Yes, I do."

"Well, he was one of them."

"But this is cruel, horrible."

"Cruelty, sheer assassination that is how those Tripoli bastards thrive on. He ordered all those that opposed his opinion about the terrible situation to go to Tripoli for a meeting and talk the matters over, they never reached Tripoli, were killed on the way."

George shook his head up and down thus expressing his feelings.

"George, here in Cyrenaica, all of us are Senussi, the sect of our king. Muammar wants to change everything that smells Senussi, even demolished their family tombs. No funds find their way eastwards of Tripoli and beyond Sirte, the new city. Although the petrol is extracted from this area, the country's income derives from here, but the Leader misuses all this income. He either purchases shares in various foreign manufacturers like the Mercedes or the Fiat or even in football clubs. He hands lots of money to the so-called revolutionary groups around the world, from Ireland to Indonesia. The Leader and his cronies take advantage of the rotten situation and use funds for personal purposes."

"That's how, that son of the Bedouin thrives."

An approaching car was slowing down and George pardoned himself, had to look after his chicken.

21: *Wind of confiscations*

Construction in the private sector not only diminished but died out completely. The long rows of trucks loaded with cut white stone from Ajdabiya stopped coming, the crushers stopped operation, and track owners parked their vehicles in their yards.

The locals envied the expatriates working with foreign companies; they had a steady income, enjoyed smuggled foodstuffs and the parties held by their consulates.

The expatriates envied the locals who owned their homes and enjoyed the fresh scanty produce from their farms.

The envy created silent enemies, suspicion, few opened their doors to visitors, relatives or not. The expatriates grouped within their compatriots, even at that visits diminished to the minimum.

"Dad, the bell, are you going to open?"

"Who could be? What's the day to-day?"

"Dad it's Monday, what, you lost count."

"If we carry on like this, I don't know what will happen to me?"

"Dad, you better see the door?'

"Welcome, what a surprise, please come in."

"You almost forgot us, what happened to you, we live in the suburbs and with the schools closed, very few cross our street and even less our doorstep," said Kate to the visitors.

Anna looked at Kate bewildered, took a seat at the oversize table, and left a sigh, she had something to say, to extricate. Demis preferred the head of the table.

"We are having Nescafe, you care for a cup?" asked George.

"Nescafe, you still have? We ran out for more than two weeks."

"Well, you'll bring fresh supplies shortly, when are you going for leave?"

"Leave, Mr. George? We cannot travel; the army took Demis' passport."

"They did what, why?"

"You haven't heard our breaking story?"

Demis and Anna lived in an apartment facing the sea front, only meters from the government office complex. Around the small square stood the buildings housing the courts, the land registration offices, and the ports administration.

"We haven't moved around these days, you know the situation, but we are all ears," said George.

Kate brought four cups of steaming Nescafe prepared with fresh milk that George managed to trade with some poultry meat. The aroma tickled the nostrils and made the eyes brighter.

"You see Mr. George, when was it, let me think."

"It's more than a week now," said Anna.

"Yes, actually six days ago, last Wednesday afternoon, it must have been four o'clock, the sun still high and you know our salon windows face west and we were sitting inside; normally we go to the balcony after seven when the sun goes down and the sea breeze is cool. Heard engine noises and looked through the window; trucks came into the small square and dumped piles of files, box files, flat files, and carton boxes. Soldiers with automatic weapons rounded the pile of paper; a tractor appeared from nowhere and pushed the whole lot into a mount. Two or three soldiers poured kerosene onto the pile and set it on fire. Out of interest or out of curiosity, took the camera and shot some photos. Must have been shooting the fourth one, when a hand grabbed the camera from behind, I was shocked and let it go."

"Turned and faced not only the one holding my camera but four armed persons. The questioning began, who I am, why take photos in restricted areas, where do I work."

"They asked questions so fast that couldn't either follow or answer them in time"

"Then he was taken away along with his passport and the camera," said Anna.

"Yes, we went to the police in Berka; there I was questioned viciously. Where do I work, who is my sponsor, why did I take those photos and so many other questions? They asked about Anna, if she was my wife, then why she lives with me?"

Kate thought that a good meal would activate the stomach and pacify the brain. She left; within than half an hour the aroma from the kitchen reached the nostrils and agitated the saliva secretion. In that short time, she prepared seven plateful with fried chicken, fried potatoes, and a nice salad; all enjoyed it and washed down food and bitterness with medium dry wine, which George prepared two years ago.

"In your house Mr. George," Anna said, after the third glass of Brusque, "I feel relaxed, secure, and revived."

"I'm glad that you feel better, you care for another drop?"

With Kate's sumptuous meal and George's understanding both felt a lot better, regained confidence. Over the coffee Demis told them the rest of his calamity.

"You know they still keep my passport."

"Don't worry, give them time, you will get your passport."

They returned his passport on his way out of the country via Tripoli since Benghazi airport was closed to international flights. Demis was put in custody for forty-eight hours, questioned on his treacherous act against the democracy of the Libyan revolution, was blacklisted for his fault, and expelled from the country.

The pile of property registration certificates smoldered for days; the sea breeze spread around smoke and ashes. The smoke reached the nostrils of those who owned the property and the ashes their eyes. A bitter feeling overwhelmed whole families, who for generations toiled to reclaim marshy areas of the city of Benghazi and found the city that a boisterous self-appointed Leader wanted to destroy.

Once they destroyed the deeds, the bulldozers moved in, and crushed hangars, sheds, and small factories, even properly built. The strong man considered all the small enterprises unnecessary. Many of those lining Tripoli road did not stand the wrath, were demolished to make room for agricultural produce. Thousands of acres lay forgotten for ages, good productive land on the outskirts of the city stood unexploited, the only few acres missing were the ones small businesses were built on.

Many saw their lifetime savings vanish within hours; nobody could utter a word, nowhere to complain. The people's committees were busy with matters that were more important.

The state owned television was busy with announcements, decrees, and shows from expeditions to ransacked villas and destroyed businesses.

The appointment of an agricultural committee gave hope to the struggling farmers, expected some assistance to improve their farms, they were bitterly disappointed.

The decree read, "in order to achieve a general improvement in agricultural production all farmers must have equal opportunities. Therefore, the high surrounding farm walls must be knocked down to no more than one meter. It was clearly stated that special inspecting groups of the revolutionary forces will demolish any solid wall above the height of one meter and the expenses charged to the owner of such farms. Any farmer failing to comply with the orders is liable to punishment." Did not mention the kind of punishment.

"This will allow the less experienced farmers of the younger generations to study and explore such farming techniques and apply them to their farms for the general benefit."

The idea behind the height of the walls was to bring down the walls to such a level that nobody could barricade himself for any antirevolutionary around Benghazi.

The farmers pulled down the extra wall and arranged wire fencing to fend burglars but the crops were left at the mercy of the scorching sand laden strong east winds.

Since the Italian colonialists left Libya, new streets had no names. Nobody bothered to have houses numbered. Such recognition was irrelevant. No house owner was interested to have his house known to the tax collector or the municipality special wardens. The sprawling town of Benghazi spread to a radius of more than ten kilometers.

The lack of street names proved that the organized town of Benghazi covered an area of about two square miles around the semi existing port. The housing organization required planning and naming the state's buildings.

The wind of confiscation swept over the Benily organization too; their offices were raided on a stormy night. They ransacked office rooms and blew up the cashier's safe, using plastic explosive, the one used only by the army. Hag Mohammed was very bitter because he served the Libyan people, drilled water wells for them to supply valuable drinking water, now they turned against him; confiscated his hotel and his villas, ransacked his company, and broke his heart.

He did not give in; instead, married to a third woman, the youngest sister of his daughter in law and saved a whole house.

Broiler growing was going reasonably well considering the limitations in vaccines and medicine. The small commission from a shrewd foreigner made supplies available.

Hag Mohammed called more often to the farm, drove his old Volvo up to the farm gate, bleeped the horn and waited patiently till one of the boys unlocked and let him drive up to the hangars. He drank tea and asked questions that interested him, like the results from the sale of a flock of chcken. Profit was reasonable and Hag Mohammed expressed satisfaction for building that farm. George run the farm efficiently and that satisfied Hag.

The old man was diplomatic, was getting old though and instead of cashing on his hard work over the years for an easier retiring, the people he helped to survive were depriving him now of his personal income; he felt bitter.

George kept him company whenever he was free.

"You know George, I am glad and really happy to see a young and energetic man working hard, reminds me of my younger age. Would like also to reveal to you that I'm happy the way you handle matters, you solve problems and keep records and books in a systematic way."

George, simply, "yes, thank you Hag, another cup of tea?"

"You said, you had vegetables, where are they? Can I have some for my new house?"

"I'll bring some myself, the boys have gone now."

"You know how much I appreciate people who plant even vegetables for their own use? Look at those trees, that I planted and look at them now, they have grown, green, nice. Who, from this government planted a single tree for fruit or for shade?"

"They just destroy, I'm afraid."

"They build nothing, produce nothing; simply stuff themselves from what they find or steal. The Prophet will never forgive them, for what they do."

"Yes, a person must look ahead, plan ahead, and think of the future for the generations to come. We are all on transit here, but whilst being here, we must build for the future, if unable to do that, at least stabilize the present. They are destroying the past and mortgaging the present. The coming generations will have to work very hard to restore what is destroyed nowadays."

Hag was bitter with the situation, despised the actions of the revolutionaries who tried to level everything. Sheer robbery, shops, houses, money, all went for the name of the revolution.

George wanted to request Hag Mohammed for his working permit; when he saw him in such a distressed condition, postponed it for a better day.

The outcry of George's landlord to leave his house, the abuses and threats disturbed him and his family to a great extent. There was a slaughtery building on the farm and George thought of transforming it into a living place. He talked it over with Hag Abdullah.

"I have no objection," he said, "provided you bear the cost."

"I'll bear the cost as such, but what is my guarantee?"

"These people are not interested in housing outside Benghazi."

George considered the idea as a solution; he brought up the idea, on a visit to Yiannis' house,

Yianni looked at George intensely for long moments, and then said, "This is not a solution, give me some time, I want to see my relative at the housing department, may help us. He is in charge of the Benina house complex."

"I am really desperate, the landlord is knocking down walls, you know, he broke the wall by his staircase and yesterday at lunch found him lying with his wife there down on the floor."

"Ah! This is very bad. Tomorrow, he will accuse you of indecent behavior that you spy on him, whilst sleeping with his wife."

George realized the landlord's intentions, must move out, but how, where?

"I promise you, to look for a good apartment at Benina complex; hope to see my relative next week."

George realized that in Libya, one cannot push matters, this is a country of tomorrow, with God's will; the age of satellites has not crossed the Sahara desert yet.

Under the present situation, George was compelled to spend more time at home with his family, to protect them as far as he could. In the evenings, paid visits to friends and acquaintances, where they enjoyed such visits and tried to relax. They visited families with a simple invitation. George wanted to talk over his problem, hoping for a solution. Most of them expressed their distress and promised to pray for them.

The schools opened and the three daughters began classes with renewed strength. Sonia was in her final year at the lyceum, Margarita in the third and final year of the gymnasium. The fast growing Mary entered the sixth and the last year of the elementary school. All were among the best in their classes respectively, and the family expected them this year to be the flag bearers for the closing ceremony.

George took an active interest in the school matters, was elected as a member in the community committee, and accepted the position of the treasurer.

The chances of finding an apartment at Benina complex rested on Yanni's shoulders. They continued paying visits to their house. Kate talked freely to Renio and Mariam; both women enjoyed talking with her.

Yianni owned an international antenna and could receive the Greek channels. George's family enjoyed listening and every time, before departing, talked about the next visit and the oncoming programs. At every visit, Kate took with her some processed chicken, hard to find on the market, which was always welcome in such large families. George never had any free coffee from them. The promise to help him with an apartment was good enough.

It was nine in the evening and all the humidity of the Mediterranean Sea settled over Benghazi, it was hot and humid. High humidity provokes bad hair that may lead to bad mood and the worse to bad headaches.

The sweat rolled down the back, followed the laws of nature, and reached the cleft of the buttocks and down the soft parts of the body. Matted hair on the skull looked thinner, open mouths gasped for air. It was humid and hot inside the house; the balcony was not a proposition and the top of the house even worse.

George suggested driving up to the farm, there in the open, conditions might be better, but Kate simply rejected the idea, she never liked dusty places.

"So what do you suggest, my dear?"

"Can you take us down to Leventakis?"

George knotted his eyebrows, though that might be a solution to their oppressive problem.

Leventakis, once the doctor of the palace and later the honorary consul of his country, Greece, lived in the center of the city in two spacious flats; although the decree about private enterprises affected clinics too, he used one of them for living, and the second as a clinic. He still got the wall plate on the right to the entrance of the staircase leading to his apartments on the first floor.

The building was badly damaged by bombs during the Second World War that hit the city. The doctor paid for the repairs in lieu of keeping the two appartments for private use. The ceiling of the flat was higher than later buildings and that gave it an advantage in the summer, was much cooler. Winters are too short, to be taken into consideration.

Although, they did not inform them of their visit, George and his family were welcomed. The doctor was always at home treating patients up to the third generation of his old customers. By the time they reached the door, all looked as if they walked in the rain.

The austerity measures created shortages, and scarcity made commodities unapproachable; the doctor was reasonably equipped, the electric fans proved that. Costas looked very relaxed in front of two sizable electric fans. The doctor was reading the Greek newspapers offered by the Greek consulate. Nicky, the second child was busy in the kitchen preparing the supper for the three. She became an expert in cooking since her mother died of cancer two years ago.

The moment they entered, the doctor asked George about the parking of his car.

"No, you better park on the side street, today there was the parade of protest against the Italians, you know, not far from here is the Italian consulate; the menace has not subsided yet."

George dashed down, the doctor was right; ahead of the parked car and only a few meters at the Christmas tree square, known as the Middan el Sagara, where a bunch of youngsters circled the tiny square and shouted slogans against the barbaric Italians and in favor of the brave revolution.

George got to his car but avoided going forward; reversed the car to about fifty meters, and hurriedly turned left. The rash turning aroused their attention. George parked the car behind the doctor's Volvo, locked it up, and rushed into the building.

"Hey, you come here, come here," heard them shouting.

George did not stop, rushed up the steps; looked back nobody followed him; once inside the house, did not utter a word of what happened. Later looked through a back window, very few persons were moving around and few cars rushed along Jamal Abd el Nasser Street. If something happened to his car, would find out hours later.

The children got together into another room, talked their own and listened to Greek music. The elders sat facing the two electric fans.

"Doctor, why this protest against the Italians today? Is there any reason or just another organized gathering?"

"No, Mr. George. This day is known as October 7, on this day, back in 1970, after lengthy negotiations between the Libyan representatives and their Italian counterparts, reached an agreement that Italy takes back thousands of Italian settlers who have settled in Libya since the Italian invasion in 1911. The day is celebrated every year under the name of Jalau'tolian. Though those settlers developed the land they lived on, still enjoyed the life here, and possessed the best land, which belonged to the Libyan people and should be returned to their owners."

"Therefore, this is a very significant day for the people of Libya. As a matter of fact I did notice something, but did not really inquire about it."

"It is wise to respect the feelings and anguishes of the people and generally the country we live in."

"Agree fully with you doctor; thank you for the proposition and the information."

The doctor spoke the language fluently and had many contacts at all levels; was a popular figure and a doctor. Even during their visit, the bell rang twice and Costas, the son answered it. Visits were at his discretion, whether the doctor would accept patients or not. He was not interested so much in money; was well off on both sides of the Mediterranean.

Costas used to send patients away by saying, the doctor was called for an emergency to the Jamahiriya hospital. Some accepted the reasoning, others complained that the excuse was a lie; the doctor's car was parked underneath.

Dr. Leventakis always recalled the golden days of the past but never scorned the happenings of today's revolution.

When George asked for his assistance to find a lawful place to move his family, the man remained silent for a few seconds, and then promised to help, with some skepticism. He might have thought that George was after his second apartment. He kept the second apartment lawfully, using his title as a cover, but used it as a private clinic under the umbrella of the consulate representative.

The doctor remained in Benghazi for the sake of his children, did not want to change their school. Children who studied abroad stood better chances of entering Greek higher institutions, and many were those who sacrificed a more comfortable living for the sake of their children.

He was an interesting person to talk to; has been in Libya since the Second World War where he served as a doctor with the rank of the lieutenant.

Upon his retirement from the British army, was appointed as private doctor at the palace; there, he successfully served medicine and his country. With his influence, hundreds of Libyans studied in Greek higher schools and academies. Also in the army, the air force, the navy, the telecommunications, the Greek universities, in medicine, engineering and so many other professions.

Athens was preferred to Cairo or Istanbul. Many of those young Libyans returned from Greece married to Greek girls. The Greek community was increasing, the European style of living entered many good Libyan houses.

Dr. Leventakis pioneered in organizing the Greek schools of Benghazi and helped to found the Greek Orthodox Church. Through his diplomatic post and professional entity used his influence.

With all his background and his gentle personality, easily could talk over a number of topics. Both appreciated Kate's reasoning; the evening past pleasantly, drank their usual tea and ate cake prepared by Costas.

On their way out, Kate invited them as usual for dinner, detailed schedule was not so important if they called earlier, all would enjoy the chatting.

Nicky, the daughter commented to Sonia that her home was warm and hospitable and the food delicious. Whenever they called, everybody enjoyed the food, the chat, and the company. Kate packed the left over food, and Costas accepted it by saying, "Madam Kate, you have golden fingers, whatever you prepare is perfect."

Yianni's home was the second family that George had the liberty of calling without prior notice, Renio and the children enjoyed Kate's company. The children mixed amicably and George sat with Yianni. The man chain-smoked and George had to keep on the lee wind, as he never smoked.

George at some point got the idea to ask if he could buy a house or apartment.

"Nowadays, impossible."

"If I buy in somebody else's name?"

"Are you crazy? Who can register a second house in his name today? Who can accept such a burden even if he does not possess a house himself? Such an idea would have been possible, say ten years ago, but even at that, don't you see what is happening?"

Yianni was the son of a Greek immigrant who crossed the Meditterranian on a small boat with a group of sponge hunters on the North Africa coast. The boy was not even ten when he landed on a sandy beach west of Benghazi. He did all kinds of errands for many years. Then drifted west towards Doheira and found a job as a shepherd with a Libyan family.

He converted by word into Muslim and married Amina, one of the seven daughters of the old Ibrahim. For dowry got a sizable piece of land, a tent for living and his first private property. A gentleman's agreement gave him the right to baptize and circumcise any sons be born. After his fourth child Andrea, the old man sold off the sheep and moved to Benghazi for a better future. At first, he opened a tiny place from where he prepared and sold Greek black coffee to sailors and sponge drivers abounding the small harbor, preparing it over sand, heated by a wood fire. There negotiated with some seagoing ship captain to bring him a coffee grinding machine.

From the front street tiny hut, moved further and installed his brand new coffee grinding machine next to the roasting one, it was a sensation for the newly growing town of Benghazi. Within a short time, he mastered the job and his name spread not only among the locals but also to the ship captains. Brought only first class coffee beans and kept the quality and his name. Later Dino, the elder son joined in and undertook the roasting.

Yianni was too young to participate; instead, he enjoyed the free life of the side streets. There, he learned to smoke and drink alcohol. Took care of his sister though; both walked from their rented home in Sid-Hussein to the Italian school ran by the clergymen of the Cathedral.

Amina was busy with her house, the cooking for the family, and sieving the raw coffee beans for her husband. Andreas'

Greek friends, who traveled up to Brazil, brought bags of good quality coffee beans; the business was thriving.

Dino was worse than Yianni, but the old man closed one eye since he was his right hand. When the old man learned about the wrong doings of his younger son, did not refrain from using his waist belt on the boy's buttocks. The effect was temporary.

Dino took a liking to nightclubs and late hours. Andrea talked to one of his compatriots, the fellow spoke to his wife, and she arranged for one of her nieces to travel upto Benghazi. She was introduced to Dino's family. Her gentle character and outstanding beauty attracted the young ram pager; he agreed to marry her. Followed the local custom, purchased enough gold from the market, and offered it to his future wife.

Mariam returned to her village on the island of Crete loaded with expensive ornaments. Her long widowed mother was not just impressed but conceited straight away that her daughter marries, the still unknown to her, the young rich Libyan.

The marriage took place in the newly completed Greek Orthodox Church of Virgin Mary, in the year 1962. Mariam's fecundity gave Dino five children. Dino gave up many of his bad habits but did not refrain from alcohol.

Andrea was quite happy with the new family; the good old method was implemented for the second son. Renio, a close relative of Mariam was earmarked and the procedure followed.

Renio, a graduate from an Athens college and a laureate in home economics, blinded with her relative's stories and ornaments, decided to pay a visit across the Mediterranean and see for herself.

Yianni, despite his rough rampage, was a handsome fellow. Recollected himself, took Renio out one evening and over a bottle of Chianti, she conceded to his request. They married in the same church in Benghazi and for several years, Renio controlled him.

With the old man gone, the two brothers had to work harder and be more careful with three families on their shoulders.

After the revolution, matters have changed in Libya; those married to non-Libyan and non-Muslim women were discriminated and branded but not required to convert to Islam. Great pressure and pestering forced such persons to change mind and character. Either the revolutionaries closed their private enterprises or black mailed them for personal interest.

Yianni turned tough and behaved rough at home. Everything was bad and horrible, beat the children for trivial reasons, and used his hands on his wife. Several times, she confessed that, with George's family visits, he calmed down and acted as a human being for a while.

"Please, Mr. George," she pleaded once, "come, more often that helps my family life." George did not understand the request but Kate explained her husband.

George's family was looking for company in this country, especially nowadays with the prevailing conditions.

George recalled the day when his daughter Mary asked him to take them upto her schoolmate Costas.

"Dad, can you take us to-morrow night, Costas is having his birthday and invited just me."

"Oh! Mary, why just you?"

"I don't know, he said only me."

"Can we come along?"

"Dad, yes, you very well know how much those people like you, especially his mother."

"All right, when I return from work, say around seven."

22: *Christian burial*

George parked outside the house at the usual place and all got off the car, but were surprised; the house sounded empty and the eight children along with their parents seemed, as they were fast asleep. It was still early and all looked at each other. George considered that both families might have gone out to celebrate Costas birthday.

"Out?" Kate said, "These people very seldom go out."

George rang the bell, none of the usual girl's giggle and competition who would open the door. Amazingly, the dog did not bark either.

"Something mysterious is going on here," said George, then touched the bell again. They waited, Kate handed the bag full of chicken to George.

They heard footsteps and Renio opened the door.

"Good evening Madame Renio, God bless you and your Costas, he has his birthday," said Kate.

"Yes, thank you," she said softly adding the usual welcome but no handshakes.

"Please come in," said Renio.

The house was dark compared to other times.

"I brought you some chicken," said Kate and George handed the bag trying to force a smile.

"Come in," she repeated, "Dino died," mumbled dryly.

George was taken aback, froze, "when, how did it happen?"

"Please talk low, Mariam does not know it yet; he died at five this afternoon and Yianni came just now from the hospital."

"Oh my God, what a tragedy?"

"Renio? Who is it?" Mariam asked.

"Nobody, nobody is here."

All were hashed into a room downstairs that served as storage place and living quarters for the younger sister of Yianni. George noticed Yianni sitting on the marble steps with head bowed down. George wanted to talk to him, to give his condolence, but Renio poking George sent him into the room and closed behind them. The strong smell of raw coffee sent George and Mary sneezing.

"The smell is too strong for you," said Renio, but could do nothing for it; she left the room briskly, but within minutes returned with her husband.

"Good evening, I'm sorry for the news, God bless his soul."

"Which God, halas, for God?" Renio snapped.

"Yes thank you Mr. George, my brother died in my hands this afternoon, he died at the Prosdoschimo hospital."

"I'm sorry."

George had no idea where that hospital was, but Yianni, still holding his hand continued, "Here are the air tickets, I arranged his exit visa and money also for his treatment in Italy." He produced two tickets to persuade George that what he said was absolutely true.

"Yes, I understand, you must have had a hell of a job to arrange his exit from the country."

"Yes, it was not easy, but managed; I have my friends in most places."

"You know most of the people."

"Returned to the shop at around one after lunch with tickets in my hand, wanted him to understand how much I care for him. He looked at me intensely for long seconds, then said,

"I hope to God, to make it to Italy, just now I feel very ill; please take me to the hospital."

"Rushed him to the Prosdoschimo hospital around two after lunch, the doctor was called from his house; its Thursday to day you know and everybody leaves early. The nurse gave him an injection to satiate his pain and put him on the saline solution. She tried her best, by the time the doctor arrived Dino was vomiting blood. The doctor checked him and said that he had liver problem, there was no chance; he expired by five, stayed with him, he was my brother, my only brother. Loved him more than myself, I am puzzled, don't know what to do."

Yianni broke down; George helped him onto the steps. He sat on the marble and with a frenzied movement threw his Libyan felt hat to the ground, but the air current caught it and landed in the dog's kernel.

"How can I help you?"

"God has sent you," Renio pleaded.

"The last time I saw a dead body was more than 40 years ago. Then a young girl fell off a bare plane tree and died."

Now George was the only person close to an established family in Benghazi and his eminence was requested to take the leading role not only for a funeral but to solve the problem of a dead man baptized and circumcised at his young age, long before he knew anything about religions. Renio, the laureate of home economics, now stood up like a statue to protect her race, her family, and her religion.

George read her feelings, her fears, and her anguish.

Renio threw her hands forward and begged George to go immediately to the hospital, ask help from anyone, and carry the body to the Greek Church.

"If the news reaches his Libyan ancestry, the whole family will arrive like a wave and demand to hold a Muslim burial with all that goes with it."

George was stunned, his undertaking was of paramount importance to them, but here George was impeding into family problems and into religious problems.

"We do not have much time," said Yanni.

"Alone cannot do it, can you come with me?" George asked Yanni.

"Now he cannot go," cut in Renio.

George was not only hesitating but also afraid to face the aftermath from the possible consequences.

"I called doctor Leventakis just a minute ago, and he agreed to meet you George, there at the hospital."

As Levantakis promised to be there with some help, George was obliged to agree.

George turned to his family sitting dead quiet in the semi-dark room, "shall I drive you home on my way?"

"No, they can stay, you will not be long."

Renio kept pressing George to go straight away; there was no time to spare.

"If you do not go now, they would put him in the cold room till Saturday, from now to Saturday, God knows what can happen."

"Al-right, I'll go now, where is the hospital and where in the hospital? Then how can I remove the dead body from there?"

Renio explained about the hospital, Yanni handed George the death certificate and said that Dr.Leventakis would be there with some help.

"Here is a sheet of linen for you to wrap the body and take it to the church."

From the moment George received the white sheet of cloth, was well in, for the rest of the operation. He drove off making the sign of the cross, the orthodox way.

Dr. Leventakis lived closer to the hospital; had experience with such cases. George found him there waiting in his old Volvo, but alone.

Both climbed up to the second floor, met the matron; Dr.Leventakis showed her the certificate, they were shown to the room with the dead man covered from head to toe with a bed sheet. George was petrified, cold sweat beaded his forehead, and some ran down his spine.

Dr. Leventakis was calm, softly and clearly said, "we are doing a great blessing to the dead man, our old friend after all and more to his family. I have to complete some paperwork while you find some cotton and stuff all the holes on the dead man's body."

George waited in the room, whilst the doctor went with the matron for the necessary paper work.

"Nurse, can you get me some cotton, please?" asked George.

She returned quickly with a ball of cotton and a Philippine nurse.

"She will help you," said and handed him the ball of cotton.

The nurse gave George a professional smile and pulled the sheet off the dead body; he moved forward and began cleaning the saliva and blood coming out of the mouth. George pulled lumps of cotton off the ball and began stuffing nostrils, mouth, ears.

Dino looked very funny with glassy eyes wide-open, stuffed mouth and nostrils. He looked as laughing on his way out of the hospital for his eternal journey. Was he laughing at those staying behind? Was he defying the upper world? Whatever were his intentions carried them with him.

The body was still warm "that is still warm," she said with a smile.

She encouraged George with her comments. When George made sure that the facial holes were properly stuffed, had to do the same to the anus. Placed his palm behind the dead man's neck and tried to lift it, at that very moment the trapped air escaped through the mouth, agitated the vocal chords and caused a ruckus, George was shocked and let the body go, forcing the trapped liquids to move with another ruckus, this time not so loud.

The nurse noticed that, "that's quite normal, it's nothing actually."

Such phenomena were unknown to George. The body was dead al-right but rumors of dead persons reviving, sent him a shiver.

Leventakis was back with some papers folded under his arm; when he saw George trying to turn the body, stepped forward to help. They were accustomed to such scenes.

The matron called two nurses and the four, placed the body on a stretcher, and carried it down to the car. One of the nurses asked for the bed sheet the body was wrapped in, being hospital property. Down in the street, George exchanged it with the one he brought from the house; they turned the body to the side and onto the pick up.

It was close to midnight, when George parked the car in the side street from the main post office.

Dr. Leventakis cautiously descended and made his way to the church entrance, it was unlocked; he pushed it open and beckoned George.

George lifted the tarpaulin and let the small door fall back. Without asking help from anyone, tried to pull the wrapped up body, the doctor came closer. Two idle persons sitting on the pavement across, stopped chatting, rose, and without being invited, approached the car.

"Need any help?"

Dr. Leventakis looked at them and with a hand gesture, invited them to give a hand. George recognized one of them as Salah, the slightly retarded young man hanging around the church neighborhood.

The four carried the dead body into the church, but as there was nothing to lay it on, George nodded them to put it on the floor, then suggested to join four chairs and rest it there until the morning, after all, the body would be then placed in a proper coffin. The doctor brought a candle stand and lit a candle, following the rituals of Christianity.

"Who is it?" asked Salah, he knew most of the churchgoers.

"One of our own," said the doctor.

The two left, were Muslim, normally not allowed in churches.

George thanked them, stood a few meters from the dead body and said,

"Rest in peace, good old friend, your worries and problems have ended."

George bid good night to the man who helped him and sincerely thanked him for his great help.

Leventakis simply said, "I like that family," and walked to his Volvo.

George hurried back to Yianni's house to inform them that the task has been achieved and collect his family.

Before he switched off the engine, Renio flung the entrance open and demanded the result.

"The body is resting in the church," said George, with great relief.

Renio exhaled a deep sigh, "thank you Mr. George, you relieved us from a great burden," without elaborating invited him to enter.

Kate was ready to depart; she suffered enough for the day.

Yianni appeared as from nowhere, "please come to-morrow early, so we can take a coffin from Rue-Saad Street."

"Where do we meet?"

"Here," intervened Renio.

George felt his blood draining, was deep in the problem, smiled and promised to be there.

Drove home with mixed feelings, wanted to help as much as possible thus assuring the community of his noble character but on the other hand undertook a great religious burden at the expense of his job.

The epigraph was written the next day, Friday 13. Several times, George passed by the Christian cemetery but never had the time to visit this reverend place.

To-day, undertook to cross the wrought iron door with the impressive designs and marble pillars. Met the caretaker, an ageing Libyan, who lived most of his sixty years in the tiny room built on the left of the entrance.

Accompanied by his two Egyptian laborers, both equipped with spade, shovel and heavy rope crossed the worn threshold.

"Yia Ibrahim, please ask the caretaker to show you the burial place of our friend."

"He asked if the deceased was the son of Andrea."

"Yes, Andrea was his father."

The old man beckoned George to approach; he obeyed to the summoning.

"Who are you?" the old man asked. Vested with authority and in a commanding tone spoke loudly.

George smiled friendly to the person in charge of this holy sanctuary.

"A close friend."

"What did you say?"

"Boss, talk to him loudly, he is half deaf," said Ibrahim.

George studied the limping approaching old figure, when close enough offered his hand for a handshake, a customary gesture.

"Boss, put something in his hand, our job will end smoothly."

George retrieved his outstretched hand fast enough, dug it in his pocket, fumbled out a five-dinar note, crunched it in his palm, and protruded the half-closed fist to Charon, if there ever was such a mythical person in front of Hades.

The old man gave his bony trembling hand, felt the paper note, pressed George's palm strongly as he could, George looked him in the eyes, smiled and shook his head, assuring the old man of his good intentions.

"You are from the family," asked withdrawing the hand scraping off the paper note that quickly dipped in his vest pocket.

George nodded and the man took back George's hand determined to lead the way to the burial place. Holding George's hand proceeded with head bent down, and talking mostly to himself than to his companion.

They passed tombs, decorated with marble slabs and crosses. Very few crosses were in their proper position, some half-broken lay over the dead persons resting place as if an abstract bond was binding the dead and the crosses.

Few tombs bore over weight massive tombstones built in artistic manner, resembling citadels, phases covered with overgrown unattended bushes indicating the place was given away to nature and its elements. On the more robust tombstones, one could read the inscribed names of the deceased, most of them Italian.

It was impossible to stop and read the epigraphs, the old man was in a hurry, walked over dead weeds and broken marble to a tomb covered with a marble slab.

"Here," cried the old man, and dropping George's hand, pointed to the tomb, "there lies Andrea, father of Murajah, and here lies his daughter, the one that her Italian husband struck to death with an axe."

George's eyes eyeballed skywards stepped back at the old man's statement.

"Approach," ordered the old man, "are you scared of the dead? They are harmless, the marbles covering them are too heavy, cannot rise, may be at the second incarnation," and with his right index circumscribed the spot for the grave. He felt at home, familiarized with the surroundings and if he ever dreamed of something, definitely his burial spot. He was a Muslim; his relatives would bury him in their cemetery, although the old man would prefer this place that became his habitat with the more humane surroundings.

Once George conceded to the burial place, turned to the two trailing Egyptians, and beckoned them to start digging.

Ibrahim with his axe drew lines for the grave.

The old man looked approvingly and said, "yes," then stepped over Andrea tombstone and made his way for his dwelling without respect to the buried ones.

"Yia, Ibrahim, got to go to the church and see how far they are with the liturgy."

"You better be off, we'll dig the grave, Ziad is a strong digger."

Before though George managed to step round Andrea tombstone, Ibrahim yelled, "yia Mister, had no breakfast to-day."

George dug another five-dinar note and handed it to Ibrahim, he looked at it, hesitated, and that upset their boss.

"Yia Mister, this is enough but there are no shops around here and it's hot, we have a lot of work."

"The dead do not need to eat that's why there are no shops around."

Ziad chuckled; the old man caught the laughter, stared at them and waved his bony arm inquisitively.

"Ask Ziad to come with me, I'll drop him at Pepsi road, there are numerous shops there, but I have no time, he has to return by foot."

"Yia Ziad," screamed Ibrahim, though the man was next to him, "go with the boss, you can walk back across the housing complex."

"I know the area," grumbled Ziad.

George dropped Ziad and rushed for the town center and the Greek Orthodox Church. Drove easily upto the main post office, turned right and parked a few meters beyond the church entrance.

The moment he stepped off his car, Yianni faced him with a pair of angry eyes. The man looked different without his Libyan fej.

"You are late, we agreed for you to come early for the coffin."

"Good morning Yianni, had to bring the laborers from the farm."

There was no response from the brother of the dead person.

"Haven't you brought the coffin?"

"Had to bring it with my car."

George only then realized the problem, a Libyan buying a coffin without disclosing for whom. Deaths, even in a city like Benghazi were events, why the relatives, the friends, the mourners, and above all the tents owners were not informed. He tried to ignore the comment and walked towards the church entrance. Heard someone shouting, but none to respond, was like a monologue. Disregarded the shouting, entered the churchyard, and looked up at the balcony from where the yelling and abuses came.

"Did you bring the dead body into my church?" screamed father Iacovos.

The adrenaline rose and reached George's ears that began burning, controlled himself though but said in a husky voice, "Yes, I brought him with the help of Dr. Leventakis."

"You had no right to place the dead man in my church."

"I always believed that this holy place is the sanctuary of all the Christians and does not belong to any particular person."

"You had no right to put a Libyan in the church."

George now felt confused, was Dino a Christian or not, stared at the priest who looked too naïve without his chalube, lost his speech, heard chatting from the corridor, looked and saw Yianni accompanied by Dr. Leventakis, George's heartbeat receded to normal.

Father Iacovos kept screaming that he would throw the dead body of the Libyan out of his church; from where he was standing, could not see the two approaching.

George never saw Dr. Leventakis before loosing his temper, walked erect despite the short of his torso, stepped into the churchyard and with a tone of authority said, "Andrea was a good Christian, and had all his children baptized, you better check the register."

The statement struck father Iacovos like a lightning, he vanished into his living room.

Seconds later appeared a second person on the balcony, taller, with sympathetic characteristics, holding a leather bound book, open.

"Yes Dino was baptized and is a Christian," that confirmed Dr. Leventakis.

"Good morning, your beatitude," said the doctor reverently.

"Good morning doctor, everything is under control and the liturgy will be held at eleven, please make the necessary arrangements."

The corpse was already in the coffin with two candles burning on either side of Dino's head with some cut flowers spread over the polished box.

The news spread like bush fire, a quarter of an hour before eleven, not only the church but the yard too was full of friends and acquaintances to see Dino off to his eternal home.

Four bearers carried the coffin with father Iacovos swinging his senser and murmuring the psalms.

George lowered the tarpaulin soon the bearers placed the coffin in the car and drove at the pace of a tortoise for the cemetery.

A few persons already lined up the entrance with the old caretaker standing in the middle of the iron gate that stood askance on rusted hinges.

George stopped the car, jumped off, and showed the old man the copy of the death certificate. The old man took it, rubbed it with his fingers, frowned his face, and looked at the paper the wrong way round, which revealed his literacy, George did not intervene, stepped aside and the bearers were on their way with Dino resting in his coffin.

The dead body must have been laid there in a hurry, nobody bothered to smoothen up his profile, they simply dumped him as such with facial openings stuffed with cotton, thus kept his funny smile, ignoring his wife's weeping, and Renio's consoling.

Yianni kept his distance, weary and nervous, scanning the surroundings for any intruders from their mother side. The clan considered Dino a Muslim, if they just got wind of the death, his body would be lying on a few planks wrapped in some colorful old bed sheet. Needless to think if Dino bothered how he was dressed or how being carried to his eternal resting place.

Whatever the mourners and friends had in mind, Dino obeyed the rituals and the rules.

Father Iacovos murmured the customary chants whilst swinging his senser sending puffs of scented fumes behind the coffin bearers. Stopped chanting when he stepped on a cobble, slipped, and almost fell, Michalis the chanter grabbed his arm and managed to steady him.

George walked ahead, Ibrahim beckoned him, had something to say.

"Boss, I must tell you, we found some bones but no skull, as we were digging, they are small size probably belong to a child."

"Did anybody else see them?"

"No, no, we hid them there under some soil."

"Well, just push them back as you cover the coffin, they won't fight."

Ibrahim chuckled lightly.

The bearers rested the coffin by the grave, father Iacovos straightened his thin body, raised his voice, and chanted the last hymns promising the dead man easy ascend to the Promised Land where everyone is equal, without any worries or problems and resurrection along with all the saintly ones.

The whole process took less than half an hour, by the time George reached his car, most of the followers vanished

1 Muslim burial

Nothing remains stable forever and so did the broiler growing, more and more farmers followed George's program. The increase in production caused congestion at the government slaughterhouse. The program for killing birds was jeopardized, and eventually dropped. Friends influenced friends and the friends bribed the officials. Even the truck drivers disobeyed orders and took the trucks to some other farm for a few dinars.

Business was degrading, birds had to be sold to peddlers with their usual problems, and they demanded larger birds and by the piece, demanded to pick the birds by themselves. Those peddlers, moved from farm to farm with dirty cars, dirty cages and dirty faces, spreading disease from farm to farm; medicine was traded on the black market.

Income dropped and so did the profit. Hag Mohamed tried to help and somehow succeeded, but was not there to live forever. Actually, had nothing to fill his long hours and developed a habit in pleasure driving. He drove up to Gimmines, the nearest town to Benghazi, along the road to Tripoli. Hag Mohamed drove along this busy road up to Gimmines and then along the seaside road, littered with four or five villages; the scenery monotonous, flat land, very few trees, scanty vegetation, deserted farms due to lack of workers and the seeping of salty water.

Still Hag Mohamed had a good round trip away from the oppressive atmosphere of Benghazi. After an hour's drive, would call at the farm, enjoy the green within the farm, and drink a glass of tea and a chat. Normally took this trip in the afternoons, but recently he did them in the morning too. On one of his usual morning trips, according to him, the old Volvo failed to take the turn the proper way and went over the escarpment. It was not that steep but enough for the Volvo to roll twice to the bottom where it landed on its four wheels. A Volvo is always a Volvo. Very little damage has been caused to the car and very much less to Hag Mohamed who opened the co-driver's door and stepped outside; some shepherds helped him up to the main road where the secretary of the local people's committee drove him in his new Toyota pick up to Al-Jela hospital where all emergency cases were to be reported.

Hag Mohamed looked in good shape and even after a quick check up by the Bulgarian doctor in charge at that particular time, found nothing wrong. The case was reported to the police office that runs on a permanent basis at the hospital's entrance, the officer in charge made a report, the son of the old man was informed and Hag Mohamed was driven to his home to rest under the care of his third wife and his youngest offspring. The Volvo was towed to Abdullah's house where after a close check up was handed back to the old man.

Hag Mohamed called at the farm after four days of absence.

"Good morning Hag," called George when he saw him climbing off his car.

"Good morning and God bless me," he said moving with a cautious pace and leaning onto his black polished walking stick with the brass handle.

"Hag, what happened?'

"What do you call him in Christianity?"

"Whom?"

"The one responsible for heaven."

"Which side of the heaven, Paradise or Hell?"

"Bring my chair George, down there under the shade."

Hag took his seat very cautiously, looked at George, and smiled, "you don't even say, God bless you."

"Hag, what do you mean?"

"Had an accident, a car accident, you did not hear about it?"

"I swear to my God, no."

"Its four days now, and you didn't hear it?"

"Wallahi, I did not."

"You mean during these four days of my absence, nobody called to see you, Abdullah did not come to see you for four days?"

"Nobody came," said George bluntly.

"Abdullah is lazy," said with bitterness.

"Could have been busy," said George, trying to defend the elder son of Hag Mohamed.

"Busy, where? Has nothing to do, apart from sleeping."

Hag Mohamed kept calling at the farm if not daily, every second day, but then stopped.

A week or so later, George called at Hag Abdullah's house and there, was informed that Hag Mohamed died that same day at Hawari hospital and were expecting the body any moment.

George respected Hag Mohamed, so he stayed along with Abdullah and the few male relatives waiting for the Mazda pick up. The car arrived in time accompanied by the younger son, Feisal.

The bystanders moved forward murmuring, 'God is great,' and 'what is for God is for God,' pulled the plain box that held Hag Mohamed's dead body covered casually with a used bed sheet from the hospital, off the small car. The moment was painful but the scene disappointing.

The man, who owned half of Benghazi, was pulled around dead, in a cascade made with a few planks of rough timber and covered casually with a used bed sheet, taken from the hospital.

There was confusion as to which house should the coffin be rested. Hag Mohamed was wise and took the pain to build a whole neighbourhood for his family, his sons' houses, the three that were already married, lived within meters to each other.

Abdullah demanded the dead body of Hag Mohamed rest in his house, being the eldest son; Feisal insisted that it would be better if his father's body were laid in his house, being much larger for the occasion. The second brother Fattallah, the most moderate and the one who inherited many of his father's merits, spoke softly and said wherever the dead body of their late father be laid did not really matter as the funeral was due to take place that same afternoon. Feisal won the argument; probably Abdullah gave in, only those two knew best. It seemed that Abdullah lost the case because he was overcome with grief and dropped on the floor, unconscious. Dropped with a thumb, his spectacles fell a meter away and his head must have hit the thick carpet. George, helped by a cousin of his, lifted him back to his chair; he was breathless. George slapped him twice, and the man opened his eyes. The bystanders looked annoyed with George's act, the fellow immediately leaned to the side, but before he dropped off, George pushed his head down, and forward, a guttural voice was heard, the man resisted somehow but George continued pressing down and calling him to his senses, reminded him that his father was an old man. It was the only time George slapped an Arab and even at that, not too hard.

Within minutes, temporary tents were under erection for the mourners. Tent hiring on such occasions is a big business but the service is prompt and goes as a package. Oblong tents covered with vividly printed cotton sheets of heavy quality, countless plastic seats, electric lanterns and huge flashlights are all included.

Normally such tents are for the male callers, whilst the womenfolk segregate inside the house. Callers trail in, late in the afternoon, as in most cases the mourning trails on for days. As they come, are received by the closest male relative, and after the customary hand shake, embrace and exchange prayers and condolence, are directed to the rows of seats, care is taken to seat every person next or at least nearby to some of their acquaintances for the normal chatting, after the first greetings are exchanged.

Callers tend to group together, are offered tea, ample food of meat and rice, followed continuously with tea, water is offered only if its requested; it is offered in plastic jugs and is drank straight by mouth after mouth.

George called at the house and paid tribute for three consecutive evenings. On the second evening, joined a group of five and shared rice and veal from the large bowl. The third evening was directed to a remote corner, the Sheikh was coming for prayers, George was the only Christian.

Kate joined her husband on the third evening; she was directed into the big house, Amina, the widow of Hag Mohamed received her. She accepted Kate as one of the family, accepted Kate's condolence and requested her to sit with her two younger sisters.

Amina's family was of Greek origin, they immigrated to Libya in the mid of the eighteenth century. Greek was her second language, and Kate found there someone to talk to in her native language. The topics were variable but Amina told Kate, in Greek of-course, that the Arabs had no brains, "Take Mohamed for example," she said, "married to a young girl, younger than his grand-daughter and look where he is now, what she did to him, she sucked him up, and that's why he died."

"George told me that Hag Mohamed died because of the car accident."

"The car accident, that was nothing, its from her," she did not even mention the name of his third wife, "now she is with a child in that big house, who will turn to visit her, here in this house, she is not accepted, I have two sons still unmarried and a daughter older than her."

Whilst talking to Kate, a helper tipped over a serving tray full of food remains and a porcelain bowl on the thick carpet, Amina's face turned purple, got very angry and did not restrain from expressing herself loudly, she spoke though in Greek, an alien language to most of the guests, "look out you filthy animal."

Kate was stunned, but Amina continued, accused the helper of being dreadful and careless.

"I told you to remove those carpets, the animals sit on mats, and more to that on a tarpaulin," added Amina's sister.

23: Choosing a higher education

By custom, the eldest son undertakes responsibility of all the related matters upon the death of the father, and that's what happened with Hag Abdullah, even drove the old Volvo, though he owned two other cars fairly new; undertook the responsibility of the family house and the young widow with her year old child.

George realized that one had to respect bonds forged over time through culture and religion, and understand the neighbor better and refrain from condemning a brother. Custom is a great guide to Community.

The man undertook also, the few remaining minor businesses, like the sandwich kiosk by the seaport and the farm, something that George resented right from the start. Hag Abdullah had no experience in farming and was very slow in taking action in emergencies. Refused to visit the farm or to visit the offices of the Poultry organization; he hated people of the lower class running important offices.

Times were getting difficult, influential persons were needed to put pressure at the organization and Abdullah raised his shoulders and said casually, "you can solve the problem."

George was disappointed, tired and felt neglected, still Hag Abdullah was his sponsor in Libya, George was obliged to work with him, rather had to generate income for him without gratitude.

When George requested Hag Abdullah to arrange his documents for registering with the authorities for his residence and work, Abdullah simply pocketed George's passport and forgot all about it. At one occasion, Abdullah expressed himself bluntly, "if you give me a good profit, I may consider your residence visa."

That sent cold sweat down George's spine, without a residence visa he could not transfer his salary allowance, his expenses were due to begin soon, his elder daughter was about to graduate the secondary school, and was pursuing further education abroad.

Although George made arrangements for her, to proceed for further studies in Greece, his suggestion was turned down, her eagerness for higher education in a British or American institution and her excellent grades forced George to reconsider his planning and give in to her demands. George began seeking information about entrance requirements and expenses of-course for an American university.

Unfortunately, the USA did not have any consulate in Benghazi; the diplomatic mission was in Tripoli, a thousand kilometers away. Communication of any kind was beyond reach, so he begged his English friend Brian to pay a visit at the Embassy in Tripoli on his next visit to that part of the country; he was working for an American international drilling company and used to travel back and forth.

Being a very good family friend brought a bundle of leaflets and brochures from the Embassy; helped George to study those pamphlets and even gave his advice, had more experience, as two of his children were already studying in British universities.

The Greek school was preparing students for Greek universities, so the English language was not taught to the required level. Sonia though diligent enough had no opportunities to take the G.C.E exams and with that shortcoming, the British institutions were remote for her. She could though sit for the TOEFL exams and apply for an American university. Still the English taught in the Greek school was of a low level; George sought advice, and got to know that the University of Garyunis at Benghazi was offering evening lessons to students intending to study abroad. Education was still a field that the popular committees have not touched yet.

Sonia enrolled for the TOEFL in the class of Peterson, an Englishman from Manchester. She was delighted; she was getting in the right educational channels, despite the hard time that lay ahead, studies and more studies. She was ready to stride forward with all her energy and did not even think about failure. Was proud to go against the odds, and make her own way through and ready to balance her expectations with her hopes. Luckily, worked very meticulously and that helped her to cope with her school lessons easily, the idea of attending an American university had a great effect on her, put wings on her shoulders.

With the enrolment of their daughter at the foreign languages institute, brought them as a family closer to foreigners and to Peterson, one of the teachers. He joined the teaching group at the institute and came directly from Manchester along with his young and attractive wife.

As there was not that much of recreation in the city of Benghazi, one could say, non-existent, in which case foreign families got together and exchanged visits, at least those that had the most essentials in the homes allotted by the Housing Committee.

Peterson was an amicable person as such, easy to approach and easier to discuss matters with. Easily extricated his esoteric world and joined the foreigners living in the town; there, he shared their mishaps, their shortcomings and even bad experiences.

At one of their visits to George's home for a meal and a glass of home produced wine, told them what happened to him in one of his attempts to pirate a heavy-duty table.

"Before leaving Manchester, we spoke with some friends about the situation in Libya and amongst other things, one of them who worked here for a couple of years, told us to lift any piece of furniture or house appliance that we find abandoned on the pavements. The locals are not that good in maintaining appliances and even worst in repairing.

To some extend were aware that moving to Libya, were plunging into an unknown world with different values.

So one evening, on the way back from the Institute, saw a very well made table on the pavement, something we were unable to find wherever we searched. The first time, did not take the table but inspected it carefully, the second night the table was still lying by the side road along with some rubbish of building material. Assumed that the owners abandoned the table, lifted it and carried it on my back. Looked funny walking bent down bearing the heavy table with its four legs dangling on my sides. Took it all the way to the building we are staying. You know, we live at the fifth floor and to my hard luck, the lift was too small for the looted furniture, so I carried it on my back up the steps to our flat. You know those flats are smaller than the small; the table was too big for any of our rooms, so placed it upright on the small balcony with the intention of cutting it in two, and thus two tables.

A few days later, we invited some colleagues from Pakistan to have dinner with us, apologized for the lack of proper furniture, and they showed an understanding. When everybody helped himself with what was available for eating, some went outside on the balcony. To my surprise, the wife began screaming hysterically, I got scared and dropped the bottle of wine on the floor, which broke with glass and liquid all over the place and rushed to the balcony, I thought some accident might have happened, thanks God all guests were there and safe, but the Muslin girl from Pakistan kept screaming at crescendo. When she saw me, with eyes almost out of their sockets and hands high up in the air asked from where did I get that sacred piece of furniture?

In a cool way, explained where I found it and even how I carried it up to our room.

"Yes, outside the mosque, it's the table the caretakers wash the dead ones on it; you better get rid of it the soonest, otherwise the wrath of Allah will be cast on your home, your family or yourself."

With her statements and threats of bad luck, the hair of my scull stood upright. Assured her though, that would get rid of it the soonest. Would have to carry it back all the way down the four flights of steps. A second thought would be to lower it by rope over the balcony but considered the trouble would have caused to the persons living in the building.

In the end defied the warnings and kept the table at the balcony, even looked around for some pieces of timber needed to repair the cut up table; I'm still looking for those pieces of wood."

"Good luck Peterson, the Muslim are very superstitious," said George and gave his visitor another glass of wine.

Only days later, Peterson himself told them outside the institute that his wife run away with somebody else to a far away city called Tobruq, some six hundred kilometers.

If the wrath of Allah fell upon Peterson or the other person lured his wife to that distant place George never found out, the institute closed for the summer holidays and George's family lost contact with the teaching personnel.

George was satisfied with Sonia's progress and began corresponding with various universities, targeting the selective ones. Unfortunately, the neighbourhood of Fuehat they lived in, though one of the most prestigious of Benghazi, streets had no registered names and of-course the houses had no numbers, only the privileged inhabitants had private post office boxes at the only one post office of the city.

George needed a postal address, thought of his friend Yianni, for permission to use his post box, the man agreed wholeheartedly and the next day handed him a key for that box.

The only entertainment around the town was between families. During those gatherings, news circulated and advice sought. At one of those gatherings George learned how difficult was to find student accommodation in Great Britain.

Thelma, the elder daughter of Brian, who went to Britain for her studies, was obliged to live in a low class hotel for more than three months before she managed to find proper living quarters and at that, had to share a room with an Indian girl. Thelma wrote to her parents that after moving from the hotel where she stayed for almost three months, that the girl student who rented the room, was murdered in that very same hotel. Accommodation was a serious problem in Gt. Britain for students, and this bewildered George.

As a regular reader of the Newsweek magazine, George used to read it right through. In the latest issue, read about the boom children of America. The article, mentioned that from the eighties and God knows until when, a third of the universities' capacity in teaching and accommodation were empty and would be available for foreign students, the article gave George a great relief, and America became the target. He talked it over with Sonia, she gave her word that she would try her best; she did very well in the class of English exams, and George wanted her to try some exam papers on TOEFL, the problem was where to search for such papers. George talked it over with Feisal; both he himself and his wife studied in the States, somewhere in Texas. Feisal promised George all possible assistance and handed him a bundle of TOEFL exam papers and several related books.

Now Sonia had almost what she needed, her aim would be a good grade in the exams. She applied for the March exams but due to the post office delay, which was the only way of communicating, the application reached rather late, was though accepted for the next one held in May. She was lucky enough, took the last TOEFL exams held in Libya, after that, the administration of the United States of America cancelled both examining posts in that country.

24: Unisa

Hag Nasser and his wife Unisa returned from London after spending more than two months in a reputable clinic. There, Unisa was treated against her liver cirrhosis, unfortunately, she returned with the operation open. From the plane took her directly to the most notable Benghazi hospital at Hawari. When George learned about it, asked Kate to join him for a visit to the almost dying patient, all the females of her family were there. George met Nasser in the corridor crying. Rose to his feet, George saw all the grief of a devoted husband in the face of Nasser, with red wet eyes, unshaven, matted hair, and chapped lips with caked saliva at the corners of his mouth stretched his arms when he saw the two foreigners approaching and two serpentines flowed down his wailing eyes.

George embraced him in a friendly way and felt the troubled body in his arms; the man leaned and cried openly on George's shoulder. George held him closer, gave him a chance to express himself that took more than two long minutes. Nasser recovered after shedding probably several times such tears in that single day, then took Kate by the hand and led her to the bedside of his dying wife, in the intensive care ward, followed by George, they passed the numerous female relatives of her and reached Unisa, she was lying in bed waiting for death. Despite her anguish, recognized Kate; smiled to her, Kate kissed the pale lifeless face, George was standing by studying Kate's face, from the expression he figured Unisa's condition, life was fading, only the strong antiseptic was looming in the stuffy ward.

Unisa murmured something between her teeth; Kate leaned forward, the woman repeated, "Madam, please my children, I trust you."

Kate was overwhelmed, tears flowed down her cheeks, and George stepped forward to prevent the unexpected, jabbed Kate, composed, leaned forward, and promised Unisa that would look after them as long as she lived near them.

Unisa felt a relief, forced a smile and two thick tears rolled down her pale face. The Bulgarian nurse came round begging them to depart; they left Unisa with tubes in her nostrils, a drip to her vein and one or two more from concealed parts of her body.

Agony struck deep furrows in Nasser's forehead; his eyes blinked constantly and at every blink, thick tears escaped and rolled down his pale cheeks.

With almost inaudible voice said, "thank you for coming, I knew that you would come, none from the neighbors, the Libyan neighbors came, they forgot Unisa, thank you, really thank you for coming.,"

Grabbed the hands of the visitors with his two cold bony hands and pressed them with all his power, then added, "if my Unisa recovers, will not only pray in the mosque but in the church too, I believe in God and God is one for all of us."

George froze at Nasser's emotional situation, his throat dried, forced down some saliva and promised to pray for Unisa and wished her quick recovery.

It was late in the afternoon, when George returned from the farm. A huge tent was already up and a second one was in progress, the street was closed to cars. He jumped off his car and rushed to his house, wanted to be near his family, Kate got very disturbed in such cases.

He found her crying, "Please Mother, she is just a distant acquaintance. She knew that she would die, you remember what she said in the hospital?"

"Yes, I do, we'll try to help; they are though different from us.'

"I know."

"Please Mother."

"Cannot help it George."

George went out of the house; Nasser's house was just across the street, puzzled, did not know what to do, how to act, he looked across.

Nasser's gate was flung open, a temporary curtain was hanging instead, some men were spreading a tarpaulin over the vine covering the yard, and a high pitch wailing was coming from there. The wailing was reaching a crescendo soon as a new bunch of women entered the yard. The elder daughter, a slim girl of not more than eleven, with pale face and untidy hair was at a loss, at one moment she rushed indoors and the next she was outside, she panicked, repeatedly cried, 'they are coming for my Mum, they are coming for my Mum.'

Her younger sister followed, too young to realize what was happening, she stared at the men erecting the tents with an indifferent gait. The elder son, a boy of twelve-stood silent near the newly erected tent, must have not understood the meaning of the tent yet. Omar, the youngest boy, not more than four, joined the by standing bunch of street boys on looking at the tent erection.

George stood petrified, could hear nothing but the wailing of the mourners and the rhythmic beating of the professional wailers, have been hired, had to play their role. George's landlord tried to talk to him without success; then he touched him on the shoulder and asked for the keys of his Peugeot, wanted to bring more chairs, the man left with the car and

George did not see him for the rest of the night. Chairs and more chairs were brought and arranged in rows inside the tent; meanwhile men were lining up like in a queue, presumably to offer their condolence to Nasser.

George joined the line, Nasser was sitting on a chair, accepted the handshakes and soft words mechanically. He stared at the solemn persons lining up, shaking his cold hand, tried to murmur something but no words were delivered, the same mandible movements, simple, mechanical. His hair was falling over his face, silvery whiskers covered his sunken face, lips parted, eyes staring the infinite, the corners of his mouth chapped with dried saliva and hands trembling, with difficulty accepted the condolence of the persons passing in front of him and very much less he recognized those who greeted him. George tried to press that cold hand more than enough, the face responded, the man looked up forced his eyes open and muttered, "George she is gone, I'll still pray for her."

George felt tears flowing, had to move along many people were queuing up.

The seats filled up, row after row, both tents, more than twenty meters long and with four rows of seats were soon occupied. From inside the house a constant thumb-thumb was filling the atmosphere, competing with the hired wailers who voiced a permanent 'Aou..Aou..Aou..'

George went back to his house and accompanied Kate up to the curtained gate with an advice not to sit for that too long, the atmosphere would wreck her, and he got a seat in such a position that could watch the exit.

The Sheikh arrived took his place and with the help of the microphone began his long perpetuating psalms that were beyond George, who was forced to remain in position with his head lowered and hands crossed over his belly. Did not dare to lift his head and face anyone, were praying in an alien language. From time to time all persons in unison gave a sigh, closed their eyes, held their hands before their breasts in supplication and set to reciting prayers under their breath, then with a mourning sound, 'God for God.' At a moment, when the Sheikh stopped his rituals, George noticed Kate coming out; she followed some other women of the neighbourhood, rose and caught her half way to their house, was distressed, he opened the entrance for her, let her pass and closed the iron door behind them discreetly. Exchanged simple words after they reached their kitchen, deep in the house

"You know, they brought professional mourners, they are the ones that make those shrill sounds, aou, aou, and each one, they are four, holds a heavy stick and strikes a table, I think that was the nice table from Unisa's dining room."

George looked with awry eyes.

"Some women told me that this is a habit and is done for two reasons, one to scare off the bad spirits and the second the mourners may extricate their grief, was asked to try at a moment when I was about to faint."

"Come on Kate, we talked about that before you entered there."

"Yes, we did, but you know…"

For the next two days people were calling by twos, by fives, by tens by hundreds, the whole of Benghazi came along to pay their tribute to their friend who lost his wife; the young television announcer during the revolution days.

On such occasions people are very particular, they call specially during the first three days to participate in the rituals, the eating, and the grief. Grudges are held for those who fail to call and even more to those who delay to call. The relatives and close friends bring in provisions for the multiple kettles of food being prepared for the visitors.

Later George was told that in the better-organized tribes, each member contributes monthly to a common account, the offering being part of the family's income and its size, the account is arranged in a bank and entrusted to a committee, normally the worthies of the family. From this account, expenses are met for emergency cases, like medical operations, a funeral, a wedding and even for a pilgrimage of some poor relative. The fund provides help so that family emergencies are met at some agreeable level.

George asked if he could offer his share, to help in some respect, considered it disgraceful to offer a live lamb or a bag of rice.

"We have everything, more than enough, more than needed," said Hag Nasser, "your presence for me is an honor, will always remember this." If Nasser meant what he said, George had to wait for years to find out.

25: *Traditions*

Since George's contract of employment allowed him a free choice between the office and the farms, so whenever he felt the office atmosphere heavy, pardoned himself and drove to a distant lonely farm, if the farmer himself was not present, there was always a helper available. Such a farm that George frequented was that of Muftah Hassan at Faakat. It was not a big farm and was not that far from the Mutamer's offices.

Muftah was a moderate person and easy to get around with. He inherited a large piece of land from his father already planted with olive trees and palm trees. His single chicken hangar, built by the family, was simple but good enough; avoided growing chicken during the hot season of the summer.

Muftah owned a house down town, but his family preferred the openness and spent most of their time on the farm. The inherited house was not that big but his six male children accommodated themselves in one room, the three daughters in the second bedroom and Muftah with Amna slept undisturbed above the kitchen.

It was a sizeable family and that kept Amna busy with cooking and bread baking, her *tenur*, the Arab type of oven, was all the time smoking.

They were so friendly and whenever George called to the farm was always welcome as one of the family.

Haja Amna, would be sitting on a mat outside, under the towering palm trees, dressed in her traditional outfit. A scarf decorated her scalp, sleeves rolled up, legs apart with her breeches reaching her ankles and busy kneading the dough for the family's pitas. Her tenur was at arms reach and always stoked by one of the girls, her job was to keep it hot enough for the baking.

Not far from Haja Amna the old dog stretched out lazily, waiting patiently for a spoiled pita. Amna called out her orders from her seated position mainly to her daughters, since the males were too busy with the football at a safer distance.

One could hear the orders, "Selma, check the kettle, see if the macaroni has enough water, don't let it dry off, Sumaya add some more twigs to the tenur, don't let the fire die down."

Khalima was not more than four; she could hardly do anything, and was free to run after her sisters.

Amna would be seated in that position for hours, very seldom was seen on her feet; even from a distance, one could not mistake her. One could hear the constant tingling of the golden bracelets; she wore four on her left arm and five on her right one, wore those ornaments day and night, never parted from them; Muftah brought one every time she gave birth to a new child.

At one time, George teased her that nine bracelets were not enough, she stopped her work and gave him a very cool answer, "its Muftah who faded out, I still have plenty of room for more, look at my arms," and she lifted her bare arms off the kneading bowl.

"Yes but you are just like brown sugar," said George in a whispering tone, she laughed her head off, lifted the dough and said, "is this black?"

That day George shared hot peppery macaroni with the family, four full bowls were steaming in front of each group, one for the mother and her daughters, one for Muftah and George and two for the six dusty, tired faces from the football team. George and Muftah were served at a distance from the family under the shade of a eucalyptus tree with the company of the dog that managed to change position from the tenur to the shade of the tree, betting for some left over. After the macaroni, Selma served tea, a medium size girl, slim, looking biblical as she moved around barefoot in her long untidy dress.

Over the tea, George and Muftah engaged themselves in a long talk about the traditions of his people. George inquired about the way of their life, the family size, the food, the living in that simple manner, the attention given to the wife, the segregation of the sexes, the indifference in cleanliness, the aloofness to politics, the suspicion of strangers, the apathetic acceptance of disasters and the strength of the kabila.

Muftah did not speak that much of English but knew very well the Italian language; they had no problem of communication.

"You ask me about our customs in a way," said calmly, " will tell you quite frankly that the customs of any nation and any people have their roots deep in the ancestry of that people and so do we." He knew a lot about his people, their history, and their way of life and how people adapt themselves to the environment, the weather and the intruders.

"You know Libya was and still is a desert country, people lived here from the ancient times and survived through the ages, the hardships of their habitat and the weather, the persecution by the invaders from the sea and the neighboring communities, since there were no boundaries, identified or natural. Land morphology played a leading role in the life of our ancestors as well as the weather conditions, the rain, the heat and the wind.

People lived a nomadic life and possessed very few things; their main belongings were their animals, mainly sheep, may be a horse and very seldom camel. You know camel were for the caravan people, the sheep for meat and skins and the horses for the fast movement.

Farming was unknown to the Libyan who had to move from place to place to find grazing land for his stock. Because of their constant relocation, never bothered about a permanent home and never built one. The mild weather was to his favor, a simple tent was enough for a roof. Sheep provided the food and the skins for the tents and traded in great numbers. The income was turned into gold ornaments that the women wore for life. To simplify things such ornaments were offered on special occasions such as the birth of a new child. By this custom, the woman acquired a role in the family, she kept the family wealth, but availed herself to dignified satisfaction, from this, and one may realize how the family wealth was turned into ornaments and how the family grew in numbers."

"You want to say that the family wealth was deposited on a female member?" asked George.

"That's right, but mind you it was not easy for a Bedouin woman to look after the family wealth as the family was always on the move. Such ornaments could be lost, though not enforced, it was very well understood that any loss, would mean heavy punishment to the woman, even death; so the wife carried such ornaments always with her and most of the times concealed, bandits were abundant those days. The idea became a habit and the habit tradition. The demand for ornaments varied from person to person, although it would be selfish to show off the wittiness of a man, because it can only be said so."

"Yes, wealth was not acquired only by growing and selling livestock, one could make money by trading, by moving goods from one area to another or even more from one country to another."

"You are right Muftah, and we come across the caravan traders who crossed inhospitable lands for the pursue of profit, many times with the danger of their lives. You mentioned the traders and the caravan people, here we see these people being the pioneers of founding the community, the village, the organized way of life."

"What do you mean, George?"

"The traders and the caravan people roamed the desert and the neighboring countries pursuing income, needed a permanent place for their beloved ones left behind."

"Yes, this is true."

"So part of the accrued income was spent into building a permanent living place, and the place had to be built in such a way to provide not only comfort to those occupying it, but protection also."

"Yes, this is right too and here we have to mention the desire, if you like the size of the family, it had to be large enough to withstand any crisis, that's why families consisted of many members and in that struggle of survival, male children were badly needed."

"And that's why a man was entitled to a second and third wife, to bring male children."

"Well this is one side of the story."

"What do you mean Muftah?"

"Nowadays males lost their vigor and agility, do not show that much interest in a productive female."

"Now, now Muftah, all the females are productive."

"No, not in those days, people lived a more natural way and nature dictates its rules, production."

"Certainly, nature dictates its rules, but also takes its toll too."

"Yes, it does, it gives but also takes, I lost three children, at a very young age though."

"So, the custom was polygamy to secure male children."

"No, that was not the only reason."

"What do you mean Muftah?"

"Can you imagine a strong male sleeping under the same tent with other females and be able to restrain himself, its unacceptable, mistakes do happen."

"So a male could easily, by mistake jump his wife's sister or mother?"

"Even his own daughters," said Muftah with reservation.

"So, that's how morals sprang."

"Yes, many problems arose from such immorality, and then the Koran permitted the polygamy?"

"The Koran came long after the custom became a legend," Muftah said, did not want to contradict religion.

"Is this the reason that females are still segregated and not allowed to present themselves in front of strangers?"

"Although years and years went by, the custom remained, females are still considered as the cause of many conflicts, and are segregated. Girls of puberty age being prone to kidnapping, very seldom exited the homestead."

"Wanted to ask you, though do not expect you to know, in those days of natural life, were any prostitutes?"

"You mean women who get fucked for money?"

"Well."

"Sure, there were for an extra piece of gold, even today there are women who enjoy the game."

"From what I got to know is when a male, say the bridegroom gets married, is obliged to offer his future wife some ornaments, is that right?"

"Yes, this is quite right, by this way the future head of the family, has to offer gold ornaments to a substantial level, to prove his ability of earning and his ability of sustaining a family."

"I see, it's a test of potentiality."

"Yes, of course," said Muftah with a sip of tea.

"What happens if a male cannot afford to buy the expected gold for his wife?"

"You mean if he has no money, well if that's the case, will either do without a wife or will try harder to earn money to create a family."

"Somehow, we deviated from our initial subject of family size, the Kabila."

"The family had to keep together for survival; all marriages were though closed marriages within the family, even cousins were allowed to get married."

"This, didn't create problems?'

"Yes, agree with you, though I am not that well informed about these problems of children being born with defects, even freaks, the freaks wouldn't survive the harsh desert conditions although closed marriages gave birth to real beauties"

"Well, it's quite natural with any species when close inbreeding is applied for several generations the eventual offspring is the perfection of nature, a harmony of limb and body, a great example was Nefertiti down in Egypt."

"Even here the Bedouin girls are real beauties, can easily compete with the Europeans."

"And more sexy, aren't they?"

"You tell me?"

"Intermarriages were a necessity for the survival of the tribe, since each tribe fought the other for some reason, over land supremacy or water possession. Many tribe members were looters; stealing animals for a tribe festive was heroism."

"No women were stolen in those days of the natural life, yia Muftah?"

"Surely, were stolen and this brought the tribes in real conflict, many tribes were wiped out from such warfare, the males, the old, the very young were killed whilst the young girls were the treasure."

More tea was brought and both Muftah and George moved the mat to a heavier shade, had a lot to discuss; George was learning a lot to-day.

"Life is simple," he said, "and time has no limits."

Muftah took the question, rotated it in his simple mind, did not change his mood, and lit another cigarette from the ones he always had, rose slightly and said.

"Of course life is simple and I don't see the reason for complicating it. Look at those boys playing football, for how long, let them play now, they get exercise, do not grumble, do no fight between them, and what else do you want. When the school opens, will go to school learn the basics and go out to struggle for their living. If they have the guts and the brains, will pursue further education; even that, what will it offer them, more sex, more valuables, better life? Do not think so.

Cannot reach the Europeans and we know it, some persons, I would say, studied abroad for years, saw your way of life, imitated it, but once back to their country, to their roots, retrieved to the good old customs, life, freedom. Do not say though to be indifferent say to cleanliness, well it matters. Certainly, cleanliness needs more than a few gallons of water that goes beyond the household. Land has to be planted with trees, trees have to be cared in order to grow, be protected from animals and devastating fires. I agree that the trees will help in improving the environment, control to a certain extend the dusty winds, give a better picture and attract wild life, this way one can create farms, improve the backyard and eventually the whole area, but this is a gigantic program, needs funds, takes time and needs education."

"Yes, but now that the tribe has settled down with a family to a permanent habitat, definitely have to work collectively for better lives, humane environment, greener scenery and cleaner surroundings for the future generations. Are the older ones satisfied with what they inherited from their fathers?" asked George.

To stimulate Muftah's interest in cleanliness, George put the question about persons pissing or even excreting next to another one.

He laughed, lit another of his cigarettes, twisted his foam pillow, and explained these habits in the simplest way.

"You must bear in mind what we said in our conversation; our people lived for long in a flat desert, really a flat desert with no natural obstacles or coverage. All humans have physical necessities several times in a day, now I ask you, what difference would it make if Farag, my boy playing over there, needs to urinate and does so within two meters from us or twenty meters?"

"I consider it abominable yia Muftah if Farag pisses next to us, as you say."

"Alright, I do not mean next to us, but say at ten meters or fifty, the scene will be the same, simply due to the land morphology."

"You, you may be right," said George and rose from the mat, thanked his friend for the nice macaroni, the well-brewed tea and the friendly conversation.

"Now I understand your people much better," and drove away.

26: *Civilization and the women's equality*

In the political arena, the confusion became unbearable, the efficient been laid aside and the smart ones undertook to run the show. The yesterday's layman was to-day's secretary of some popular committee, was indoctrinated in some army camp by some experts from the Soviet block, offered a Toyota with official plates and free petrol to pay visits to his uncle's tent or that of his cousin. There, praised the merits of the great revolution and asked his shepherd relative to report any unusual or suspicious movement in his area; the man received a coupon for foodstuffs, a television or a gas cooker. Now that the alien suckers were driven out of the country, all locals were entitled to a house, a television set, a gas cooker, and a home refrigerator.

Electricity poles marched overnight and reached the remote shacks, television entered the lives of the Libyans; day and night, the viewers watched their Leader preaching his doctrines, and his visits to remote villages talking at the Mutamarat, known as people's meetings. Everybody learned how to raise his clenched fist and shout, 'Al-fatah.'

The Libyans thought themselves privileged in comparison to their brothers in neighboring countries; it was though a short- term illusion. In return for all those goodies, all males had to register for the army by their eighteenth birthday. There, the machine of propaganda was very busy. Day and night, the young recruits heard green, saw green, thought green, ate green, drank green and probably green was their…. The green revolution entered their skin, their entities, many were those who washed themselves with a rather bad smelling green soap, hoping for their skin to turn green. The key driver of the green revolution was to improve the potential to provide sufficient for everybody, which was not understood and even not appreciated by all those for whom the green revolution was intended.

After the males, the females had to enroll in the army, it was by law, so the daughters of the shepherds, and those of the water carriers were enlisted in the glorious army, torn away from home to some distant camp for training. Yes, these young women must be freed from the customs and taboos of their tribes and predecessors. No more confinement within the walls of their dwelling, no more obligatory serving to the male members of the family, they have the right to be freed from all that. Their recruitment in the glorious army will prove beneficial to themselves and their country. Dressed in the dedicated uniform, they paraded, practiced, and brought live on the television. At their occasional home visits spoke highly of their skilled training and their indoctrination to the aims of the revolution. Food was free and plentiful; the slim put on weight and the kilos provoked their dim knowledge on sex. It was hay time for the sex hungry superiors. Problems began with pregnancies, and a whole wing at the Jamahiriya hospital was cordoned off for the brave military illegal birthgivings. Taboos set aside, families torn apart and illegal houses operated in the old town sector.

Besides the handing out free of so many things by the army, amenity trips were available to many of the most courageous female soldiers to visit the friendly country of Turkey, after all, the boats running trips to and from that country were owned by the government of the revolution. Turkey was the only friendly country around the Mediterranean and the only place offered for an exodus. Rumours spread around how those brave female cadets got loose in an oriental city like Istanbul with one leg in Europe. The worst news came when a large group took the trip to Turkey and decided to remain behind for a few more days, the days became weeks, and despite the advice and pressure applied by their radical headers, they dispersed and vanished underground. Money was not a problem, had enough to trade and many were those who offered themselves in the dark alleys of the city. Their loose behavior enraged the local organized prostitutes as their income dropped dramatically.

The government of Libya was obliged to send militants who rounded them up, and by force brought them back to their home country and distributed them to various prison camps for reforming. After a while the law of compulsory army service was dropped.

"Kate, what happened? You look so excited?"

"For sure I'm, was invited to attend the wedding of Mariam."

"Moreover, who is she? Do I know her?"

"Yes you do, is Naziha's cousin, but no men allowed, my dearest."

" What is she getting married alone? Without a man I mean?"

"You are terrible."

George kept sipping his Nescafe, with fresh milk that he managed to get through a friend directly from the government dairy farm.

"And was the marriage arranged, did the brothers agree to marry their children when they were still babies?"

"No, Mariam met Hassan, her future husband at the university."

"Very interesting, this sounds to be new trend, the young ones get educated and creep away from taboos and customs, and when is the wedding dear?"

"The actual one is on Thursday; probably you may be invited to the rajala party."

"What do you mean actual wedding, is there any other kind of marriage?"

"Weddings in Benghazi area, I'm not sure if they differ from other localities; anyway here they have the *hafla* that is the first night of the parties. During the *hafla*, the bride wears her traditional costume, long and simple with a matching kerchief. Guests are served with *rishda* a kind of macaroni, hot and spicy. Have live music."

"Amplified music?"

"Definitely yes, and it's the night of all the women guests. Young and old get on the dancing floor. Tie belts or colorful shawls round their hips and skimmy away a kind of Libyan belly dancing.

At Aisha's party, a little girl with long hair had her own style. Kept bending over from the waist, shaked and skimmied her non-existent hips like a pros. Tossed her hair fast in circles, first one side and then the other, so that her hair became a whishing halo."

"Did she really, female here love dancing."

"It's their chance to show off. You should see the elders watching the young ones dancing, especially those who have sons of marrying age."

"And you've been invited to this one too?"

"I've been invited to all the parties."

"And how many are there?"

"Actually five."

"And which are these?"

"The *hafla, the nejma, the goufah, the dokla and the sabahiyya."*

"You told me about the hafla."

"The nezma is the day the bride gets hennaed."

"That one, I know."

"There are details to it George. They prepare the henna and apply it to certain parts of the body."

"Apart from the hands and feet, where else?"

"You are terrible, I told you. Interesting, is the custom where a boy proceeds carrying a tray holding candles for light, eggs for fertility and a knife to keep away the bad eye."

"These people are really superstitious."

" Not more than any others, George."

"Well, what's next?"

"Then follows the *goufah,* where the groom's family invites family and friends who bring gifts to the bride. The bride at this occasion wears the white dress. There is also the *rajala day*, the men get together and eat couscous."

"Then follows the *dokhla,* when the bride gives a party in her own home before the groom comes to pick her up and take her to his house. This happens normally on Thursdays, the decorated bridal car accompanied by many other drivers drive through the main streets of the city-all honking and shouting in an attempt to rouse others that the groom takes the bride to his house. Inside the groom's house, family members will treat them, some reciting prayers from the Koran."

"And then is the *sabhiyyaa.* "

"That's right and the day the groom's family expects proof that the bride was a virgin."

"What do they ask her or the groom?"

"Here, word does not count, the family demands proof, something to see."

"What, the bride lifts up her….."

"George, are you going to listen or give your gnome?"

"Please go ahead."

"A tray is presented with the blood stained sheet."

"And everybody applauds."

"And the women ululay."

"What a treat, I wouldn't like to be there."

"You'll never be invited."

"Why, because I see the crudity of the custom?"

"Of-course the couples nowadays go on a honeymoon like we did."

"Wouao, *shahar al asal or shahar al basal?"*

"What do you mean with this?"

"You mean *asal* is honey and *basal* is."

"Onion, tears you mean?"

27: Benina the new residence

George's landlord was pestering him about that extra flat which he rented to those foreigners, he was afraid of being confiscated by the ministry of housing; reached the point of threatening George with beheading, the poor fellow tried hard along with so many other hardships to find a lawful shelter. When the fever over Unisa's death went into second rank, the threats were intensified. The Arab began his tricks with the water supply, the electricity, and the cleanliness, many a time advised his urchins to shit outside their door entrance. Kate had a serious problem to keep the house clean. Quite often, a turf of soil would land through the kitchen window or into the hall, despite her close watch out was unable to catch anyone.

George called at Yianni on his way back from work, though quite late, Yianni was taking his afternoon shower. When Renio answered the main door and faced George in that composure almost fainted. With trembling voice asked, "what happened Mr. George? You look washed out."

George told her in brief about the problem, she hurried indoors and called her husband.

Yianni learned from George the treacherous tricks of the property owner, the threats not only to George but to his family too.

"You know his tribe, Mr. George?"

"I think, Senussi."

"Ah, bedouins."

Renio brought coffee for two and they drank it there on the staircase, Yianni advised George to return to his home and that he would talk to him that same night, gritting his teeth.

Less than half an hour later Yianni was talking to the Senussi man; George did not resist to eardrop and overheard Yianni saying that if anything happens to his friend he would have to face him; the property owner assured the visitor that nothing would happen but must assist with his connections to find another house for the Greek.

George stepped down the steps and walked straight up to them; both smiled and welcomed him, Yianni spoke first and said.

"Look Mr. George, promised my friend Ibrahim that I will help you to find another house for you very soon. The moment I secure such a place you will have to hand this one over to my friend, you know he has a very big family, has growing girls, and needs his house."

"You see Mr. George I do have a big family and need this apartment very badly," said Ibrahim with a mellow voice, almost begging for his flat.

Yianni turned to George and spoke in Greek very fast and repeated what he told to the man, the message was given, since that moment Ibrahim did not bother George or his family, but did not greet him either, a very bad sign in that part of the world.

The month of Ramadan was approaching and no news from Yianni; from long experience, George knew that during the month of Ramadan everything goes into hibernation, the system gets slower than the turtle speed of the normal times, had very little hope for any help whatsoever and restricted himself in his house for obvious reasons.

Whilst George waited for his girls outside the Greek school, Yianni left his car, something very unusual and walked over to him.

"There is a great possibility of a flat being freed at the building complex of the Benina prefabricated houses, will let you know very soon. You better pack whatever possible and stay at home over the next few nights."

George thanked him with some reservation and remained at home waiting for the promising news. Informed his whole family and a wave of expectation flowed over the dinner table, though George still had his uncertainties.

It was eleven at night, when the bell rang for more than one minute, George ran down the flight of steps and met Yianni dashing upwards with gleaming eyes, "I secured an apartment for you at Benina, you must move now, straight away, I mean now."

George heard the good news with profound relief, grabbed Yianni's hand and shook it warmly.

"You better hurry up, get a truck, and start loading your material."

Yianni broke the news to Ibrahim almost the same time. Ibrahim promised to find a Mitsubishi Canter straight away and advised George to find some helpers. Ibrahim left for the Canter and George left for the farm to call his laborers, Yianni in his turn promised to go and guard the flat. Housing was not just scarce but was valued at the time, more than gold.

Kate began rolling mattresses without consideration and tying them up, many of the household were already prepacked in boxes and suitcases

By the time, George returned with his two broad shouldered Egyptians, the Canter was already by the entrance. Ibrahim volunteered to help with the loading but Kate bluntly refused. Wardrobes, beds, refrigerators, tables, boxes, suitcases went on the Canter. Ibrahim, the Egyptian carried all the heavy home appliances single-handed down the steps and on the truck. By the time they reached Benina, it was four in the morning; Yianni was there chain-smoking, and really stood up to his promise.

There was no light in the flat, Kate provided her help as usual, and her candles came handy. The helpers unloaded all the material, carried it up two flights of steps, and piled it as it came to them. The flat itself had a terrible bad odor, smelled like a chicken hangar and Ibrahim the Egyptian teased George about it. Drenched in sweat the two helpers looked up at George for their work "I'll see you to-morrow Ibrahim."

"At least for cigarettes," winked Mohamed in a witty manner.

George handed them a five-pound note each and winked back smiling, they pocketed the paper note, got in the Canter, and were on their way to the town, the property owner arranged the transport truck.

Yianni refused a cup of coffee, "it's too late for you," he said and drove off for his early breakfast; was respecting the holy month of Ramadan.

The whole family was dead tired, all drenched in sweat like all the others but the relief of freeing themselves from the continuous intimidation forced a smile on all faces; luckily the water was still running, one by one took a cool shower and dropped asleep on temporary arrangements. The stench was pungent, George opened a couple of windows but the fiendish mosquitoes visited them several times, the newcomers were visited over and over, the sun was high up in the sky when the family woke up, Sonia was the first to rise; very little was spoken about the flat condition.

George, Sonia, and Margarita drove off to collect the rest of their belongings, to their surprise, the door was forced, and the flat ransacked. Margarita was the first to notice the absence of her beloved dolls, began screaming, two of Ibrahim's daughters walked timidly up the steps; Margarita caught the elder one from her long matted hair and demanded the dolls. Did not let the girl until urine ran down her spindly legs; the girl then directed Margarita to the adjacent flat and pointed to some shelves holding the traditional huge aluminum kettles. George followed the female procession and helped to lower the kettles, inside which the dolls were crumbed. Besides the dolls, the family retrieved some worthy tablecloths, two porcelain vases, and some table napkins and George's shaving kit.

Sonia threatened the elder girl, "I will put you in the pot and close you up there to die."

She got so scared and dropped down, George thought for a moment that she fainted, lifted her up, talked to her softly, she recovered, they collected their few belongings left over and George inserted the key into the lock secured the door closed then pressed the key to its side and broke it, they left as fast as they could.

Margarita seated herself by the car door and just as the car was about to move away threw a sizeable stone, which she kept hidden in her pocket and vexed with mockery, "to hell with your house, wretched Ibrahim."

The anger was profound on all faces, but nobody expected Margarita to depart from that horrible place in such anguish, she sent the house owner to the anathema.

Now the family had a new house, a new address, Benina prefabricated homes. These sets of flats were built of solid concrete walls fitted together, the locals despised them, no place for any chicken or for a couple of sheep; the walls were too hard even for a nail, where one could hung his flour sieve or even his beret.

The Housing committee rented the seven thousand apartments to the so-called foreigners, Palestinians, Egyptian schoolteachers, Bulgarian nurses, Indian doctors, Greek companies' employees, Russian military experts, and an occasional promoted militant.

Now George's family had a lawful flat through the Housing Corporation, Yianni kept his promise. Kate took George by hand, and led him round the rooms. The daylight revealed the state of the flat, the walls were almost black, the Egyptian bachelor schoolteachers that lived there, for the last two years, prepared their food on kerosene stoves and from the look of the kitchen walls, they moved the stove from place to place as if to blacken all the walls on purpose. The bedrooms held more than two hundred kilos of rubbish, old mattresses, underwear, and debris of all kind. The bathroom needed a week's scrubbing and disinfecting. Kate left the pantry as the surprise of the tour, the last occupants kept goats and sheep on the floor and pigeons on the shelves, meant for their supply of meat. The ventilating window served as an exit for the feathered captives.

Kate was furious with the condition of the apartment and George had to explain the terrible situation of housing in the whole of Libya not only in Benghazi. All the family members offered a hand to transform the stable into a sociable home.

Yianni called to visit them, he laughed his head off with the bad situation, advised them though, to thank the almighty God that they secured even this dirty flat. He called it a privileged one, as it was near the police station area, which could be seen across their window.

George walked up to the station with Yianni. At the basement, was the post office and the public telephone booths, on the first floor the local police station, the second floor was occupied by the housing department and at the third floor, enthroned was the army general responsible for the housing and the area in general, he was a close relative of Yianni from his Libyan mother.

The paper work was completed; George paid two month's rent in advance and promised to settle the rent bill in time. Yianni spoke to the person in charge at the housing office to fix the electricity, to George's surprise it was connected before his return.

"I called here on my way to you," said Yianni, had some influence around the place; George appreciated his friend's help very much.

Back to the house, George turned on the electric breaker but not a single bulb was in place, he connected the refrigerator plug, put some water to cool, that was badly needed. The whole family got down to hard work, ceilings were scrubbed and hand washed, walls were scraped and drenched with soapy water. The girls worked at the walls of their rooms, to their height, George undertook to muck out the kitchen and the pantry, the sheep were gone but the sheep ked were left behind in the dirt, in the crevices, these devils thrive on human blood also. He packed carefully, all the debris in plastic bags and down to the car; then with really hot water, scrubbed all the wooden shelves, several of these abominable insects dropped to the water-flooded floor, bailed all the dirty water through the kitchen sink.

After a light lunch, George went to the farm, had a quick look around, and then picked a gallon of disinfectant, a hand brush, and a bucket. Bubaker, the main farm worker was surprised to see George carrying a whole gallon of disinfectant for his house. The Nigerian visited George's previous house several times accompanied by his wife and was very well aware of Kate's cleanliness.

In his hurry to return to his house, George almost forgot to unload the debris; Izzy, the other Nigerian shouted out about it. Was advised to unload it carefully and burn it off.

From one of his friends, George purchased a whole drum of white plastic paint, half a drum for the ceiling and a gallon of oil paint for the doors along with paint rollers, brushes and a plastic tray. Everybody was with sleeves rolled up when George reached the new home.

"Oh, well done Daddy, that's what we need," said Sonia when she saw the paint, "we need a step ladder now."

"I really don't know where to find one."

"Try at Yianni, I think they have two aluminum ladders of the folding type," said Kate.

"Cannot go there now and ask for the ladder?" George said.

"Not necessarily now, we can go to-night," said Kate. "I'll ask Renio."

"When we get the ladders, in two days I think we can do the ceilings, for the walls we can use the rollers."

"Well that needs some practice."

"Do we have time for that?" asked Sonia.

"Daddy, don't worry, we'll manage," said Margarita.

"I must confess that I'm thrilled, we are a family."

"We are and always will be," said Kate.

"Yes Daddy," added Mary, dropping for a moment the brush she was using for cleaning the wall. She was not even twelve but understood the meaning, embraced her father with tears rolling down her eyes; all the family worked as one person, all acted in common for the ultimate objective, the success of the family.

George had a bunch of stuff on the stove right there, the friends were pitching to help; the family was excited about things to be done and were supporting their father all the way.

For three days and three nights, Kate, Sonia, Margarita and Mary worked non-stop, they scrubbed, washed, cleaned, and painted. George helped only intermittently; was too busy in another field.

When the housing inspector called to hand over the contract and saw the new look of the apartment said without reservation, "I will suggest your company undertakes the maintenance of all the flats of the Housing Department."

Accepted a glass of fresh lemonade and left more than pleased.

All the family worked hard, they put the flat in shape, now they could relax, sleep, no pestering by the urchins, no threatening, no sleepless nights to keep guard against any unexpected visitors. They all thanked Yianni, his help was colossal and his support immense during those difficult days.

"You thank me for such a small thing, what can I say or how can I thank you for your help?"

"Mr. George, if you did not act properly that evening, I don't know where would we all be now," said Renio

George was accepted as a friend, and respected as a gentleman.

"What Yianni appreciates most, is the way you do things, was asked by many members of the community how Dino's body was placed in the church that evening, nobody got to know how it was done, you do things your own way and that's what Yianni likes best."

"Well, thank you Yianni," said George casually.

George was almost in tears, was the endowed one, and Yianni helped him and his family at a very critical time.

After the family settled down, George had to solve another big problem, the residence visa. Hag Abdullah was having his passport for more than two months without any indication that was willing to arrange for the much-sought visa. George called at his home, discussed the farm problems for which he showed an understanding but when he was asked about the passport, Abdullah turned sour and forced George to second thinking.

A few days later when both George and Abdullah were on their way to the newly formed Poultry Farmers union, George brought up the subject, Abdullah got very angry, stopped the car and yelled, "don't mix up things, you understand?"

George got infuriated, concealed his anger but made up his mind to terminate their co-operation, though he was quite well aware that the situation was very bad, had to carry on, the family expenses were rising steeply, but he knew also, that Hag Abdullah pocketed nine thousand dinars in less than six months.

28: Electrocuted

The Libyan winter lasts just forty days according to the elders; this year though, the weather was extraordinary, heavy rains flooded the town and the fields. The road, cutting across the fields to the farm became impossible; the car skidded on the wet red soil, the wheels spinned badly and hurled mud meters away. George was forced to use the long way through the nearest village, some fifteen extra kilometers, the villagers most of them sheep shepherds were surprised to see the foreigner cross their domain. Soon had to give up this route as a portion of the road subsided; eventually George was forced to cross the fields at high speed, sending the car to all directions, the daily calls to the farm were necessary, the high humidity in the hangars and the lugging of the laborers could not be neglected. To his bad luck, a lightning struck the fuse on the transformer just outside the farm and the electric supply was cut off; no lighting for the houses and no current for the electric water pump. George reported the failure to the electricity authority twice but nobody called for repairs.

The water in the overhead tank ran out by the third day, George went again to the electricity board offices, despite their promise, they never called; it was four in the afternoon and the birds had no water. At a closer inspection, George spotted the fault and decided to fix it, it was just a fuse; he repaired the same fault not very long ago.

The rain never meant to stop, the fuse was broken, and the chicken had no water. Braced himself against any mishap, and drove the Peugeot pick up under the double electric pole holding the transformer. Arranged a wooden ladder inside the car box, put on his rubber boots, gloved himself in heavy rubber gloves, took with him a good pair of pliers with a heavy protective handle coating and climbed up the ladder with Kate staring at him. As he climbed up to the level of the high voltage lines, embraced the wooden pole for support, then checked for the fault, there saw the fuse broken and decided to get hold of it, pull it and pass it over the heavy wire, he made the fault of his life. With his free right hand took hold of the fuse but the live current flowed through his body. First, he felt the current flowing through his eyes, and then through his ears and mouth. Lost his senses, his muscles were becoming stiff and probably that saved his life. As his muscles stiffened, his arm holding the wet pole was forced away from it and that disconnected him from the flow system. His right arm dropped off the fuse and momentarily found his senses, caught the pole and let himself slide down the ladder, luckily, he slipped down otherwise a fall in the car metal body would definitely mean his death. Once down in the car and away from the invisible danger, tried to move his legs, were moving; he looked around, things seemed normal, the fields were flat, the sky clouded, still alive, rather resurrected, only his beloved wife was in bitter tears and continuously making the sign of the cross. He did not bother to lower the ladder, got in the car, and asked his terrified wife to climb. Switched on the engine, tried his legs on the pedals, they were co-coordinating, shifted in first gear and battled off the wet field, when he reached the asphalt road only managed to shift the car into second gear and in that drove all the fifteen kilometers to his home

"Please go home, I'll see Hag Nasser, will ask him to take me to the hospital."

"I'd like to come with you, please let me come," said Kate.

"If Nasser comes with me, the car takes only one male."

"I understand you."

"Please Kate do not refer anything to our children, leave it between us."

"Hag Nasser, Hag Nasser, where are you?"

"My Dad is upstairs, you want him?"

"Yes please, if he is not busy."

"He is watching television, as usual Mr. George," said the younger girl and ran up the staircase to call her father.

"Yia George, come up, the film is very good, you know."

"Please come down, need your help, need you to take me to the doctor."

"The doctor, what is wrong, who is sick?" asked Nasser rather agitated.

"It's only me, nothing really wrong."

Nasser ran down the steps, shook hands with his foreign neighbourer, "really what is wrong?'

"Got electrocuted, rather went to Ades, and returned."

"When, where?"

"Can you come with me to the doctor and I'll tell you about the problem on the way."

Both climbed in the Peugeot and George drove up to the El-Kish clinic, it was the nearest one. There George met an Indian nurse to whom he explained his problem; she began laughing, "Well your problem just now is not a problem, a short electric shock invigorates the heart."

"Please, can I see the doctor?"

"Yes sure, please follow me."

"When did this happen?" asked the doctor.

"About twenty minutes ago."

"Normally electric current kills instantly," said the doctor in the most casual way.

The doctor's casual way of dealing with George's problem upset him.

"Anyway lay down, I'll check your heart beat."

"Everything is normal," was his diagnosis.

"Do I need any medicine, say vitamins," George could not think of anything else at that moment.

"No, nothing, but if you are addict to vitamins, I'll prescribe them for you, the problem the clinic pharmacy is closed now." He scribbled some vitamins on a piece of scrap paper and handed it to George.

Back to the car with Hag Nasser, George felt a flash on his face; tried to feel his pulse but with the heavy traffic, failed to get a good reading. Back in their street, George thanked Nasser for his great help and made his way for his home. There, he tried to act as cool as possible but did not escape Sonia's sixth sense.

"What happened, Dad?"

"Oh, nothing!"

"What do you mean nothing, you look very pale."

"You think late Dino sent me a message?"

"Lately you talk in your sleep, really what happened."

"Oh, nothing my dear! How is your studying?"

"You always change the subject, Dad."

Mary prepared his usual cup of Nescafe; had a knack of preparing her Daddy's coffee.

George got hold of the cup and began sipping very slowly; the little girl noticed it,

"Daddy, anything wrong with the coffee?"

"No love, it's wonderful."

Kate came back from the kitchen and with inquisitive eyes asked her husband what was the doctor's diagnosis.

George told in detail as to what the doctor said and what he prescribed.

"George, you look pale."

"Will get over it, I do feel better, the Nescafe refreshed me."

29: The Greeks of Benghazi

"Dad, you have a message from the president of the committee," said Sonia and handed him the folded paper.

George unfolded the note and read it aloud to all the members of his family.

"To all members of the Greek community, a general meeting will be held on May 13th, at 16.00 hrs, in the Greek Orthodox church.

Subjects of discussion, a) the economic situation of the community,

b) School teachers' rest room,

c) Salary of father Iacovos

d) Salary of the Arab attendant

The presence of all members with constructive, suggestions will be highly appreciated.

N.B. The committee will meet on May 12, at 19.00hrs for summing up the results.

Signed

President"

George read the announcement, and as a member of the committee had to prepare himself, was elected as the cashier of the community, though he did not have much to do with money that was dealt by his assistant, had though to close the books and prepare the report.

Mrs. Nicholas received George in an amicable way whenever he called to their house. Her husband, a professional bookkeeper was working as an accountant in one of the Greek companies operating in Libya was the assistant cashier, quite reliable and George let him keep the records.

"Nicholas will be here any moment, he is rather late tonight," said the Greco-Egyptian lady in her Cairo accent, "please take a seat Mr. George."

"Thank you Mum."

"Shall I get you something to drink?"

"Thank you Mum, a Greek coffee will be fine"

"You normally do not drink this black stuff, Mr. George."

Old Nicholas arrived before George managed to finish his coffee.

"Oh, Mr. George, what a pleasure to see you in our home, it's an honor."

"Hello Mr. Nicholas, thank you for your kind words, came to talk over about the next community's meeting."

"You mean about the money."

"Well, the whole world rolls on money."

"Correct, correct, but those people never had money," ha, ha, ha, cackled old Nicholas in his characteristic laughter, "welcome to my house," repeated for the second time.

"Thank you Mr. Nicholas, and do pardon me for not informing you prior to my visit, but you know telephones are a luxury here."

"Yes, here they have a long way to go yet, civilization is approaching by camel."

"Mr. Nicholas….."

``"No, Mr. George it's true. Just now as I was driving home, one bumped into the rear of my car, when I stopped by the road side, he was gone, where are you going, you donkey, I shouted as he was speeding away."

"Did he hear you?"

"I doubt it."

"Nicholas, shall I get you something to drink?" asked his wife who patiently stood by for his command.

"Would like a mint tea, please."

"You know about the meeting Mr. Nicholas?"

"Yes, I do," said the old man in an indifferent way.

George kept sipping the remains of his coffee.

The old lady brought her husband's tea, he was taking his time. They talked about the human values, the increasing corruption, the scarcity of foodstuffs, the bad situation of the Greek community, also about their lack of interest in participating on the important matters as the proper running of the schools, the church and even the welfare of their families.

"You know Mr. George that there are persons, company employees, who spend night after night gambling, spending their salary and neglecting their families?"

"Heard about them, one of those lives near us," added George and asked old Nicholas for the community's books, the receipts, the vouchers, and all other expenses with detailed reasoning.

"Yes, have them all here for you," said old Nicholas and pulled a drawer at the wardrobe near him and lifted a flat file, "here, I have everything for you," and went through one by one, giving detailed explanation on every item.

George listened carefully to an old man's patience. Mr. Nicholas was old but really professional and very particular about the details, took out the documents from the file by saying that he might need them for future transactions.

"You know Mr. George, I have no benefit from the community, and I'm exploited."

George did not like to comment on his complain, picked the necessary papers, rose, bid good night to the old lady, thanked her for the nice coffee, shook Nicholas hand and requested him to be available at the meeting.

Nicholas enjoyed his position in the community, despite his bitter complains, was present at all the school functions, he was seated at the front row, an honored position and he enjoyed it.

George called at Dr. Leventakis' home two days later and discussed several matters with him. For several years, this man was the honorary consul of Greece in Benghazi. He was aware of the community's economic situation as well as the problems with the authorities and knew very well many people of Benghazi.

Dr. Leventakis always praised the Greek teachers who came from the mainland and called them as mentors of the Hellenic civilization; those persons left their homes, their home country and came over to teach and keep the torch of goddess Athena alight.

Kate once reminded him that those teachers were paid extra for teaching abroad.

"Money is an incentive," he said solemnly, "but you see many other employees come over for work and what do they offer to the community?" he paused for a long moment and added, "several of them disrepute the name, I mean the name of the Motherland."

Rumours went around that several married Greek women made money the good old way and the veteran doctor of the Libyan palace despised that.

During his employment as the Royal palace doctor worked hard to improve relations between the two countries and was always a courageous advocator of the traditional ties.

Many were those who dreamed of a villa at Fuehat neighbourhood, preferably east Fuehat and Yianni was one of them; his brother Dino urged by his wife, hammered the idea more than enough. The villa progressed rapidly; the upper storey was almost complete when Dino left this world. Yianni, alone now had to carry on and fulfill the family dream. Single-handed toiled in the shop from morning to late in the afternoon; did not like to employ anyone for reasons known only to him. During the good days, Dino was roasting the coffee in a much-specialized manner, for that, many a person from the whole town queued up for their supplies; and Yianni ground and sold the famous product. Just those two knew the art of roasting and grinding coffee of prime quality; the secret of their success kept it to themselves, and safeguarded the family business. The two brothers supplemented one another, now with Dino gone; Yianni could not stand the long hours at the shop and the demands of the two families. The demands were enormous, taking eight children to the school in the morning and back at lunch time, to look after the families' necessities, the importation of the material, the municipality, the electricity and telephones and so many other chores, Yianni was worst than a farmer who spent a whole day in his fields.

As they were enjoying a local brew of ouzo and some Greek meze, Renio asked George if he could pass by their home on his way to school and take with his car the three children of her late brother in law Dino. George was deeply indebted to Yianni, he helped him in the acquisition of a home, so, when he was asked, agreed without reservation, never gave it a second thought, agreed to transport the three children, although the car could not carry six persons plus the driver.

Since George's family moved to Benina, they all felt relaxed, no abuses from the landlord, no urchins to piss on their door, no sheep on their roof to run up and down; they had a positive supply of electricity and water and above all security. Most of their problems eased off; only the volume of work and responsibility lay heavier on George's shoulders. Was forced to drive for more than six hours daily from the house to the school, to his work and the various authorities down town and then the evening lessons for the girls and the regular visits to some friendly family. His great satisfaction was that all the members of his family appreciated what he managed to offer.

Spring was well in advance, the days grew longer, and the weather turned hot. The Greek community most of them of island origin, were sea lovers and did not resist the idea of spending their weekends by the sea. Every Friday there was a catholic exodus, tens of cars carried young and grown up to the long sandy beach. That was the only time, the community kept together; at least those that George knew. They swarmed the beach near the small village, some twenty kilometers from the town centre. Access was easy to the beach, at least near enough to carry their bundles close to the water line. Many were those who drove there early in the morning, when the sand was still wet, almost to the water line, the late ones were forced to park half a kilometer or so away from the splashing water, the stubborn drove on the hot soft sand and got stuck in the soft sand. Nobody showed any real concern since some good friend with a four-wheel drive car would pull the stuck one out of the sand.

Few dared to carry their paraphernalia for roasting and cooking; the majority satisfied their appetites with sandwiches and fruit. George drove with the family, normally to the nearest point, early in the morning. Helped them unload their stuff and take it up to the water line, return to the farm for a few hours and then join them for a splash and a long bask in the sun. By this time, the beach was crowded with assorted colored umbrellas and swimmers of various nationalities. The Europeans kept together though nobody ever pestered them. Nurses of many nationalities frolicked in tiny swimsuits, exposing normally concealed parts of their plumb bodies, provoking the sex starving single males of the community.

As the summer progressed, camping was organized from Thursday evenings to Saturday mornings. Erected tents at a regular pattern considering the wind and the togetherness protection, although not far from there, were two army camps, manned with local soldiers of dubious character and desires. During the long hot days, everybody enjoyed the clean warm water and the cool breeze. The children had the time of their life, the shallow water, the sandy beach and the parental care gave them every opportunity to enjoy swimming, playing, or competing in all sorts of sports and games.

The nights were the most enjoyable for young and old. Logs of timber were collected from the beach and great bonfires were kept going for most of the night. The fire was so strong, that the whole group of campers could squat around and listen to the multitude of jokes and logo games. Music was available most of the times and many were those who attempted a dance on the sandy place that many a professional dancer would envy; the swing of the bodies was so expressive that lured the not so experts to join ad lib. Guitarists were happy to fumble the chords and singers joined in voicing their strength against the swishing waves and the cool breeze.

Thursday nights were the most popular; the well-established members of the community arranged birthday parties and anniversaries with barbeques of all sorts with lamb chops, veal stakes, marinated chicken and home brewed wine. Home-distilled firewater was seldom brought and very much less consumed, as its high alcohol jeopardized the good atmosphere.

George the curious, that is how he was known in the community, acted as the leader and many were those who followed his requests; one of his undertakings was to organize the food arrangement of the next Thursday.

The Greek consulate provided hints as which member was due for a birthday or an anniversary; many were the excuses for another barbecue.

Many times Kate marinated enough plumb chicken to feed a contingent. Sizzling barbecued chicken portions were not just eaten but devoured by young and old. Jacket potatoes were dug out of the ashes, hot, delicious with salt and lemon.

Several members took to fishing, old George's tiny dingy with its overboard motor was used to take the fish hunters deep into the sea, where they were dropped and left to catch enough fish to feed the campers. Catches were reasonable and fresh fish was there for everybody. Old George was the master organizer and the expert chef; in his blue trunks and sandals moved from one end of the fire to the other, with his long fork and turned the cutlets, the chicken portions, or the fish brought by the skin divers. Eating, singing, story telling and with few games, the nights went by happily.

Very seldom, a minor misunderstanding created friction. Once old Costas, an elder divorced Greek who sided with comrades of the then eastern block, brought along several of his Polish girlfriends, mature nurses, and well acquainted with the human anatomy. They preferred European company; were better treated and better subsidized to their meager salaries.

That particular night, a starlit night, with temperature soaring to thirty-five Celsius, old Costas brought veal for the group and wine from Vasilis' cellar, another lonely Greek on that North African beach. That night, the tents were erected in a semicircle around the fire. The pressure lamp was weak under the full moon and the starlit sky. The wine was a success and plentiful. After several rounds of the red stuff, three of those Polish nurses crept into their nearby tent, switched on their battery-operated fluorescent, and engaged themselves to change their tiny bikinis to another fancier type. The dim light of the torch circumscribed their plumb bodies and all greedy eyes watched the wriggling of those females and the struggle to shed off the tight swimsuit, to wipe the sweat from all the body parts and compare their skin color.

It was dead quiet around the campfire and George took the opportunity to break the silence. He began singing part of the well-known song of Delilah, 'I saw the flickering light across her window, I saw the loveliest legs I've ever seen,' everybody burst into laughter except old Costas, irritated got up, run into the tent and turned off the light and with that the show.

Old George was smart enough to drench George the singer with a glassful of wine. He did not complain, simply ran into the water, and gave a splash to himself; did not like anyone licking the wine off his salted body. Wine was plentiful and George had a couple of extra glasses and felt easier after that; he was advised to stay at the camp that night, there was a lot of checking on the road to Benghazi.

Kate resented staying overnight on the beach and tried hard with her reasoning but old George solved the problem, invited them both to share his tent. There was a lot of laughter around the fire and the teasing went beyond bearing, Old George's wife intervened and proposed the sleeping arrangements. Old George would sleep in the far end, and then his attractive wife, next to her Kate and George would sleep at the other end. She turned though to George and commented, "You don't have long hands, do you?"

George caught the comment and stretched his hands forward; she was not that far from him but did not reach her.

"You see, they are not that long, anyway you are not afraid of the night, are you?"

"With two men around, never," she said and giggled away, an old tune was fumbled on the guitar and she was ready for a hop on the sand.

It was four in the morning when the party began waning away and old George did not let the time check up go unnoticed.

"Anyway, you can share our tent just for a couple of hours; we will be safe when the sun will be out."

A roar of laughter went round the fading fire. The humidity was piercing even the most sunburn skins, one by one crept into their sleeping bags and rolled away to the tents, George followed the lady's arrangements, waited for the three to enter, got in and dropped the flap, sleep came almost instantly.

Not long after, the commotion around the camp was enough to wake up even the heaviest sleepers, George woke up, took a splash in the cool water followed by Kate, they left for the farm as it was on their way home; there George took a quick look around and left it to the workers.

"Come on folks, tonight is my night, get the fire stronger, we'll need a lot of ambers, brought some lovely stakes," said Antony.

The youngsters needed no more to pile more timber from the heap a few meters away.

Preparations were in full progress when George Curis came panting along the sandy pathway.

"Hey, you are late."

"You won't believe it."

"What, you got stuck in the sand?"

"I wish it was that."

Most of the campers surrounded George Curis and with inquisitive eyes demanded an explanation for his delay. The barbecued chicken was ready and many were those who ran out of saliva.

Kate, for that evening marinated thirty plumb chickens, specially picked by her husband from the last flock he grew.

The seaside bench was set as a banquet table, two piles of large dishes, and four large bowls of salad.

George grew enough vegetables on his small garden on the huge farm he worked, the piles of chicken manure and the water turbine helped enormously.

Although he succeeded in brewing a perfect wine, refrained from bringing any, too many roadblocks; despised sweaty hands searching his new car.

The food was ample and barbecued excellently, old Vasili put all his expertise for the night. More salad had to be prepared with fresh cucumbers, tomatoes, and sweet pepper.

Figs and grapes followed the main course.

Whilst nibbling berries off the grape bunches, George found himself under interrogation, not that the campers were that much interested but for the fun of it.

"You know that Greek ship that arrived last week with live cattle."

"That was not much of a ship," said Yiannis from the consulate.

"A large boat, so to say. She was about to sail with all paperwork arranged; we were stopped the last moment. Two customs officials walked into my office and demanded to stop the ship from sailing."

"Our brothers in Lebanon need food, medicine and support very badly," said the younger one authoritatively.

"The papers have been arranged for the sail, personally I cannot change the orders," said.

"We'll change the orders," said the elder and grabbed the sailing documents lying on the table.

The blood rose to my ears, with trembling hands searched for cigarettes, the younger one offered me one from those they get from the incoming boats.

"You wait here, we'll come back."

"When it was dark enough, they brought a brand new tank, craned it onto the ship. On top of that, piled foodstuffs, just name them, rice, flour, oil, sugar, tea, tinned fish, and boxes of cheese and do not know what else. They handed the captain fifteen thousand dollars there in front of me, and ordered him to leave immediately; the poor fellow had no other choice."

"To-morrow night the mujahedin of Abu-Nidal will attack the Christian sector for sure," said old Vasili.

"You see who supports guerilla wars?" said Yianni "we cannot intervene, let's have a drop of arrack, I have a bottle buried in the sand by the sea line."

"I hope it's still there, the kids were playing around that

"I was watching them and I believe it's still there."

30: Challenges in all formats

Sonia took her TOEFL exams with great success, and received response from several American universities; some accompanied their replies with brochures and extra information. The United States was a far away country for George, beyond the Atlantic; apart from reading about this economic and cultural giant, had a vague knowledge about their way of life, the cost of living, and the dangers for juvenile people, and even their educational system. He tried through the pamphlets and reading between the lines, to find the answers in order to decide for the university he would apply for Sonia. She was even more lost than her father was; George went over the correspondence repeatedly, in the end, decided to apply for the University of South Carolina. Sonia was scared of overcrowded mega-cities. George went through the encyclopedia and found out some information, although scanty, it proved though useful, he got to know the size of the city and the activities of Columbia.

Both father and daughter found the information to their expectations, Sonia accepted the suggestion, the application was made and posted from Cyprus by a traveling friend; post offices of Libya were rather slow and non-reliable. Many expatriates who lived for long in the country, told stories about letters reaching their destination, months after posting, envelopes torn and very often censored.

Old Leventakis told of one occasion, where he received a Christmas card sometime in November from Australia, after studying the postmark the letter was delayed just one year.

The school year was drawing to closing for the summer holidays, a fever of exam preparation was high in George's home; Sonia was graduating the lyceum, Margarita the secondary school and Mary the primary, all three girls and each one at her level were studying hard. Kate and George were on a stand by mode for any advice, for a problem or analyze some awkward subject, their assistance was rarely sought, all the girls, despite the volume of their work went about with great ease. The exams finished and all enjoyed a few more beach camping.

When the results came out for the year 82, that year was named, 'The George's year.' At the customary elaborate school closing ceremony in the specious schoolyard, George was more than happy. At the parade, Sonia was leading the Lyceum pupils holding the Greek flag; Margarita led the gymnasium holding a second Greek flag and Mary led the elementary school holding the third Greek flag. All three led their fellow pupils, marched as leaders of their sections; their consistent hard work and long hours brought them to the top, their aggregate marks were the best for many years.

A few days later, a group of selected pupils gave a theatre act at the national theatre hall of Benghazi and two days later a banquet was held at the city sports club in honor of the graduating pupils; Sonia, Margarita and Mary were honored with gifts and certificates signed by the Greek minister of education. George felt as much proud as Kate; overwhelmed with happiness and tears, kissed their daughters one after the other wishing them to continue their wonderful success.

Success in Benghazi, was always rewarded with a piece of gold ornament from the dazzling gold market, the girls worked hard enough, they deserved it.

The success of the poultry farming did not follow that of his daughters, overproduction created competition at the government slaughter, prices dropped dramatically, proper medicine was not available, and disease spread very easily and the summer heat took its toll. On the 24th of May between two and four in the afternoon died 4824 chicken out of the 5000 housed, birds ready for marketing, they simply died from the high heat. The birds died in the most abominable way. Overwhelmed by the rising temperature, kept drinking the hot water, breathed the hot air, huddled under the automatic waterers, lifted the drinkers with their bodies, the water overflowed, wetted the litter; probably the birds used the ingenuity of their tiny brain, the hot water did not help at all. The overheated birds just squatted, stretched their necks over the wet litter and gasped desperately for air, nothing helped them, unable to react, to move or run outside, the scorching sun was hot for any living creature, the birds died in that squatting position.

The farm profit dropped and so were the relations between George and Hag Abdullah, he accused George for everything and anything even for the hot summer. George was bitter with his partner, his lack of interest, his inertia and his accusations, things were turning sour every day. With the onset of the summer, the water supply from the municipality got less and less to the point that George was forced to buy water daily; the balance sheet could not afford such an expense.

Hag Abdullah failed to fulfill his promises, refused to register George under his name with the authorities, George demanded his passport, and Abdullah demanded the money from the sales of the birds.

“I will report you to the police,” threatened George.

“I will take you there, have no problem.” He threatened George with expulsion from the country since he did not have a residence visa for more than eighteen months.

Bubaker and Dandy left on the same day, the first one graduated from the university and had to return to his country, Dandy arranged to travel to Holland to some relative of his, with an ultimate scope of reaching the United States; he dreamed of Miami Beach in Florida. Holland helped as the jumping board. George was pleased with their work, their performance, and their willingness for that extra effort at difficult times; paid them the salary in full and gave them a good bonus. Embraced their employer and with emotional tears left for their destination. Now the work was on the shoulders of Izzy; he was not that reliable. An effort to recruit new blood failed, so George was forced to employ Egyptians from the agricultural field, Izzy left the same day; despised that nationality, 'I'm not going to work with that dirty lot,' he said and left.

The volume of work diminished and even George lost interest in the farm and with that his future in Libya. Had a considerable amount of savings but was now entering the most crucial period of his family expenditure. Sonia was due to travel to the States for studies, Margarita required evening lessons and Mary demanded to join the evening classes too.

George finished his work, the Egyptians went to their room; he sat right on the ground under the acacia tree, the one, late Hag Mohamed planted and was proud of it. The strenuous work and the confusion overwhelmed him; he dozed off. There, where he was asleep and closed to himself, heard a voice calling his name, for a moment he took it as a dream, rose and turned to the perimeter wall side from where the voice kept coming, the voice was real, from a Palestinian he knew for a long time, one of his competitors.

"Tired yia Yiunani?"

"Her yia Yasser" said George, "a little bit."

"You are working too hard take it easy, relax," he said and tried to jump over the perimeter wall. George rose and went to him, there over the wall got engaged in a long talk, the bad times in the country, the bad times in the poultry industry and the very bad times working in Libya, discussed matters, simply for warming up.

George knew very well, the situation of the farm Yasser was working as the manager. George knew also the farm owner and the Indian veterinarian employed there. It was that Indian, who bribed the lorry driver of the government slaughter house and drove the lorry to their farm instead of Hag Mohamed's, they sold their birds and those of George's were left at the mercy of the scorching sun, a whole flock died in front of his own eyes.

Yasser was not a person to be trusted, his composure evoked suspicion; wore thick lenses, had an untidy long moustache, and his long hair reached his shoulders matted and uncombed, he shaved only on holidays. His piggish eyes behind those thick lenses blinked continuously, one moment reaching his bushy eyebrows and the next down to his moustache. Whenever he knotted his eyebrows, a rat never envied him. His sagging belly, the hideous clothes, his coarse and fat face, his lying, impertinent looks, and his plebian manner of speaking obliged anyone to conclude of a non-reliable person.

"You know why I came to find you," he said after the long discussion about futile matters.

"Could not say in the least."

"Heard that you are quitting Hag Mohamed."

"No he left me; you know he died a couple of months ago."

"I know that, I mean you are leaving Hag Mohamed and came to ask you to work for us, I mean with Hag Ahmed."

The proposition to work with Yasser came to George like the thunder of last winter, he kept calm though and said, "But you already employ a veterinarian."

'The Indian left, sucked long ago."

George knew the Senussi farm from the days they imported day old chicks from Cyprus, at that time, was known as 'Hawari Dairy Farm.' It was one of the larger if not the largest farming enterprise on the outskirts of Benghazi; it belonged to the late King Indris family and covered an area of more than ten square kilometers with more than six wells. Egyptian families, Tunisians and Palestinians, farmed it; they grew vegetables, melons and kept sheep. The dairy herd vanished long ago.

Yasser, was acting as the farm manager, arranged partners for vegetable growing, monitored the supplies of seeds, insecticides, fertilizers and the sales; he made a good living out of the whole business and lived comfortably with his nine children off the main road. The house, a contemporary one, was drowned in the green of acacia trees. He drove a Volvo, something abnormal for a Palestinian.

George knew that they had problems with their poultry, but the invitation brought him skepticism. If the water supply were restored on Hag Mohamed's farm, George would like to continue despite all the shortcomings.

"I was thinking of a move," said George with some reservation, "here, we do not have water."

"Come to us, we have nine wells now with two to four inch pumps."

Water was a major factor in Libya, Hawari area was renown for the water availability, reasonably good water, after all the area got its name from an artesian spring that existed long ago, the word *hawar* means artesian spring. The lack of water and the uncertainty of his relations with Abdullah lured George to agree for a meeting with Hag Ahmed. Never met him in person, but knew his farm quite well, as well the ancestry of the owner. Hag Ahmed known for his nobility, now if nobility was a royal characteristic or acquired, George had to find out.

Ahmed, tall, lean, well groomed, properly dressed in clean, well pressed shirt and trousers, received George warmly and politely.

"Mr. Senussi?" asked George timidly.

"Come in Mr. George, was waiting for you."

"Good afternoon, thank you," said George, warming up.

Hag Ahmed spoke perfect English and that allowed the two to communicate freely and directly. Over the customary glass of tea, discussed the problems prevailing with the poultry industry; George avoided even the slightest comment on the political situation. When the primary talk was over, George promised to look around the farm, at the poultry houses, study the situation and return for further talks.

"I'm glad that you tackle the problem systematically, Mr. George."

The chicken farm, consisted of four contemporary hangars built by an Italian company, were of sound construction with automatic feeding and watering, with hot water system and regulated windows on either side, even a dimming light system was available which helped a lot in the electricity bill. The rest of the houses were built the local way of very poor standard and use. The farm owned a hatchery with a capacity of ten thousand day old chicks weekly and a semiautomatic slaughter of five hundred birds per hour along with a cold store. George met Yasser at the cold store, which was under his direct supervision, and only he had access to it. To George's request, unlocked two of the three cold rooms and had the chance to study the packed frozen chicken; they were not chicken, rather carcasses of skin and bone, the size disclosed the age, the weight and the poor quality.

Yasser tried to explain the poor chicken condition, the lack of proper medicine, the poor feed, but not his poor management.

"It can happen," said George casually.

"Correct, correct."

Yasser asked George about the discussion with Hag Ahmed, George looked at him, the man was bluffing.

"Have to think it over."

"It's a great chance for you, Hag Ahmed likes you, and is a very good man, I'm working with him for more than seventeen years non-stop."

"Is it so? Seventeen years, you must be very happy here."

"Yes I am, now not so much, not as before." He still dreamed of the good old days when the old King was in power and the family thrived on nepotism; the days his boss moved around with royal respect, the days the import and distribution of foodstuffs were in their hands. The Benghazi transport system and the Volvo agency were theirs and so many others.

They walked up to the farm office but Hag Ahmed was gone, George felt easier, would have some time to think over the offer and clear up with Hag Abdullah.

On the way home, thought the whole matter repeatedly; the size of the farm and the prevailing problems. Definitely, Hag Ahmed needed someone with experience to undertake his poultry unit; was looking for an employee most probably not a partner and a salary whatever the number, would not be enough for the family and the upcoming expenses. On the other hand, George needed a job and someone who would arrange the residence visa for him and at a later stage for the family, without a residence visa, could not transfer money for his daughter. George thought of a combination of a reasonable salary and a royalty on the number of chicken; here he was at a dilemma, to ask on the number of birds housed or on birds finished, the first would suite George and the second the farm owner. The second idea would be rather risky for George, with the limitations of feed and medicine; before he reached home, decided on the second plan for a reasonable salary to cover the basic expenses and a royalty on the finished birds that could be transferred, if he managed to secure a visa. Worked it out that his average monthly salary would be a thousand dinars plus. The size of the farm did not scare George, after all, Hag Ahmed promised every support, a factor that George heard with great reservation, it was common amongst the Libyans;

many were those who promised a lot but provided very little. Yasser was actually controlling the supplies of feed, day old chicks, medicine, and the slaughter.

George, during his presentation would stress the poor chicken quality, the high mortality, and the wastage. About the figure on the chicken toll, would leave it flue, would risk this on the marketed chicken.

The meeting went smoothly and Hag Ahmed offered more than George expected, even spoke on his desire to see George working for him long ago. He discussed the matter with his friends at the Poultry organization, who advised him positively, so right on the spot, they signed a contract binding both sides on all points along with a clause of informing either side of any dissatisfaction at least with a month's notice.

George made it clear that he would be managing the poultry unit without interference or hindrance, which was wholeheartedly accepted. The question of the residence visa remained in suspense; Hag Ahmed rejected the matter rather diplomatically. The agreement was signed on 30 July and George requested right on the spot for a fifteen days leave to accompany his daughter to the States. Hag Ahmed did not see that very favorably, but accepted the request. The agreement was signed, Hag Ahmed pocketed his copy and drove off, Yasser was waiting outside the office and hurried to ask details on the agreement, George gave him a vague outline and lied that they would need to meet again to finalize the terms of employment. Yasser knew even the details of the agreement through the secretary; the Arabs have their own way of communicating, gestures.

George now had to finish his co-operation with Hag Abdullah, there were still chicken on the farm that had to be sold, close the accounts, and retrieve his passport.

News travel faster than one expects, Hag Abdullah knew the very same day that George signed with the Hawari farm and expressed his discontent when George called to his house; at first he refused to receive George but his wife reasoned with him and eventually sat down to discuss the outstanding matters. Hag Abdullah demanded the money there on the spot and discuss any other matter later on, George insisted on closing the books, receive his passport, and deliver the share due to Hag Abdullah. The Libyan got nervous and shouted at George. His wife brought the second glass of tea with homemade biscuits, laid down the tray, normally very calm and quiet, but in her own house possessed some royalty. She paused right there in the sitting hall, looked at her husband and told him in Arabic calmly and clearly that his shouting would not help anyone, even advised him to find an arbitrator.

George caught the idea and straight away suggested Hag Nasser, his good old neighbourer, assured Hag Abdullah that everything would be ready for the meeting, accounts, money and any information needed, stressed the delivery of his passport, the Libyan had no other way out but to agree.

The same evening George called at his neighbourer who was glad to see George in his house, they talked about many matters and the farm problem with Hag Abdullah, his default in the business and the present situation.

"You know Hag Nasser, matters reached the breaking point, decided to give up his farm."

"And what are you going to do George, where will you work now, times are very bad, Libyans are becoming very selfish."

"Arranged to work with the Senussi."

"They are from the king's family."

"Yes, I think so."

"They are a good family, docile people."

"Believe so."

"Yes they are, although now they are having a hard time. During the king's reign were very strong, active in many businesses, now I think they have just the farm on the Hawari road."

Nasser took a sip of his tea and added that Muammar had an eye on that farm, an enemy's farm.

George felt cold sweat down his spine; had not yet joined the farm and was to be confiscated. Nasser must have noticed George's reaction and said laughingly, "George don't worry it's just a rumor."

"Even the revolution began with a rumor," said George

"Now George, don't take things that serious, you've made the agreement already, you go with those people, and they are good people."

"Yes, I will go, that is not a problem, I called here for something else."

"I hope it's for good, say, what is it?"

"I want to clear up with Hag Abdullah and need your help; mean to act as an arbitrator, so to say."

"Anything you want me to do George, you are my brother."

"Always felt that way," said George with moistened eyes. "Got his telephone number, can we call him up and arrange for a meeting, he knows that I was coming here to request your help."

Nasser phoned up Abdullah and after the exchange of the customary long greetings and wishes, agreed for a meeting on Thursday next, at lunchtime.

George asked, "What time is lunch time?"

"After one o-clock."

"All right, I'll be here."

Abdullah arrived with his brother, wore his floating national clothes; Nasser answered the bell and led them to the sitting room with the armchairs. Before they sat down, Nasser asked them if they had any preference, a European salon, or the customary Arab one.

"George prefers an arm chair," said Nasser, they agreed to a European salon.

They exchanged greetings in a cold atmosphere; Abdullah knew that Nasser belonged to the other group, the new masters of the city, so he sat politely and quietly.

George did not waste time. Opened the book, showed Feisal the accounts, the receipts, the bills and raised the plastic bag containing the money and placed it near Nasser who was sitting very close to George, he was his partner now. Within minutes, checked accounts, found them in order, Hag Abdullah's share was handed over by Nasser and there, the passport was pulled out of the deep pocket of Abdullah's gellebiya and thrown onto the small table lying in the middle of the room. Nasser's face turned red like a ripe tomato, picked the passport, fumbled through, and passed it to George.

George got hold of his precious document, went through page after page, and mumbled; '*O.K.*' Nasser accompanied his Arab visitors up to the house gate, closed the gate firmly after them and returned to the sitting hall, he found George still holding his passport.

"Bad people," said as soon as he entered the room, "you did all the work, I saw you running day and night, all they do is to fuck and sleep and collect the money, and still not satisfied, Muammar is treating them the right way."

George rose, tried to thank Nasser, wanted to be on his way, but Nasser pushed him back to the armchair, "food is ready, its chicken, George's chicken."

George tried to find an excuse to leave without success. The food was hot, nicely cooked and liberally flavored. They ate with a fork from the same bowl; George shared food many a time with Hag Nasser on several occasions before and after Unisa's death.

'Tell me George, when are you going for vacation."

"We are not going for holidays this year, mean my family, only Sonia and myself, as you know she graduated, and will follow further studies in a university abroad."

"Greece, Cyprus?"

"In Greece, I hope." George lied; such lies were easily accepted in Libya.

"God help her, she is a fine girl, what I was going to say, is that, if you were going to Cyprus, to take my children with you for a month or so."

"Hag Nasser hopefully next year, when all the family will be going."

"Please don't forget them," said with a sad voice, "since my Unisa died, nobody turned to see us or visit us, not even from the family. Nobody is interested to see if we are dead or alive, sick or God knows what."

He was bitter with his wife's family. He begged George for a second time to take all four children to Cyprus for a few weeks, "even a day out of Libya, to get the feeling that someone cares for them."

George was aware of the great difficulties and the many problems with strange children of another cast, another religion, but Nasser touched his soft heart and he conceded. Hag Nasser was his invisible guardian helped him on many occasions and supported him, George was obliged to him and his family, but four kids were too much.

"Will get them return tickets and will arrange traveler cheques for their expenses."

He already planned their exodus a year ahead; George had to agree.

"Your children are like my children," said George. "Will arrange to take them with us to Cyprus, but next year."

Nasser lifted the tray with the chicken bones, the forks, and the empty food bowl, went to the kitchen but returned with all his four children talking aloud to them about George's promise to take them to Cyprus. The elder boy jumped up and down, he thought it was for that year; Nasser tried hard to explain that the holiday was for the next year, the boy felt downhearted, George had to intervene and praise Cyprus and the great time they would have on the island.

George's family began weaning; Sonia flew away like the full-grown birds that are lured to take the plunge into the open world. Yianni arranged a final exit visa for Sonia. She was to leave for Athens, spend a few weeks there with her aunt until George would be able to arrange his residence visa. He did not like to get out of Libya without securing a residence visa; did not like to leave Kate on suspense with two children in Libya, to secure a new visa to enter Libya those times was rather remote.

George talked the matter over with Yianni, he promised to help; needed time for it though and probably some money. Since Hag Ahmed refused to arrange George's residence visa, George had to consider of buying such a visa for himself and his family.

"Yes, I spoke to my friend Mohamed, is a good man, and he promised to do it." George saw a ray of hope after being without a residence visa for almost two years, rather risky. He avoided every liable rough spot that might endanger the disclosure of such an offence, though that was not enough, his driving license was expiring within a few weeks, for its renewal a residence visa was needed, and even the minute traffic offence would reveal his illegal stay in Libya.

George called at Yianni's house on his way back from the farm; informed George that his friend agreed to register him and his family in his name, provided George helped him on his poultry unit in return.

"Who is Mohamed who owns a farm and requires my help?" asked George.

"Oh, you know him; will be here in a minute, called him by phone."

George was curious about the farmer who owned a farm, and a telephone; very few Libyans engaged in farming owned such houses where telephones could be installed.

The bell rang and there entered Mohamed Magdi, a well known poultry farmer; owned a large farm at the foot of the low mountain range, the large hangar was fully automatic as a matter of fact, it was the only hangar around Benghazi with automatic feeding, watering, ventilation and light dimming.

Mohamed was a quiet person, soft spoken with advanced ideas in poultry farming; the main problem for this farm was the distance from his home in town. He lived in Fuehat east with a brood of seven children, could not stay away from home, had grown up sons and daughters. To his bad luck, Tareq the eldest son, whom he sent to Gt. Britain for further studies, turned into a drug addict and was expelled from the college. Nobody trusted such a person at home with his father away. Mohamed tried to lure him to the farm without success, Tareq might stay at the farm for rather a short period, ranging from days to weeks, was inconsistent and unreliable, and his bad habits brought him face to face many times with his father.

Mohamed was ready to help George if he could call at his farm as often as he could to assist Tareq in running the farm. George made himself clear that could offer his expertise as far as management went, he could advise on medication, vaccination and down to earth chores, but did not have the time to do any work on the farm. Mohamed accepted George's offer.

"If you manage Tareq, and I know you can, I will register your visa in my name not only for the last two years but also for the years to come."

George saw a window of hope and said, "I will try my best Mohamed, I talked with Tareq once or twice in the past, and will try…"

"Thank you George," and took the passport, "will tell you in a couple of days, if there is any problem."

"Can we meet here?" George turned and asked Yianni.

"My dearest, of-course, this is your house."

George accepted almost every promise with a good pinch of salt; smiled at Yianni and thanked Mohamed for his willingness to help under such difficult times.

Two days later, George went to Yianni's house, Mohamed was already there enjoying a drink of firewater with the host.

"Good evening gentlemen."

"Hello George, welcome, you care for a shot?" said Yianni, leaning forward with goggled eyes; must have had his dose.

"No thanks, not tonight."

Mohamed looked at George with a shrewd smile and dug out of his vest pocket some forms, requested George to sign them, asked for some dinars for the stamps, and made it clear that George had to pay his taxes and social insurance, fees known as INAS subscription. George agreed on the spot and with great satisfaction. Yianni sensed it and offered a round of firewater to celebrate the deal; called out his wife for some more roasted groundnuts.

More firewater found its way to the glasses and the chatting changed to other subjects about the situation, the weather, and the coming religious festive. The matter of George's visa was already a second rating matter until George called for his family for departure. Everybody rose to see George's family leaving; Yianni took George to the side and told him that Mohamed needed some money to buy feed for his chicken farm.

"I do not have any money with me just now, but how much does he need Yianni?" George did not realize the request and blindly confessed that he had at home some eight hundred dinars.

"But, I cannot lend him all that money, you see I have to travel and must leave some money to my family, in any way, can lend him up to five hundred."

"I'll tell him that," and returned to Mohamed who was enjoying his firewater, they exchanged a few words and Yianni called out, "half kilo."

George got the message, five hundred, and "OK tomorrow evening."

George was free those days, so the family joined him to deliver the promised amount of money; something was telling him that Mohamed did not need the money for purchasing feed.

Renio opened the door, greeted all of them wholeheartedly and Margarita with Mary joined the two daughters of the house. Yianni was in the shower. Renio looked restrained for some reason but George avoided any comments about the money, she gave in and said, "You know Mr. George, Libyans work this way, for every service they get paid."

"Realized that," said George with a smile.

"Look at him, they take his money, and he keeps smiling."

"What else can I do?" George said, casually.

Yianni came along puffing at his cigarette, greeted them in Arabic, very friendly and asked George if he brought the money. George nodded his head; Kate was the one who carried the family money in her bag, her good old bag that could easily take up to ten thousand dinars, read the gestures of Yianni and tapped at her bag, assuring him of the contents.

"The boy is not here yet."

"Which boy?" George asked patiently, for the moment he thought that Yianni was referring to young Tareq.

"That's how we call them here, boys, and young persons."

By the time they took their coffee, Mohamed was parking his old Peugeot outside Yianni's house.

"There he is," said and got up to open the gate.

Mohamed got inside like a lame duck, shook hands with George, and dropped on the nearest chair. Yianni opened the meeting by offering the newcomer a cup of coffee; began warming the conversation with the usual common themes, politics, foodstuffs, the weather, and the bad situation with the poultry industry. Mohamed talked about the Labor office, the Immigration office, and the trend of bribing to get any job done.

George winked at Kate; she pulled out of her bag the bundle of five hundred dinars, got hold of it and handed it to

Yianni, he sized the bundle in his right hand and handed it to Mohamed.

"Why is it in five dinar notes?" asked Mohamed.

Yianni was quick enough to comment that the Benily never paid in notes of ten dinars.

"What, he hides them under his dining room tiles?" said Mohamed cackling.

"The old man cannot hide anything now; he is hidden under the marble."

"What, did he die?" asked Yianni looking straight into Mohamed's eyes.

"Yes, you did not know? He is dead alright, it's more than four months now."

"Never heard about that one."

"Ah, it was when you were abroad."

"Yes, you are right, went for a check up."

Since the green revolution wiped out the nightlife, most Libyans, at least those who could afford it, went abroad for a check up and to saw their wild oats.

George began work at his new job, with the Hawari poultry farm, as it was known. They welcomed him as the savior and he rolled up his sleeves, hoping for a success. George made a new program for the broiler farm, taking into consideration the capacity of the hatchery and the slaughter.

Hag Farag agreed and promised his full support. Was not happy with his manager and the Tunisian labor; they were polite but sluggish, were not used to organized work, and resented the new face on the farm. George kept a low profile but strict on the daily schedule; it was hard to keep those disobedient young Tunisians confined to their hangars. Explained them why he was adamant on this, tried to reason his instructions on disease problems and the different ages of the chicken; still they crept through any corner to meet their friends, drink tea, and chat for hours. George reported them to the farm owner who threatened them with dismissal, actually sacked one of them, but even that did not help that much.

The first flock of chicken grown under George's supervision went very well. Mortality was less than two per cent and the food ratio was two to one. The slaughtered birds, resembled those in the glossy pictures of the magazines, in shape and size, the account was made but Hag Farag did not give George his share with the excuse that he purchased a large quantity of feed at that time.

George visited Yianni the same evening, there he learned that his passport was arranged even with an exit entry visa endorsed, they called Mohamed on the phone, and within an hour, the passport was in Kate's bag.

The next day, George went down town and arranged his travel ticket for Athens, reserved a seat and afterwards called at the farm. Nobody was around, went to the hangars, took a routine check up and found two hangars without water for some unknown reason and another hangar without feed, the feed chain was rotating idly, though the food bin was brimful, no feed was flowing through and the chicken went round and round chirping nervously. George asked the old Tunisian in charge what was the problem, the old fellow shrugged his shoulders and puffed at his cigarette stab.

George tried to poke the feed, to break the liable feed bridge, to his surprise the stick he used struck something hard, looked at the Tunisian angrily, suspected him of dropping a bag of feed into the bin on purpose and that might have blocked the flow.

"Ahmed there is something hard there, you better empty the bin."

Instead of following the instructions, got angry and abused George; even threatened him with a broomstick. George did not give in, forced the old man to stand by and he himself began emptying the bin, the Tunisian gave a lazy hand, when the bin was half empty a horrible stench rose, it was unbearable, birds were pulled into the bin by the chain, those birds died, and formed a bridge over the chain. When George asked him about the stench, he pretended of stuffed nose and stepped away, afraid that George's closed fist might land to his nose.

"You better come with me to Hag Farag,"

The Tunisian vanished, did not even collect his dues, and nobody saw him again. George went back to the hangar and arranged for the birds to get a proper feed supply. On his way out of the farm two Tunisians threatened him for sending their friend away, George did not stop, went to his home, the next day referred it to Hag Farag, he called them for an explanation. The farm had to succeed and that is how their salary could be paid. Big promises given on the spot along with hefty handshakes and all promised to try their best for the common good.

Two days later, George switched on his parked car to return home. Though the car was brand new, he could not accelerate more than ten kilometers an hour, with great difficulty returned to his home. The same evening requested a Greek mechanic to take a look, after a long check up, he found the exhaust barrel filled up with wet sand, the Tunisians did their trick.

George referred the problem to Hag Farag, got the customary comment, and "did you see anyone? Our laws dictate this."

George informed his employer that he would be going abroad for at least two weeks, Hag Farag grinned, twisted in his chair, tried to warn George that if he delayed might lose his job, the least to worry about, thought George, promised though to be back at work in time.

"Good afternoon Hag Ahmed."

"Good afternoon Mr. George."

"Really, I admire the magnitude of your power, reading your holy Koran in a quiet place."

"I always loved to read my Koran on such quiet afternoons with all those rascals away."

"Well, there is some work on the farm that I have to do; everybody is away as you've said."

"You are welcome, when you are through, I'll wait for you, for a cup of tea."

"Thanks Hag Ahmed though cannot predict when to be back, depending what one encounters in the hangars."

"I'll be here, have enough to read."

It took more than two hours for George to inspect the six hangars; Hag Ahmed was still there, bent over his gold gilded holy book."

"Shall I brew the tea, Hag Ahmed?"

"Please."

George took his time, cleaned the tray, the saucers, replenished the sugar in the bowl, brewed the tea to what he considered best, and brought it over where Hag Ahmed was busy with his holy book.

"Thank you Mr. George, now I'll close this and enjoy a cup of tea with you, please be seated."

George poured the tea in the traditional way to make froth.

"Hag, do you always come here for your reading?"

He smiled with appreciation, looked George straight in the eyes, sipped some tea, and said, "You know my surname."

"Yes, certainly."

"What else do you know?"

"That you belong to the royal family."

"You asked me why I study my Koran alone, I'll tell you, you are a Christian, is that right?"

"Yes, I am."

"Greek Orthodox I believe?"

"That's right."

"Christianity is a sound and established religion."

George looked at him awry.

"And we respect your religion; it is after all one of the three religions of our area, along with Islam and Judaism. As we all know, at least those who studied the theme, religions are based on rituals and concepts handed down from generation to generation which at some time were put on paper in the language spoken at the time. Many of these writings are ambiguous and scholars who studied them over the years gave their own explanation. From such explanations sprang differences that led to sectarianism what we see today as sects although Islam is a religion of coherence not like Christianity that is belingered by conceited separation. The ordinary people, mostly illiterate, blindly followed any fiery speaker who expertly adapted his preaching to suit his followers and so the man created a clan. Many such clans exist in Islam."

George eyed him but waited patiently for Hag to elaborate on his idea.

"Here in Libya and more specifically in Benghazi area, there are the Senussi to which my family belongs since we originated from the great founder of the sect.

The Salifists were introduced much later that the self proclaimed Libyan Leader imposed on the believers.

I am sure you noticed what is happening on Fridays inside and around the mosques. They imported Imams from other countries, mainly from Egypt, gave them a good salary, added extra loudspeakers and all those whom Qadhafi feeds, swarm the mosques not for the preaching but to be seen by the radicals.

Personally, do not like to pray under such conditions. You very well know that the government controls most of the mosques, even those endowed by prominent families. I prefer the austere solidarity of my office and read what my clan believes.

"Yes, I do, but our deeper roots, go back to the Senussi-Sufi order founded back in 1837, according to the western calendar."

George smiled and waited.

"It is actually a sect of Islam; the order began as a religious reformation and ended up in establishing new Muslim States.

The Senussi order was started in 1253(AD 1837) in Mecca. It advocated the prohibition of music, dancing and smoking but discouraged exaggerated forms of ascetism. Encouraged commercial living where each member of the lodge would engage in a useful community activity such as cultivation, education, or commerce.

They are opposed to the use of force; follow orthodox Sunni orders, advocated austerity, simplicity, and the free Shari'a law.

The Senussi order exists in Libya as a spiritual movement.

Tribal customs and undecendants are more important than sectarian beliefs in maintaining unity among people. Koran is God's revelation, is not secretive or allegorical but philosophical according to the reasoning of their leaders, fanaticism and social antagonism of ages of degeneration.

Bedouins tend to follow tribal customs, rather than Muslim jurisprudence and know little of religion beyond the recital of words they have memorized but scarcely comprehend; they are chiefly concerned with deriving a scanty living from the hostile desert. For them, water is more important than religion.

King Idris, my uncle, became the chief of the Senussi order in 1916 following the abdication of his uncle Sayyid. Was recognized by the British under the new title of Emir of the territory of Cyrenaica, a position confirmed by the Italian rulers in 1920. As a spiritual Leader and following the sect's rituals, spent much of his carrier attempting to negotiate independence for his territory Cyrenaica, came in contrast with the rulers, who began waging military campaigns against the Libyan brotherhood.

Was forced into exile in Egypt that served as his base from where he staged a guerilla war against the colonial Italian occupants.

During the World War II, Idris supported the United Kingdom and brought the Cyrenaica nationalists to fight alongside the Allies against the Axis, which had occupied Libya. With the defeat of the German army, he was finally able to return to his capital, Benghazi. Then was invited to become Emir of Tripolitania, another of the three traditional regions that now constitute modern Libya.

He accepted the invitation and began the process of uniting Libya under a single monarchy. From Benghazi, Idris led the team negotiating with the United Kingdom and the United Nations over independence. That was achieved on Dec. 24, 1951 and Idris was proclaimed the King of Libya.

Idris maintained close ties with the West despite the chagrin of the Arab nationalists at home and supporters of Pan-Arabism in neighboring states.

A threat to his regime was his failure to produce a male heir to succeed him to the throne.

Under his rule, prosperity thrived from the oil production in the presence of the United Kingdom and the United States, but the king started to suffer from poor health.

His nephew crown prince Hassan was to succeed him on Sept. 2, 1969, the coup led by Qadhafi pre-empted Idris instrument of abdication dated August 4, 1969.

Unfortunately, people tend to forget very easily. Many of those who parade in the streets dressed in that dirty green from top to toe, lived in tin sheds a few years ago, utterly illiterate, with many suffering from various ailments like eye problems, liver infections, lung disturbances and intestinal problems, benefited from King Idris' desire to help the needy.

Within the economic possibilities of his time, established hospitals, housing complexes, roads, gave great emphasis on the supply of water, electricity, education, judicial courts.

In agriculture advocated in organizing production, allowed the foreigners to continue their engagements, whether in business or agriculture, and implemented regulations so that the knowledge possessed by those people be transmitted to our people.

People easily forget, are blinded by empty speeches from unproven, unworthy, treacherous persons. Regretfully, I say that people are ungrateful.

"If this is what they want, let them get it, in time will only realize what is coming to them, which I'm afraid won't take that long, though many will be yearning the past that very seldom turn back. Once the water passes under the bridge tends to follow its course, requires an extraordinary force to reverse the flow.

Moreover, you see those who ride on the necks of our people watch every democratic movement, and annihilate suspects and non. When the civilization weakens and is stagnated, religion suffers also."

"Are you watched or any family member, Hag Ahmed?"

Lifted his head, smiled in a bitter way, and swallowed his saliva that caused his Adam's apple rise and fall, and then said, "Why do you think I prefer to read my Koran here alone?"

George returned the smile with pitiful eyes, discreetly consulted his wristwatch, it was turning dark; his wife was alone in the apartment, surrounded by non-friendly people.

"I'm greatly indebted to you; you took time to explain many hazy matters and made clearer the situation."

"Thank you for listening Mr. George, appreciated your understanding, the tea was perfect, thank you again."

"Good night Hag Ahmed, though things do nod seem to improve in the near future still everybody hopes that people will come to their senses and reconsider their frenzied support to the regime."

"People are forced to express lip support, though I believe their innate feelings are entirely different."

31: Going to America

After his round in the poultry farm, George dropped at the office to record his findings, to have a cup of tea and talk with the owner if he happened to be available. The habit of late rising still loomed over the offspring of the Royal clan of Libya.

To his surprise, Hag Ahmed was there chatting with a handsome young man, over a cup of tea.

Both greeted George as he entered and Hag invited him to have tea.

"This is Ramses, my younger brother; George is a poultry expert and joined us recently."

George offered his rough hand with the dirty fingernails, did not have the chance to wash.

Ramses was tall, lean with a sympathetic face and pleasant smile, greeted George amicably in perfect English with an American accent.

Hag Mohamed drained the teapot for George and called his male secretary for more.

George excused himself, wanted to clean his hands, when he returned found only the young fellow fumbling a copy of Newsweek.

George took a seat, lifted his cup, took a sip, and asked the young fellow about his magazine.

"Brought it with me."

"You came from where?"

"From the States, studying there, but had to cut short my studies, our father died, was obligatory for me to be at his funeral,"

"God bless his soul," mumbled George.

"Thanks a lot."

George kept sipping the thick sweet tea in small gulps, wanted it to last.

"You come from Cyprus, was told."

"Yes, that's right."

"And how have you landed here on this desolate country?"

George was startled with the description of Libya by a person who should be more Libyan than any should, smiled, and said, "We come from the north part of the island…"

"The invaded part, I know."

Silence reigned for a while and the fellow kept fumbling his magazine.

"And how do you find your country after being in America?"

"Terrible, deteriorating, suppression, disorientation, hypocrisy, even religion is misused, life has no value here. The city is full of crooks, too many serpents."

"From what you say, I don't see you staying here for that long?"

"Unfortunately, I'm stuck here; they do not allow me to leave the country."

"But you were studying there; you've got to finish your studies."

"Studying or not, we are branded, although none of our family thought of opposing or feel hostility to the new regime; it's in our religious sect, they have illusions."

"And…"

"Count time, trying to find a way to return to my country."

"Is this not your country?"

"Not any more, the imposed dictatorship disrupted the country's development, education is subdued, dignity wiped out, the hooligans became masters and the elite imprisoned. There is no life here, no scope, and no future."

"And what are the virtues of the country you are studying, Mr. Ramses?"

"First and above all, its democratic, there is freedom in all walks of life. Freedom in every activity, freedom of movement, freedom of thought, freedom of expression, freedom of speech."

"There is a notion that once a person joins the American society, is like falling in a wheat mill funnel, is transformed to a working robot, is that right?"

"There is no underground life, one has to work, to produce, to deliver, to survive."

George eyed him thoughtfully, himself was struggling to set a foothold on this land and save others too.

Hag Ahmed came in, beckoned his brother, both left in a hurry, George lifted his tired body off the plastic chair and dragged his heavy feet towards the chicken hangars

Yianni saw George off at Benina airport, within an hour he was in Athens. His sweet daughter was at the passengers' exit shining with his arrival, by taxi they went to George's sister; he got a very warm welcome by Tim, his brother in law. Gia could not help expressing her affection by allowing several valuable drops of tears to roll down her cheeks. They spent the evening sipping the customary Greek alcohol, ouzo, which turns white when water is added to it.

The next day George called at the United States embassy, the reasoning for the visa was accepted but being Cypriots, were obliged to go to Cyprus and apply form their country. George did not waist time, called at Olympic airways and got return tickets for Larnaca, caught the plane just in time.

The next day their application was approved, they returned to Athens straight away and took the next plane to New York.

The Boeing reached JFK by six in the afternoon local time, but the traffic, the people, the commotion were beyond George's imagination. Had to ask, how to get to La-Guardia airport for the next part of their trip for South Carolina, 'through the exit to a taxi for El-Guardia,' said the dark girl behind the counter. Sonia and George dragged their heavy luggage through the exit and came to a street, the rain was pouring. George stopped perplexed, did not know whom to ask and which direction was the second airport, waved to a taxi, but got no response.

A couple of Indians were battling with an oversize bundle, trying to reach the taxi stand across the street. George watched them, then followed them, there, he asked a black fellow standing idle, he pointed to the taxi stop some fifty meters away, the rain was now heavier, could not wait, the next plane had to be caught, the flight was due in less than half an hour. They managed to catch the Eastern airlines flight for Charlotte and the plane joined the queuing up of planes for various destinations. For the first time George saw such heavy air traffic, their plane moved a few meters and stopped, then a few more meters and stopped again, George fell asleep, Sonia woke him up when the plane was in the air, she said softly, "Dad we are off."

George dipped his hand in his pocket; the traveler cheques were still there.

On their way from Athens sat next to an American Italian, got acquainted and he gave them a picture of the problems they might encounter, stressed that stealing was the worst vice in crowded places.

The plane delayed in taking off and they missed the connection to Columbia, the company put them in a motel for the night. They were given a single room with a double bed, George called the reception and explained that he was accompanying his daughter and not his wife, got no response, was obliged to sleep on the floor.

Early in the morning went downstairs for some breakfast since the airline representative promised them that. George received two coupons and was advised to get the breakfast from a catering truck outside the motel. There was a small confusion, people did not keep any queue, had to ask twice for something to eat, in the end was handed two hot dogs with dripping fat. Ate the fatty stuff and rushed for their luggage, boarded the shuttle bus for the airport, the plane reached Columbia within half an hour.

Outside the airport a hefty black driver climbed off his cab, helped George to pile the luggage in the boot. George explained where they wanted to go; he suggested the Holiday inn, the one near the university campus and the administration building.

After washing up, took their credentials and headed for the administration building as directed by the hotel receptionist. She was very friendly, she confessed that she liked Greek people, and was married to a Greek fellow who died in a car crash.

At the administration building, a young woman with Lebanese roots received them, very friendly, very co-operative. Sonia had a small problem in catching the accent; people spoke with a melodious tone, whilst her Dad orientated himself in no time.

"Your are Cypriot? We have a girl named Sophie from Cyprus, she just passed through, let me see if I can catch her for you?"

Closed her office, and slipped through a back door, returned within minutes with the girl, "this is Sophie, I mentioned to you, she is Greek."

George and Sonia were surprised to meet, all out of the blue, a Greek Cypriot girl in a remote state down south.

Within minutes Sonia was talking to a girl, she met several years back in a village in Cyprus. Old memories revived, both girls embraced, Sonia's reserved face gleamed now, met a compatriot, an old friend.

The young woman helped George in many ways, since they came from a different environment. They hired a taxi went to the mall where Sonia purchased several personal things. George inquired about the university, the campus, and the life around there. Sophie was a great help for Sonia and a great relief for George, he felt relaxed; Sophie would help, advise and support his daughter in that distant, unique, multinational but democratic country. He saw a change in Sonia, saw her reviving, spreading her wings, felt relaxed, and talked about her ambitions, her targets.

"Here, you will not have any difficulty in achieving your target as long as you study, you don't even need to study that hard, because people have no real stress, they go around relaxed, secure. Anyone who avoids the rough places lives a happy life, jobs are available, and people pay a good wage for a reasonable day's work. What they do not have is the social security on a national basis but as a student, you are covered by your student's ID," said Sophie.

"Sonia don't worry, you have friends here. My sister is here too, you will meet her soon, let's go down this alley we are close to our dorm."

Within minutes, they met Andrei, Sophie's younger sister; she was very busy, a term exam was coming up. They left Andrei with her studying, walked up to the hotel, there in the lobby the girls chatted about Cyprus and the good time at Sophie's native village, about the university, the lessons there, the university's activities and the students from so many countries.

The next day, within an hour or so, everything, really everything was arranged. Sonia's registration, her dormitory, the shuttle bus, the bank facilities, and even George's return route to Athens. George was amazed with the organized system, the promptness of concluding a job, the clarity of the people and their willingness to offer their assistance even over a phone.

When George requested the receptionist to advise him how to book his return ticket, she simply said, "I'll give you the phone numbers of the airlines and you can do it yourself without any hindrance; if you encounter any problem, please contact me."

George had everything arranged within minutes; rang up the receptionist and thanked her for her support.

The University of South Carolina was founded in 1802, and was the favorite institution for many faculties; Sonia was more than pleased when Sophie informed her about the university's reputation.

Through Sophie, Sonia met an old Greek Cypriot woman living in Columbia for a long time. She lived with her unmarried daughter in a nice brick built house of the older generation when labor was a lot cheaper and people built houses of a more permanent structure. Were invited to attend the Sunday mass at the Greek Orthodox Church, they went and had a very warm welcome by notable members of the established Greek community. After the mass enjoyed a wonderful lunch with the Antony's family at their house and proposed with Cyprus wine.

George kissed his daughter good bye, wished her good luck, and promised her every support in front of the Humanities centre. Tried hard to conceal his emotion but was impossible, father and daughter teared freely; let the tears roll down their cheeks. George began walking away, tried hard not to turn his head back but could not resist, Sonia was bolted at the same spot, motionless, even from that distance, George's blurred eyes could see her tears rolling down forming visible serpentines,

"Please Sonia, you will miss your class, please go, I will write to you soon, very soon."

"How soon? Libyan post office moves at a camel's pace."

"My beloved, I'm afraid is the only way to communicate from there."

George remembered the advisory letter that he prepared the night before and forgot to hand it to his daughter. He turned back and hurried towards her. She run forward and embraced her father, she thought that he turned back for another hugging; George let her hold him for a few long seconds, there he handed her the letter, with the advice to open it after he was gone, now it was Sonia who advised her father to go, he might miss his plane.

"That letter, keep it, read it as often as you need, good buy my love." Said George and walked straight, steadily away with clear conscious, had to catch the flight for New York.

From JFK reached Athens by Olympic airlines, spent two days with his sister and Tim, and enjoyed the ouzo with the plentiful meze at their home balcony.

At the Hellinikon airport George found himself battling with another hundred passengers to board the flight to Benghazi, the good old way of manners did not change, the seats were numbered but all passengers wanted to be first on the plane. Though aware of the conditions, still he was shocked, why should that start right from the boarding of the plane, he was still in Europe, paused shocked and looked at the mass of noble creatures in front of him, wondering if they were humans or not.

From Benina airport George got a taxi for his home, Kate was thrilled to see him back, so were Margarita and Mary, the small presents were welcomed. After supper, George recited in detail about the university, the town, the life there and the conditions of the student life. He assured his family, that Sonia met an old friend of hers, an old playmate, and that she settled down quite nicely. Explained how they met Sophie, then the Antony's family, how they found the church and the quiet life of the town of Columbia.

32: *The Barber of Berka.*

George called early at Hawari; the offices, the farm, the whole place seemed deserted. Walked round the houses, the chicken were there, some chirped happily but others cried in complain. Waited there between the hangars for more than half an hour, the workers began work at their leisure, and the early risers opened their hangars at 7.30, the lazy at around 9.00. The early risers welcomed George and expressed their feelings to see him back; the late ones cursed his return at low tones and complained of some ailment as the cause of their delay. Just after ten Hag Farag arrived at the office, was very happy to see George, they took tea and talked about the United States, a country he visited during better days. They talked about the farm, the workers, and the condition of the chicken flocks that George did not find to his satisfaction. The same day he began chasing everybody, good, and bad, he had to impose his standard in sanitation, ventilation, feeding, watering, and medication.

The Tunisian workers disliked George's tempo but Hag Farag applied his pressure, George's success was parallel to his and his numerous family, as chicken farming was their only source of income.

The first lot of chicken was about to finish, the growth was good, the birds looked even and the mortality low, George was happy. When they killed those birds and the meat sold very easily, Yasser did not appreciate George's achievement. The old farm manager preferred poor farm conditions, in that way he dominated and when the finished product was not marketable, was stored in a poor refrigerator from where he sold it at will at negotiable prices, had his side income in that way.

George's program was to produce poultry meat of prime quality, to market it directly or the earliest and collect his share.

Yasser tried to dishonor George to Hag Farag, George stood up to all accusations with facts. His Arabic improved considerably and was able to hold a conversation and understand the arguments and the accusations. Yasser accused George of mistreating the workers and that was the reason some of them ran away, Hag Farag answered for his manager, "I am not sorry if some of those dirty workers leave the farm, stealing will stop, tell the rest to go today if possible."

Until that moment, Yasser was standing, moved about occassionally, simply to attract attention, the moment he got the answer, walked, and found a seat for himself at the far end of the office.

"Yes Yasser, you have anything else?"

"I tried to trade our old stock of chicken meat with the fresh one, but George intervened and the man left without purchasing even half and half."

"George proved something we could not understand ourselves up to now, produced marketable chicken, does not even need a refrigerator, you see the difference, produced chicken that can be sold and bring money, money badly needed."

"I only tried to trade the old stock and help the company."

"You wanted to solve your problem, the chicken you grew and could not be sold; for how long are they in the cold store, one month, two months? You see with George the results are clear, from ten thousand day-old chicks we have now for sale, this very moment 9645 birds, which is 96.5 per cent of the ones housed, a percentage to be more precise that you never achieved."

"We did Hag Farag, we did."

"Do not remember, may be I'm getting too old?"

Yasser sank to his seat, propped his elbows on the table and hid his face in his palms.

George stood up to his reputation, won the battle but created a formidable enemy, Yasser, had though to defend himself, needed the job, was entering an era of expenses, his daughter entered the university. Kept to his program, handled the workers with a firm fair hand, and the ones who followed his instructions and produced good chicken, got a prim from the farm owner.

Another crop finished with as good results, Hag Farag was pleased, but the hawks were after George, the chicken peddlers lost their lick, the peasants lost their take away, and the stray dogs got thinner.

Although chicken farming demands work seven days a week, most of the workers slipped away by ten on Fridays. George tried to arrange a rotation program but religion was brought up, how could a non-believer like George take off on Fridays whilst a Muslim work amongst the chicken? Was the only Christian, had to shoulder the Friday morning work and call in the afternoon too for a check up, which took not less than three good hours.

Hag Farag normally called at the farm on Friday afternoons, dressed up in his traditional white outfit, shining in cleanliness, from the traditional white cap to his linen shirt, the heavy cotton baggy trousers embroidered on both sides and the bottom ends, even white polished sandals and solemnly read his Ko-oran. Paid no attention to anyone whilst reading his psalms, hardly greeted George when he entered the office, and George avoided unnecessary visits to the office, why Hag read alone and for what, only he knew.

The hot summer was almost over, rather the summer, the customary school summer holidays were over, the campers returned to their confinement, back to their tiny apartments, behind locked doors. The freedom of the expansive beaches was over; freelancing and skin colors were brought back to the city.

The school reopened as usual but the schoolteachers delayed their return from the motherland of Greece. Even some of the pupils delayed their arrival for the simple excuse of lack of teachers.

On the opening day, father Iacovos, the Greek consul accompanied by two of his disciples, the community council and most of the parents gathered on that hot September afternoon to hear the new schoolmaster's speech, to take a soft drink with sweets from the nearest confectionary and chat about their summer holidays.

Father Iacovos never missed to say a prayer and sprinkle first the consul and then the other dignitaries with his holy water that he brought all the way from down town as the school water system was cut off since the community did not pay their bill in time.

It was a real gathering, where the Greek women married to locals, came along wearing their heavy golden ornaments and the females of the expatriate employees prostrated their new hairstyles and deep tan. The children got excited and ran up and down the schoolyard like newly freed goat kids. Bunched for a moment at one spot and the next moment at the far end, greeting each other loudly and telling exaggerated stories from the motherland.

Margarita registered in the first-class of the Lyceum and Mary entered the gymnasium, both girls passed to their new classes with no difficulty at all. Margarita had no problem whatsoever in following the curriculum, Mary was the top class pupil in the elementary but going to a higher class in the secondary school had her reservations, looked retracted and George spared no time to assist her. He enjoyed sitting with her, helping her sparingly and attempting to involve her in a deeper and further analysis of the subject in question.

"Hello Margarita how was your first day at school?"

"Hello Margarita...?"

"You don't look that enthusiastic, are the lecturers not back yet?

"They are back, alright."

"Then, what is it?"

"I'm fed up with this bloody place, I'm fed up."

Kate kept on with her usual home chores, left Margarita fumbling her new acquisition, her book on poetry by the Greek laureate Odysseus Elytis.

Margarita was not studying the book, just fumbled through.

"We live in a place like prisoners, deprived of everything, cannot go out of the country because Dad has no working permit yet, have no entertainment whatsoever, and even the so called basics in other countries."

"My child what happened to you today?"

" Child, I'm not a child any more, I'm seventeen, please mother."

Margarita kept challenging and pushed the conversation to the edge; put her questions sarcastically and irritation swept over her.

Kate was fully aware of the situation, tried to reason with her teenage daughter and find out the reason of today's bad mood. Gave time to her daughter; tried to circumvent exploration and waited for the right opportunity.

"Are all your schoolmates back?"

"Yes, they are back alright."

" Did they bring new stories and imaginations from abroad?"

"Yes, new models of clothes, new hair cuts and don't know what else. This is the third summer we have not been able to get out of this prison."

"Now I get you, you are right, we live here as in isolation. Life turned to boredom and social decay. The system does not inspire much confidence."

"These people have no brains, no speech, no guts, he took their money, their properties, closed their shops and businesses and they sit like ducks waiting for what?"

"My dearest, that is none of our concern, please don't you ever express yourself against the regime, it's a dictatorship, too many informers and God bless anyone that falters."

"Yes, God, mother."

"I feel as bad, no where to go except a visit to a family, the people got tired of us."

"Why did he close the hair salons, the confectionaries, the book shops?"

Kate shook her head in appreciation. "So your schoolmates returned groomed in new styles, Margarita?"

"Yes mother, now look at my hair, needs badly a cut."

"Did you refer it to your father?"

"My father overworks himself with the joint venture with that filthy rich Libyan. I hate those rich people who exploit the needy ones, Muammar treated them accordingly, took their money, confiscated their property, some of those deserved it."

Kate realized that Margarita was building up an argument with facts.

"We all appreciate how hard your father strives to earn our living and save money for your further education."

"Education and education."

"It is the only thing we can afford just now; you know very well what we lost with the Turkish invasion. Mary do you need a haircut too?"

"Thank you mother, my hair has a natural flow, but could do with a trim."

" I'll talk to your Dad later in the day, promise."

George had to drop the girls at home and rush back to the farm, was expecting a new load of chicken feed from the local feed mill. Had to count the number of bags delivered and see how many short. The previous time, the delivery was by fourteen bags of fifty kilos short; when he complained about it to the head of the mill, was told that the weighbridge does not operate properly and some bags come out overweight, and in order to have their ingredients balance correct, deducted from every farmer some bags of feed; a very cheap explanation. Nobody complained about bags of underweight, no farmer possessed a proper weighing scale to be able to check.

Later in the evening, Kate talked to her husband about the matter, George knotted his eyebrows, remained skeptic for a while then said, "they left nothing in its place, wherever one goes meets people mumbling, teeth gritting, cursing, and many really begging for a piece of bread, life is intolerable, everywhere the secret police, informers."

Kate listened with her head down, concentrated on the mending of her husband's threadbare socks, the sweating of his feet worn them out.

"I'll talk to Mohammed, my barber; I hope he agrees to cut our girls' hair."

"Heard of some Yugoslavian who does this from house to house, she worked at Fellah's salon, but cannot recall her name just now."

"Even if she does this, probably around the town center, may not like to come up here. To-morrow will talk to Mohammed; you remember his shop was close to Aquila's restaurant in Berka."

"They were demolishing that quarter, last time we went through there."

"Not his, you know they demolished the whole quarter but left his tiny shop, the army bulldozer stopped at his door."

"Must be one of them, then."

"Quite true, after all his shop is adjacent to that dreadful Berka police station."

"That's where you went with Ramadan to report the Libyan who attacked you?"

"Yes, and they kicked me out simply because I complained against a Muslim."

"They are bad, bad, bad."

"We cannot change them, will solve that by themselves. Mohammed must be one of them and I'm always careful with him, most of his customers are plumb and carefree..."

"What does that mean?"

"The pros are fat..."

"And the cons are thin."

"And rugged."

The next day George called at Berka, parked his car at a fair distance and walked the narrow pavement for Mohammed's barbershop, found it closed, tried the door without success.

"Went to the hospital," called a passerby.

George smiled at him, "hope nothing serious."

"His wife has leg problems."

God, these people have no secrets, thought George, "you know if he opens in the evening?"

"Yes, come after five," said the stranger and disappeared into the police station.

George referred it to his family, Kate advised both daughters to accompany their father to Berka, assuming that Mohammed would be there waiting for them.

"We can go down to Berka after I return from my work."

"George, please come early."

"The timing of my work does not rely on me, you know chicken farming, Kate."

"Today, try to be here early George."

George forced himself, finished earlier, talked to Ibrahim about his departure but warned him not to leave the farm whatever happens.

George drove to Berka with the two girls next to him, advised them to remain in the car until he checks on the barber. The shop was open; George greeted the two sitting and waited. Mohammed turned, saw him in the mirror, raised his eyebrows acknowledging the new customer, George smiled, stood there and waited. When Mohammed finished with his customer, George approached but the customer in queue got up with an angry face. Mohammed raised his finger and George was allowed to reach Mohammed and talk to him. The man nodded positively but before George walked out, Mohammed caught him, "you better wait till these two go."

George left with half a heart, Mohammed did not assure him but did not reject him either, walked to the car and faced four inquisitive eyes.

"We have to wait for a little here, has two customers to finish."

"Did he say, he can do it?" Margarita asked eagerly.

George had no answer, "we just wait my dear."

Before one customer came out, two others entered the tiny place.

"Oh God," said George, but the two came out faster.

When George considered the time right, asked his two daughters to try.

Nervously, all three climbed the three steps and entered, Mohammed nodded approvingly, and George's heartbeat returned to normality. The customer paid and found his way into the busy street.

Mohammed pushed the door closed and looked at George from behind his thick spectacles.

"I never did this before, it's strictly forbidden, but for you…"

George felt a relief; Mohammed nodded Margarita to get on the chair.

Hesitatingly climbed the step and sat with a thumb, did not like the treatment at all, but under such conditions one has to bear the limitations.

Mohammed placed a towel round her neck and secured it with a safety pin. With both hands lifted her overgrown hair and asked her looking in the mirror, how she wanted him to cut it. He spoke in Arabic and George had to intervene for the translation. Within seconds, Margarita agreed and Mohammed cut the hair in a rough way. He brushed the hair and Margarita approved the cut with a forced smile.

"How about the small one?"

"Mary would you like yours to be cut?" asked George.

Mary explained the barber what she would like him to do with smiles and gestures.

George gave Mohammed a ten-dinar note for both haircuts but Mohammed kept only five. George gestured with a movement of his hand but Mohammed answered with another gesture that he took enough.

George smiled at his two daughters; both thanked Mohammed and turned to leave. Before exiting, George turned and whispered something to his friend.

"She cannot come here? I may land in jail."

"Can you come to my house?"

"Have no car," he bluffed.

"I can take you."

"Very risky."

George felt his Adam's apple going up and down twice.

"If you come tomorrow at about seven in the evening, will see what we can do, but I want to warn you, it is very risky."

George left with his daughters and Mohammed pulled the shutters of his shop.

The next day George called at the shop as agreed, Mohammed nodded him to take a seat. Sat and waited until

Mohammed finished with the customer on the chair, looked at George, smiled at him, and said, "My friend Salah will take me, you just go ahead, where you stay you said?"

"At Benina complex," smiled George.

"A long way," exclaimed the man who stood up and fumbled his bunch of keys.

"Let's go," ordered Mohammed.

Kate's hair was taken care by Mohammed in the middle of their salon, George gave him five dinars; the man looked at the note but said nothing, expected more.

Margarita appreciated her father's effort to solve her problem, Kate was pleased to have hers cut to her liking, Mary said, "I love the way he cut mine."

33: *Haoua's Dad*

George registered Margarita at the evening classes for English at the higher Libyan institute. The system of registering was very simple; the student took the entrance exams and placed to the level according to his or her knowledge of the language. Promotion to an upper class could be done any time during the running course, considering the progress of the student.

When George suggested that Mary could attempt the entrance exams, she was astounded. George took her to the English teacher, who advised her to take the exam and just write what she knew, the girl agreed grudgingly, her father urged her to try, and Mary entered the examination room, George hang around, passed by the window smiled at her, she came out of the class in tears.

"What happened, my child?" asked George softly.

"Dad, knew nothing of the sort, so, I drew a cat in the middle of the answer sheet."

"That was very thoughtful of you," said Kate.

Mary was accepted for the primary class, within two months was transferred to the junior class, and was much happier in the classroom than waiting in the car until her sister finishes her class.

Registering Mary in the second year was not that easy. The desert winds have blown harder ruffled the desert sand and carried away with them many virtues of the decent people.

People were obliged to follow the imposed changes and abide with the created turmoil.

George drove to the town center where the old palace was turned into teaching classes of Garyunis University, accompanied by his wife and young Mary.

There was limited activity around the street and the small square with rather few cars and very many less people around. He easily parked the car in front of Lenghi's square, where not very long ago would be rather hard to find a parking place; today a lot of space to be spared.

Kate remained in the car parked in that poorly lit side street of the small square, the square with the only fountain in the whole Benghazi. A small electric pump helped the water up to the top of the sand stone column with the chiseled ears of wheat and sylphium.

No street crime as such was experienced and Kate did not run any problem of disturbance.

George smiled at Mary who was too eager to be registered at the vocational classes for foreign languages. Up the stone staircase, they encountered very few persons; the lessons have not started yet. They stopped at the head step, looked along the corridor with George trying to find his bearings and the registration office.

As there were no signs on the doors that looked moreless alike, apart from the flaked green paint, they walked along the corridor with George straining his ears for any conversation indicating the required office. The place was too quiet. He pepped through one half open door and saw two persons sitting on the same table with some papers in front of them, paused for a second contemplating to enter or not.

The woman sitting in a more comfortable way than the fellow sitting to her left, lifted her head and stared at the two who dared to inquire fore something.

The head that looked at them was not that attractive. Under the bare light of the oversize lamp, hanging from the ceiling by a single wire, luminated a face covered with rough skin, unattended pimples and a pair of chapped half-open thick lips that revealed two poorly kept rows of strong dentine. The eyes were sharp and penetrating, shaded by a pair of untidy bushy eyebrows. The forehead was broad with deep furrows meeting in the middle with a pair of perpendicular crevices. The hair composed of curly, raven untidy mane spread to a diameter of twice the size of the head. The picture was not an inviting one at all; spoke in an authoritative manner and asked the two standing at the front of their door if they came for registration.

George answered positively and that gave him courage to enter. He always respected the person facing him, spoke with clarity, and addressed them sincerely.

"Tfatal," meant an invitation.

George was holding Mary's certificate of attendance of the previous year, a birth certificate translated in Arabic, his Libyan temporary residence card and the family book acquired through a friend.

The very first question asked by the female official was if George was a comrade.

The question surprised him, felt his face hot and red, swallowed the extra saliva, but before he managed to give an answer, the fellow with a more sympathetic composure, smiled in an alluring way and said.

"If you are a comrade, you get a discount of fifty per cent. Normal charges are eighty dinar, so if you are, you pay only forty."

George felt more puzzled now, was that a political catch, or did the fellow wanted to give him a discount.

He was battling to earn the family living under those difficult times; forty dinars was a considerable amount, paused, and hesitated to cast his political belief.

"Are you or are you not?" came the question short and sharp from the woman.

George recollected all his courage, let his Adams apple rise and fall, smiled as sincerely as possible, and answered, yes.

The woman pierced him with an icy look and George felt his adrenaline down his bowels.

Without any further questions ordered the fellow next to her to do the registration.

"Your name, please?"

"Did not come for myself, it's for my daughter."

Another long inquisitive pause and George's color was turning red again, felt droplets of perspiration down his spine, stood though erect and repeated the sincere smile.

"O.K." was the second bark from the woman.

Mary was registered in the third class of the English language and George paid the requested sum of forty dinars against a receipt.

The lessons began and the shuttling between Benina building complex and Benghazi center was twice a week, Sunday and Wednesday.

George made it a habit of calling there early, so he could park as close to the main building entrance as possible. Always stood by his car; too many youngsters got the notion of bullying the foreign females.

Noticed that another elderly couple parked their car close to his with registration plate numbers were those reserved for locals, an identification procedure was implemented by the regime; cars driven by foreigners could be distinguished from far away.

Both persons sat in their car waiting patiently but looked somehow different.

George greeted them as he passed by their car and both responded.

"We came for our daughter."

"We came for the same purpose," answered the man, "Ah, there she comes," he added.

George noticed a girl walking next to Mary coming towards him.

"Hello there," said George audibly enough and with a smile.

"Good evening," answered the girl.

"Dad, this is…."Mary tried to introduce her companion.

"Haoua," added the girl with a broad smile and offered her delicate hand for a handshake.

"Sorry, did not catch your name," apologized Mary.

"That's alright; our names are not that familiar with Europeans."

The group of three moved towards the car, the man who greeted George was there waiting.

"Hello Haoua?" greeted the man.

"Mary, this is my father, Dad, this is Mary, my classmate."

George stood aside, the man greeted Mary mentioning his name, and George caught only the second part was Qadhafi.

Another member of the family thought George and with restrain gave his hand for the introduction.

"How are the lessons?"

"Oh, they are alright, the lecturers are British."

"Then you will learn something," said the man.

"Dad, I believe so. Don't you think so Mary?"

"Yes, definitely," added the young one, who was not more than half the age of her classmate.

The street was not a place for comments or discussion, the old man urged his daughter to move along.

"Hope to see you again," said the man.

"Oh definitely, will be coming here as long as the lessons hold."

"Where do you live?"

"George..." said Mary's father, "we live at the Benina complex."

"We live that way too."

George looked at him rather inquisitively; the man explained that they live in Fuehat sharkia (East Fuehat).

"Very nice," said George, rather indifferently.

Fuehat known as the rich suburb of Benghazi, hosted the more affluent in huge and impressive villas.

"To-night, we have to pay a visit to a relative, otherwise you could have come through Fuehat and have a cup of tea with us."

"Thank you very much, very kind of you."

"Next week, by the will of God," said the man.

"Yes, we have plenty of time, very nice to meet you and very kind of you to invite us for a visit to your home."

"You are welcome and there, we'll get to know each other better."

"Definitely! Good night Mr Qadhafi."

"Good night Mr. George, good night young lady."

"Good night sir, good night Haoua."

"Good night Mary, good night Mr. George, pleased to meet you."

"Good night Haoua and thank you for your assistance to Mary."

"She is doing fine, much better than most of our classmates."

"What have you been discussing all this time, got tired sitting in the car," complained Kate.

"Hello Mum?"

George switched on; on the way, explained about the meeting, the introduction, and the invitation.

"We will see," said Kate in her reserved manner.

Haoua was absent from both next lessons, Mary looked downhearted, lost her classmate.

George tried to justify the absence without success; the country was going through a very rough time.

The week after, George parked at his usual side, sat there with Kate and waited for the shriek buzzing declaring the end of the classes.

He noticed the old white American car parking across the street. As he parked across from George, both drivers turned and their eyes met. George briskly climbed off his car and greeted the new acquaintants.

"Haoua missed two lessons," said the woman sitting next to the driver, "Unis was not feeling that well."

George widened his eyelids and strained his ears.

"You know, he has a heart problem, last year had an operation in Switzerland."

"Hello Mr. Qadhafi, I hope you feel better now."

"I'm alright, Aisha is exaggerating."

The woman looked at George with a mournful eye, and then looked at her husband.

George gave another broad smile and wished good health to the man in the driver's seat who looked very quiet.

The bell rang and the stampede on the stone stairs was noisy.

"Here they come, I better go over," said George.

"Haoua will bring your daughter," said the woman in a confident way, "she is such a fine child."

"Hello girls, lessons over?"

"Oh yes," said both classmates.

"We agreed with Mary that you all come along to our house for a cup of tea and a chance to get better acquainted, my parents suggested it anyway" said Haoua looking into George's eyes.

Mary stood there in a pleading way.

"We'll ask Mum, I believe she will agree," said George.

By the time George walked to his car accompanied by the two girls, Mr. Qadhafi was talking with Kate and she agreed for the visit.

"Just follow us," said Mr. Qadhafi, "if you get lost in the traffic, we live in East Fuehat, not far from the old English school, near Ibrahim Magrebi."

"I think, I know the area," said George with some skepticism.

They reached the place; George followed closely the old American car.

Qadhafi stopped in front of a large impressive iron door, honked twice and both gates were flung open. The girl got off the car and her father drove through; she beckoned George to drive in.

"There is plenty of parking spaces inside," said with a soft gesture and a broad smile. The gates closed behind them.

A large double storey house stood in the middle of a huge garden with flowers, decorative plants and many palm trees.

The lady of the house stood at the base of the broad marble staircase waiting for her guests.

"Please come, please Madam," said pleadingly to Kate.

"Kate, just Kate," said Kate with her inviting expression.

"We live upstairs."

The four women were half way up the steps when Qadhafi took George's hand in a friendly way, urging him to climb.

By the time, the two men entered the spacious salon, the two girls and Kate were giggling from across the corridor, Haoua was touring them through the large house, Aisha was heard handling cutlery from across, busy with the tea preparation.

George was not surprised, house helpers were forbidden under the decree of non-exploitation.

The men sat comfortably in the enormous Italian sofas that looked small in the large salon.

A nice chandelier was lit, and the small lamps shone softly on the heavy furniture, the large wall paintings, the thick carpet, and the impressive bureau with shining articraft.

"We just had a tour of the house, everything is so nice and orderly," said Kate with a smile that reached her earlobes.

"Thank you Madam," said Qadhafi in a low tone.

The two girls were taking a tour of the balconies and their chatting was heard from downstairs.

Aisha pushed a kitchen trolley over the thick carpet loaded with porcelain cutlery, teapot, and all the rest of the same vintage. Addressed Kate, after the exchange of a few phrases, they agreed on the color of the tea, the amount of sugar and the number of scones she was going to get.

Before, Aisha addressed George, expressed his gratitude for inviting them to their house that looked wonderful, took a cup of tea with some milk and half a teaspoon of sugar. Was not surprised to notice that his teacup was of Royal Dalton; the silver plated spoon must have been of the same quality.

"We make the pastry by ourselves ever since they closed down the confectioneries," said Aisha with a tinge of bitterness.

"We still have a male Sudaneese on the grounds of my previous status."

"More due to your illness, my dear."

George's eyes darted from husband to wife.

Without asking her husband, poured for him a cup of tea without milk and just a scone on his plate.

"Haoua, can you serve Mary, please?"

The talking was in perfect English. To George's surprise, Haoua spoke fluent English and that inspired him to ask why she attended evening classes.

She responded with a broad enigmatic smile, looked at George with hazy eyes and confessed that due to the closure of every private activity and people were obliged to confinement, the taking of such classes gave her a reason to get out of the house, then turned to Mary and said.

"Look, how lucky I am to meet this wonderful young lady and your good selves."

George, Kate, and Mary responded as if presaged.

"We are the lucky ones, who have met you, the kind people."

Silence reigned over the large salon.

"How did it come and you are in Libya?" asked Qadhafi.

"We lived in the north part of the island of Cyprus and due to the Turkish invasion were forced to emigrate."

"Why to Libya?" asked Aisha.

"My husband is a poultry expert, was managing a large poultry farm in our home country, and came to Libya to start a franchise, here in Benghazi."

"And due to family necessities, we are here now for twelve years," said George.

"You came after the revolution," intervened Unis.

"Well, I visited the country several times, even before the coup, in 68 and 69

"You had contacts since then?"

"My first contact was the Hawari farm."

"Ah, of the Senussi family, belonged to the late King's sister," said Aisha.

"That's what I learned years later, but did not come with them, came with a certain Abdurrahman Buzer, whom I met in Beirut."

"Knew the family, his father was a school teacher," Unis said.

"He, himself was the same," said Aisha.

"But our marriage did not last that long for various reasons."

"And now with whom do you work Mr. George?"

"I work with the Farmers Union as a poultry expert; it was the only kind of employment that could keep me going in Libya. We have considerable expenses with two girls studying at an American University."

"Ah, you have two daughters studying in the States?" asked Aisha with great interest.

Kate gave a short description of the two girls studying abroad.

"Our son Mohammed studied there," said Aisha and a deep sigh escaped her burning lungs.

A deadly silence spread over the softly lit salon.

George lifted his cup mechanically, took a silent sip and replaced cup and saucer as delicately as possible on the side table.

"He finished his studies four years ago. Went with some friends of his to Derna, to visit another fellow student who returned a month earlier, on their way back had an accident, somebody else was driving, hit an electric pole, the high voltage electric wires broke and fell on the ditched car.

Mohammed was not hurt, got off the car in an attempt to help one of his trapped friends, got electrocuted, and died on the spot."

"My God," exclaimed Kate and grabbed Aisha's trembling hand.

"How tragic, I'm sorry to hear it," said George, "God bless his soul."

"Thank you sir and Mohammed's death brought the heart problem to Unis."

There was no more tea in George's cup.

Aisha got up, "shall I pour you another cup to drink it in memory of our Mohammed?"

"Yes please and God bless his soul."

"He was such a fine boy."

"May be, and that's why God took him in his arms," said Unis, who was rather quiet.

The atmosphere was tense, George gave the signal, time was getting late, had another ten kilometers or so and two road check points.

"Do they harass you Mr. George?"

"Not more than any other."

"May be they see where you work and show a better understanding?"

On their way down the stairs, the two women engaged in the usual talking. Aisha asked Kate about the Greek community and talkative Kate grabbed the chance to talk. She mentioned the people from the Greek consulate, some schoolteachers, and Dr. Leventakis.

"You know Dr. Leventakis?"

"Yes, we do, we are family friends."

"Next time you see him, give him our best regards, you know he was our family doctor for years and years."

"We know that he was the doctor of the Palace," said Kate, beaming of the acquaintance with Dr.Leventakis.

"Yes, that's right, he was also our doctor. You know Unis was the last but one Prime Minister and Dr. Leventakis was our doctor, he gave birth to our three elder children."

"Did he really?" exclaimed George.

"Would like very much to see him," said Unis.

"We haven't seen him for so many years."

"Since they closed his clinic," said Unis cynically.

"We may see him on Thursday next; usually brings his children over for a get together."

"He is such a kind fellow, lost his wife three years ago, I think," said Aisha.

"I don't remember exactly, but I know she died abroad."

"In Italy, I think, went there for therapy," said Aisha.

"Please bring Dr. Leventakis next time and Aisha will prepare something for all of us."

"Can only ask him," said George.

"I'm sure when you ask him will give a positive answer."

"We meet almost daily outside the Greek school."

"Is the Greek school still there in Fuehat?"

"We found it there."

"I signed the permission for the school, when I was Prime Minister."

"I'm sure the Greek community is grateful to you, Mr. Unis."

"In general they were a progressive community and want to believe still are."

"The old guard is weaning, the newcomers are on temporary basis."

"George, shall we go?" called Kate.

"Good night Mr. Unis, I will try my best."

"Good night Mr. George, would like very much to see our old friend and doctor."

On their way home, George thought that one understands a man better after a visit to his house.

Unexpectedly Dr. Leventakis called on Thursday evening for a cup of tea. Kate prepared a nice dinner that everybody enjoyed.

When George mentioned Unis Qadhafi, the doctor's body jerked as if struck by an electric current.

"You met Unis Qadhafi? And went to his house?" asked with great interest.

Kate explained how they met Unis' family.

Dr Leventakis congratulated Mary for her desire to learn and her audacity to get acquainted with her classmates.

Mary blushed and conceded to a humble, thank you.

Before departing, the doctor of the Royals insisted that, a meeting should be arranged the soonest.

Kate eagerly expressed great interest also and that obliged George to make the necessary arrangements.

"These people are always watched and one has to be very careful when talking to them and even more when calling to their house," warned the veteran doctor of the Royals.

George felt an invisible fear.

Kate's enthusiasm subsided, remained silent, bid farewell to the departing family, and returned to her domain, the kitchen.

Cautiously, the necessary contacts were made and all agreed to call at Fuehat on Thursday evening.

"Don't delay, so we have plenty of time to talk," said Aisha.

"Agreed," added George.

The doctor called at George's house at the agreed time alone. George refrained from any inquiries about his two grown up children.

"Can we all fit in your car, Mr. George?"

"I believe so; we are not that many now."

"Please Madam Kate, sit in the front."

After the exchange of who would sit where, George intervened and asked the doctor to sit in the front, at least he would guide them on the way.

"What, you don't know the place? I have not been there for years; though still remember the big house with the beautiful garden."

With the touch of the bell the gate was opened and George drove through, before he even switched off the engine, Aisha met them gleaming.

"Welcome doctor, welcome to our house, welcome all of you, please."

The man shook hands with her and thanked her sincerely for the invitation.

"We are really pleased that you managed to visit our home, it's how many years now?"

"The pleasure is mine, time flies, can't recall the last time."

"Thanks to these kind people who helped for this meeting."

George quickly mentioned that all should thank the two young ladies; they began the contacts.

"Whoever began this, God bless them," said Aisha, "we've prepared something for dinner, so we might as well move to the dining hall."

Unis, until then, was sitting quiet facing politely his guests with a fathomless look probably traveling to the past, more glorious days.

Aisha smiled considerately, caught the message, rose elegantly, and with a polite gesture invited her guests.

The table was set accordingly, though Dr. Leventakis was very well acquainted with the ex-prime Minister, and his family, still the table setting took a ceremonial layout.

Traditional dishes, expertly prepared followed one after the other in sequence and custom.

Halfway, the doctor with an expert eye, surveyed the table and the occupants, Aisha caught his quest and said, "Our Mohammed died, its four years now."

"More than that Aisha," added Unis.

"Yes, I was in Italy at that time, that's when my wife died."

"She died in Italy, then?"

A deadly silence reigned over the table and the elegant dining hall.

"Yes, we went to continue the therapy, but the disease caught on us."

"This is an incurable disease."

"At least for now, medicine is advancing and hope one day will come up either with a drug or a vaccine."

"It's the horror of our times, I believe."

"You had another son, I remember."

Aisha almost dropped off her sofa, Unis looked at her in a sympathetic but austere way.

Leventakis, George, and Kate withheld their breathing, turned to Aisha and gave her time to compose herself.

"You know our Usef is in jail in Tripoli, its more than two years now."

"Why, he is just a boy, how old is he, twelve, thirteen?" asked Leventakis with a husky voice.

"He turned fourteen last July, the 14th of July actually."

A deadly silence reigned over the large salon; the small group of visitors withheld even their breathing.

"You know doctor; our Usef was accused of conspiring to assassinate that son of a bitch at the inauguration of the new supermarket at Rue Saad. The boy was silly enough to express himself against the great Leader in his classroom along with Omar, a close relative of Haroubi. Some classmates, informers, reported them and on the day of the inauguration were approached by the secret police and carried them away, took them to Tripoli, informed us only two weeks later. It took us more than ten days to find out where they were held and that we managed through Unis contacts. When they took them away, were not even twelve."

"Do they allow you to visit them?"

"Once a month; sometimes we fly there and return without being allowed to visit our Usef."

Four pairs of eyes pierced Aisha, eager to learn more about Usef's custody.

"They procure all kinds of excuses, wretched persons."

"How are the conditions in that horrible prison of Abu-Salim, probably worse than the Quefia one."

"Quefia may be considered a holiday camp compared to Abu Salim of Tripoli. Not just our Usef, but also many others too of his age are held prisoners. Imagine, they are allowed to visit the toilet just twice daily, get very poor food and the worst, do not allow them to read even school books. They get either the Holy Koran or that horrible Green book of the new philosopher. He solved all the other problems and engaged himself in a new theory, on politics."

"They try to preach the Green book, in reality it's a combination of socialist and Islamic theories, rejects democracy and political parties, they call it the Third Universal Theory.

"Was produced to promote Muammar as Leader de facto chief of the state and guide the revolution."

"You know the story that Muammar tried to sell it to the Soviets, was turned down, too cheap for theories and he landed in Yugoslavia with his friend Tito?"

"And ordered his disciples to ship his tent and his animals; typical Bedouin behavior."

"And the people here had to watch all of that on the state television, what a laugh?"

"Heard that the detainees are badly tortured in the most horrible ways."

Many people talk about the falaga, beating on the soles, pole stretching, electric shock, cigarette burning, biting by aggressive dogs, death threats, psychological treatment, threats to the family members."

"They use radio transmission at high volume for long periods so that detainees cannot sleep, and have the 'car torture' where they force them to sit uncomfortably on boxes for days even weeks with hands tied to their backs."

"Underground rooms are used for interrogation and torture, from what I heard down at the Halige, the offices of the newly formed oil company."

"Detainees are held incommunicado and their whereabouts remain unknown, when relatives call at Abu Salim prison, they send them to Ain Zara or to Al-Ataba

"These people are off their mind, the train is about to get derailed," said Leventakis, "haven't you applied to international bodies to visit them and investigate such atrocities?"

"We applied. Actually, Aisha's brother did, he lives in London, and representatives from the International Red Cross and the International Amnesty came; we were informed and went to Tripoli. When those officials requested to see the prisoners, you know what they answered, 'what prisoners, no juvenile prisoners are held, we have a few grown up held for civil offences. The people waited a whole week without success."

"They denied categorically such accusations. We tried in vain through some of our people to find a loophole, nothing, were even threatened; with broken hearts returned to our prison," said Unis.

Aisha was sobbing, Haoua with bent face down studied the food remnants of her plate, Kate looked stealthily at the parents, George kept a sober face, wanted to say something, but Dr. Leventakis saved him.

"Heard of the dreadful conditions but would never imagine such hatred and misery."

"You know very well, that many other prisoners are held in solitude for years, where even family members are not allowed to visit them."

"Heard of Ahmad al.Thuthi was denied of family visits for three or four years."

The group moved to the salon where the two women served tea.

Mary did not utter a single word, looked very sad; from time to time Haoua took her hand in hers.

"Are you still helping patients, doctor?"

"Whenever possible, times have changed. Accept few patients but it is rather tricky and no one can tell who is knocking at your door. However, occassionally, I'm requested to call at the hospital. Last week was called to see a dead girl at the Jamahiriya hospital. The girl, the younger daughter of Usef Harati, joined the army under the new law. She was not even eighteen when recruited. Young as she was and with very little social experience, got pregnant. The parents were shocked and demanded an abortion. Under her parents' pressure and the neighborhood, went to the hospital for the occasion, she had the abortion but died of sipsimia, very poor conditions in that hospital now. There is a shortage of medicine and hygiene is almost non-existent. Most of the medical staff is Asians with doubtful interest."

"And she is not the only one, there is a whole ward dedicated for maternity. Many female recruits ended up for abortion; very few denied that and gave birth to such illegitimate children."

"This is new and disgraceful to our people. It was a fallacy to enroll females in the army at this stage. They were not ready for such a venture, poorly educated and misinformed about the grievances and pitfalls of the army. Totally disagree with the situation, though was not happy with the closed life and prearranged marriages either. There are cases of first cousins getting married under the pressure of their parents with disappointing results. Quite often, such marriages give children with noticeable defects."

"In your opinion, Hag Unis, are they trying to change the system, the course of legendary customs?"

"From the look of it, certainly, but customs and taboos cannot be changed overnight, any hasty action normally brings poor results."

"Customs are not written on stone."

"Nobody likes perpetuation of the stereotypes."

"Yes, true, wherever people are deprived of their rights and customs, progress is either retarded or hindered."

"In another case, was asked to visit an old woman, her son came to our house, rang the bell in that characteristic way, Costas answered the bell, the man entered and pleaded persistently. We went to an apartment in Abdel Nasser Street, in the building of old Mavrakis. The place looked disgusting; the sewage flooded the entrance, the lift out of order, and the steps dirty, muddy, and slippery.

We managed to climb to the fourth floor; the man opened the door using his own set of keys. The apartment was very badly kept, the place untidy and depressing. The woman was suffering from chronic arthritis. Checked her and advised on some medicine, suggested though to move to a better place, that apartment was damp with a bad smell of decay. You know what the son said, 'Doctor, to go where, everything is under control, we are going through very bad times and nobody knows when it will change,' the army fellow expressed himself, kept my opinion to myself."

"It is bad for everyone, since that bloody fool from Cuba visited him, things have deteriorated, gave him new ideas," said Unis.

"Yes, people say that Fidel advised Muammar to restrict even foodstuffs, so people will run after him with open palms, begging for alms."

"They are both Bedouins," said Unis.

"Last week, heard noises down the street, by the Christmas tree square, looked through the window and saw those "rogues of his" slashing car tires and smashing wind shields, windows and head lamps, even the body work were damaged. It is the new trend against the bourgeoisie with the big cars."

"Heard about it," said Unis with a sad voice.

"Noticed that too," added George solemnly.

"We talk about hospital hygiene; you heard what happened at the At-fal hospital, rumors go round that hundreds of children have been infected with the disease of aids."

"Yes, Dr. Hakim told me that, about four hundred, many died already and they accused a group of Bulgarian nurses."

"Also, Dr. Ashraf, a young Palestinian, with a degree from Cairo, clever fellow, met him just before they imprisoned him along with the six nurses."

"What a disgrace, the medical personnel are not responsible for the deteriorating hospital conditions. Corruption is thriving, medicine, equipment, material vanish overnight. Facilities have been neglected, how cleanliness can be sustained without sanitary products and above all, water."

"You remember the standard of that children hospital when the Americans built it?"

"Yes Unis, I remember, management, maintenance, cleanliness, personnel, everything ran like a bee hive."

"Now the water system does not work, the sewage system is blocked, electricity is not staple, and the locals do not call for work, a sheer disgrace."

"With fiery speeches nothing can be achieved, show me deeds, results, people lost their values," said Unis.

"George is running a chicken farm, properly cared and luckily we have enough meat; you know how many persons call daily requesting chicken meat?" said Kate.

"It is hard to find chicken, especially good plumb chicken," said Aisha, "and do you supply them?"

"Not to everybody. George cannot kill everyday."

"The man who kills chicken does not call for work everyday," said George, "personally avoid killing birds, I am a Christian."

"You would have done a better job, I'm sure."

George blushed but refrained from any comments.

It was almost midnight and the guests considered the visit long enough. Unis though was eager to talk, to extricate, to relief himself, and requested the two male guests to move to his study, for a cup of tea.

Dr. Leventakis conceded to the request and George nodded positively. All three moved to the spacious office furnished with heavy polished furniture.

Unis begged his guests to take a seat, walked to his chest of drawers, pulled a drawer and took out two flat files of considerable thickness, held the files with both hands reverently and placed them on his desk. Both files looked old; the top one had the name of "Brown and Roots,'" printed in block fading letters.

The company's name rang a bell; it was the British based consulting company for the famous Great Man Made River, which Qadhafi boasted notoriously.

Both guests were not surprised about the files since Unis Qadhafi was Prime Minister of the country.

Without introduction or loss of time, Unis opened the second file and said, "you see these files, have been in my possession since 1954," and pointed at the dated stamp on one of the letters lying in the file.

"These people talk about achievements of the green revolution, I can tell them, the study about the desert water was done and concluded in 1954, look how many years back. We know, water was there in the desert but needed money, a lot of money for drilling, pump installation, and pipe lying. During those hard years, we did not even have money to pay the government employees. We know very well about the quality and quantity of the water and the study about the existence of the water in the desert. One theory was that the White Nile, before kicking off towards Egypt, water seeps via underground ducts and finds its way to the Libyan Desert around the Tajerbo oasis, which is the most broadly accepted. The second theory was that the water in that area was the byproduct of the submerged ancient forests, from the fossils came the oil and water. In the course of time the two elements separated by some natural process and the water is now available. As mentioned to you, we did not have flour how we could make bread.

King Idris and his government worked very hard to build the nation, invested in exploiting the natural resources and organize the country."

"Knew that plans were laid for that water reserve," said Leventakis, "but did not know that was concluded decades back, still it's a gigantic project, a lot of money was needed, but has become a reality and water is available in many households in Benghazi and very many other inhabited places along the east coast."

"It's true that water is available for the people, at least it's money well spent."

"It's a gigantic project, probably the biggest Libya ever experienced. We visited one of these trenches about three hundred kilometers from Ajdabiya. Huge machinery operate day and night. The diggers open trenches seven meters deep and seven meters wide to accommodate the four-meter diameter concrete pipes. The extracted soil is fed into a crusher and piled close to the trench; is used for bedding and backfilling," George said.

"Mr. George is more technical than myself," Leventakis said.

"Thank you for the details," added Unis.

Gorge noticed the resentment, stopped talking.

The women finished cleaning up and the elders came over to the office.

Aisha cautiously smiled and in a low tone said, "Unis don't you think it s rather late?"

"Yes, we better go, the later in the night the greater the danger to meet the inquisitive obnoxious secret police," said the doctor.

"They get very notorious at night, that's what I heard too," said Unis.

"I am very glad that I was able to see you after so many years, times are hard, I'm waiting for the children to finish their schooling and will be moving, the place stings with ammunition."

"Good night Madam Kate, very nice of you to help Aisha, let God be with you."

"Oh, the pleasure is mine and you are invited to come to our house, I'll prepare something."

"Madam Kate is a wonderful housewife and an excellent cook, she cooks wonders," said Dr. Leventakis.

Kate blushed, George stepped forward, "she tries with whatever is available, but assure you that she may please even the most demanding palate."

"Good night Madam Kate, thank you for your help, I'm sure you are a great wife."

"Just Kate, please."

The two girls were chatting by the car.

The helper opened the gates; George drove through cautiously, and took the shortcut to the main street.

Several times, George met Unis taking his exercise walk along the Hawari road always accompanied by Haoua. Whenever they met, George stopped the car discreetly and chatted with them.

Haoua did not attend her evening lessons regularly, probably did not find them so interesting for her.

When Mary inquired in her class about her close classmate Haoua, was told that her father died, and gave up her lessons.

34: *Sayeed's revenge*

Despite George's great effort and hard work to put the Hawari farm on its feet, the marriage with Hag Farag did not last that long. George mastered the management of poultry but the intrigues and black mailing suppressed his efforts, with Yasser, the master of the game. His popularity dropped dramatically through the practice of the good old Arab method by circulating rumors on various subjects, involving religion too. That was enough to provoke his reverence Hag Farag against a non-Muslim; he could not defend George or even support him in front of the Muslim workers, and times were not that favorable for such a confrontation.

Though production improved to a very high level with George's income being more than tenfold, had to subjugate to the invisible pressure. Hag Farag called George to the office and announced bluntly that he was not happy with the efforts and his achievements; George did not argue with him, requested to close the accounts, give him his share and promised to be available if Hag needed any help.

Two days later George called at the farm as agreed to collect his share, was told that Yasser was sacked and that Hag Farag was undertaking full responsibility of his enterprise, within a few months not even a single chicken was grown on the farm, it was closed down due to poor performance.

George took a long due rest; stayed at home for a whole week, taking the girls to their school and in the afternoons to their English lessons and spent the evenings with friends. He talked the matter with Yianni who listened carefully and promised to help him for a new job.

A couple of days later Yianni, asked George to meet a certain Ahmed Quafi, who owned a big poultry farm on the Hawari road. George knew the farm from the days of slaughtering chicken and agreed to meet the owner. After the coffee, both drove in George's car to Ahmed's place. The fellow recognized George and was quite friendly. Was honest in his past dealings and George saw a ray of hope to start afresh, needed urgently to work, the expenses were mounting.

Ahmed demanded that George deposits a sum of at least two thousand dinars, pay the laborers and share the net profit fifty, fifty. George agreed to all the demands, the only drawback was the two thousand dinars, promised though to deposit the amount within the first three months, Ahmed hesitated but Yianni intervened and guaranteed the transaction.

"I have already an order of two thousand day-olds, if you like, you can grow those, and then we'll see," said Hamed, that's how his friends called him.

George accepted the offer and requested to inspect the hangars, Hamed joined him to the chicken farm with the six hangars cordoned off with chain link wire, the houses properly built and equipped, the only drawback that George saw were the roofs, were of zinc sheet and without insulation.

"We have a water spray system for the hot days," said Hamed.

"This is very helpful on hot days; the problem is the humidity in the houses during winter with simple zinc sheet roofing."

Hamed looked at him with surprise, did not expect the comment.

George began work on the next day, began arranging the hangar for the next batch, repaired some windows and cleaned the water tank, water was plentiful and always available, George for the first time felt at ease. He repaired the lighting, the water tubes, and the rolling shutter doors.

Hamed, in his forties, carried around hundred and forty kilos, walked slowly with both hands braced behind his broad buttocks, looked kind hearted but liked his alcohol.

Close to the chicken farm was an enormous water tank from where the Tunisian partner watered the cash crops. Adjacent to the water tank, Hamed built a room downstairs that he used as an office and store for some poultry equipment, medicine and a refrigerator that served as a meat depot for his drinking habits. Above the office another room was built, here a gas stove was kept busy seven evenings a week, except during the holy month of Ramadan, when Hamed abstained from alcohol. The room was equipped only with the most essentials, a plate holder, a gas stove, two refrigerators, and a round table with some poor quality folding chairs. The steps leading to this upstairs room were of solid concrete with very small elevation between them; Hamed could not lift his legs that much. The staircase led to a closed veranda, walls covered half way with zinc sheets and the rest with glass, a small door opened to the uncovered water cistern. The covered veranda was the meeting place of the customary visitors who called almost daily; the big gatherings took place on Thursday nights.

An Iraqi, who worked as a poultry attendant, specialized in cooking meat in an underground hearth oven. It was actually a barrel buried down in the soil with an opening, through which they fed wood for heating and with two pipes protruding that helped as ventilators. When the heat was at the right level, flat stones were placed over the ambers and chops of marinated meat wrapped in aluminum foil along with jacket potatoes were laid over the stones. The opening was then covered with a piece of zinc sheeting and sealed with mud, the whole process took about three hours depending how smart was the Iraqi.

At the first yelling, the Iraqi opened the oven and rushed the first chunk of meat up the steps, the calling followed according to the consumption and the clients, alcohol required food and was provided in abundance. Remnants from the table went into the water for the fish, mosquito eggs and larvae were eaten as a desert.

George was worried at first, noticed a great disparity between his previous boss and Hamed, the one highly religious and the other not in favor of the Koran; had to wait to find out the real difference.

Another abnormal phenomenon on the farm was the young male camel living permanently within the enclosed area of the poultry unit, along with two ponies; they ran freely all over the place. The ponies were not a problem but the camel grew into a nuisance. Over the years of George's working the unit, *sayeed*, that is how the camel was known around the vicinity, caused many problems to many persons, including George himself.

The first small flock of birds came out very well; from those two thousand chicks, they made a profit of more than two thousand dinars. Hamed could not believe his eyes and his ears when George showed him the results; he was delighted and openly congratulated George. "You made more from this small flock than what we could make from a ten thousand flock."

Flocks were going and coming, George was pleased with the results and his earnings. He hired a young Tunisian to look after the older chicks and he took care of the smaller ones. Normally, he worked the six houses in pairs with a gap between the flocks of not more than two weeks. Applied a program, so that the oldest birds were sold before the new batch of day-old chicks arrived, though occasionally flocks overlapped one another.

Hamed was always at reach, his presence guaranteed the smooth running of the farm, guarding from thieves as well as from any awkward customers.

Within three months, George deposited his share of capital in the farm business as he promised, though the set forth program demanded very much more capital, Hamed could always arrange feed on credit, this helped tremendously in running the farm.

The only period that Hamed was away from the farm, was the month of August, during this month would pull his speedboat loaded with all the camping paraphernalia, his fishing gear and the barbecue for preparing the badly needed cushioning for the drink. Would spend the whole month with few members of his tribe on a far away beach; the land cruiser could pull the boat to any spot of the endless Libyan sandy beaches. The preferred spot was beyond the small town of Gimines, a place that not so many could reach.

During this month, George had to put up with *sayeed* the camel. The Iraqi and Hamed undertook personally the young orphan camel when the mother died a few weeks after its birth. Why it was called *sayeed, the happy one,* nobody gave away the secret, though given a Muslim name no circumcision was done, it grew on a milk bottle into an amicable animal hanging near the entrance of the poultry unit.

Just a few meters from the entrance, Hamed placed two prefabricated small houses, the one served as a dwelling for the laborer and the other one as an office and store for George. Across the yard, not very far from the two small prefabs laid an old Mercedes saloon car that Hamed left after his last journey to Tunis. This car, *sayeed* decided to make it the resting spot during the day. *Sayeed* slept next to it overnight, the most astonishing was that during the resting time. In the most boisterous manner the animal placed both front legs over the engine cover and stayed there for hours, not even the two ponies could go near *sayeed*. If anyone dared to approach the old car he would growl harshly and flap its tail vigorously, would hoist its long neck high up, hold its head to one side and with a glaring eye warned off man and beast. The grey color of the zinc sheet faded off from the constant rubbing of *sayeed's* long neck and the red undercoat revealed.

During Hamed's absence the animal kept a self-centered portrait, did not accept food from many people, the owner offered *sayeed* Nescafe from a plastic cup and occasionally a short alcoholic drink whenever Hamed wanted to show off to his friends. With a second cup, *sayeed* would get a bit tipsy and ran up and down the farm for hours, groaning. Another bad habit of *sayeed* was the sniffing at the exhaust pipes of running engines, then lifting its head high, twisting backwards both thick long lips and showing its two rows of strong grey teeth and exclaim a characteristic erotic sound, nobody dared to disturb it during this special moment.

Occasionally *sayeed* would follow a moving car out of the farm, twice George had to beat it hard with a heavy electric cable to force it back to the farm. The punishment for its disobedience created abhorrence between George and *sayeed* and did not take long to express its revenge for the slashes from George's whip.

One evening the brute slipped through the farm gate into the adjacent yard where several private cars were parked. Hamed had a gathering. George's car was one of the six or seven other cars, *sayeed* did not miss its target, with its strong teeth bit both windshield cleaners and cut them off. When George came to his car it was dark and did not notice the damage but saw *sayeed* running up and down in an unusual manner holding something between its strong mandibles.

"What is that bloody animal after now?" George asked himself and proceeded to his car, to his surprise, both the cleaners were gone; he got furious, switched off the engine, and ran to find the brute, too late the animal was at the far end of the chicken farm. Aware of what might happen to it, was alert and ready to take on its heels if George approached to a threatening distance and that is what happened. George was enraged and with a long piece of wood in hand tried to creep near *sayeed,* too late, the young camel was too fast for anyone. George chased the animal more than twice round the farm, Hamed noticed the uneven struggle from the top of his drinking parlour and called out, "what happened?"

George stopped chasing the brute and went for the upper room, explained Hamed what the camel did, Hamed could not hold his fat belly from laughter and that infuriated George very much more, he said,

"I will charge the two broken parts on the farm account."

Hamed laughed even louder that made not only his belly rock up and down, but his drunken head too, then turned round and entered his drinking parlour, George drove for his home, was already late.

Two days later, George sneaked behind the animal and hit it twice before it managed to run away kicking its hind legs upwards and swinging its powerful tail.

Sayeed never left accounts unsettled. The very same night that George hit it, the animal pushed the rear door of the chicken hangar and squeezed itself inside. Once inside, treaded on several small chicks, tried to eat off the feeders and whether by mistake or deliberately, unhooked the burning gas brooder that dropped onto the littered floor, the wood shavings caught fire, the chicks cried, the animal got scared and ran off with a groaning sound. Luckily the Tunisian heard the commotion and ran out of his home, heard the chicken chirping; acted fast enough to prevent the worst, he hit the animal though rather badly.

When George called at the farm the next day, *sayeed* was standing at the far end of the farm, a sign that it did something mischievous.

Munir, the Tunisian explained what happened, the loss was about hundred chicken, now the animal had two persons to face, George and Munir, it could be the other way round.

Several days later whilst Munir was busy repairing a knapsack sprayer, *sayeed* encroached, bit Munir's scalp damaging the skin, and took some hair off it. Despite the pain and the blood oozing, Munir tried to chase the animal, looked for revenge but never managed. Munir was taken to the hospital for treatment and a jab of tetanus; it took more than a month to heal. Ever since *sayeed* kept away from Munir and Munir always carried a good piece of electric cable.

George's turn did not take that long to come. It was Friday afternoon, not a single soul on the farm, Munir had the half day off, and so George called there to tend the chicken. He fed and watered the small ones, checked the other two hangars, opened the water line to irrigate his small vegetable garden when he noticed *sayeed* hanging around. George tried to ignore the animal and kept himself busy with the watering and weeding the vegetables, he dropped the weeds over the zinc sheet that sheltered the small garden from the ponies and *sayeed*. The ponies ran forward and began nibbling, the horrible animal eyed from a distance, whilst on previous occasions, the animal would scare the ponies away and have the lot for himself, but today the brute stared from afar.

George noticed *sayeed's* indifference, but nothing passed through his mind about the animal's behavior. He left the water running and took the wooden ladder, reached one of the hangars housing the older birds, laid the ladder against the wall, wanted to climb onto the roof of the hangar to check the water level in the tank; he medicated the chicken two days earlier. Normally the climbing and checking took only a few minutes. George was about to close the tank lid when he heard a thumb, paid no attention for the moment but was surprised, when he reached the point where the ladder was supposed to be, the ladder was gone, it was laying on the ground two meters below the eave of the hangar. George looked around; saw *sayeed* staring at him from the distance of about ten meters in the most vengeful manner.

"You stupid animal," screamed George from the top of the roof.

"Prrrrr," was the reply of the brute

George wanted to jump off the roof and kill the brute but the height stopped him. From that height, he scanned the vicinity for a passer by, but nobody could be seen, it was Friday afternoon and people went to the beach or to the city; was left on top of the hangar sweating it out.

It was hot and his fury was mounting, he longed for a sip of water, tried from the tank ball valve with no luck. Did not want to bring water to his mouth with a dirty palm, released the ball valve, the water stopped running as the chicken were on medication. The water from the pipe was hot, brought though some in his palm and rubbed his hands, and repeated the process until he managed to remove the thick layer of dirt from his hands. The liquid was too warm for the mouth; he was mad, angry, looked down at the animal, and screamed, "Just wait till I climb off this roof."

No response from the animal, did not understand Greek or any other language, did not move from its position, not even flipped its ear or swished its tail. George noticed only the grey eyelids closing twice over the large eyeballs and resting back in the usual position.

Sayeed was enjoying George's anguish; stood there headstrong, stiff neck, unbending, unshakeable. In vain George tried to ignore that, sat on the hot tin roof sweating it out until the brute ran twice round the chicken farm to arouse George's attention, then returned to its previous position and resumed the same obstinate witty posture.

George's worry was how to descend from the hot tin roof and quench his thirst; *sayeed* was not his main problem just now. Two and a half hours later, an old customer called to the farm by chance to check if any chicken were ready for the market. George felt a relief when he saw the old pick up van approaching the chicken hangars.

"Salem," shouted George from the top of the hangar, the moment the man stepped off his car.

Right from his position George explained what happened; Salem equipped himself with a long stick and entered cautiously through the side gate, reached the fallen ladder keeping an eye on the animal. An angry roar was heard when *sayeed* saw the ladder been lifted, then darted to a safer distance. Salem held the ladder for George to climb down.

"Salem, thank you very much, if you allow me I need some water, let me get some and then we discuss the rest."

"Welcome, George it's your farm."

"Thanks old boy."

Salem warned George about the treacherous animal, "many people got knocked down and treaded over by these crazy animals, anyway its still young and hope Hamed gets rid of it before it grows older."

"Hope so too, it's giving us a lot of problems."

"It's a male, isn't it?"

"Yes, I think so."

"By the great Allah, camels are traitorous and male camels are killers, especially during the mating season."

"I hope Hamed takes it away or kills it."

"I know Hamed, he grew it up, he is attached to it, he will not agree to any of that."

"I'll ask him to tether the bloody animal."

"Camels are difficult to tether, they tend to attack their attendants."

Salem, an Arab, knew a lot about camels, he told stories of camels attacking the caravan personnel overnight, killing anyone who ill-treated them.

"During mating season, male camels are dreadful, may attack even the caravan leader, a mere groan of a camel may send fear all around," said Salem

"You know them better than me, Salem; the last time I saw a camel was forty years ago."

"There are no camels in Cyprus?"

"Scarcely any, I think there is one at the zoo."

"In Sudan there are too many, the Sudanese drive them here for slaughtering when there is a shortage of meat."

"So those herds we see from time to time come from Sudan?"

"Yes, all the way from Sudan, they are killed here, some people are fond of camel meat, I'm not very fond of it, though there is nothing wrong with it, and camel is a forager."

"Apart from its requital the meat is edible, and the elders prefer it to bovine."

"The people who really know the camel are the caravan people, they train them in many ways apart from being very friendly, and understanding to them, is the only animal that can walk on sand."

"I know that the camel was the boat of the desert and for hundreds of years it was the means of transporting goods across the desert; the camel was exploited by man anyway."

"Camel is an intelligent animal and remembers not only the bad but also the good experiences, you know the caravan people train their camels to dance?"

George craned his neck and strained his ears, how can a camel be trained to dance, this slow motion animal.

"It's simple; the elders tie the camel's eyes and drive them over an area covered with live coal. Normally the dry manure is used for the purpose, in a desert wood is scarce. Well the animal with its eyes tied is driven over the live ambers, whilst another person thumbs the tarbouqa. The animal's soft feet pads get hot and moves them up and down hoping to step on a cooler spot but the caretaker leads it by the rope over and over the burning coal to get the feeling, a feeling that is never forgotten. The practice if repeated two or three times then the animal treads to the tune of the tarbouqa without stepping on burning ambers. Many animals were trained to dance in this way; it is the amusement of the caravan people in the desert."

"So the caravan people and I would say the Arab caravan people, have exploited the animal senses long before Pavlov."

"This fellow used a whistle whilst feeding his confined dogs; the dogs got used to the sound and simulated it with food. Every time they heard the sound began barking and saliva ran down their cheeks."

"It looks to be the same idea, the fire, the tarbouqa, the tied eyes, and the animal later treaded to the sound of the tarbouqa without eye blinding."

"Yes, that's right."

"So the Arabs studied animal behavior many years before your, whatever you call him, was born."

George agreed fully with Salem, had no other way.

"The chickens are still small, you may come back, say in two weeks time," said George.

Salem was disappointed; left with a droopy face, George's live chicken were the most preferred in the market.

With Salem's advice about camels, George changed his mind and decided not to hit the animal but instead gave all the weeds from his small garden to all the three animals, *sayeed* was not satisfied with some weeds, being vengeful targeted the small vegetable garden.

When George finished his work with the chicken, enjoyed spending an hour or so in his garden. Today he got furious, approaching the green patch, noticed the zinc sheet bent inwards, at a closer look, saw most of his half grown lettuce wilting on the ground, he jumped over the fencing thinking that a mole was burrowing his patch of ground. He lifted one of the wilting lettuces, then another and then another, all were roughly cut from the stem at ground level, the camel's footsteps revealed the culprit. *Sayeed* just stepped over the low zinc sheet fence, cut off the lettuce plants and let them lying there on the spot, and the animal barely ate any, though it could have done so, but the savage beast acted with hatred. George left the gate of the farm half open that night and *sayeed* was never seen again. Hamed assumed that the animal followed the exhaust pipe of one of his friends' car and got lost; could have been stolen. Nobody *saw sayeed,* the camel again, Hamed lamented over it, but George was relieved.

35: Commonwealth War Memorial Cemetery

Libya witnessed many bitter fights during the second world war, thousands of soldiers from both armies succumbed, in memory of all those brave soldiers who lost their lives in battle, their countrymen built cemeteries around the town of Tobruq as well as in Benghazi town. The Commonwealth countries with the metropolis of London in the lead, built a specious, solemn and imposing cemetery, the Germans built their own in the form of a castle, the French and the Yugoslavs their own not far from the Commonwealth one.

The upkeep under the auspices of the Commonwealth War Memorial cemeteries was done in the most appropriate manner, the grass was groomed, the trees pruned and watered systematically.

On Remembrance Day, normally held on the second Friday of November, the service took a ceremonial procedure in the town of Benghazi. Many members of the communities with compatriots lying in peace at the cemetery attended the ceremonies. English, Greeks, Indians and Cypriots all dressed formally, took part in the reverential area of the cemetery. Solemnly they crossed the stone entrance with the engraved words, *Commonwealth War Cemetery,* and walked to the far end with the imposing marble cross standing on the elevated stone enclosure. Normally a piano was brought specially for the day and pupils of the local English and Greek schools orderly paraded, a choir was assembled, and flags were flying on the masts at low level and with eyes turning from the wristwatches to the street, waited for the British ambassador.

He was punctual, at 12.00 noon the black Rolls Royce rolled in with the British ensign flapping on both sides. He would descend; walk slowly, steadily, and solemnly to the platform, in a way appropriate for the day. Hymns were sang by the choir, many of the attendants got enthusiastic and rose their voices to crescendo, trying to rouse both the dead and God, of their presence on that not very friendly country. Tried to remind their presence and sustainace to the ever-lasting memory to those whose white marble crosses standing above their cenotaphs bore the words, *the brave ones accept any place for burial,* and the question comes forward, did the dead soldier decide where to be buried? Not really.

In an attempt to decapitate such western ideas, as remembrance ceremonies and gatherings by those aliens, the Leader advised the popular committees, how to deal with such problems. The brain washing was at its zenith, so the committees decided to close down the cemeteries, and provide land elsewhere for such western ideas.

The four ambassadors of the countries concerned were hurriedly summoned to the Leader's tent. The committees iterated the decisions to the foreign dignitaries and demanded from them a decision there on the spot. The French consul was asked to speak first, bearing in mind that no Frenchman was buried in Benghazi and the Leader expected him to comply with the idea, the consul opposed the demand.

Then the British ambassador rose to his feet without being summoned, cleaned his throat, straightened his tie, and receded to his seat. The meeting was concluded, the Commonwealth War Memorial cemetery is still in its place.

The next day the water supply was cut off, the flowers and the grass died out, vandals broke off several marble crosses, and many Europeans commented that *he who cannot beat the live ones strikes the dead.*

After the failure to remove the Commonwealth War Memorial cemetery, the Mayor of the city of Benghazi undertook to uproot the Christian one. Neither the consuls of the two major communities, the Italian and the Greek, nor their communities managed to avert the wrath. A paper notice was glued on the falling iron cemetery gate, informing all those concerned that the area was to be developed into a housing complex, badly needed for the people of Benghazi. Very few managed to exhume the remains of their beloved ones.

Nothing remained upright, from the majestic entrance to the guard's room, up to the magnificent tombstones, cenotaphs, memorial marble plates. Everything above and whatever remained below the ground were ripped, loaded onto army tracks, and dumped in the marshy area near the old vegetable market, in the heart of the old city of Benghazi, the city the Italians founded some seventy years ago.

Many locals regained their nocturnal habits, and despite their strong superstition, jumped over the boundary wall and pirated crosses, plates and plants from the tombs. Sheep were allowed to roam the area, consume the edible green, and litter the gravestones.

A Korean company contracted the erection of prefabricated multi-storey buildings, within a few months the resting place of so many souls was transformed to a residential place for more than two hundred families.

The confiscation of private property, land, villas and apartments, created a huge shortage of housing. The lists of applicants got longer and longer at the Housing department, the persons in charge got fatter and fatter, priorities were jeopardized, *baksheesh(bribing)* was very full of zip.

Superstition remained high among the Benghazi people, no believer in Allah dared to request accommodation built on non-believer's burial ground, for this reason many people from other localities secured a roof on the bedeviled flats, then the locals shook off their scary beliefs and rushed for a new, clean and modern flat. Families are still living and multiplying above the non-believer's burial ground, nobody got scared off by phantoms of the day or the night. If the cemetery demolishing was brought up at any assembly, the comment was, *he does not leave in peace the alive ones, never mind the dead.*

36: Legal status

The depression was loaming everywhere, even the pirating of foodstuffs from the co-operatives declined, there was no one with extra money to buy such stuff, not many items were there to steal either, no television, refrigerator, cooker, vacuum cleaner or furniture were imported for a long time. The black market thrived, the dollar, known as green money, soared from thirty piastres to three hundred and forty, all expatriates changed their hard currency to purchase foodstuffs; the dealers bought them and pirated whatever they could from surrounding countries, Malta was a favorite, many discontented Libyans went there and made all kinds of small businesses.

Under such poor conditions and so few opportunities, forced many to join the ranks. The towns turned into a fertile breeding ground for follower groups who argued that patience and acceptance have achieved nothing.

For several years, Muslims from African countries were allowed to flow in and work freely. So many African Muslim immigrants flowed in which led to xenophobic hostility, and a steep rise in crime, house breaking, car stealing, pocket lifting, just name it. With to-day's austere measures, the person who earned around five Libyan dinars daily could send half of that to his family, which meant about two hundred to two hundred and fifty dollars per month. Now, with the dinar rocking, many of those who walked thousands of kilometers across the formidable desert took the long way back, penniless, it was a way to scare off the unwanted. Labor got scarce and the blacks were not considered farm workers.

After the immigrants came their leaders, some officially and others incognito. Called at Tripoli trying to sell their ideas to Muammar and collect their reward millions of dollars, with a thin promise to raise Muammar's name in their country. The income from our petrol, our natural product given away, leaving our people living just above starvation, on macaroni and tea. Take Wendy, I think that's her name, the ex-wife of Mandela, she knows how to manipulate our Leader.

That Mugabe calls here very often to indoctrinate him how to be more sympathetic.

Even the farm workers did not escape the avalanche, a new decree was passed which read clearly that any foreigner engaged in agriculture could transfer to his foreign account the equivalent of not more than sixty Libyan dinars per annum which meant officially two hundred dollars. This sent another wave of workers homewards. The few that hid somewhere, were herded from house to house, and from farm to farm; stripped off their personal belongings and deported.

George was interrogated on a Thursday afternoon on the farm, a farm he ran with so much zeal. The only thing that kept him out of jail was his diploma in poultry husbandry gained in Scotland several years back. Luckily, was properly translated in Arabic, and certified by the Libyan People's bureau in Nicosia.

"You better bring it with you on Saturday morning at the Hadik police station," said the revolutionary in a commanding tone.

George waited for Hamed to return from his outing to the sea, he was back at nine in the evening. When he was told what happened to Munir, their Tunisian labor, Hamed got very upset, and cursed the boy for roaming outside the farm, then turned to George and asked,

"You told me, you had a diploma in poultry or agriculture, what was it?"

"Yes, I do."

"You better bring it to me tonight."

"Alright, will you be at home?"

"Yes, I got nowhere else to go."

George drove to his house and brought the diploma.

"This is the original, so please..."

"Don't worry, I will not give it to anyone, will only show it to them."

By mid-day of Friday, although a non-working day for the locals, Hamed handed George a letter of appointment duly signed, stamped, and certified that he was an employee at the *Mutamer of Fellahin*, known as the Farmer's Union along with his diploma.

"Put it in your pocket; show it only when you are sure about the person who asks for it."

"How about to-morrow, on Saturday?"

"What about it?"

"They asked me to call at the police station of Hadyk."

"You go, take your diploma and the letter, show first the diploma, and if they insist for more then present the letter."

George realized how Hamed got the letter despite the three official stamps on it and as many signatures.

"Don't worry. I'll wait here, if you do not return I will see someone."

George was not the type to be scared off, but his obligation to call to a police station put wind up his bag. He was alone on the farm, had to shoulder the whole work, and it was too much, had though to do it for the sake of his family and his promise to Yianni.

Kate's fragile health was not that good those days, she hardly managed to cope with the house chores and stay awake for water collection.

On Saturday morning, George left the house early, before six with Margarita and Mary for the farm. There, he explained his two young daughters, how to feed the chicken in the large hangar, it was not an easy job for the two schoolchildren to distribute four hundred kilos of feed in an hour and continue to their school, after that.

George battled to attend the two houses with the small chicks, then take his girls and pick up Dino daughters to the school and return for a grueling of another two hours.

It was after ten, when George tired, soaked in sweat and hungry, drove to Hadik, to face the possibility of being deported. They were surprised to see him, never expected him to call. When the police officer, who instructed him to call to the police station, recognized him, asked George to follow him to his office, there was offered tea, and was asked to present his diploma.

The man took the diploma in his hands, studied it from both sides, read the translation, and saw the certification at the back page. Then, rang up someone and referred the case, adding his comments about George's voluntary presentation, that he was a Greek Cypriot, possessed a diploma duly certified by the Libyan People's Bureau in Nicosia. Eventually, the police officer commented that he guaranteed the man in front of him. After returning the receiver to its cradle, smiled at George, handed him his diploma and in a polite way, said,

"You can go; there is no problem with you."

George thanked him in the most casual manner and drove to the farm, Hamed was there waiting.

"Show me your paper? These bastards will not leave anyone in peace," he said with a rough voice.

"I have my friend, will arrange a job for you, an official one with the Mutamer, so that you can transfer at least half of your salary, it's the best I can do," said Hamed in a very amicable way.

"How about the farm?" George asked.

"Never mind, you will work there just in the morning and in the afternoons you can ran the farm if you want to."

"Yes, if you think that is feasible."

Hamed did not catch the detail.

George asked Hamed to help him with some laborers.

"I will see the Chadian," said Hamed and drove off.

George took a round in the hangars and left for the school. At home, George discussed the whole matter with Kate, she was very sad.

"They do not give you a brake, George," she said.

Muftah Mohamed belonged to the group; he arranged the letter of employment for George and Hamed advised where to meet Muftah as Hamed could not carry his weight to the second floor of the Mutamer offices at Fuehat. George knew the place very well; it belonged to the Benily family.

It was not difficult to climb to the second floor, but at the head of the step, both entrances were closed with heavy iron doors and locked. George looked across the corridor to the left not a soul; he heard only voices and laughter. To the right, the matter was somehow different, doors could be seen open, and occasionally a girl would cross the corridor to somewhere. George waited with the faint hope that someone would notice him in this heavily guarded building.

The minutes flew by and the hours and George waited at the same spot, trying to catch someone beyond the iron door, with little success. After an hour or so, a person came up climbing the stairs. George looked downwards, when the fellow reached the top where he was standing, noticed that the man was dressed in European style, in a grey suit, a shirt without tie and a light overcoat despite the high temperature. He was more less George's size, their eyes met, George drew a soft smile and got a response, greeted him, and the man gave him his right hand, in his left hand held a grey envelope.

"Tfatal, please," he said softly.

"I am looking for Mr.Muftah, Muftah Mohamed."

The man twitched his face at the name and added the usual Arab saying, "Tfatal."

"Is that you?" smiled George.

"Yes. Tfatal."

"I come from Hamed."

"You are George, come in," and invited him to go towards the double locked doors.

"Yia Mohamed, Mohamed?" yelled Muftah.

"Aioua, aioua." Was heard and an elderly fellow rushed with a bunch of keys in his hand. The door was flanged open and George followed Muftah, they went directly to the door from where the laughter was coming, Muftah pushed the door open, and both entered.

It was a large room with a conference table in the middle and about ten persons sat round in two rows. Muftah passed from person to person and greeted them impartiality. He stretched over the table and greeted the ones beyond, then moved to the head of the table and greeted an elderly fellow sitting there; he seemed to be presiding over a meeting.

Muftah leaned over and told him something in a soft tone, both looked at George, it was the introduction, they exchanged a few words and Muftah came back to George, took him by hand and led him to the adjacent room, it was an office but absolutely empty, "you wait here, they have a meeting just now."

"Yia, alright thank you Mr Muftah."

He sat there for more than an hour, listening to the laughter and the loud talking, the minutes were endless, at last, the laughter and the arguing subsided to almost zero. He heard people walking in the corridor, came out of the room, and caught the rears of three men near the exit, rushed to the meeting room, it was empty, hurried down to the corridor and tried to spot Muftah, he was half way down the steps. George rushed down and got him at the first floor head step, when he saw George showed indifference, George felt a grip in the pit of his stomach but picked up courage and called out, "Mr. Muftah?"

The man turned his body, and looked apathetic, George smiled, the man responded, "Ah, you want Ahmed? He is...." he looked up and down the steps and added, "Ah, he is down there."

"My dearest, just a minute," said George puzzled.

"Yia Ahmed," called out the man, but got no reply.

"Ta'al, come quickly," shouted the man and both rushed down the steps, they managed to catch the refined president of the meeting, just as he was about to get into his brand new Peugeot 504. Muftah had another word with him; the man looked at George who held a smile though his face was tomato red from their oblivion.

"Please, to-morrow, come to the Mutamer," the man said.

"What time you want me to be there?' asked George politely.

"About ten in the morning," said the man and closed the door, the man at the wheel drove off. Muftah noticed George's disappointment and said softly, "he is on his way to the Minister of Agriculture, of Benghazi, he is in a great hurry, you will meet him to-morrow, there is nothing to worry about."

"Thank you Muftah," said George wryly and walked the opposite way, out of the yard. When he reached the farm, nobody was there, except the two ponies standing behind the chain-linked wire fence.

The next day George parked his car before 9.30 within the Mutamer's surrounding in such a way to watch the only entrance. Many cars pulled in but not the new Peugeot 504. At ten, he got off his car and tried to ask the bystanders for the person who came for, not a single person knew who George was looking for, typical Arab custom, they never give away information or secrets, whatever those could be, especially about persons. George was disappointed with their attitude, looked around and saw a young fellow getting off a new Audi; he was dressed in a clean shirt and pressed trousers, George walked straight to him, the fellow turned his face away, and George thought that the young man tried to avoid him. To his surprise, the right eye of the fellow was faulty, that was the reason. George greeted the man who stopped, listened, and said, "Ahmed Mohamed is at the Qufra buildings, you better go there now."

George shot off, up the second floor, called out *Mahmoud,* with some confidence, was allowed in and walked to the door where the meeting was held the day before, nobody was there. He asked Mahmoud, the old man beckoned him to follow him, pointed to a side door, George entered, and three Arabs were sitting round a table sipping tea, since George could not remember Ahmed's face so he asked for the fellow.

"You have an appointment?"

George was caught unaware, had a meeting but not at this place, he erred, "yes."

"Yes or no?" demanded the Arab.

"Yes at ten."

"Ten, eleven, Ahmed has no time, just wait?"

Ten minutes later George saw two persons coming out of an inner office, the one was his person, he rose to his feet, but the man was indifferent.

The Arab, with whom George talked a few minutes ago, called Ahmed by name, the fellow craned his neck and uttered, "Just a minute."

He saw his companion off, and turned round.

George went for him and greeted him quite friendly.

"Yes, come in," they entered the office and he closed the door, "you like tea, here is some ready."

A tray lay on the table with six tea glasses of some color, George handed him the letter and picked one of the glasses, the one that no fly was alight on, at that moment.

The fellow read the letter carefully, asked for the diploma and George gave it to him.

"You have experience in poultry you said?'

"Yes, for many years."

"Very good, we need a good person to work at the Mutamer."

"Yes thank you," said George.

"I have to go, have an urgent meeting," George thought the man was avoiding him, looked at the man, who was pressing a button and Mahmoud appeared.

"Aioua, yia Hag."

"Call me Masrati."

A tall slim fellow came in with a big ball pen in his hand.

"Aioua, yia Hag."

"Yia Masrati," said Ahmed, " Mr…." Turned to George and asked for his name.

"George."

"Mr. George will work with the Mutamer, you arrange the contract and all the other documents for registration, make sure you do that today," and handed George his diploma.

"This, you put it in your pocket," said and rose to his feet.

"What is the salary?" asked Masrati.

"Three hundred, is that good enough for you Mr…?"

"Make it four hundred; I'll have to use my car."

"Three hundred and fifty and I'll see about the use of your car."

George did not answer, car expenses could not be considered salary, could not be accounted for currency transfer, but needed though an official job to remain in Libya, so he agreed in silence.

Ahmed was gone through a side door, George followed Masrati the way he entered, crossed the room with the three Arabs still sitting and sipping tea. In Masrati's office the papers were typed, George signed the contract, took back his original diploma and left for the farm.

Hamed was there sitting under the zinc sheets of the old garage with a black fellow, George greeted them and Hamed asked if he met Ahmed.

"Yes, and all has been arranged."

A smile revealed Hamed's rotting teeth.

Under the Libyan law every foreigner obliged to change employment, has to file an application requesting the authorities to close his present working permit, travel abroad, obtain an entry visa from the Libyan People's Bureau in his country and return within a reasonable time hoping his new application be accepted.

Upon his return has to reapply through his new employer for a working permit and a new temporary residence, so that he may apply for his social security, driving license, pay his taxes and eventually allowed to transfer the permissible percentage of his salary to his bank account abroad.

Besides the application for the work permit, the applicant has to undergo the necessary medical tests. Such ones are for Aids, hepatitis, tuberculosis and eyesight. Such tests require time and are expensive.

Masrati, who undertook to draw the contract of employment for George, asked him to take the medical tests

George was fit as a fiddle, never complained about any disorder or ailment, and did not detest any medical tests or even blood taking.

He knew though, the poor standard of hygiene and negligence of the personnel, which made him reluctant.

On his way out bumped into Muftah Mohamed, thanked him for the employment and mentioned the demand for the medical tests.

"Do not worry. I'll arrange that," said Muftah and closed partly one eye.

With that, George realized Muftah's power and status.

"I'll talk to Masrati."

When George returned two days later to check on the progress of his documents, Masrati handed him a set of papers, duly stamped and signed. Requested him to go to Berka Madrassa (school) and see Omar the teacher.

Masrati explained that Omar was appointed by the Mutamer to handle the paperwork for the Labor office and Immigration department.

George drove to Berka madrassa, which was not difficult; he knew the locality reasonably well.

Parked his car at a fair distance from the school, knowing the behavior of the urchins around Arab neighborhood and walked along the pavement opposite the school wall that rose to more than two meters, anything could fly over the wall.

The time was not even eleven and saw youngsters fleeing in all directions, holding school bags.

Looked across the street for the school entrance, and was not surprised to see boys jumping off that perimeter wall landing on the ground. School bags landed immediately after, some came down like bricks, hitting the pavement and bursting, with the contents splattering all over.

The owner collected his belongings in a hurry, cursing his fellow pupil still behind the wall for the improper throw.

George proceeded, reached the closed iron gate, and banged at the zinc sheet with a pebble. Someone yelled from inside, aioua, aioua. The bolt was pulled back and the gate partly opened.

George greeted the armed soldier who confronted him and asked him if he could see Omar the teacher. Showed him the bunch of papers and allowed him to enter. Once inside, requested the guard to show him Omar's office.

"Just go to the second floor, there someone will tell you."

George obeyed the directions and hurried to meet Omar the muders.

From the balcony of the first floor, George heard short sharp orders, looked down, was amazed, children of not more than ten, were hard at the training of arms handling.

George blinked his eyes, considered the arms as imitation, no were real ones.

Through his curiosity missed the steps and had to turn back as instructed by a person who looked rather as a watchman than teacher.

This wondering gave George the chance to take a look through windows in empty classrooms, no pupils, no lessons, only a few bunches of urchins gesturing and talking.

With the help of an older pupil, George eventually entered Omar's office.

"Mr. Omar? Good morning."

"Good morning, tfatal."

"I come from the Mutamer.."

"Ah, for your papers."

"Yes, sir."

"Muftah told me last night."

George bewildered thought that Mufath signed the papers only half an hour ago.

"You have the papers?"

"Please."

"There are one or two missing, no problem, I'll arrange that. Did you bring enough photos?"

"Have four."

"That's not enough, need another six, do you need a driver's license?"

"No, thank you, already have one."

"That's OK, then bring another six tomorrow, after tomorrow, no hurry. There is tea ready, have a cup."

"You have no lessons, is it break time?"

"Lessons?" whispered the master of education, "it's a long time since we stopped giving lessons, now the military people undertook another kind of training, the new heroes of the great revolution, are trained here and everywhere."

"But those are just kids."

"That's the right age; they catch these arts very fast."

George delivered the requested photos the next day and Omar promised to arrange his work permit and residence within a week.

It was Tuesday and the week finishes on Thursday, impossible, thought George, avoided though the slightest body movement, thanked Omar who undertook to arrange his documents in that strange country.

Have a drink.

"This is Issa," he said, "show him the work."

George studied the fellow, he was thin, weather bitten, slow in motion and somehow retarded.

"George, there are no people around now," said Hamed aloud.

He passed the message; George turned to the black man and said, "Tfatal."

He followed George to the small caravan that served as sleeping place for the laborer, then the little store, the hangar with the small chicken, there he asked the man if he worked with chicken before, the fellow fed his grandmother's chicken back in their village.

"Village chickens do not need any real attention," said George, Issa laughed.

"The black fellow has to be trained, has no idea what is a gas brooder or an automatic waterer," thought George.

Invited his new laborer into the house and began explaining step by step the various chores of the daily routine, the fellow seemed indifferent, the language was not to his understanding. George tried hard to inspire his interest in the job; after more than half an hour of preaching, released the poor guy and told him to call the next day for work, just to press him somehow, asked him to call for work at seven in the morning. Without response or complain the man agreed to be there even earlier, his vegetable adventure was not very bright.

The next morning Issa was at the farm gate, greeted George as he climbed off his car. They went into the houses and George explained Issa firstly and primarily, how to walk amongst the chicken, the black guy had long feet; then George explained about the gas brooders, how to increase the flame and how to decrease it and more to that when to do that, the fellow tried to read George's lips not his eyes. They moved to the older birds, there George explained him how to feed them and how to check the waterers, how to clean the pans, how to push the wheelbarrow loaded with feed amongst the birds without killing any and so many other points to take care for. Times were bad for everyone; George had to battle on many fronts if he wanted to survive.

Mutamer, was the official body between the government and the farmers engaged in private farming. George was on their employment list because of his knowledge and experience in poultry but far more due to his partnership with Hamed, all those officials spent many a happy evening drinking and feasting at his lofty hideout.

Within a few days, George met the whole committee, Khalifa the secretary, Osman the chairman, Hussein the financial controller, and Fathi with the faulty eye acting as the internal auditor. Khalifa was the most active one; he arranged the feed supply, the medicine, and the distribution of these items as well as the equipment. He made the contacts with the Ministry of agriculture since his brother was the Minister; any proposal or conclusion of his, was highly respected.

Khalifa was soft spoken and always smiling in a witty way. The brother used him in every transaction; in raw materials, feeds, seeds, fertilizers, equipment, medicine, turnkey projects, just name the transaction. Along with his four brothers owned five agricultural projects, including a layer farm fully automatic.

George undertook to register all the poultry units, big and small, around Benghazi area and arrange to visit them regularly, study their problems, and advise them accordingly, the advice had to be in the simplest way, down to earth, one could say.

On his visits, advised them on cleanliness, the value of clean potable water, the cost of thoughtless use of feed, culling of the birds, the medication in time and proper vaccinations. Advised them to fend off the peddlers, they carried disease from farm to farm. The proper use of light with layers, the sensitivity of eggs to odors, the proper way to collect eggs, the house and equipment maintenance and so many minor matters but of vital importance to turn a poor flock into a profitable one, George was accepted as their savior. He enjoyed his rounds, met the poultry farmers in their cradles, listened to their bitter complaints, drank tea with them, and shared their food and expectations.

The Mutamer committee was too busy with their commissions and internal bickering, never asked for reports on the farms; whenever George presented any reports, nobody cared to study them or even look at them. He wrote the reports in English, a language none of them could read, so any problem had to go through George, if it ever arose.

His employment obligation was until two in the afternoon; George talked to Khalifa about his girls at school and allowed him to leave any time after twelve.

"Very few farmers call at the Mutamer after that time," said Khalifa.

Though the farmers were the clients and were the ones who generated the side income of Khalifa and his group, in reality he despised them; probably Khalifa knew them better than George, even his transplanted European heart a couple of years ago in Zurich did not have a soft spot for his fellow countrymen.

On the contrary, George enjoyed their company, their uncomplicated logic, simple life, and hot temperament; they would argue for hours over trivial matters and within minutes would shake hands with the adversaries and drink water from the same plastic jag.

Many a times, George was invited to share a meal in the evenings and at one occasion asked Ahmed why people preferred that time of the evening for a meal.

"Very simple," he said, "you know George we are by custom, people of segregation, prefer to have males separate, away from womenfolk. Have a family of nine children, six of them are girls, and the house is not that large to have extra guest rooms, you see, I have two problems already, too many females in the house and not enough space. Above that, cannot cook a small lamb like this in the house, who would eat and who would not. Here you see we are only four, have two friends coming for dinner and the lamb, the way is cooked will be just enough for us, mind you the head of the lamb will go to the Chadian, the innards stewed with onion and tomato, are good to start with. Let's have a sip of grappa, our national illegal alcoholic drink, till Mustafa and Mahmoud arrive."

He filled the two glasses from a bottle that he pulled out of the water well.

"Lowered the bottle there to cool down, but I'm aware of those bastards who come along uninvited. Most of the times sneak in the farms on horseback, searching for illegal workers or the forbidden drink."

"They themselves, don't drink?"

"Oh, if they lay their hands on it..."

"Then why are they so particular about a beverage consumed extensively?"

"The actual problem is not the consumption of a good alcoholic drink; it's the badly produced stuff by many opportunists from all sorts of material like raisins, sugar, rice, dates and so on. Consumption of such poorly produced stuff causes health problems, stomach disorders, eye problems, muscle and nervous disturbances..."

"Even brain distortion, paralysis, death..." added George.

"That's why one should be careful from where to obtain reasonably good stuff."

Were on the third glass of grappa when the headlights of an approaching car appeared at the end of the farm road; Ahmed returned the stopper on the half-empty bottle and hid it under the plastic mat.

"Drink it up quickly," he said, "you don't know who is coming."

The approaching car put off its headlights and was moving slowly just with the sidelights. It stopped at a good distance, the lights went off and two doors opened, the inside light revealed the descending figures. Before the doors were slammed closed and the light go off, George noticed something moving in the back seat, looked as a human figure, but only two came out of the car and the one shouted from afar, "Yia, Ahmed, yia tess, you filthy one, you ate all the meat?"

"No, it's still in the hearth; you are just in time, you two beggars."

The exchange of decent and non-decent words continued until the two were close enough to notice George's figure in the dim light of a hurricane lamp hanging on the nearest acacia tree.

Ahmed rose and shook hands with both visitors.

"This is Mr. George," he said and pointed to George, with a gesture was invited to greet the visitors. One of them leaned forward, wanted to study the stranger before greeting him. "Ahlen, ousahlen, *welcome,*" said George.

The man shook George's hand, smelled his breath and said heartily, "he is one of us, the Greeks like their drink."

"Sure they do," said George laughing.

The second one did not bother to greet George; he simply dropped to the nearest cushion and lifted one of the glasses off the tray with a blip as the tray carried a film of water. George could not say if this film of water was there intentionally, probably to keep away the walking flies.

The fourth glass was lifted now and a round of alcohol was served, the newcomers poured it down their gullets and rose for a refill, a saying came to George's mind that the late visitor drinks to catch up with the others. A second round for the two and down it went quickly and got ready for the third one.

George withdrew his glass, but Ahmed insisted, allowed him fill it up.

One of the two called, "bottoms up," in English, and lifted his glass.

George followed him, though he felt, he had enough for the night, and had some forty kilometers to drive with roadblocks on the way. Brought the glass level to his mouth, turned sideways and damped the liquid behind him, glasses were lowered on the tray, another round and then another, the bottle was finished.

Ahmed rose, called the Chadian for the stewed liver, and made his way to the water well; bottle and liver arrived together.

"Tfatal," urged Ahmed, round loaves of bread were lifted, pieces were chopped off and dipped into the stew as long as there was sauce in the frying pan.

"Issa, bring more bread," shouted Ahmed.

"Yia Ahmed, are you going to fill us up with bread?" asked the elder, Mustafa was his name.

The Chadian brought more bread, but Ahmed got up, unhooked the lamp and unsteadily walked with his worker to a few meters from their layout. In the dim of the light, they shoveled soil and a zinc sheet was revealed, it was removed and the air filled with the smell of roasted meat, the westerly breeze brought it to the nostrils of the guests and made their mouths water.

"Aioua, that's better," called Mustafa.

Ahmed with the Chadian lifted a metal tray and carried it to the middle of the group, it was still steaming, and the aroma of meat, and the spices raised the appetite.

"Khul, eat," said Ahmed inviting the already stretched out hands onto the cooked lamb. The meat was cooked to such an extend that parted from the bones at the touch. It was not that spicy, it was delicious, for more than fifteen minutes nobody uttered a single word, laughed or sneezed, hands were going and coming, chunks of flesh were lifted, rolled into the mouths and before swallowed fresh pieces were ready half way up. All were too busy when the Chadian came along with a tray full of fresh cucumbers and tomatoes.

"Are these from the farm?" Mahmoud asked with his mouth full.

"No, we brought them from France," cackled Ahmed, "eat up and shut up."

Cucumbers were crunched and eaten, tomatoes squirted when bitten, it was a laugh, and all members were as on a competition of consumption, the top part of the carcass was stripped of every bit of flesh.

Ahmed just grabbed the legs of the cooked animal and turned it over, "tfatal," he urged all, "eat now when it's still warm."

Ahmed pulled off the hind leg of the carcass, called Issa for a tray, added cucumbers, and tomatoes, and ordered the worker to take it to the person in the car.

Four hands dug in with the desire to deflesh the rest of the carcass. George ripped off a good piece though it was much bigger than what he expected. The lower side of the animal, lying on the charcoal got rather overcooked.

George began biting and chewing, found it more delicious, whether it was overcooked or absorbed the flowing juices from the upper part, had to be sorted out later; with difficulty he finished that piece, his belly was full with lamb meat, fresh tomatoes, cucumbers, green hot pepper and cool water from the well, the bottle was finished long ago.

Issa took the tray for the person in the car and briskly returned to his boss. Ahmed pressed the carcass near the ribs and lifted the animal's head, twisted it and separated it, "take it and call the other two friends, is it enough for you?"

"Inshallah, by God's will," said Issa with respect and hurried away with the dripping head.

George stopped eating, could not eat any more, and so did the other two; Ahmed urged all of them to finish it off without success.

Mustafa got up and walked towards the car, Mohamed lifted the tarbouqa and began beating it in that customary monotonous rhythm, to George's surprise Mustafa returned with a woman; she was around forty with ample flesh round the hips and oversize breasts, the hurricane lamp was too weak to luminate the face, remained standing away from the light. From a glimpse, George noticed the darkened parts around the eyes, the bruised lips, and the cheap outfit.

The tune got louder, more vivid, Mustafa threw at her a long scarf, she caught it expertly with a giggle, passed it round her hips, tied both ends to the right side of her thigh and began trotting to the tune of the tarbouqa and the clapping of the two Arabs. With great expertise, the woman trotted and rocked her buttocks up and down in a very sexy way. Her arms were the one-minute open out like a flying bird and the next over and above her head rolling one arm over the other. The monotonous tune kept rambling for more than fifteen minutes, the *girl* got tired, her trotting and arse rolling got slower, her face was sweating and George sensed the rest of her body was so too. With a brisk movement removed the scarf and dropped it on Mohamed, he caught the scarf with one hand and with the other grabbed the *girl's* leg, she giggled and dropped on the mat

Mohamed revived the tune and Ahmed responded to it, tried the scarf the way the girl did though the end pieces were hanging lower, he was much slimmer, but trotted the usual way.

A third bottle of grappa arrived, glasses filled and drank, raising them high and when empty, boasted of their achievement, the girl joined the drinking spree.

The tune stopped and Mohamed removed and dropped the scarf to George, the tarbouqa was now beaten much harder and all three Ahmed, Mohamed and the girl clapped to a crescendo shouting.

"Hayia, hayia George," he was very reluctant to dance but the urging got crazy.

Rose to his feet, tied the scarf round his buttocks, the ends of it reached almost his shoes; tried to rock his buttocks. George was never a good dancer, could not synchronize his movements with the tune or the clapping. His arms were like the wings of a wounded dove, went round and round three four times, pretended that he slipped and landed on the mat, got a liberal applause and handed the scarf to the girl, she rolled her eyes with expertise and rose for another dance.

Tied the scarf the same old way, the tune was different, more seductive, the buttocks rocked faster in a sexier way, moved her legs for that, her breasts went up and down with rhythmic shoulder movements, the clapping was deafening, George joined the frenzied group. Ahmed would stop clapping for a second, fill up the glasses and urge everyone for a quick drink; George managed to empty the contents of his glass beyond his shoulder.

Mustafa kept the tune, this time the girl could not hold any longer, fell down panting, two hands grabbed hers, and two stroked her from face to breasts. The tarbouqa got soundless;

Mustafa threw it over their heads and landed with a crush on some stones a few meters away. The girl stretched out on the mat, hands and legs open, closed her eyes, the game was about to start soon, she giggled and wriggled when she was tickled.

George rose and took the lantern from the tree, wanted to find his shoes, at last he got them, dipped one foot in and tried to push in the second foot, felt the shoe wet, lifted it and sniffed, it was grappa, must have been the liquid he tipped over his shoulder. He uttered no word, placed the lantern on the ground and slowly made for the Peugeot, before entering his car took a sneaky look back, saw a mass of bodies on the mat mingled with considerable giggling, he left the farm unnoticed.

37: Operation- El-Dorado- The great attack

Attempt after attempt to organize a movement against the Leader failed, many considered the rumors of antirevolutionary movements being staged, in this way the radicals would round up the defectors and exterminate them in one way or another. Several days after an event, via rumors one would learn that so many, numbers were never disclosed or defined, have been executed because they were found guilty by the military court of wrong doings.

The exact reason would never be known, neither the place nor where the court was seated, just a brief announcement would be made over the radio and television that the guards of the alfatah revolution revealed the treacherous plans of dissidents.

A horrifying announcement informed the disciples of the great revolution a group of crossed the Tunisian border, in an illegal way. The Bedouin shepherds, real patriots and lovers of the great revolution, reported the matter to the revolutionary guards, who caught the intruders within hours, along with their ammunition and antirevolutionary printed matter. Nothing was made public, neither the number of persons nor the quantity or type of their vulnerable armaments or the revolutionary matter; days, weeks have passed with very little released about the matter.

One Thursday morning the news broke around Benghazi that three of the infiltrators would be executed at the closed arena of the Benghazi sports stadium. Very seldom, the names were made known and nobody could make out who were be the condemned ones, apart from one called Mohamed Sheriff, a young fellow of twenty-six.

Mohamed, according to rumors originated from Benghazi; lived in the United States, there he studied aeronautics, returned to his hometown, and acquired a job as supervisor at the servicing of civil aircraft. As a supervisor, traveled abroad quite often, the guards of the great revolution got jealous and began watching him, reported him of having connections with the enemies of the great revolution. Mohamed was rounded up, questioned and placed under custody, defied their threats and insisted on his innocence, his defiance cost him his life, he was condemned to death by hanging in public.

Benghazi people considered Mohamed a descent fellow; loved his country and that is why he returned to serve his people; the cronies would listen to nothing of that.

On Thursday of February '87, was to be hanged along with another two traitors, in the closed arena of the stadium; anyone who wanted to witness the punishment of the traitors could obtain permission from the officer in charge and enter the arena.

Usef Aquila, a man of sixty, a very docile fellow, decided to witness the act. He was a distant relative and as Mohamed was an orphan, lost his father long ago, Usef got the right permission to pay tribute to this undeserved execution.

George knew Usef, he lived in the same street at Fuehat garbia, and owned a farm outside Benghazi. Met him several times at the Mutamer where George worked as a poultry advisor. It was weeks later, when George on one of his rounds visited Usef's farm, the man looked prematurely aged with grey untidy beard and long matted hair. George sat with him, shared his lean breakfast, drank tea with him, and listened to his bitter story.

"I went there on my own, entered by showing my cousin's identity card; it was recorded and was allowed to enter. Many people were there, but believe me, most of them were just dogs of his. The three stands were ready with three loops; the guards formed a semicircle, and kept the place free by force. At a moment, some people were hushed in and directed to the front facing the hanging spot, strained my neck and what I saw was unbearable, Gallia, Mohamed's mother and Saber his only brother, a boy of not more than twelve were brought in and ordered to stand there facing the ropes.

Only minutes later, the three were brought in, hooded, with their hands tied behind them and ushered by hefty dogs, two for each condemned, placed them in front of the stands and one by one had his hood removed, then was ushered up the wooden stool and the loop passed through his neck.

An army officer standing by, announced the name of the first condemned, along with a few words about his terrible crime against his country and his people and the court's decision, *to be executed by hanging in public,* the stool was kicked away, and in seconds, the body was squirming from the rope.

A shrill, *Allah,* was heard from the bystanders and the lifeless body hanged still. The second fellow was treated exactly the same way and had the same fate."

George crouched lower, shriveled up and kept looking into Usef's watery eyes, the man continued.

"It was the turn of Mohamed; his hood was removed, a pale face was revealed, but young and sympathetic, with two searching eyes. The boy craned his neck and saw his mother, recognized her and left a feeble voice, *Mummy, Mummy,* he called also his brother's name. The little brother tried to stand up, but a soldier held him down and placed a pair of heavy hands on the boy's shoulders. Gallia did not move, tried to call her son's name, and raised her arm but the soldier struck the arm limp.

The army officer, indifferent, announced the death penalty and the executor passed the rope over Mohamed's neck. Gallia screamed *ibni,* son, and fell off, dropped down dead, she died before her beloved son Mohamed was hanged.

At the scene of Gallia's death, the crowd began at first timidly murmuring that Mohamed was innocent, the voices got stronger, louder, and the military officer hesitated for a moment. It could be Allah's wish that the mother died at that very moment, left an intuition that Mohamed was innocent.

A fat bitch with a green scarf round her untidy head screamed, *hang the bastard, hang the bastard.*

The order was given, the stool kicked off but to everybody's bewilderness, Mohamed's body did not squirm like the others, the body remained stiff; another shrill cry was heard, the fat screamer was stabbed to death on the spot, the crowd retreated, many found their way out and with them the assassin, who was never found."

"The drama did not end there."

"What do you mean yia Usef?"

"I'll tell you, just the way I lived it, be patient. I told you that Saber the boy had a shock and ended up in the psychiatric ward of Hawari hospital."

"Poor boy, that's a mad house there."

"Just listen to the rest of the story and then you ...The bodies of the hanged were lowered and taken away to be disposed in some dubious manner as in so many previous cases; the bodies were never handed to their people for a descent and customary burial.

When the soldiers freed Mohamed's body, noticed that the body was still warm, alive, though unconscious. Even the dogs have a heart; they rushed him to the hospital where an Indian doctor attended him. The man gave him treatment, Mohamed was reviving but the bastards who call themselves guards of the revolution found out what happened, drove to the hospital and insanity overcame them, they cut off the supporting tubes to Mohamed's body, oxygen and solutions and dragged the body with them, nobody saw that body ever after."

Usef, managed to finish his monologue, with trembling hands searched for his cigarettes but did not find them, then fainted.

George had to use his first aids knowledge, managed to help Usef back to his senses, offered him some cool water brought over by one of his daughters, who watched from a certain distance as long as their father had a visitor and was reiterating.

"As far as I know, if a person survives the executioner, the person is considered innocent and given a chance to live, and this is by God's will or Allah's if you like," said George in a low tone.

"The two are the same," exclaimed Usef, "Yes, this is acknowledged and taken care of, in a civilized country, here, where is civilization? Where are you yia Idriss?" and lifted both hands to the sky saying, "'Allah, Allah."

"Such erroneous doings…" George tried to say.

"These are not just wrong doings, these are acts of Satan, you know Satan, you have the same in your religion, and I know that." Usef tried to draw comparison between the two religions.

"Of-course we have the devil," agreed George, "what happened was abominable, treacherous and inhuman, and nobody tried to bring forth worldwide acceptable laws, human rights and international courts, such as that of Hague?"

"And who will be the one to take the Satan to an international court?" Usef sighed, "and where is the money?"

"Before, we grew chicken and managed to meet our family's expenses, at least the basic ones, now, we don't even grow chicken," Usef was bitter with the corrupt system of the

Mutamer. "The favorites take the day-old chicks, the feed, and the medicine; our requests are postponed, postponed for ever."

George expressed his deep regret to Usef for what happened to his young relative, for the bitterness he suffered, the bad dealings of the Mutamer; the man had six growing children, the farm was idle for most of the time and the pressure increasing.

The girl who brought the water for her father was around fifteen but her outfit, her behavior and composure did not much that of a ten year old. How tragic, at such an age, could not read or write her own language, not to mention any foreign ones.

Usef regained his senses, George bid him patience and drove away; had a very sad visit to day, he kept away from that farm for several weeks, too many informers roamed around the area.

The strong man miscalculated his strength; he believed that with a few hundreds of Russian tanks, a few Migs, several missiles of uncertain capacity, few mercenaries, and some meaningless speeches over the television would scare off his American enemies. Did not realize, that politics is a tricky, complicated, and dangerous business. He listened to none, relied on false gallantry, forgot that Libya was a sandy land, fathomless without infrastructure.

The first rapping did not take that long to come, two of his fighter planes were shot down with their brave pilots within the gulf of Sirte, a disputed area; this came as a shock, the latest model of Mig planes could not combat the enemy. The military machine was pulled into action; tens of tanks and antiaircraft artillery were positioned around the city of Benghazi. Every single acacia tree harbored two, no room left for the tents; the whole mobilization proved worthless, the very same moment international media gave away even the registration number of each tank, its position and capacity. Overnight, the tanks returned to an open field in Fuehat, since then nobody ever saw them move and the operators were given long-term leave to rest.

The oil income kept flowing, its quality, and proximity to Europe lured buyers for a constant supply. The oil revenue provided power and was accused of supporting the mozaheddin. The Libyan Desert was turned into a training centre, madrassas for the mujahedin; many joined their counterparts in the Bekka valley to fight their eternal enemy.

Lebanon was devastated; Beirut, the renowned Paris of the Middle East was turned to rubbles. Tension was mounting against Libya, Muammar was left with his mathematics, he thought that a bomb here or a terrorist attack there, like that in Rome, Vienna and in a West Berlin disco, would bring his name to the front lines; the equation was not the expected one.

On April 16th and exactly at 02.00hrs, two groups of F16 flew the long way from Britain and in top secrecy reached their targets in time, one group headed for Tripoli and the second for Benghazi, at both places, predetermined targets were hit and within minutes were on their way. The targeting was specific and accurate.

Before a storm everything is quiet, says a common saying, which is exactly what happened. George would never forget the experience of that night. At that time, he lived with his family at the Benina housing complex, in one of those prefabricated houses. It was an apartment at the first block of the complex facing east and across the oval parking in a similar block lived a group of Russian military experts. Everyday the army buses rolled in and picked those persons to their posts, exactly at 07.30 am. On the 15th of April, Kate, who was always at home, noticed army buses picking up not just the males but the families too, told this to her husband the moment he went home for lunch.

"The Americans are coming," said George ironically.

"You think so, George?"

Bearing in mind his wife's concern, George tried to make fun of what he said; took a quick lunch, returned to the farm and urged Hamed to arrange some extra feed.

Due to some misunderstanding between the French construction company and the Libyans, the Benina housing project was not completed, just over three quarters was executed. Left the water supply to the expected water pressure for the upper floors; the pressure was not enough beyond the ground floor during the day, so the tenants of the upper floors were forced to keep guard overnight in order to collect water for their needs. In George's home, Kate as a considering wife undertook this task, was awake on a constant basis and that is what happened on April 15.

George and Mary were asleep, at a moment they jumped off their beds from the sound of the explosions and the flashes, Kate screamed, "wake up, wake up, it's a war."

All three slipped into casual clothes and rushed downstairs. At the basement, other tenants joined them, Palestinians, Egyptians and locals, all terrified. Womenfolk in tears, the mothers tried to huddle their kids, all agreed to remain under the staircase and put off the lights. By the time, they agreed on these simple things, the operation was over, the explosions seized and numbness reigned.

George crept to his car that stood a few meters from the building entrance, switched on the car radio and tried to tune to some foreign station. It must have been 04.30am, when he managed to tune to some Spanish station, the speaker repeated that the North Americans bombarded Qathafi's living quarter in Tripoli, no mention was made about their mission and that they flew out of reach and out of sight.

George was still sitting in his car trying to tune the radio, turning the knob from left to right and then back again when he heard a whizzing noise from the main road, looked across but caught only the glimpse of a fiery thing flying with high velocity at low level towards Benghazi. Within seconds, heard the same ear piercing sound and saw a second rocket following the same route, at about fifty meters off the ground, both exploded with a devilish sound not very far from George's car.

With the break of the day, it was known that both those missiles hit a petrol station, tore down the scanty structure, and killed the station's night guard.

The locals fired several of the rockets that just managed to cover the distance of twenty kilometers or so. The news broke with the passing of the hour, the Americans struck Libya, details were not given about the targets hit or the damages caused.

It was announced later, that the worst hit was the Leader's quarter and a child was killed; an illegitimate child of a house helper, the strong man himself was somewhere down in Saudi Arabia. The aftermath about Benghazi was one dead, a petrol station guard, a house was hit near the petrol station, an ammunition depot next to the rehabilitation hospital, several Migs at Benina airport and tens of car accidents caused by frantic driving with seven dead and many wounded.

A lot of teeth gritting and Muammar realized once and for all, that his military machine proved worthless, even the radar warning system failed, the missiles useless and the military personnel though double trained in the eastern block were caught asleep.

The only thing left to Muammar was to invite his Arab friends and guide them through the ruins of his one time stronghold; received the visitors in his tent nearby, and the devil retreated to his habitat.

Retaliation was threatened through terrorism, which was the decision of the People's committee, the black sheep that bore the blunt of every blunder. Libya responded by firing two missiles at U.S coast guard stations on the Italian island of Lambedusa which exploded short of their targets. Abu Nidal in Beirut executed two British hostages along with an American by hanging. Another two were executed in Jerusalem. Gaddafi went into oblivion for a while, a disguised move. In top secrecy, plans were laid down, revenge. The hijacking of Pan Am Flight 73 in Pakistan on September 5, 1986, followed by the bombing of Pan Am Flight 103 on Dec 21 1988 over Lockerbie were listed against him. Two Libyans were alleged in 1991. The Libyan Government formally accepted responsibility and offered 2.7 billion US dollars to compensate the families of the 270 victims.

Many nations condemned the attack on Libya, all Arab countries as well as Britain, France and the Soviet Union.

Margaret Thatcher was bitterly criticized for approval of the use of the Royal Air Force bases and Qadhafi himself commented that, "Thatcher is a murderer...Thatcher is a prostitute. She sold herself to Reagan."

The End

About the Author

The author has retired after living in Libya for three decades. With his book "Camel Milk" unfolds in a realistic way a dictatorship that cost numerous innocent lives within the country and leveraged disturbances, wars and coups in many parts of the world. His personal experience gives a vivid picture of that section of the Arab World. He lived the loudness, but also the deafness of the desert. Shared the native entertainment, the local food, and the traditions. Offered condolence to Muslim and Christian alike. Enjoyed the sensational heartfulness of the simple people. Traveled along the caravan routes and visited a thousand year old mosque; walked along the alleys of ancient cities built by his ancestors. He experienced the real Libya, which deserves to be read and talked about.

Printed in Great Britain
by Amazon